T0325762

Artificial Intelligence and Security Challenges in Emerging Networks

Ryma Abassi
University of Carthage, Tunisia

A volume in the Advances in
Computational Intelligence and
Robotics (ACIR) Book Series

Published in the United States of America by
    IGI Global
    Engineering Science Reference (an imprint of IGI Global)
    701 E. Chocolate Avenue
    Hershey PA, USA 17033
    Tel: 717-533-8845
    Fax: 717-533-8661
    E-mail: cust@igi-global.com
    Web site: http://www.igi-global.com

Library of Congress Cataloging-in-Publication Data

Names: Abassi, Ryma, 1980- editor.
Title: Artificial intelligence and security challenges in emerging networks /
  Ryma Abassi, editor.
Description: Hershey, PA : Engineering Science Reference, [2019] | Includes
  bibliographical references and index.
Identifiers: LCCN 2018027791| ISBN 9781522573531 (hardcover) | ISBN
  9781522573548 (ebook)
Subjects: LCSH: Computer networks--Security measures. | Internet--Security
  measures. | Malware (Computer software) | Artificial intelligence.
Classification: LCC TK5105.59 .A78 2019 | DDC 006.3--dc23 LC record available at https://lccn.
loc.gov/2018027791

This book is published in the IGI Global book series Advances in Computational Intelligence and Robotics (ACIR) (ISSN: 2327-0411; eISSN: 2327-042X)

British Cataloguing in Publication Data
A Cataloguing in Publication record for this book is available from the British Library.

All work contributed to this book is new, previously-unpublished material.
The views expressed in this book are those of the authors, but not necessarily of the publisher.

For electronic access to this publication, please contact: eresources@igi-global.com.

Advances in Computational Intelligence and Robotics (ACIR) Book Series

ISSN:2327-0411
EISSN:2327-042X

Editor-in-Chief: Ivan Giannoccaro, University of Salento, Italy

MISSION

While intelligence is traditionally a term applied to humans and human cognition, technology has progressed in such a way to allow for the development of intelligent systems able to simulate many human traits. With this new era of simulated and artificial intelligence, much research is needed in order to continue to advance the field and also to evaluate the ethical and societal concerns of the existence of artificial life and machine learning.

The **Advances in Computational Intelligence and Robotics (ACIR) Book Series** encourages scholarly discourse on all topics pertaining to evolutionary computing, artificial life, computational intelligence, machine learning, and robotics. ACIR presents the latest research being conducted on diverse topics in intelligence technologies with the goal of advancing knowledge and applications in this rapidly evolving field.

COVERAGE

- Heuristics
- Adaptive and Complex Systems
- Robotics
- Neural Networks
- Computer Vision
- Fuzzy systems
- Artificial life
- Brain Simulation
- Automated Reasoning
- Agent technologies

IGI Global is currently accepting manuscripts for publication within this series. To submit a proposal for a volume in this series, please contact our Acquisition Editors at Acquisitions@igi-global.com or visit: http://www.igi-global.com/publish/.

Titles in this Series

For a list of additional titles in this series, please visit:
http://www.igi-global.com/book-series/advances-computational-intelligence-robotics

Advanced Metaheuristic Methods in Big Data Retrieval and Analytics
Hadj Ahmed Bouarara (Dr. Moulay Tahar University of Saïda, Algeria) Reda Mohamed
Hamou (Dr. Moulay Tahar University of Saïda, Algeria) and Amine Rahmani (Dr. Moulay
Tahar University of Saïda Algeria)
Engineering Science Reference • ©2019 • 320pp • H/C (ISBN: 9781522573388) • US
$205.00

Nature-Inspired Algorithms for Big Data Frameworks
Hema Banati (Dyal Singh College, India) Shikha Mehta (Jaypee Institute of Information
Technology, India) and Parmeet Kaur (Jaypee Institute of Information Technology, India)
Engineering Science Reference • ©2019 • 412pp • H/C (ISBN: 9781522558521) • US
$225.00

Novel Design and Applications of Robotics Technologies
Dan Zhang (York University, Canada) and Bin Wei (York University, Canada)
Engineering Science Reference • ©2019 • 341pp • H/C (ISBN: 9781522552765) • US
$205.00

Optoelectronics in Machine Vision-Based Theories and Applications
Moises Rivas-Lopez (Universidad Autónoma de Baja California, Mexico) Oleg Sergiyenko
(Universidad Autónoma de Baja California, Mexico) Wendy Flores-Fuentes (Universidad
Autónoma de Baja California, Mexico) and Julio Cesar Rodríguez-Quiñonez (Universidad
Autónoma de Baja California, Mexico)
Engineering Science Reference • ©2019 • 433pp • H/C (ISBN: 9781522557517) • US
$225.00

For an entire list of titles in this series, please visit:
http://www.igi-global.com/book-series/advances-computational-intelligence-robotics

IGI Global
DISSEMINATOR OF KNOWLEDGE

701 East Chocolate Avenue, Hershey, PA 17033, USA
Tel: 717-533-8845 x100 • Fax: 717-533-8661
E-Mail: cust@igi-global.com • www.igi-global.com

Editorial Advisory Board

Table of Contents

Detailed Table of Contents

    Muhammad Ubale Kiru, Universiti Sains Malaysia, Malaysia
    Aman B. Jantan, Universiti Sains Malaysia, Malaysia

This chapter focuses on the world's most frightening cybersecurity threat known as ransomware. Experts popularly describe ransomware as scareware that makes data and resources on a victims' computers inaccessible and forces the victims to pay a ransom with bitcoins or through other means by frightening and intimidating them. Ransomware these days needs no introduction. The perpetrators behind ransomware have done more than enough damage to critical infrastructures and collected billions of dollars from victims across the world and are still collecting. As such, this research aims at uncovering the underlying mysteries behind the sudden growth and popularity of ransomware through the in-depth study of literature and efforts made by experts globally in understanding ransomware and how to fight and stop it. Moreover, the research seeks to bring together the collective professionals' views and recommendations on how to set up strategic defense in-depth for fighting against ransomware.

    Antonio Muñoz, University of Málaga, Spain

This chapter reviews current technologies used to build secure agents. A wide spectrum of mechanisms to provide security to agent-based systems is provided, giving an overview with the main agent-based systems and agent-oriented tools.

An evaluation of security mechanisms is done that identifies security weaknesses. This review covers from the initial approaches to the more recent mechanisms. This analysis draws attention to the fact that these systems have traditionally neglected the need of a secure underlying infrastructure.

Chapter 3

Zuleyha Yiner, Siirt University, Turkey
Nurefsan Sertbas, Istanbul University – Cerrahpaşa, Turkey
Safak Durukan-Odabasi, Istanbul University – Cerrahpaşa, Turkey
Derya Yiltas-Kaplan, Istanbul University – Cerrahpaşa, Turkey

Cloud computing that aims to provide convenient, on-demand, network access to shared software and hardware resources has security as the greatest challenge. Data security is the main security concern followed by intrusion detection and prevention in cloud infrastructure. In this chapter, general information about cloud computing and its security issues are discussed. In order to prevent or avoid many attacks, a number of machine learning algorithms approaches are proposed. However, these approaches do not provide efficient results for identifying unknown types of attacks. Deep learning enables to learning features that are more complex, and thanks to the collection of big data as a training data, deep learning achieves more successful results. Many deep learning algorithms are proposed for attack detection. Deep networks architecture is divided into two categories, and descriptions for each architecture and its related attack detection studies are discussed in the following section of chapter.

Chapter 4

Thangavel M., Thiagarajar College of Engineering, India
Pavithra V., Thiagarajar College of Engineering, India
Guru Roja R., Thiagarajar College of Engineering, India

Network scanning commonly implies the use of the computer network to collect information about the target systems. This type of scanning is performed by hackers for attacking the target and also by the system administrators for assessment of security and maintaining the system. Network scanning mainly analyzes the UDP and TCP network services that are running on the target, the operating system that is used by the target, and the security systems that are placed between the user and targeted hosts. Network scanning includes both the network port scanning and vulnerability scanning. Network manipulation is an effort that is made by the user to modify the network or structure of a network and thus using online network tools to achieve the target. Software-defined networking is a term that comprises several network technologies with the aim of making it adapt the features of flexibility. Key terms for SDN implementation include separation of functionality, virtualization in the network, and configuring programmatically. This chapter explores network manipulation using network scanning in SDN.

Chapter 5

The Usage Analysis of Machine Learning Methods for Intrusion Detection in Software-Defined Networks

Derya Yiltas-Kaplan, Istanbul University – Cerrahpaşa, Turkey

This chapter focuses on the process of the machine learning with considering the architecture of software-defined networks (SDNs) and their security mechanisms. In general, machine learning has been studied widely in traditional network problems, but recently there have been a limited number of studies in the literature that connect SDN security and machine learning approaches. The main reason of this situation is that the structure of SDN has emerged newly and become different from the traditional networks. These structural variances are also summarized and compared in this chapter. After the main properties of the network architectures, several intrusion detection studies on SDN are introduced and analyzed according to their advantages and disadvantages. Upon this schedule, this chapter also aims to be the first organized guide that presents the referenced studies on the SDN security and artificial intelligence together.

Chapter 6

Toward Formal Verification of SDN Access-Control Misconfigurations

Amina Saadaoui, University of Carthage, Tunisia

Software-defined networking (SDN) allows centralizing and simplifying network management control. It brings a significant flexibility and visibility to networking, but at the same time creates new security challenges. The promise of SDN is the ability to allow networks to keep pace with the speed of change. It allows frequent modifications to the network configuration. However, these changes may introduce misconfigurations by writing inconsistent rules for single flow table or within a multiple open flow switches that need multiple FlowTables to be maintained at the same time. Misconfigurations can arise also between firewalls and FlowTables in OpenFlow-based networks. Problems arising from these misconfigurations are common and have dramatic consequences for networks operations. To avoid such scenarios, mechanisms to prevent these anomalies and inconsistencies are of paramount importance. To address these challenges, the authors present a new method that allows the automatic identification of inter and inter Flowtables anomalies. They also use the Firewall to bring out real misconfigurations.

Chapter 7

A Review of Dynamic Verification of Security and Dependability
Properties 162

Antonio Muñoz, University of Málaga, Spain
Jamal Toutouh, University of Málaga, Spain
Francisco Jaime, University of Málaga, Spain

This chapter reviews the notions of security and dependability properties from the perspective of software engineering, providing the reader with a technical background on dynamic verification and runtime monitoring techniques. The chapter covers the technical background on security and dependability properties with system verification through dynamic verification or monitoring. The authors initially provide a short overview of the security and dependability properties themselves. Once definitions of security and dependability properties are introduced, they present a critical analysis of current research on dynamic verification by presenting general purpose and security oriented dynamic verification approaches.

Chapter 8

A Formal Ticket-Based Authentication Scheme for VANETs 188

Ons Chikhaoui, SUPCOM, Tunisia
Aida Ben Chehida, SUPCOM, Tunisia
Ryma Abassi, SUPCOM, Tunisia
Sihem Guemara El Fatmi, SUPCOM, Tunisia

Vehicular ad hoc networks (VANETs) enable vehicles to exchange safety-related messages in order to raise drivers' awareness about surrounding traffic and roads conditions. Nevertheless, since these messages have a crucial effect on people's lives and as we cannot disregard the probability of attackers intending to subvert the proper operation of these networks, stringent security support should be applied on these messages before they can be relied on. Authenticating these messages before considering them is one of the key security requirements since it enables the receiver to make sure of the received message's integrity and the genuineness of its originator. This chapter presents a conditional privacy-preserving authentication scheme for VANETs.

Chapter 9

Toward a Security Scheme for an Intelligent Transport System........................221

Amira Kchaou, SUPCOM, Tunisia
Ryma Abassi, SUPCOM, Tunisia
Sihem Guemara El Fatmi, SUPCOM, Tunisia

Vehicular ad-hoc networks (VANETs) allow communication among vehicles using some fixed equipment on roads called roads side units. Vehicular communications are used for sharing different kinds of information between vehicles and RSUs in order to improve road safety and provide travelers comfort using exchanged messages. However, falsified or modified messages can be transmitted that affect the performance of the whole network and cause bad situations in roads. To mitigate this problem, trust management can be used in VANET and can be distributive for ensuring safe and secure communication between vehicles. Trust is a security concept that has attracted the interest of many researchers and used to build confident relations among vehicles. Hence, the authors propose a secured clustering mechanism for messages exchange in VANET in order to organize vehicles into clusters based on vehicles velocity, then CH computes the credibility of message using the reputation of vehicles and the miner controls the vehicle's behavior for verifying the correctness of the message.

Chapter 10

Ryma Abassi, SUPCOM, Tunisia
Sihem Guemara El Fatmi, SUPCOM, Tunisia

Specifying a security policy (SP) is a challenging task in the development of secure communication systems since it is the bedrock of any security strategy. Paradoxically, this specification is error prone and can lead to an inadequate SP regarding the security needs. Therefore, it seems necessary to define an environment allowing one to "trust" the implemented SP. A testing task aims verifying whether an implementation is conforming to its specification. Test is generally achieved by generating and executing test cases. Some automated testing tools can be used from which model checkers. In fact, given a system modeling and a test objective, the model checker can generate a counterexample from which test cases can be deduced. The main proposition of this chapter is then a formal environment for SP test cases generation based on a system modeling, a SP specification (test purpose), and the use of a model checker. Once generated, these test cases must be improved in order to quantify their effectiveness to detect SP flaws. This is made through the generation of mutants.

Preface

The recent rise of emerging networking technologies such as social networks, content centric networks, IoT networks, etc. have attracted lots of attention from academia as well as industry. In fact, the attractiveness of such networks leads to the increase of security risks in particularly privacy and security threats. According to Gartner (2018), within 2017, leading global companies have seen sales and revenue impacts as high as $300 million due to malware-based cyberattacks.

Besides, recent years have seen a dramatic increase in applications of artificial intelligence (AI), machine learning, and data mining to security and privacy problems.

In fact, cybersecurity products are increasingly incorporating AI in order to detect new malwares reducing by the fact, the amount of time needed for threat detection and incident response. Without this help, organizations can waste as much as $1.3 million per year responding to "inaccurate and erroneous intelligence" or "chasing erroneous alerts" (American Institute of Aeronautics and Astronautics, 2018).

Besides, AI can be used by attackers: "We're still in the early days of the attackers using artificial intelligence themselves, but that day is going to come," warns Nicole Eagan, CEO of cybersecurity firm Darktrace. "And I think once that switch is flipped on, there's going to be no turning back, so we are very concerned about the use of AI by the attackers in many ways because they could try to use AI to blend into the background of these networks." (CNBC 2018)

The purpose of this book is to study the relation between artificial intelligence and cybersecurity and thus by highlighting research challenges and open issues using AI for cybersecurity purposes and/or cybersecurity attacks.

ORGANIZATION OF THE BOOK

The book is organized into 10 chapters. A brief description of each of the chapters follows:

Chapter 1 deals with ransomwares and uncovers the underlying mysteries behind the growth of such malware. More precisely, authors brought together the professionals' views and recommendation on how to set up a defense in depth against ransomware.

Chapter 2 reviews current technologies used to build secure multi agent systems. An evaluation of security mechanisms is also done in order to identify their main weaknesses.

Chapter 3 considers attack detection in cloud networks based on artificial intelligence approaches. In fact, a review of some machine learning algorithms used for attack detection is first presented. However, due to the lack of efficiency of such algorithms, deep learning algorithms are then reviewed.

Chapter 4 deals with network manipulation using network scanning in Software-defined Networks (SDN). In fact, network scanning is used by attackers and administrators in order to assess the security of a given system and to collect information about it. Hence, this chapter explains thoroughly the possible attacks in SDN and defensive measures the organization needs to implement to avoid such attacks.

Chapter 5 focuses on the use of machine learning methods for intrusion detection in software-defined networks and proposes a guide referencing studies on both the SDN security and artificial intelligence.

Chapter 6 proposes a formal verification of software-defined networks access control misconfigurations. In fact, although software-defined networks centralize and simply network management, they may create security challenges, too. This may be the case due to misconfigurations. Hence, authors presented a new method allowing to automatically identify inter and intra Flowtables anomalies and used firewalls to bring out real misconfigurations.

Chapter 7 reviews dynamic verification of security and dependability properties and more precisely abductive reasoning for generating explanations. A critical analysis of current research on dynamic verification is also presented.

Chapter 8 introduces a formal ticket-based authentication scheme for Vehicular Adhoc NETworks (VANETs) preserving privacy. In fact, such network enables smart vehicles to exchange safely related messages to raise drives' awareness about surrounding traffic.

Chapter 9 presents a security scheme for intelligent transport systems. In fact, the performances of such systems may be affected due to messages falsification and/or modification and cause accidents, jam, etc. Hence, a secured mechanism base on clustering and trust is proposed in order to evaluate the credibility of a received message and increase the confidence of each vehicle on others.

Chapter 10 proposes a formal environment for Security Policies (SP) testing based on test cases and mutants generation. In fact, specifying a SP is the bedrock of any security strategy but can be inadequate regarding to the security needs leading by the fact to vulnerabilities. Hence, testing the SP before its real implementation seems to be necessary.

Ryma Abassi
University of Carthage, Tunisia

REFERENCES

American Institute of Aeronautics and Astronautics. (2018). *Artificial Intelligence for Cybersecurity.* Retrieved 16 October 2018, from http://www.aiaa.org/protocolAI/

CNBC. (2018). *Weaponized drones. Machines that attack on their own. 'That day is going to come'.* Retrieved from https://www.cnbc.com/2018/07/20/ai-cyberattacks-artificial-intelligence-threatens-cybersecurity.html

Gartner. (2018). *Cybersecurity Q&A: The New World of Cyber.* Retrieved from https://www.gartner.com/smarterwithgartner/cybersecurity-qa-the-new-world-of-cyber/

Acknowledgment

The editor would like to acknowledge the help of all the people involved in this project and, more specifically, to the authors, reviewers and editorial board that took part in the review process. Without their support, this book would not have become a reality.

Hence, I would like to thank each one of the authors for their contributions to this book, their time and expertise.

Moreover, I wish to acknowledge the valuable contributions of the reviewers regarding the improvement of quality, coherence, and content presentation of chapters. Some of the authors also served as referees; I highly appreciate their double task.

Finally, I am very thankful to the team of IGI Global for accepting this book proposal and giving me the opportunity to work on this book project. Particularly, I am thankful to Amanda Fanton (Assistant Development Editor), Courtney Tychinski (Special Projects Coordinator), and Jan Travers (Director of Intellectual Property and Contracts).

Ryma Abassi
University of Carthage, Tunisia

Chapter 1
The Age of Ransomware:
Understanding Ransomware and Its Countermeasures.

Muhammad Ubale Kiru
Universiti Sains Malaysia, Malaysia

Aman B. Jantan
Universiti Sains Malaysia, Malaysia

ABSTRACT

This chapter focuses on the world's most frightening cybersecurity threat known as ransomware. Experts popularly describe ransomware as scareware that makes data and resources on a victims' computers inaccessible and forces the victims to pay a ransom with bitcoins or through other means by frightening and intimidating them. Ransomware these days needs no introduction. The perpetrators behind ransomware have done more than enough damage to critical infrastructures and collected billions of dollars from victims across the world and are still collecting. As such, this research aims at uncovering the underlying mysteries behind the sudden growth and popularity of ransomware through the in-depth study of literature and efforts made by experts globally in understanding ransomware and how to fight and stop it. Moreover, the research seeks to bring together the collective professionals' views and recommendations on how to set up strategic defense in-depth for fighting against ransomware.

DOI: 10.4018/978-1-5225-7353-1.ch001

INTRODUCTION

Ransomware is popularly described as a type of malware that makes a file on a victim's computer or device inaccessible and then demands the victim to pay ransom mostly in the form of bitcoin or other means of payment to regain access to the hijacked system (Micro, 2017). However, Liska and Gallo (2017) describe ransomware as a new type of extortion, hence describe it as a criminal practice for obtaining something especially money or its equivalence from an individual or institution through coercion or threats. Hackers and people with malicious intent are responsible for spreading ransomware. However, we know from experience that employees also contribute to the spread due to human error and or ignorance caused by lack of awareness (Fimin, 2017). Some of the conventional methods of spreading ransomware include exploiting system's known or unknown vulnerabilities or by visiting compromised sites or deep webs.

Studies suggest that the sudden rise of ransomware attacks recently is a signal that ransomware has come back with full force in both complexity, impact and size (Downs, Taylor, & Whiting, 2017). The year 2017 was the year history will never forget as per as internet security breach is concerned. It was the year in which the world saw some of the most dangerous attacks in the history including WannaCry pandemic, Petya, NotPetya, Cerber, Cryptomix, Locky, CrySis and many others. The aforementioned ransomware attacks were massive global ransomware attacks that mostly affect Windows operating systems that were unpatched or unsecured. More importantly, the WannaCry attack became prominent following the leaked exploit kits which were stolen from the United States NSA by the infamous group known as 'Shadow brokers' which opens pandora's box for other variants of ransomware to be created and eventually affected thousands of devices across the globe. (Barracuda, 2017). These events led different social media observers and professionals in various domains to name 2017 as *the year of ransomware* (Cabaj, Gregorczyk, & Mazurczyk, 2017).

The damages erupted by ransomware did not catch much attention until recently when hundreds of companies and security agencies across the world have begun to cry out (Brodsky, 2017). So far, the popular variant known as WannaCry had rapidly spread to around 200,000 to 300,000 machines in over 150 countries across the globe since its first appearance (Yaqoob et al., 2017); making it the world's largest attack in history if measured in terms of wide coverage, complexity and impact. Earlier in 2016, the FBI reported that over $206 million was paid to ransomware criminals in the first quarter of 2016. In another report by the United States Department of Justice, there are over 4000 ransomware attack reports per day, and that every month new variant of ransomware is being produced, which makes it more likely to increase with 100% by Q4 of 2018 (Harpur, 2017). Perhaps, the emergence of IoT devices has also contributed as well as accelerate the wide spread of ransomware and the modern security challenges we are facing today (Yaqoob et al., 2017). The vast availability of devices on the internet has open access to all perpetrators who have malicious intent to start ransomware campaign at a massive scale.

The question many people keep asking is why is ransomware prevalent and unbeatable in every part of the world? The reason is that antivirus and anti-malware are no longer capable of detecting ransomware because modern ransomware use polymorphism and machine learning to avoid being detected. Secondly, the advent of Ransomware as a Service and the Exploit kits as a service in black markets make it even more difficult to deal with the situation. With RaaS, anyone including script kiddies can lay their hands on ransomware codes and reproduce their own. According to MacAfee Lab (2017), the writers of 'Cerber' (one of the most dangerous ransomware family) release a new variant of ransomware every 8 days on average, selling with bonuses and offers of 20% discount (Ashford, 2015; Singh, 2017).

Having said that, the objectives of this research include identifying new trends in ransomware attacks, the root causes of the attack, methods of the attack, mode of operation, attack vectors, and to identify popular suggestions given by experts on how ransomware attacks can be dealt with professionally using the simplest, cost-effective and most successful techniques for mitigating ransomware attacks. Other objectives include identifying the most suitable approach for ransomware mitigation as well as exposing and uncovering the mystery of ransomware to the users so that they become aware of how to recover in the aftermath of the attack. To break down these information, the sections are arranged as follow: Introductory section gives an overview on the focus of the entire research, a literature review section which comprises of ransomeware timeline, types of ransomware, mode of operation and other relevant information about ransomware. The methodology section comprises of detailed information on the techniques used in conducting the study. Other sections include ransomware management techiques section which explores the various preventive and detective techniques. And finally, the recovery and incidence response techniques.

METHODOLOGY

This section discusses the research design, area of study and method for data collection and information gathering. The researchers choose to adopt a state-of-the-art research review method, as it allows the researcher to analyze and summarize previous and emerging trends in a given field of study. The aim is to have a critical look at the existing literature and draw conclusions Dochy (2006). To achieve that, a survey must be conducted. As defined by McBurney (1994), survey means accessing public opinion or individual characteristics using primary or secondary sources of information. In this case, the subject of this study is ransomware. At the time this chapter was written, not much have been written about ransomware until recently. Hence, it was necessary to explore all boundaries without limit. Data was collected and analyzed, and conclusions were drawn from the analyzed data. The information collated for this research were sourced from contemporary works of research including journal articles, webinars, online interviews, online tutorials, security reports, bulletins, interagency intelligence reports, news articles, magazine articles, commentaries from ransomware experts in different domains and disciplines.

REVIEW OF LITERATURE

A recap of the previous years' data has shown a disturbing concern about how ransomware attacks have significantly increased from the last five years. If we trace the impact and growth from 1990 to 2006, ransomware cases were in fact insignificant to be recorded. Soon, however, the scale turns the other way round. In a report by Symantec (2017), they highlight that ransomware landscape increased these years dramatically with the appearance of the two variants of self-propagating ransomware threats namely WannaCry and Petya. The two threats have caused what Symantec called a "global panic". As many have seen on the news and other media outlets (O'Brien, 2017), ransomware damage costs were estimated to have exceeded $5 billion in 2017, and according to Microsoft (2017), it had risen from $325 million in the year 2015 (Morgan, 2017). Before these massive attacks, ransomware was not seen as a threat of any serious concern, as it was merely a malicious scam campaign. Until in 2016 when ransomware programmers started offering ransomware variants as a service with the advent of exploit kits and its wide availability in the black market. According to a report by Symantec (2017), one in every 131 emails contained a malicious link or attachment that could infect a device with a variant of ransomware. Within a short period, security agencies and private companies like Symantec and Kaspersky had blocked and intercepted over 22 million attempted ransomware attacks worldwide (Mort, 2017), and 57% of the victims were individuals while 43% were organisations. The report adds that 59% of the ransomware infections were delivered via email phishing with malicious attachments or compromised URLs embedded within the emails (Cyber_Intelligence_Team, 2017). We must undoubtedly accept the fact that the year 2017 had seen what many will call the 'fall of security infrastructure'. So far we must say that modern technologies have failed woefully and proved insufficient and inefficient in the fight against ransomware (Downs, Cook, Wright, & Kent, 2017).

Figure 1. Ransomware timeline

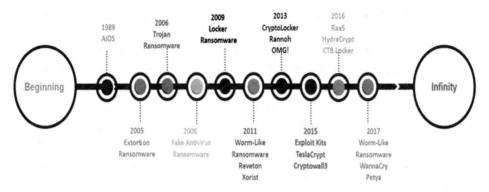

Ransomware Timeline and History

The majority of computer scientists around the world assert that ransomware might have originated from Russia and was limited to Russians until in early 2012 when several reports proved its presence in other parts of the world including Asia and North America (Micro, 2017). The sudden growth of ransomware was triggered by the tons of malware variants that are produced because of the stolen exploit kits from the NSA arsenal which allow reusability, hence reinventing new variants of ransomware become easy. (See figure 1 for ransomware timeline)

The early discovered ransomware was known as AIDS. It was first discovered in 1989. It was not spread using the famous phishing attacks, instead, its writer Joseph Popp used ordinary floppy disk and sent the malware via postal service to a gathering of world health organisation conference held in London. This early ransomware was characterised with encrypting system directory by replacing AUTOEXEC. BAT on the infected machine (Liska & Gallo, 2017) making the system unstable. Later after infecting the system, a message displayed demanding $189 ransom which is to be sent via a Post office Box number in exchange for the decryption key (NoMoreRansomware, 2017b).

After a long disappearance of ransomware, it was reported that extortion ransomware emerged in 2005. Most extortion ransomware at that time were mere apps that posed as fake spyware removal tools such as SypSheriff. Others posed as performance enhancement tools and registry cleaners. Their major targeted machines were Windows and IOS Computers. The hackers' trick was an exaggeration of serious issues on the machine. Next, they asked if the user wants their problem fixed for $30 to $90 (Savage, Coogan, & Lau, 2015). Somewhere in May 2005, a new variant of crypto ransomware that encrypts and demands ransom surfaced known as Trojan.GPcoder. It used a custom-encryption method which was considered weak and easily breakable. Perhaps it was not successful due to the failure of the hackers to make it more effective. Therefore they kept on modifying the version for a long period (Hampton & Baig, 2015; Savage et al., 2015).

By the quarter of 2006, more sophisticated ransomware variants had emerged and started to use more complex and rigid RSA encryption algorithms. Reported cases from Moscow revealed that a variant of ransomware called TROJ_CRYZIP.A was discovered. This variant was characterised by certain activities whereby data is copied into specific password-protected archive files (Micro, 2017); therein the original files are deleted along the line; leaving a password key saved in a text file for unzipping the files. Other ransomware variants were reported in that period including TROJ.RANSOM.A, Krotten, and Cryzip (NoMoreRansomware, 2017b).

Furthermore, several ransomware occurrences continued to be the topic of discussion, even in early 2008 to late 2009 when a new threat emerged. Here, the hackers were said to have switched from using malicious software to using fake Antivirus programs that appeared legitimate to the users. The fake programs were used to perform a virus scan on the system after they claimed to have detected a large number of security threats that needed immediate action. Thus, users were asked to pay money amounting $40 to $100 to fix their faked threats (Savage et al., 2015). Nevertheless, this technique did not last much longer; as many users decided to ignore the recommendations and chose to address the problem using other available means.

The first locker ransomware surfaced in the last quarter of 2009 and later became prevalent from 2011 to 2012. During that period, attackers no longer use fake antivirus or fake luring-application-software to attack their targets. For the first time, perpetrators were able to hijack systems remotely and locked it up. This time, worm-like ransomware equipped with remote-locking-capability started spoofing the Windows Product Activation notice emerged (NoMoreRansomware, 2017b). A report by TrendMicro suggested that these new variants of ransomware known as TROJ_RANSOM.QOWA and Trojan.Randsom.C have compromised many systems, and both were capable of popping messages that compelled the users to dial a premium-rate phone number and paid some amount of money through electronic cash voucher before the victim's machines is released (Micro, 2017; Savage et al., 2015).

More reports suggested that hackers had continued to be inventive; hence, introduced a new variant of ransomware known as Reveton. This variant began to impersonate law enforcement agencies including the police. The victims were befooled into thinking that they had broken the law by simply visiting a prohibited site or by downloading a copyrighted item or by visiting a pornographic environment. Hence, the hackers used a lot of social engineering techniques in carrying out these attacks as it had to do with convincing and deceiving the victims. It is vital to note that, Reveton ransomware was the first of its kind to introduce different payment methods for victims. A study by TrendMicro shows that victims were asked to pay the ransom through Ukash, PaySafeCard, and MoneyPak (Micro, 2017).

As technology grows, new types of ransomware known as crypto-ransomware and cryptoLocker also emerged in Q4 of 2013. These new variants were considered as the best generation of ransomware since the disappearance of fake antivirus ransomware and were also rated as quite profitable. Previously, ransomware was considered inefficient due to unstandardized use of weak infrastructure. This latest ransomware changed the scales of ransom, thereby, collected an unimaginable sum of $300 from each victim, and before the end of the year had earned more than $3 million for its creator. According to Symantec, between 2013 to 2014, there was a massive increase of 250% in the new crypto ransomware. The newcomer infected more than 250,000 systems within two months (Lord, 2017). This time the hackers successfully used more complex encryption algorithms such as RSA 2048 which requires two-way encryption and decryption key (AES+RSA encryptions) (Micro, 2017). In fact, the year 2013 was indeed the beginning of the present-day sophisticated ransomware attacks.

The rise of crypto-ransomware led to the reinvention of even more sophisticated and well-enhanced ransomware in 2015 through 2016. For the first-time hackers started designing exploit kits which were used for creating other series of ransomware variants. Typically, crypto-ransomware does not affect the functionality of the targeted system, it, however, encrypt crucial files to force users into paying the ransom (Kaspersky, 2016a). Thus, the emergence of cryptocurrency in 2009 and its widespread in 2015 has open door for modern ransomware writers to remain untraceable on the web. Popular ransomware in that period comprised of Teslacrypt, CTB-Locker and Cryptowall which earned over $18,000,000 from its victims according to an FBI report (FBI, 2015). A new variant called Locky came and overshadowed Teslacrypt and CTB-Locker and became one of the most used and most popular ransomware variants of all times (Fortinet, 2017). It had collected over 1 Billion USD before the end of the year. CryptXXX earned 77 million USD, while its counterpart Cerber collected over 54 million USD (Crowe, 2016; Korolov, 2017).

New breeds of ransomware were born in 2017; ransomware has become first on the list of every organisation; be it private or public sector, and it continued to dominate and grew exponentially throughout the year. This spike according to several security experts is because of the emergence of the two new breeds namely WannaCry 2.0 and Petya. The former emerged due to a leak of an NSA exploit kit (Known as EternalBlue) responsible by a group of hackers who identified themselves as Shadow brokers. WannaCry or WannaCrypt has a worm-like feature and a self-propagating capability which gives it the ability to spread itself rapidly and widely across the network without any user interaction which makes it invincible and abruptly challenging to stop (Perekalin, 2017b). Petya according to popular assessment is nothing new, it was the handy work of the same exploit kit used by Shadow brokers.

Although, the two variants shared specific properties in common viz: Petya also adapted self-propagation technique, it incorporated other SMB network spreading methods, and it used public key based64 encoded algorithm alongside Salsa20 which makes it extremely difficult to decrypt (O'Brien, 2017). Petya was primarily designed to target organisations in Ukraine, but it later spread to other regions including the US, Russia, France, Germany and few others.

Types of Ransomware

The types of ransomware vary according to different scholarly opinions. The most prominent and popular types of ransomware can be classified as (1) Locker or Lock Screen Ransomware and (2) Crypto or encryption ransomware (Brunau, 2017; Harpur, 2017; Rubens, 2017a; Shinde, Veeken, Schooten, & Berg, 2016).

Locker Ransomware

As the name implies, locker ransomware is a variant of ransomware which overtakes the system or device and eventually denied access to the user lest ransomware is paid. In most scenarios, the infected system is left with limited resources to use for interacting with the hacker(s). In few cases, personal files are not tampered with, while in some cases files may be stolen.

Crypto Ransomware

This type of ransomware encrypts and deletes the personal files and folders in the affected machine. Even though not all types of files are encrypted, specific variants of ransomware trace certain types of file formats such as .doc, .xsl, .xml, .zip, .pdf, .js and encrypt them only (F-Secure, n.d.). Traditional crypto ransomware, on the other hand, encrypts the entire directory.

Ransomware Variants

Since the emergence of ransomware, new variants of ransomware are being released every day. Perhaps it is important to note that, types of ransomware should not be mistaken with variants of ransomware, the variants are the distinctive types of ransomware family which possess unique features and patterns of operate. In tracing the different variants of ransomware family, one might say they are infinite. The earlier variant of ransomware was said to have emerged in 1989 in the form of a Trojan. Since then, hundreds of ransomware variants have been produced annually, coming in different forms, pattern and structure. Various assessments by security agencies

Figure 2. Ransomware families (Symantec ISTR Report 2017)
Source: Symantec, 2017

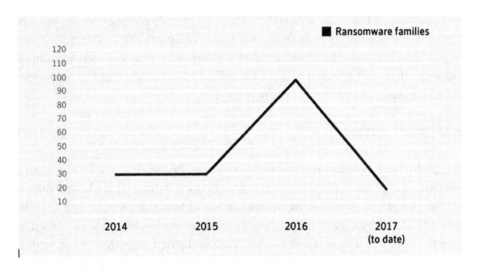

show that a massive increase in ransomware production was seen in the Q4 of 2015 through 2017 (Crowe, 2017; National Cybersecurity and Communications Integration Center, 2016) especially with the advent of Ransomware as a Service (See Figure 2). As mentioned earlier, RaaS gives unskilled hackers the tools to manufacture any variant they desire. Thus, New Jersey Cybersecurity and Communications Integration Cell (NJCCIC) reports that it has profiled 197 ransomware variants since the second quarter of 2015 (NJ Cybersecurity & Communication Integration Cell, 2018).

The following are some of the popular variants of ransomware as profiled by NJCCIC (see Table 1).

Table 1. Popular ransomware variants, attack vectors and dates

Alias	Attack Vector
1. Cerber	Spam campaign, RIG Exploit kit, Magnitude Exploit kit
2. WannaCry	Phishing campaign, EternalBlue
3. Jaff	Spam campaign
4. Sage	Spam Campaign. Botnet, RIG exploit kit
5. GlobeImposter	Spam campaign
6. Locky	Spam, Neutrino exploit kit, Nuclear exploit kit
7. Mamba	Targeted attack, network compromise
8. CryptoXXX	Angler exploit kit
9. CryptoWall	Spam campaign, Angler, Nuclear, magnitude exploit kit, Malvertising

Source: New Jersey Cybersecurity and Communications Integration Cell (NJCCIC), 2017

Ransomware Modus Operandi

Studies indicate that several variants of ransomware have their unique Modus operandi (Method of operation). Several experts describe (Fruhlinger, 2017; Sarah, 2017) how ransomware works in many academic works. However, for easy comprehension, we decided to follow an approach which is described by Liska and Gallo (2016) Figure 3 illustrates how ransomware works in reality.

Deployment: Phase 1

In the deployment phase, a payload is deployed on the targeted machine in form of a malware or legitimate file with malware embedded within. This phase cannot be achieved except one or two of the following actors is put in place (Liska & Gallo, 2017): (1) Drive-by download – Here, a piece of malicious code is embedded within the codes of a comprised site and is downloaded onto the system without the user's authorisation. (2) Phishing - This is one of the popular methods for ransomware campaign. Through this means, legitimate emails are sent to users with malicious attachments or compromised links. With a single click, the system becomes infected. (3) Exploiting system's vulnerability - This includes conducting a reconnaissance of the target network or system and exploiting the vulnerability

Figure 3. Stages of Compromise (Liska A. and Gallo T. (2017)
Source: Ransomware: Defending Against Digital Extortion- by Liska A. and Gallo T. (2017)

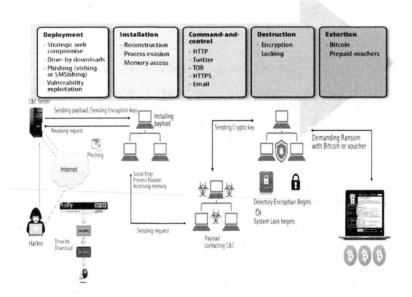

found. (4) Malvertisement- here, malicious codes are embedded within legitimate advertisement websites to be used for luring victims (Savage et al., 2015).

Installation: Phase 2

In this phase, as soon as the malicious malware is delivered to the target, the impacting process also begins. Usually, the infection is being propagated using a method called DDM (Download Dropper Method). In this method, a small piece of the file is dropped which is designed to evade detection. After impact, it establishes a connection between the infected system and a server in a remote location known as Command-and-control server where the main malware and instructions are stored. (Liska & Gallo, 2017).

Communication and Exchange Phase: Phase 3

In this phase, communication is established between target and a remote server called C&C server. The C&C server acts as the commanding officer-in-charge of operations. It ensures that smooth communication channel between the target and server is established. Meanwhile, the payload begins to request for instructions on how to carry further action. The instructions include identifying the types of files that are to be encrypted, which encryption algorithm they should use, and whether they should continue to spread at the beginning of the process or not. More so, a synchronisation process often takes place in some ransomware variants, where the malware report back significant information such as system information, domain names, IP addresses, operating system banners, information about installed antivirus, and so on (Liska & Gallo, 2017; Sophos, 2017).

Destruction: Phase 4

In this phase, all malicious files that will carry out the operations in the form of encryption and deletion are put in place; the targeted files are also identified. The encryption keys have also been supplied to the malcode. Now encryption or deletion will begin. In most cases the malcode will encrypt files with extension such as .doc, .jpg, .gif, .pdf, .xsl, .xml, .zip, .exe and many more (Mattias, Frick, Sjostrom, & Jarpe, 2016).

Extortion: Phase 5

In this phase, however, it is expected that the hackers have eradicated all backed up files, encryption of sensitive files have also taken place. The next is to generate a notification on the victim's screen informing them that they have been compromised. The different variants of ransomware have their unique ways of displaying their demand messages. However, in this notification, the victim is informed on how to pay the ransom for the release of the system which is now paid using bitcoin. If the first allotted time expires, the ransom is doubled (Comtact, 2017; Klein, 2017; Liska & Gallo, 2017).

Ransomware Infection Vectors

Attack vectors are basically the transmission channels through which a machine is being infected by a particular attack or another (Zimba, Wang, & Chen, 2017). All types of attacks come with their different and unique campaign strategies. Our case study here is ransomware. There are various attack vectors which are peculiar to ransomware. Perhaps the majority of experts believe that the most commonly used attack vector for ransomware attacks is known as phishing attack (Brodsky, 2017; Mehmood, 2016; Zimba et al., 2017), and according to a study by Barracuda networks (Goodall, 2017), 90% of anonymous emails received in the last two years are email phishing. Although, among the newly discovered ransomware variants, exploit kits are now used in the last few months for carrying the attacks. Malvertising has also become very handy these days, as many have fallen victims of this method (Paul Zindell, 2017; Rubens, 2017b). Experts have also identified other types of attack vectors, and they comprise of the following:

1. **Smishing**: This is a technique used by hackers to deceive victim into navigating to a site and providing their personal information. This attack is mostly carried on Android and IOS based mobile devices (Vanderburg, 2016).
2. **Vishing**: This is an automated voicemail attack that lures the victim into calling a premium phone number. The caller in the other end usually impersonates a customer representative of a fake company, who directs the victim into installing the malware on their machine (Vanderburg, 2016).
3. **Drive-By Download**: This method allows the victim to download malware on their machine from a legitimate website that is compromised by malicious codes (Lawn, 2016; Vanderburg, 2016).
4. **Network Propagation**: This is an instance whereby worm-like ransomware is spread across a given network and affected all the vulnerable machines on the network (Vanderburg, 2016).
5. **Freeware Trojans**: Hackers sometimes share bad software with bad codes on the internet with free value and access, to trap unsuspecting individuals. These kinds of software are available for free to download Use of such could open backdoors and eventually lead to a massive attack.

6. **Flash Player**: FP is a small program that is provided by the software giant Adobe Systems. It is intended to support multimedia files on the internet. Several reports came in explaining how some group of hackers used fake FP to coordinate attacks (AdobeForum, 2017; Collins, 2017). Adobe system confirms that victims were diverted from legitimate websites of Adobe to compromised ones where they get the fake software downloaded on their systems (Symantec, 2017).

7. **Messaging Apps**: Hackers embed malicious JavaScript in messages conveyed through Facebook Messenger containing images in Scalable Graphics File (SVG) format. With a click, the image directs the victim to a spoofed YouTube site and deceive the victim into installing a codec file (Rubens, 2017b) which eventually compromised the system.

Indicators of Compromise (IOC)

In every instance of a ransomware attack, attackers always leave a trail. Those trails are what experts refer to as indicators or sign of compromise. Rigorous study and assessment of some selected compromised machines have provided hints on the indicators that prove a machine has been compromised. According to a SANS's periodic white paper some of the early indicators of compromise are obvious to the user while some are not obvious enough. When a machine gets infected by a variant of ransomware, system files extensions begin to change; bulk file renames occurs, explicit ransom notice appears boldly on display screen. While in other cases, possible denial of services also occurs (Majd, 2017). Similarly, Cisco Systems further describes that when the machine is compromised specific behavioural indicators begin to show themselves. Some of these indicators include disappearance of wallpaper background, document file establishing network communication, files being modified in the system directory, VBA Macro uses CallByName, artifact flagged by antivirus engines, a submitted document caused a crash dump file to be created, heavy traffic created by unknown programs, occurrence of DNS traffic, unknown processes running unknown activities, system eventually slowing down and many more (CISCO, 2017). Ericka Chickowski, a columnist at Dark Reading News, while reporting on the indicators states that other critical signs include *unusual outbound network traffic, anomalies in privileged user account activity, geographical irregularities, other log-in red flags, swells in Database read Volume, HTML response sizes, large numbers of requests for the same file, mismatched port-application traffic, suspicious registry or system file changes, DNS request anomalies, unexpected patching of systems, bundles of data in the wrong places, web traffic with unhuman behavior* etcetera (Chickowski, 2013). Some of the indicators above can easily be traceable on the system, whereas others can only be identified with the help of some tools.

Common Ransomware Targets

In the last few decades, the targets of ransomware were very specific and few. Most of them were either organisations, government sectors or individuals. Now, ransomware has widened its attack coverage to other areas. Nowadays, ransomware target could be anyone or anything including individuals (Mehmood, 2016), law Enforcement (Krotoski, 2017), government agencies (Ravindranath, 2016), retailers (Kaspersky, 2016b; Starr, 2018), telecoms companies (Wall, 2018), manufacturers (Perrett, 2018), entertainment, construction and charity organizations (Murray, 2017), transport systems (Williams, 2016), educational institutions (Robbins, 2017), hospitals (Davis, 2016), and financial institutions (Harpur, 2017; Kaspersky, 2017b) (See figure 3 for illustration on ratio of ransomware attacks and targets). Lately, the focus of the attack is on cloud databases and storage systems (As we have seen in September 2017 when ransomware attacked against MongoDB databases and hijacked over 45,000 MongoDB databases. (enisa report, 2017)) as well as IoT devices and gadgets due to the versatility of their platforms and other factors including zero-day exploits. Subsequently, Kaspersky Security Bulletin: Threat Predictions for 2018 predicts that by 2020, billions of cars will be constructed and there is a chance that 98% of the cars will be connected to the Internet. So with this indication, there is a clear sign that automobiles would be the next ransomware targets (Kaspersky, 2017a).

Figure 4. Ransomware attack targets (Kaspersky, 2017)
Source: Kaspersky Security Bulletin, 2017

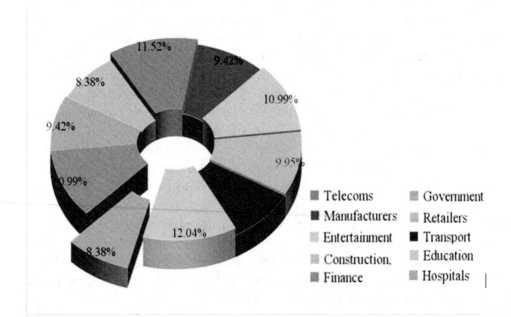

Mode of Payment for Ransom

Initially, it is essential to know that from the time of compromise some ransomware give the ultimatum of 72 hours to pay the ransom. If the deadline is over, the ransom gets increased. The mode of payment for ransom in most cases is categorised based on the hacker's choice. Perhaps, the mode of payment keeps changing dramatically over time. For instance, the earlier ransomware victims were asked to pay the ransom through what was known as Traveler's cheque until later in 1990 when it was completely abolished. Later as technology evolves, a computer scientist and expert in cryptology by the name Satoshi Nakamoto invented a unique digital Cryptocurrency popularly known as Bitcoin in 2009. Since its invention, hackers began to use it. They use the cryptocurrency because no bank or third party is needed, and it is untraceable, safe and reliable for anonymous transactions (Kshetri & Voas, 2017). Other recently discovered modes of payments include iTunes and Amazon Gift Cards. Although, both payment methods are not considered any more (Olenick, 2016).

Causes of Ransomware Attacks

It is believed that the most recent ransomware campaigns that hit many targets were due to insider threat or corrupt staff. According to a report, 90% of organizations today feel vulnerable to malicious insider threats (Insider threat report, 2018). Malicious insider in an organization can hire hackers from outside to help bring down the organization through phishing emails and or other types of attacks. In some of the reported cases, the adversories successful launched the attacks with the help of insider's credentials (Cohen, 2018). However, experts have analysed hundreds of ransomware cases and concluded that among the likely causes of ransomware attacks are a failure to patch up systems' vulnerabilities regularly and added that lack of proper security policy management is also factor, too, which is absolutely true as we have seen in the case of Wannacry victims. Other undeniable factors are included in Table 2.

Table 2. Causes of ransomware attacks

Common Causes of Ransomware Attacks
1. Lack of Staff Training
2. Lack of support from top management
3. Staff negligence
4. Using pirated software and applications
5. Inadequate security infrastructure
6. Bad security policies

RANSOMWARE MANAGEMENT TECHNIQUES

In this section, we propose the state-of-the-art techniques for preventing systems/devices and users from ransomware attack risks through a range of protective, detective and preventive measures as identified by this study.

Preventive Measures

Preventing Malicious Insider Threats

Insiders can either be accidental insiders or malicious insiders. Simple training and awareness seminars can help prevent an accidental insider from being hacked. While malicious insiders are unpredictable and undetected, hence are not detected early. To prevent such attacks, use User Behavior Analytics tools to track suspicious behavior in the organization. Also, use log and event manager to monitor users who don't follow security protocols and reduce their excessive access privileges in case they decided to abuse them. In addition to that, implement IDS/IPS on sensitive assets to detect insider exploits on the network (Insider Threat Report, 2018). Recently, IDS have proved to be efficient in detecting insider threats.

Conduct Training and Create Awareness

It is worth noting that end users are usually targeted or used as a gateway into the infrastructure when it comes to ransomware attacks. Meaning, people are the weakest link (Westin, 2017). It is believed that lack of knowledge of ransomware has contributed to many ransomware attacks in these recent years. Therefore, they training of employees and making sure they are aware of how to identify and manage ransomware situations would help in preventing ransomware attacks (Bambenek, 2017; Dawes, 2017; Kalember, 2017; Saurbaugh & Liska, 2017; TrendMicro, 2017; Yaqoob et al., 2017). However, the training of personnel should be focused on specific areas. Hence, it is recommended that trainees should be taught how to deal with certain types of situations such as phishing attacks, social engineering attacks, espionage, malvertising, advanced persistent threat attack, etcetera (Downs, Cook, et al., 2017).

Backup Data

So far so good, backup has proven to be one of the most effective and reliable means of preventing ransomware damage. Hence, perform regular backup and verify the backup to ensure integrity and validity of the backed-up files. Also, ensure that backup storage are not connected to network (Bambenek, 2017; Brodsky, 2017; Dawes, 2017; Haley & Sherman, 2017; Januszkiewicz, 2017; NoMoreRansomware, 2017a; Perekalin, 2017b; Phil, Chris, & Amber, 2017; Singh, Grantz, Payne, Laing, & Wolf, 2017; TrendLabs, 2017).

According to Unitrends, an effective backup strategy known as 3-2-1 rule is one of the best approaches nowadays for ensuring data safety during ransomware outbreak. Many including TrendMicro considers this strategy as one of the best methods for backing up data. The backup can be done systematically as follows: 3 copies of your data, store in 2 different types of media storages and store 1 copy of data in an off-site location. User must test back up several times to ensure that backed up data is valid and restorable (Fimin, 2017; Goodall, 2017; Harpur, 2017; Jordan, 2017; Kalember, 2017; Micro, 2017; Saurbaugh & Liska, 2017; Singh, 2017; UniTrend, 2017).

Haley and Sherman (2017), on the other hand add incremental backup as a solution to backup issue especially on endpoints. Similarly, Watson believes users should back up their data using what he refers to as Volume Shadow Copy Service-based backup. VSS is an application based backup system in windows machines which uses two methods namely clone and copy-on-write to create shadow copies of backup from snapshots (Watson, 2017).

Apply System Updates, Security Patches and System Upgrades

Recently, we have seen how failure to patch systems had contributed considerably to the WannaCry and Petya ransomware pandemic in 2017. Henceforth, ensure that all systems' operating systems are patched up and up to date. To achieve a successful patch up, use software assets management solution like Symantec Endpoint software manager, TripWire, Corvil which can understand which version of software needs to be patched and on which computer. Also, make sure that firmware and third-party software including Adobe Flash, Java, Web browsers are patched too (Beek & Furtak, n.d.; Dawes, 2017; Goodall, 2017; Kalember, 2017; Saurbaugh & Liska, 2017; TrendLabs, 2017). Likewise, ensure that any application on the system that connects to the internet is always up to date and fully patched(Liska & Gallo, 2017). On top of that, users should beware of fake security patches and updates which are downloadable via torrents and popular sites which masquerades the official patches. Such files' extensions are labelled as Patcher, so beware of those.

Use Robust Anti-Malware and Anti-Virus Solutions

Security giants like Trend Micro, Kaspersky, and McAfee claim that using a robust anti-malware and or antivirus could help detect and block ransomware from attacking.

According to the giants, they boasted that their labs had successfully blocked over 4 million variants of ransomware from 2015 to date (Abiodun et al., 2018; Dawes, 2017; Januszkiewicz, 2017; Kalember, 2017; Perekalin, 2017b; Westin, 2017).

Proper Security Policy Implementation

Poor security policy implementation could open direct access to the organisation's infrastructure especially when Insider threats exists. The first step to tackle this issue is by making sure that security policies are properly administered by experts and are administered on every critical system in the organization's infrastructure. Then make sure all administrative privileges are appropriately assigned to the right users. Also, make sure that the policy of least privilege assignment is handled efficiently (FBI, 2016a). This will automatically reduce the power of malicious insiders. It is reported that variants of ransomware take advantage of this privileges and exploit the systems. Henceforth, users should use administrative privileges and administrative accounts only when it is necessary (Fimin, 2017; Harpur, 2017; Phil et al., 2017; TrendMicro, 2017; Westin, 2017).

Furthermore, it is advised that access control is configured on files, directory and network share permissions; make it read-only on those directory locations (FBI, 2016b; Leong, Beek, Cochin, Cowie, & Schmugar, 2016; Mehmood, 2016). Also, set up software control policies to prevent programs from executing themselves automatically without user's authorisation especially %AppData% and %LocalAppData% folder (Harpur, 2017). Likewise, enforce UAC (User Account Control) feature found in windows OS; as it helps prevent malware from executing itself. If it manages to execute itself, UAC will pop up an authentication dialogue box for the user to sanction it (Downs, Cook, et al., 2017; Harpur, 2017).

Disable Unwanted Functions, Features and Services

It is indisputably true that operating systems do come with many features and services that are not always used by the operating system or the user. For instance, communication ports and some active directory services etc.. These features and services can be exploited by hackers when they are not secured or idle. Assessment of malware cases shows that different variants of ransomware have used Microsoft office Macros as a point of entry to exploit the system. Hence, disable macros so that files sent through email cannot have an impact on the macros. Likewise open attached emailed documents using a simple office viewer rather than using the whole Office suite (Downs, Taylor, et al., 2017; Harpur, 2017; Kalember, 2017; Saurbaugh & Liska, 2017; Singh, 2017; Westin, 2017). Also, disable WMI, by doing so it will be impossible for ransomware to spread over the network.

Decentralize Resource and Isolate Network Components

Decentralize and segregate critical files and other resources including network resources and devices, throughout the organisation. That could be achieved by implementing logical/physical separation of resources and network items based on organisational units and or departments within the corporate organisations (Dawes, 2017; Downs, Taylor, et al., 2017; Fimin, 2017; Harpur, 2017; Saurbaugh & Liska, 2017; Stenhouse, 2016). Also, at the physical layer of the network, implement VLAN as another effective method for segmentation of critical infrastructure (Stenhouse, 2016). This method if appropriately implemented could prevent ransomware from spreading over the network. Meanwhile, if it happens to spread, it could easily be contained within a given space.

Set Up Security Support Team

It is highly recommended that every organisation should have at least a team of IT support personnel who can analyse and deal with the threat before it escalates. Also, IT personnel are advised to join the dark web so as to acquire knowledge on new threats and vulnerabilities; that will make them aware of how to address new threats (Downs, Taylor, et al., 2017; Singh et al., 2017). However, it is a good practice to keep your IT support team on speed dial. That sounds funny, but it can save you time and reduce the impact of attack if help comes quickly.

Avoid Using Freeware

Visiting compromised sites to download freeware could endanger your entire organisations. Visit only sites that are trusted. To ensure trustworthiness of a site, the user can tighten security by configuring security zone in the internet option from the system's control panel. Raise the zone security level from the default (medium) to High. Users can also use third-party software solutions for monitoring compromised sites such as Kaspersky internet security.

System Hardening and Hygiene

Usually, poor security hygiene is in many cases the cause of cybersecurity risk on systems. Therefore, maintaining proper security hygiene is vital (Westin, 2017). Some of the good practices for sanitising and hardening system's security are explained as follows. Part of system hygiene is blocking ads and unnecessary web contents from accessing your browser because criminals use legitimate sites for malicious intent (Harpur, 2017). Likewise run system check up and diagnosis periodically, this could help uncover premature risks and vulnerabilities. Perform periodic penetration testing on your organisation's resources. That could help identify vulnerabilities that could endanger the infrastructure (Haley & Sherman, 2017).

Protective Measures

Implement End-Point Security

One of the significant roles played by endpoint security (EPS) is reducing or eliminating chances of getting exposed to untrusted sources. Implementing endpoint solutions could help control access to critical and sensitive information within and outside the organisations (Beek & Furtak, n.d.; Brodsky, 2017; Downs, Taylor, et al., 2017). In light of that, End-Point solution could be any form of solution, such as ransomware behavior monitor, vulnerability shielding system, malware profiler, web server protector, email and gateway protector, spear-phishing protector etc. (Brodsky, 2017; Dawes, 2017; Goodall, 2017; Saurbaugh & Liska, 2017; TrendLabs, 2017; Westin, 2017). Another strategy for endpoint protection is the implementation of DNS sinkhole. The sinkhole is a trap designed on the DNS server to prevent resolving hostnames of some selected URLs. Some of its common functions include blocking access to Drive-by download websites, controlling and blocking access to C&C channels and other malicious traffics (Mazerik, 2014).

Filter and Monitor Incoming Emails

Provide a solution that can filter and monitor all incoming emails and make sure links and attachments are not malicious. Moreover, do not attempt to open any suspicious link or attachment unless you are sure of their authenticity or forward them to the IT department for further evaluation (Downs, Taylor, et al., 2017; FBI, 2016a; Goodall, 2017).

Use Virtually Controlled Environments

It is a good practice to execute suspicious items in a controlled environment such as virtual machines and sandboxing tools to limit and control the impact of the damage it might cause. (FBI, 2016a) Another smart move is to make Notepad the default program for opening script files such as JavaScript, PS, WSH etc. (Harpur, 2017; Leong et al., 2016). You can also use a type of endpoint solutions that have sandbox embedded in them which provides a micro virtualised platform for testing email attachments, word docs and so on (Liska & Gallo, 2017).

Implement Program Whitelisting

The implementation of application control using AppLocker for whitelisting programs, software and applications could help a lot in restricting unauthorised and unknown programs from executing. WannaCry, Petya, NotPetya have benefitted from this vulnerability. Moreover, many experts view it amongst the most effective ways of preventing ransomware from launching itself on the system (FBI, 2016a; Harpur, 2017; Leong et al., 2016; Singh, 2017; Stenhouse, 2016; Westin, 2017).

Migrate Data to Cloud-Based Service

Migrating data to cloud-based data protection services is the smartest move for protecting data in the era of ransomware. Although it has certain ramifications including cost and espionage. Nevertheless, the benefits are boundless as it enhances recoverability and reliability of backups as well as security and compatibility (Reavis & Nielsen, 2017). Alternatively, you can implement DRaaS. According to Rouse, (2017), DRaaS is a physical or virtual server machine that provides third-party failover services in the event that the main systems fail. DRaaS has the ability to backup data with less user interaction and also in the event that the system fails, it quickly restores the data back to its original form.

Detection Techniques

Deploy Firewalls With IDS/IPS

By deploying an effective firewall equipped with intrusion detection and prevention capabilities, and then feeding them with updated signatures. The user has a very high chance of detecting and stopping ransomware from establishing a connection with the C&C server (Brodsky, 2017; Dawes, 2017; Harpur, 2017; Saurbaugh & Liska, 2017). Alternatively, the user could impose spam filtering as well as web gateway filtering to tighten the security.

Deploy Heuristic Detection Solutions

There are a variety of solutions out there that help you detect ransomware. Perhaps the choice of heuristic detection solutions would give an added advantage to the user. Heuristic solutions have the ability to learn and adapt to any situation. Their learnability is what makes them unique. Thus, budget for tools and solutions that detect known and unknown variants of ransomware family and ensure they can automatically feed their repository with latest signatures of new variants of ransomware (Harpur, 2017; Reavis & Nielsen, 2017).

Monitor Events and System Logs

Event logs have been so valuable and resourceful when it comes to uncovering cybersecurity mysteries. We must say that; events and logs monitors have helped uncover many ransomware activities and helped stopped them from further damage. However, security experts believe that lots of security failure come due to reluctance to analyse event logs. Hence set log filters and monitors to track the activities of your system to find anomalies or untrusted activities (Ambre & Shekokar, 2015; Brodsky, 2017; Grimes, 13AD).

Traffic Analytics

Traffic analytics are cloud based solutions that monitor and track the activities of network resources. When implemented on DNS they are very handy when it comes to detecting anomalies especially when the attack is in motion and communication has been established between the malcode and the C&C server. So by blocking the communication chain, you have automatically stopped the attack(Robert Lemos, n.d.). Likewise they are adaptive with third party cloud service providers such as azure. They can work alongside virtual networks and network watchers.

Deploy Honeypot

Honeypot is a decoy set in the network to help proactively detect suspicious activities in the network before they could make any serious damage (Stephen Rouine, 2017). Ideally, honeypots are not deployed to prevent ransomware from attacking; instead, they are a line of defence that gives the administrator a baseline to signal that something is about to happen. Hence, deploying honeypot could give the administrator time and opportunity to quickly shut down computers and network devices before they get infected (Darragh Delaney, 2016; Moore, 2016; Stenhouse, 2016; Surati & Prajapati, 2017).

HOW TO RESPOND TO RANSOMWARE INCIDENTS

Responding to Pre-Attack Phase

Design Incident Response Plan

The response plan is a piece of paperwork containing contingency plans about how an organisation can quickly respond to a disaster in case it occurs. So, usually, it contains some routine exercises that are to be carried out during the response period. In talking about incident response plan, the National Institute of standards and technology has published a 79-page response guideline. In one section, it describes the major stages of incident response process which comprises of preparation, detection and analysis, containment, eradication and recovery, and post-incident activity (See Figure 5). Read more from the source (Kruger, 2017; Paul, Tom, Grance, & Karen, 2012; Union & For, 2016).

Similarly, Harpur (2017) says a response plan should have the following checklist of 10 exercises: (1) respond quickly, (2) isolate infected device to contain infection, (3) preserve the encrypted data, (4) determine if you have backups, (5) identify the ransomware, (6) determine if a decryption tool is available online, (7) restore or decrypt, (8) last resort is to pay ransom, (9) review and strengthen the infection point, and lastly, (10) fully wipe and re-image infected device (Harpur, 2017).

Figure 5. Incident response plan (Computer security Incident handling guide, 2012)
Source: National Institute of standards and technology, 2012

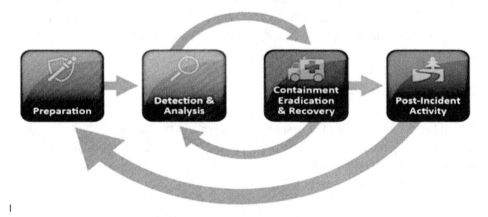

Get Cybersecurity Insurance

Some organisations when attacked cannot respond quickly due to a shortage of resources to facilitate an effective and quick response. So in order to stay put, it is advised that the organisation avails an insurance policy to enable the organisation to put in place all the resources required for a full response and recovery (Hamlin & Rutledge, 2017).

Responding to Campaign Phase

Situation Analysis Through Tabletop Exercise

Hold a special meeting among high ranking organisation's members to discuss emergency situations. Hence, set up a team to analyse the situation at hand by focusing on the following: (1) What exactly you are dealing with, (2) how did the attack happen, (3) what part of the system is affected, (4) how to deal with the incident. (5) determine whether a Legal action will be taken (6) and lastly, how to improve the situation and get back to work (Hamlin & Rutledge, 2017; Saurbaugh & Liska, 2017).

Report Suspicious Activities

One of the good etiquettes that are often associated with a good staff is the ability to report suspicious activities upon discovery. Suspicious activities could be heavy traffic, idle ports becoming actives suddenly, system misbehaving on its own etc. (Downs, Taylor, et al., 2017; Singh, 2017). Thus, establishing an efficient process of reporting incidents as soon as they are detected on the systems (Hamlin & Rutledge, 2017).

Impose Human Firewall

Put all hands-on deck. Get the best IT support team to try and do everything at their disposal to stop the ransomware from propagating itself at its early stage (Hamlin & Rutledge, 2017). Train some of your staff on how to handle emergency situations and how to recover from them.

Responding to Infection Phase

Use Sandbox

Sandboxing allows the user to execute the suspected ransomware in a controlled environment using a special virtual system and analyse the behaviour of the malware. However, one of the best practices for responding to ransomware attack is to sandbox the threat, reverse engineer it and analyse it (Maass, 2016; TrendLabs, 2017; Westin, 2017). This gives you a clue to answer questions like who designed the malware, what encryption algorithm it uses, what similarities or difference it has from other variants, what weaknesses or strength it possesses, and in what way does it affect the system.

Report Incidents to Law Enforcement

The Internet Crime Complaint Center in their public service announcement dated September 2016 had urged the public to report any cyber incidents to www.IC3. gov quickly. Likewise the FBI request victims to submit the following information while reporting the threat: Date of infection, ransomware family or variant, victim company details, how the infection happened, ransom amount, attacker's bitcoin wallet address, overall losses, and impact statement (Harpur, 2017; NoMoreRansomware, 2017a; Ubale & Isyaku, 2017).

Reset Passwords and Entry Codes

Upon realising that the entire system has been compromised, it will be smart to quickly change login passwords, entry codes, authentication keys and what have you. A study reveals that some ransomware not only deploys a malware but also use that opportunity to steal other information including login credentials, financial information and so on (Mark Dargin, n.d.).

Exit User Accounts With Admin Privilege

As soon as an attack is detected on organisation's computer, sign out from all user accounts with administrative privileges. Moreover, if there are IoT appliances that are managed by computers, like the elevators, room conditioning system, temperature controllers, gas controllers etc., stay away and shut them down too. If one or two files or script is responsible for controlling them, they could jam off as the system goes down.

Responding to Communication (C&C) Phase

Disconnect Machines From the Network

Upon discovering any strange activities on your system, simply disconnect it from the internet as some ransomware variants have to retrieve the encryption key from the C&C server. Hence, wait a moment and understand the situation or call IT support for help (Harpur, 2017; Januszkiewicz, 2017; NoMoreRansomware, 2017a; Ryan Harnedy, 2016).

Block Untrusted Domains From Firewall

Firewall is your first line of defence, hence use the firewall rules to block incoming and outgoing communications that might be established with the C&C server. That could help terminate the exchange between the malcode and the C&C server from taking place (McAfee, n.d.). However, this is where the role of network monitoring tools come, they have the ability to trace the URL through which the malcode is trying to navigate to. Hence, you can be able to break or block the connection.

Block Tor Browser

When you realise that you are under attack, block access to tor. Experts learned that Tor could be used by ransomware to obfuscate communication to the C&C server. Which means Tor is clearing the passage for the crypto to be delivered (McAfee, n.d.).

Responding to Encryption Phase

Isolate Infected Source and Control Spread

If the response team can quickly identify the infected machine, then, it is recommended that the infected machine is isolated from the rest of the machines to avoid rapid spread (Stenhouse, 2016). Also, detach all network connectors from the machine, disabling all shared drive and disconnect external attachments in the form of devices if the infection has not spread yet (Mark Dargin, n.d.; Reavis & Nielsen, 2017).

Use Threshold Alert for Crypto API Calls

Some variants of ransomware usually use one of the windows feature known as Windows Crypto API to manage encryption. In the process of encryption, some unusual calls are made to the Crypto API. So by creating a threshold alert to trigger an alarm whenever suspected calls are detected, the user can link the alert to an endpoint solution which will be able to stop the encryption or inform the admin about an ongoing attack (Liska & Gallo, 2017).

Using Bait for Honeyfile and Honeydirectories

A Honeyfile is also an intrusion detection technique which uses a bait file that is deliberately kept for ransomware to access. A group of files with different formats like doc, pdf, Jpeg are stored in a decoy file server, and the files are given names that can be attractive to anyone with malicious intent like company salary list or Top Secret. As soon as the ransomware hit and begin to encrypt them, an alarm is triggered and is sent to the IT team for further action (Saurbaugh & Liska, 2017).

Responding to Payoff Demand Phase

There have been controversies over the issue of whether victims of ransomware attack should pay the ransom or not. Lots of experts and even law enforcement agencies have differed in this regard. Liska and Gallo assert that ransom should not be paid unless the system or device plays a significant role in the organisation's network or content of the device or system is critical. A commonwealth article discloses that paying the ransom has both pros and cons. Hence, by paying, the victim might get their files back while sometimes they do not get them back. If the victim refuses to pay, the price gets increased and eventually lose their files (CommonWealth, 2017). The popular European site known as No more ransom also discourages paying the ransom as there is no guarantee for restore of data, and also, problems might arise in future especially if the malware used in operation has a payload which is designed to steal information from users (No-More-Ransom, 2017). Notwithstanding, paying the ransom should be an option when the situation is unavoidable and seems to be the last choice. Hence, a few suggestions are given on how the victim should pay the ransom:

1. Before making the payment, find out the exact family or variant of the ransomware you are dealing with by searching online or consulting cybersecurity experts. A few security agencies often released ransomware decryption tools on their sites.
2. Check whether you have backups, if you do, just wipe the system clean and install new OS again. After that, discard the ransom demand.
3. In the absence of a backup, visit websites like No More Ransomware for free ransomware decryption tools as they update their reservoir frequently.

4. As part of your contingency plan, learn how cryptocurrency works, how to buy a cryptocurrency especially Bitcoin.
5. If paying has become the last option, reach out to an expert who knows how Bitcoin works, that is, if victims cannot pay for themselves.
6. Yaqoob et al. (2017) recommend that as part of the payment procedure, the victims should try to negotiate minimum ransom payable to the hackers as report shows that some hackers allow bargaining with the victims (Bambenek, 2017; Yaqoob et al., 2017).
7. Arrange the purchase and go ahead and make the payment. At the very time, the researchers were writing this paper one bitcoin is 11,182.23 USD.

CONCLUSION

So far, we have seen in the above discourse how detrimental ransomware could be if unleashed on our businesses, lives and our security. It is undeniably true that what we have witnessed so far is just the tip of the iceberg. Surely ransomware is growing bigger and smarter every day (Singh, 2017). It is sophisticated enough to evade pursuit; it is becoming more difficult to tackle than ever. With the disturbing WIKILEAKS news about how a million dollar hacking project arsenal comprising of viruses, trojans, malware, weaponised zero-day exploit kits, as well as malware remote control frameworks and related documentation got stolen from the NSA servers (Wikileaks, n.d.). Since then, many have a fear that the next generation ransomware will not just hit small targets, instead it will target critical infrastructure like nuclear power plants, cruise missile controllers, submarines, drone controllers and so on. When that time comes, we will not just be dealing with crypto ransomware anymore, instead, we will be dealing with weaponised ransomware and AI-based ransomware that will be capable of mass destruction.

REFERENCES

Abiodun, O. I., Jantan, A., Omolara, A. E., Mahinderjit, M. M., Abubakar, Z. L., & Umar, A. M. (2018). Big Data : An Approach for Detecting Terrorist Activities with People ' s Profiling. In *Proceedings of the International MultiConference of Engineers and Computer Scientists* (Vol. 1). IMECS.

AdobeForum. (2017). *A new strain of ransomware nicknamed "Bad Rabbit" asks to update Adobe Flash Player*. Retrieved from https://goo.gl/oSq6zr

Ambre, A., & Shekokar, N. (2015). Insider Threat Detection Using Log Analysis and Event Correlation. *Procedia Computer Science*, *45*, 436–445. doi:10.1016/j.procs.2015.03.175

Ashford, W. (2015). *Ransomware growing rapidly, warns Intel's McAfee Labs.* Retrieved October 25, 2017, from https://goo.gl/NjFjmE

Bambenek, J. (2017). *Ransomware in the Age of Wannacry: What Fintech Needs to Know.* Retrieved May 18, 2017, from https://goo.gl/A5HwbU

Barracuda. (2017). *Understanding Ransomware.* Retrieved October 25, 2017, from https://goo.gl/qUisCG

Beek, C., & Furtak, A. (n.d.). Analysis of a targeted and manual ransomware campaign. *International Security.*

Brodsky, J. (2017). *Detection of Ransomware and Prevention Strategies.* Retrieved October 20, 2017, from https://goo.gl/mpExdZ

Brunau, C. (2017). *Common Types of Ransomware.* Retrieved January 17, 2018, from https://goo.gl/Kczkyz

Cabaj, K., Gregorczyk, M., & Mazurczyk, W. (2017). Software-defined networking-based crypto ransomware detection using HTTP traffic characteristics. *Computers & Electrical Engineering*, *0*, 1–16.

Chickowski, E. (2013, September 10). Indicators Of Compromise. *Dark Reading News*. Retrieved from https://goo.gl/aE2TqQ

CISCO. (2017). Indicators of Compromise and Where to Find Them. *Cisco Blogs*. Retrieved from https://goo.gl/VULXTo

Collins, K. (2017). *The latest ransomware presents itself as an Adobe Flash Player download.* Retrieved January 22, 2018, from https://goo.gl/MeLQmQ

CommonWealth. (2017). To Pay or Not to Pay: How to Survive a Ransomware Attack. *Common Wealth Financial Network*. Retrieved from https://goo.gl/VzXLfk

Comtact. (2017). *How Ransomware Works.* Retrieved January 21, 2018, from compact.co.uk

Crowe, J. (2016). *Ransomware by the Numbers: Must-Know Ransomware Statistics 2016.* Retrieved January 6, 2018, from https://goo.gl/Nn3CRk

Crowe, J. (2017). *Must-Know Ransomware Statistics 2017.* Retrieved from https://goo.gl/FBVFns

Cyber_Intelligence_Team. (2017). *Ransomware: What you need to know*. European Cybercrimes Centre.

Darragh Delaney. (2016). *5 Methods For Detecting Ransomware Activity*. Retrieved February 18, 2018, from https://goo.gl/qcxpUE

Davis, J. (2016, October 5). Ransomware: See the 14 hospitals attacked so far in 2016. *Healthcare IT News*. Retrieved from https://goo.gl/TJFie5

Dawes, S. (2017). *WannaCry Ransomware: How to Detect the Vulnerability and Exploits*. Retrieved October 21, 2017, from https://goo.gl/A1ukWN

Downs, J., Cook, D., Wright, J., & Kent, J. (2017). *Protecting Data in the Age of Ransomware*. Retrieved October 13, 2017, from https://goo.gl/YJ2f94

Downs, J., Taylor, A., & Whiting, I. (2017). *Fighting Ransomware & Responding if the Worst Happens*. Retrieved October 1, 2017, from https://goo.gl/WSrVM3

F-Secure. (n.d.). *Crypto-ransomware*. Retrieved January 17, 2018, from https://goo.gl/amkNiU

FBI. (2015). *Criminals Continue To Defraud And Extort Funds From Victims Using Cryptowall Ransomware Schemes*. Retrieved from https://goo.gl/b7GSog

FBI. (2016a). *Ransomware Victims Urged To Report Infections to Federal Law Enforcement*. Retrieved from https://goo.gl/8vNpVo

FBI. (2016b, April 29). Incidents of Ransomware on the Rise. *Federal Bureau of Investigation*. Retrieved from https://goo.gl/z8Z1Bf

Fimin, M. (2017). Are employees part of the ransomware problem? *Computer Fraud & Security, 2017*(8), 15–17.

Fortinet. (2017). *Threat Landscape Report*. Author.

Fruhlinger, J. (2017). *What is ransomware? How it works and how to remove it*. Retrieved January 19, 2018, from https://goo.gl/UJJ1C8

Goodall, D. (2017). *Ransomware: The Best Defense*. Retrieved October 14, 2017, from https://goo.gl/z8qyso

Grimes, R. A. (13AD). *Detect the undetectable: Start with event logs*. Retrieved February 13, 2018, from https://goo.gl/eeNyPq

Haley, K., & Sherman, M. (2017). *Defense Against a Ransomware Attack: Latest Research and Best Practices*. Retrieved February 14, 2018, from https://goo.gl/4fHm8h

Hamlin, M., & Rutledge, B. (2017). *How to Recover from a Ransomware Disaster*. Retrieved February 14, 2018, from https://goo.gl/n98EAj

Hampton, N., & Baig, Z. A. (2015). Ransomware: Emergence of the cyber-extortion menace. *Australian Information Security Management Conference, 13*, 47–56.

Harpur, R. (2017). *Cybersecurity Threats: Ransomware*. Retrieved October 21, 2017, from https://goo.gl/xFTKKN

Januszkiewicz, P. (2017). *Ransomware Protection – Top 3 Prevention Techniques to Use*. Retrieved October 24, 2017, from https://goo.gl/PWMQWc

Jordan, M. (2017). *5 Ways Backup Kills Ransomware Threats*. Retrieved July 24, 2017, from https://goo.gl/XdxKay

Kalember, R. (2017). *Ransomware – The Billion Dollar Thief*. Retrieved May 19, 2017, from https://goo.gl/a39FDh

Kaspersky. (2016a). *Kaspersky Security Bulletin 2016*. Retrieved from https://goo.gl/MBUcbe

Kaspersky. (2016b, December 8). Attacks on Business Now Equal One Every 40 Seconds: Ransomware is Kaspersky Lab's Story of the Year 2016. *Kaspersky Lab*. Retrieved from https://goo.gl/NKHKrn

Kaspersky. (2017a). *Kaspersky Security Bulletin: Kaspersky Lab Threat Predictions For 2018*. Retrieved from https://goo.gl/nbXMo6

Kaspersky. (2017b). *Kaspersky Security Bulletin: Review Of The Year 2017*. Retrieved from https://goo.gl/z6yg8W

Klein, T. (2017). *5 Phases of ransomware attacks*. Retrieved January 21, 2018, from https://goo.gl/bGbwkm

Korolov, M. (2017, January 5). Ransomware took in $1 billion in 2016--improved defenses may not be enough to stem the tide. *CSO*. Retrieved from https://goo.gl/26DA32

Krotoski, M. L. (2017, May 22). WannaCry Ransomware Cyberattack Raises Legal Issues. *The National Law Review*. Retrieved from https://goo.gl/gdYnLp

Kruger, Y. (2017). Cyber incident response. *IT Web*. Retrieved from https://goo.gl/vc1ekX

Kshetri, N., & Voas, J. (2017). Do Crypto-Currencies Fuel Ransomware? *IEEE, 19*(5), 11–15.

Lawn, S. (2016). *Ransomware: Current Strains, Attack Vectors And Protection.* Retrieved January 21, 2018, from https://goo.gl/m2tVh7

Leong, R., Beek, C., Cochin, C., Cowie, N., & Schmugar, C. (2016). *Understanding Ransomware and Strategies to Defeat it.* McAfee Labs.

Liska, A., & Gallo, T. (2017). Ransomware: Defending Against Digital Extortion. O'Reilly Media, Inc.

Lord, N. (2017). *A History Of Ransomware Attacks: The Biggest And Worst Ransomware Attacks Of All Time.* Retrieved January 3, 2018, from https://goo.gl/A8o978

Maass, M. (2016). *A Theory and Tools for Applying Sandboxes Effectively.* Carnegie Mellon University. Retrieved from https://goo.gl/Hqcahd

Majd. (2017). *Kaspersky Security Bulletin: Predictions For 2017- 'Indicators Of Compromise' Are Dead.* Retrieved from https://goo.gl/CoLVkB

Margaret Rouse. (2017). *What is Disaster Recovery as a Service (DRaaS)? - Definition from WhatIs.com.* Retrieved February 17, 2018, from https://goo.gl/85dRV2

Mark Dargin. (n.d.). *How to protect your network from ransomeware.* Author.

Mattias, W., Frick, J., Sjostrom, A., & Jarpe, E. (2016). A Novel Method for Recovery from Crypto Ransomware Infections. In *2nd IEEE International Conference on Computer and Communications* (pp. 1354–1358). IEEE.

Mazerik, R. (2014). *Understanding DNS Sinkholes – A weapon against malware.* Retrieved February 13, 2018, from https://goo.gl/JwKDoi

McAfee. (n.d.). *Understanding Ransomware and Strategies to Defeat It White Paper.* Retrieved from https://goo.gl/7vdx3d

Mehmood, S. (2016). *Enterprise Survival Guide for Ransomware Attacks.* SANS Institute InfoSec Reading Room.

Micro, T. (2017). *Ransomware.* Retrieved from https://goo.gl/nZaoAa

Moore, C. (2016). Detecting ransomware with honeypot techniques. *Proceedings - 2016 Cybersecurity and Cyberforensics Conference, CCC 2016,* 77–81.

Morgan, S. (2017). *Ransomware Damage Report.* Retrieved from https://goo.gl/um3tBe

Mort, M. (2017, May 16). Symantec Blocks 22 Million Attempted WannaCry Ransomware Attacks Globally. *Business Wire.* Retrieved from https://goo.gl/BG56TR

Murray, S. (2017, November 8). Charities unprepared for cyber attack risk. *Financial Time*. Retrieved from https://goo.gl/kJmZcm

National Cybersecurity and Communications Integration Center. (2016). *Ransomware and Recent Variants*. Retrieved from https://goo.gl/UBXGBi

NJ Cybersecurity & Communication Integration Cell. (2018). *Ransomware*. Retrieved January 18, 2018, from https://goo.gl/EPUW9G

No-More-Ransom. (2017). *Prevention Advice*. Retrieved October 25, 2017, from https://goo.gl/GK8LzU

NoMoreRansomware. (2017a). *Prevention Advice*. Retrieved February 8, 2018, from https://goo.gl/f16kF3

NoMoreRansomware. (2017b). *The History of Ransomware*. Retrieved January 1, 2018, from https://goo.gl/1Aqxzg

O'Brien, D. (2017). *An Internet Security Threat Report Special Report*. Retrieved from https://www.symantec.com/content/dam/symantec/docs/security-center/white-papers/istr-ransomware-2017-en.pdf

Olenick, D. (2016). *New ransomware demands payment in iTunes, targets older Android software*. Retrieved September 11, 2017, from https://goo.gl/CnomUi

Omolara, A. E., Jantan, A., Abiodun, O. I., & Arshad, H. (2018). *An Enhanced Practical Difficulty of One-Time Pad Algorithm Resolving the Key Management and Distribution Problem*. Academic Press.

Paul, C., Tom, M., Grance, G., & Karen, S. (2012). *Computer Security Incident Handling Guide*. National Institute Of Standards and Technology. US Ministry of Commerce.

Paul Zindell. (2017). *Stopping Ransomware at the Door (and Every Other Threat)*. Retrieved October 16, 2017, from https://goo.gl/S8FSD7

Perekalin, A. (2017a). *Bad Rabbit: A new ransomware epidemic is on the rise*. Retrieved February 9, 2018, from https://goo.gl/Fzg5oL

Perekalin, A. (2017b). *WannaCry: Are you safe?* Retrieved September 20, 2017, from https://goo.gl/hguon9

Perrett, M. (2018, January 22). Food manufacturers warned over 'cyber hurricane' events. *Food Manufacture*. Retrieved from https://goo.gl/2zBPVh

Phil, R., Chris, G., & Amber, B. (2017). *How to Recover from the WanaCrypt Ransomware Attack*. Retrieved September 26, 2017, from https://goo.gl/iRRxzm

Ravindranath, M. (2016, September 21). Ransomware Attacks on Government Agencies Tripled in Past Year. *Nextgov*. Retrieved from https://goo.gl/6HC5tF

Reavis, J., & Nielsen, A. (2017). *Backup & Recovery: Your Get out of Ransomware Free Card*. Retrieved February 14, 2018, from https://goo.gl/CjkLe2

Robbins, G. (2017, January 10). Los Angeles college pays $28,000 in ransomware. *San Diego Union Tribune*. Retrieved from https://goo.gl/HLj3R3

Robert Lemos. (n.d.). *Ransomware: 5 strong tactics for defense and response*. Retrieved February 19, 2018, from https://goo.gl/qEfN9w

Rubens, P. (2017a). *Common Types of Ransomware*. Retrieved January 17, 2018, from https://goo.gl/EiQjE3

Rubens, P. (2017b). *Understanding Ransomware Vectors Key to Preventing Attack*. Retrieved January 21, 2018, from https://goo.gl/j6Gxjp

Ryan Harnedy. (2016). *How to Recover from Ransomware: The First 5 Things You Should Do*. Retrieved February 15, 2018, from https://goo.gl/Xr3VeF

Sarah. (2017). *Spotlight on Ransomware: How ransomware works*. Retrieved January 19, 2018, from https://goo.gl/mQX8dJ

Saurbaugh, M., & Liska, A. (2017). *Defending Against Ransomware with Intelligence, People, and Automation*. Retrieved July 17, 2017, from https://goo.gl/6wRDwz

Savage, K., Coogan, P., & Lau, H. (2015). The Evolution of Ransomware. *Security Response*, 57.

Shinde, R., Van der Veeken, P., Van Schooten, S., & Van Den Berg, J. (2016). Ransomware : Studying Transfer and Mitigation. In *International Conference on Computing, Analytics and Security Trends (CAST)* (pp. 90–95). Pune, India: IEEE. 10.1109/CAST.2016.7914946

Singh, A. (2017). *The Second Coming of Ransomware - Insights into New Developments*. Retrieved October 19, 2017, from https://goo.gl/p5GMvd

Singh, A., Grantz, M., Payne, C., Laing, B., & Wolf, R. (2017). *How the US Secret Service combats advanced ransomware*. Retrieved October 14, 2017, from https://goo.gl/hLqj5z

Sophos. (2017). *Ransomware: How an attack works*. Retrieved January 21, 2018, from https://goo.gl/KLDJ4r

Starr, R. (2018, January 16). Hackers Will Target Small Business Through the Internet of Things in 2018, New Report Says. *Small Business Trends News*. Retrieved from https://goo.gl/n87Qg7

Stenhouse, J. (2016). *Master of Disaster Webinar - Recovering from Ransomware in Minutes*. Retrieved February 14, 2018, from https://goo.gl/1hBKdF

Stephen Rouine. (2017). *A guide on how to prevent ransomware*. Retrieved February 18, 2018, from https://goo.gl/PKgJ53

Surati, S. B., & Prajapati, G. I. (2017). A Review on Ransomware Detection & Prevention. *International Journal of Research and Scientific Innovation, 4*(9), 2321–2705. Retrieved from https://goo.gl/JwDUyV

Symantec. (2017). *Fake Adobe Flash Update Installs Ransomware, Performs Click Fraud*. Retrieved from https://goo.gl/Qn9fbe

TrendLabs. (2017). *Ransomware: Past, Present, and Future*. TrendLabs.

TrendMicro. (2017). *Ransomware Recap: Patcher Ransomware Targets MacOS*. Retrieved October 29, 2017, from https://goo.gl/L1dk85

Ubale, M. K., & Isyaku, S. M. (2017). A Situation Analysis on Cybercrime and its Economic Impact in Nigeria. *International Journal of Computers and Applications, 169*(7), 975–8887.

Union, E., & For, A. (2016). *Strategies for incident response and cyber crisis cooperation*. Academic Press.

UniTrend. (2017). *White Paper: Beat Ransomware in 5 Easy Steps*. Author.

Vanderburg, E. (2016). *The top 10 ransomware attack vectors*. Retrieved January 21, 2018, from https://goo.gl/JDSntN

Wahdain, E. A., & Mohamad Nazir, A. (2014). User Acceptance of Information Technology: Factors, Theories and Applications. *Journal of Information Systems Research and Innovation, 31*, 17–25.

Wall, M. (2018). *Firms buy insurance "in mad panic" as cyber-attacks soar*. BBC London. Retrieved from https://goo.gl/6oqEiG

Watson, G. (2017). *A Foolproof Ransomware Recovery Strategy*. Retrieved February 13, 2018, from https://goo.gl/ifiMUt

Westin, K. (2017). *How to Stay Ahead of Today's Ransomware Realities*. Retrieved October 21, 2017, from https://goo.gl/DoUg29

Wikileaks. (n.d.). Vault 7 : CIA Hacking Tools Revealed. *Wikileaks*. Retrieved from https://wikileaks.org/ciav7p1/

Williams, C. (2016, November 27). Passengers ride free on SF Muni subway after ransomware infects network, demands $73k. *The Register UK*. Retrieved from https://goo.gl/bg6UKF

Yaqoob, I., Ahmed, E., Rehman, M. H., Ahmed, A. I. A., Al-garadi, M. A., Imran, M., & Guizani, M. (2017). The rise of ransomware and emerging security challenges in the Internet of Things. *Computer Networks*.

Zimba, A., Wang, Z., & Chen, H. (2017). Reasoning Crypto Ransomware Infection Vectors with Bayesian Networks. IEEE, 149–151.

ADDITIONAL READING

Cabaj, K., Gregorczyk, M., & Mazurczyk, W. (2017). Software-defined networking-based crypto ransomware detection using HTTP traffic characteristics. *Computers & Electrical Engineering, 0*, 1–16.

Erridge, T. (2016). Ransomware: threat and response. *Network Security, 2016*(10), 17–19.

Furnell, S., & Emm, D. (2017). The ABC of ransomware protection. *Computer Fraud and Security, 2017*(10), 5–11.

Laboratories, T. B., David, J., Lindup, K., Cohen, F., David, J., & Myers, T. (2017). … Marietta, M. (2017). Ransomware and IoT among leading threats. *Network Security, 2*(9).

Liao, K., Zhao, Z., Doupe, A., & Ahn, G. J. (2016). Behind closed doors: Measurement and analysis of CryptoLocker ransoms in Bitcoin. *eCrime Researchers Summit, eCrime, 2016–June*, 1–13.

Mercaldo, F., Nardone, V., & Santone, A. (2016). Ransomware inside out. *Proceedings - 2016 11th International Conference on Availability, Reliability and Security, ARES 2016*, 628–637.

Orman, H. (2016). Evil Offspring - Ransomware and Crypto Technology. *IEEE Internet Computing, 20*(5), 89–94. doi:10.1109/MIC.2016.90

Scaife, N., Carter, H., Traynor, P., & Butler, K. R. B. (2016). CryptoLock (and Drop It): Stopping Ransomware Attacks on User Data. *Proceedings - International Conference on Distributed Computing Systems, 2016–August*, 303–312.

Yang, T., Yang, Y., Qian, K., Lo, D. C.-T., Qian, Y., & Tao, L. (2015). Automated Detection and Analysis for Android Ransomware. *2015 IEEE 17th International Conference on High Performance Computing and Communications, 2015 IEEE 7th International Symposium on Cyberspace Safety and Security, and 2015 IEEE 12th International Conference on Embedded Software and Systems*, (1), 1338–1343.

KEY TERMS AND DEFINITIONS

Defense-in-Depth: A layered approach to tackling security issues using different layers of defense.

Detection: The ability to identify something that is hidden or obfuscated.

Exploit Kit: These are sets of tools deployed to exploit security vulnerabilities on machines primarily to spread malware.

Hacker: A person who gains unauthorized access to a machine with the intention to cause harm or steal.

Malware: Any malicious software that is used to inflict damage on computers and devices.

Phishing: A technique used by hackers to obtain confidential information from victims by sending illegitimate emails that look legitimate.

Ransom: A sum of money paid especially to criminals before a captive is released or freed.

Chapter 2

A Review of Security Mechanisms for Multi-Agent Systems:
Security Challenges in Multi-Agent Systems

Antonio Muñoz
University of Málaga, Spain

ABSTRACT

This chapter reviews current technologies used to build secure agents. A wide spectrum of mechanisms to provide security to agent-based systems is provided, giving an overview with the main agent-based systems and agent-oriented tools. An evaluation of security mechanisms is done that identifies security weaknesses. This review covers from the initial approaches to the more recent mechanisms. This analysis draws attention to the fact that these systems have traditionally neglected the need of a secure underlying infrastructure.

INTRODUCTION

Agent-oriented paradigm (AOP) is known as the paradigm in which the software is built on the concept of software agent. A widespread definition of software agent is a piece of software that acts for a user or other program in a relationship of agency, this implies that an agreement to act on one's behalf is involved in the relation. This definition can be materialized in different ways as intelligent agents,

DOI: 10.4018/978-1-5225-7353-1.ch002

autonomous agents, distributed agents, multi-agent systems (distributed agents that work together to achieve an objective that could not be accomplished by a single agent acting alone), and mobile agents (agents that can relocate their execution onto different processors).

Mobile agents are software entities with the ability to migrate from node to node in computer networks. Nodes are provided with an environment for execution of agents, these nodes are known as agencies or hosts independently. Agents act both autonomously and in cooperation with other agents to perform a set of tasks. Nowadays a large number of applications based on agent technology exist such as peer-to-peer computing, web crawlers, etc.

First Multi-agent systems (MAS) applications appeared in the middle 80s. These pioneer systems covered a wide variety of environments (manufacturing systems, process control, air traffic control, information management, etc), but almost the totality of them were built upon non secure infrastructures. At that time, considering the foreseen scenarios and threats, agent technology developers assumed that the underlying infrastructure was secure, but now it is obvious that it is not. Some other agent-based applications lacking a security infrastructure were even proposed for nuclear plants (Wang, 1997), aircraft control (Schwuttke, 1993) applications, multilateration of internet hosts (Banks, 2011), personalized HealthCare agent technologies (Ivanovic, 2017), microservices as agents in IoT systems (Krivic, 2017) and correlating driver stress and traffic accidents (Pavlovskaya, 2017).

Multi-agent Systems (MAS) represent a promising architectural model to build web applications and distributed applications. MAS can contribute with relevant benefits, especially in highly distributed scenarios. Indeed, the autonomy and auto-organization features of mobile agents provide an excellent support for the development of flexible and dynamically adaptable systems, in which security and dependability are essential requirements. In this sense, we focus on the use of mobile agents in ubiquitous computing scenarios and ambient intelligence solutions because these are the basis for numerous applications in which dependability and security are essential features. Despite of the attention that the scientific community has paid in recent years to this field, its acceptance has not meet the initial expectations. However, this technology has been applied in several relevant scenarios if real world. We believe that this fact is motivated because security aspects play an essential role in multi-agent systems and are one of the main problems to solve before this technology is mature to be used by the industry but this aspect is not currently appropriately solved. A variety of agent infrastructures exists, among them there are platforms like Aglet (Clements, 1997), Cougaar (Helsinger, 2004), JACK (Shepherdson, 2003), the popular JADE[1], JAVACT (Alechina, 2006) and AgentSpeak (L). We have to consider that all of them shares a common disadvantage is the poor security provided that results insufficient for real world applications.

MOBILE AGENTS

A mobile agent is an agent that can simply carry out our tasks for us as users remotely. By remotely, we can mean many other remote locations. A mobile agent is thus simply one that is created at one place, carries its code and state over to another place and resumes its execution. It does not require the remote code execution approaches for this; instead it propagates itself over the communication network to carry out its tasks (Lange, 1998). White (1996) and Milojicic (1998) state that a mobile agent system has agents and places, and a place is where the agent visits in its journey. At each of these places, there exists an agent environment to allow its execution. The environment allows processing on the basis of a policy. Marrow (2000) define the mobile agent computing approach and give the features of the actual setup and features that are required. Traced from what has been discussed and by mobile agents have certain fundamental features. Taking a general idea that a mobile agent moves from place to place, a mobile agent requires the elements of mobility, communication and task association. A mobile agent is fundamentally mobile and can migrate from place to place as specified. Similarly, a mobile agent needs to communicate and co-ordinate with agents and the execution environment to execute.

Mobile Agent Benefits

The application of mobile agents provides a number of benefits to distributed and component based systems and technology (Kotz, 1999) are numerous. Mobile agent proposes a computation with many possibilities as White (1996) widely describe. Among the most relevant features reduction of network loading is highlighted. Unlike traditional approaches that require many communications between client and server, a mobile agent carries the set of interactions to the server. A mobile agent is capable for executing commands locally reducing the set of instructions to the server, this reduces network load. Some authors claim that protocols do not need to be enhanced for mobile agents that are migrating and they can utilize the protocols at hand as for other mechanisms the protocols need to be upgrade according to the specification of the communication required, but I advocate for an enhanced secure migration protocol. Besides dynamism provides by mobile agents the capability to configure according to environment requires making them fault-tolerant and achieving robustness. Finally, the underlying specification of mobile agents is independent to the agent itself, this allows a higher heterogeneity integration with other devices and systems.

Mobile Agent Applications and Limitations

Several applications are possible because of mobile agents. Indeed, mobile agents can use their advantage in reduction of network bandwidth and can enhance these for several network services that future or next-generation telecommunication networks (Pham, 1998). Mobile agents are used for the evolution of client/server-based network management approaches to a more distributed approach. Mobile agents can be used for retrieval of information over a network and the Internet. The mobile agents can carry queries and can retrieve particular information. This can be extended for cache management and searching as well. There is other work in progress in many dimensions as seen in the literature on them. Mobile agents can be used in Global Information Systems for tracking, in Grid Systems, in Intrusion detection systems, for distribution of multimedia and so on. Also, agents have a broad research potential (Kotz, 1999).

Unlike mobile agents have their immense applications and there are several benefits because of them but they still have their limitations. Their possibilities are hindered by several challenges (Schoder, 2000). Some of these are limitations to the technology and some are because there are missing solutions to numerous issues that arise in mobile agent systems concepts and design (Rothermel, 1997). Various authors have written about the mobile agent dimension limiting and the reasons that cause the limitations to their adoption (Gray, 2004). Also, the reason has been highlighted as because of applying it in the wrong regard despite having a clear concept to their use (Johansen, 2008). For this the reasons listed in (Vigna, 2004) define the limitations and their reasons quite well. A generalization states that agents may reduce network bandwidth consumption and so on, but this is not true in every scenario, then performance issues can be limiting. There is a lack of a systematic approach to design a mobile agent, making it difficult to develop. Implementing agents is also hard work as so many unpredictable interactions are present in its journey to so many places consisting of adverse environments. The testing and debugging of such systems are extremely complex. This is due to the fact that the approaches become so unpredictable. Authentication can be based on so many things the agent is associated with, for this the authentication mechanism may be weak. Corruption of the agents is possible as the agent transfers over the various places it visits. This means an agent can lose its information or actually deviate from its goal. Since information might be lost, the agent cannot be trusted with secret information either. The information can be leaked on its way. Mobile agents remotely execute at one place and go to the next; this is very much like a worm that actually can cause so much damage to the system if they are allowed to process.

Security as the Trigger for a Widespread Settling of Agent Paradigm in Current Panorama

This chapter focuses on one of the most relevant weaknesses of Multi-agent systems in terms of security (Vigna, 2004). A huge amount of researches has either raised the notion of security of mobile agents or has tried to solve it in one way or another, but the results are not sufficiently satisfactory. You can wonder the relevance of security in mobile agents, I claim for the security as a cornerstone for achieving a mature status of this technology, let us introduce an example to show the importance of this feature. Mobile agents that are roaming a network can be used as malicious objects for accessing private or confidential information and resource, for causing corruption like viruses and worms and so on. In this regard if an agent is supposed to be non-malicious, it is impossible to carry proofs that it did not visited malicious hosts that altered its behavior. Many different theoretical approaches were covered in the literature regarding mobile agents and mobile agent systems, we briefly describe the most relevant approaches evaluating pros and cons and proposing alternative solutions.

Some authors (Brooks, 2004) have limited to four the main approaches to mobile code security solutions (Sandboxes, code signing, use of firewalls and Proof-carrying code (PCC)), but, our perspective of the problem is wider and this oversimplifies a complex problem. Thus, I faced the study of the topology of these attacks as follows. Different attacks according to the source that origins the attack describe every category. In this line I have identified:

- **Malicious Host:** Several security threats can be included in this category like masquerading or posing as a correct platform and also the corruption or misuse of the agent, spying on the agent and its data (Robert, 1996). As a variant of this attack, other agents may modify agent and so may the environment (Jansen, 1998).
- **Malicious Agent:** In parallel to agent protection the host on which the agent is executing has to be protected (Robert, 1996) since the agent may misbehave on the host and its resources (Jansen, 1998).
- **Malicious Network:** Communication channel between agents and hosts is the network, and we have to inspect the security within the network on which the mobile agent is transferred to other platforms. Once it has been introduced the possible source of attacks, let me outline the most relevant attacks in practical agent based systems, which encompass 96% of real attacks of these systems.

- **Spying Out Code:** The requirement that states that agent code has to be readable by the host exposes agent security. Although this requirement can be restricted to the next instruction at a single point of time, this does not solve the problem since some hosts see almost all of the code because they execute most of the commands. In our example the host visited last executes nearly all the code. If the agent code is characteristic not only for a single, but a whole class of agents, the whole code of the agent may be known even before execution time. If an agent is generated out of standard building blocks (which is a good idea regarding code migration costs and ease of agent construction), the detail specification is available for building blocks like libraries or classes. Furthermore, these blocks can be explored by blackbox tests. Knowing the code leads to knowledge about the execution strategy of the agent, knowledge about the exact physical structure of code and data in the memory of the host and sometimes (by using data statements like initial variable assignments) to knowledge about parts of the agent data *(spying out data).*

- **Manipulation of Code:** If agent code is readable by the host code memory is accessible, then agent code is modifiable. A malicious host could alter the agent code, and agent behavior on that particular host or for next hosts. If the host knows the physical location of the data in the memory and the semantics of the single data elements, it can modify data as well *(Manipulation of Data).* In our example the host could cut down the shop list after setting the offer of the local flower provider as the best offer.

- **Manipulation of Control Flow:** Some malicious hosts are able to manipulate the control flow conducting agent behavior. In a simplified version host can access the entire code of the agent and its data, it is possible to determine next steps for agent execution and use this information for an attack *(Spying out control flow).* Data can be protected using cryptographic functions, but, protecting the information about the actual control flow is a hard target to achieve. A malicious host can deduce information from agent knowledge

- **Incorrect Execution of Code:** A malicious host may also alter agent code way of execution, as a result agent behavior can be conducted by the host even without changing agent code or the flow of control.

- **Masquerading**: A third party may intercept an agent and perpetrating a masquerading attack this agent can be transferred and started as the correct receiver host. This threat is possible since a host is liable to send an agent to a receiver host ensuring the identity of the receiver.

- **Denial of Execution:** Host is responsible to allow agent execution, in some cases the agents are passive and the host can simply not execute the agent, this is a vulnerability to denial of execution attack.

- **Spying Out Interaction With Other Agents:** The agent may buy the flowers remotely from a shop situated on another host. If the interaction between agent and the remote flower shop is not protected, the host of the agent is able to watch the buy interaction even in the case the host cannot watch the execution of the agent. In our example, the host could read e.g. wallet and spend the stored money.
- **Manipulation of Interaction With Other Agents:** If the host can also manipulate the interaction of the agent it can act with the identity of the agent or mask itself as the partner of the agent. In our example the host can e.g. redirect the buying interaction to another shop, or it can interrupt the interaction e.g. to prevent spending the money by the agent.

Once the problems have been presented, let us have a look on the spectrum of possible solutions. Firstly, I dissect those approaches that pretend prevention of single attacks. In the next section I introduce an approach that pretends restoring the autonomy of the agent, the so called blackbox approach.

SECURITY ENGINEERING TOOLS

TROPOS Methodology

Tropos (Matulevicius, 2012) is an agent-oriented software engineering (AOSE) methodology based on a secure architecture by means of a description language for agent systems (Bork, 2017; Banks, 2011). Tropos covers every stage in software development process based on two essential foundations. The most innovative aspect is the consideration of agent notion with all related mentalistic notions, including goals and plans. Tropos methodology covers every phase, that is, from requirements analysis, this allows a deeper knowledge of software environment, will all interactions that should occur between human and software agents.

Tropos methodology spans four phase. The first stage is the early requirements gathering. This involves to concern with the understanding of a problem. Early requirements analysis has two different diagrams: the goal and actor diagrams. The goal is a refinement of the actor one with emphasis on the goals of a single actor. An advanced requirements gathering phase takes place.

A system's global architecture is provided including every identified subsystem, data, connection, control and other relations between them (Pavlovskaya, 2017; Krivic, 2017). This phase is articulated in three steps the definition of the overall architecture as general overview, the identification of the capabilities the actors require to fulfill their goals and plans and finally the definition of a set of agent types and assignment to each of them one or more capabilities. Last phase is the description of a detailed design of the architecture. In this step is detailed the of every component from the architecture. A micro-leveled specification of each agent is given, describing in detail the goals, beliefs and capabilities of the agents, along with the interaction between them

Jade Security Model (JADE-S)

JADE [2] (Java Agent DEvelopment Framework) is a software Framework fully developed in the Java language. JADE simplifies the building of multi-agent systems using a middle-ware that complies with the FIPA[3] specifications and through a set of graphical tools that support the debugging and deployment phases. I define the concepts that determine the diverse security levels to a better understanding of the role of security in the transmission of private and critical information through an open environment like Internet: (i) Confidentiality is the property that ensures that only those that are properly authorized may be access the information. (ii) Integrity of the property that ensures that information cannot be altered. This modification could be an insertion, deletion or replacement of data. (iii) Authentication is the property that refers to identification. It is the link between the information and its sender. (iv) Non-repudiation is the property that prevents some of the parts to negate a previous commitment or action. When you are dealing with Multi-Agent systems (MAS), these properties are especially important, due to the autonomy and mobility of agents. A MAS without security support could not be used in an open environment such as Internet if it deals with critical data, because communications could be spied or even the identities of agents faked. JADE-S consists on a plug-in of JADE that allows to add some security characteristics in the development of MAS, so that they can start to be used in real environments. It is based on the Java security model and it provides the advantages of the following technologies:

- JAAS (Java Authentication and Authorization Service) allows to establish access permissions to perform certain operations on a set of predetermined classes, libraries or objects.
- JCE (Java Cryptography Extension) implements a set of cryptographic functions that allow the developer to deal with the creation and management of keys and to use encryption algorithms.
- JSSE (Java Secure Socket Extension) allows to exchange critical information through a network using a secure data transmission such as SSL.

Several considerations might be taken into account when dealing with JADE security. A JADE platform may be located in different hosts and have different containers. JADE-S structures the agent platform as a multi-user environment in which all components (agents, containers, etc) belong to authenticated (through a login and a password) users, who are authorized by the administrator of the system to perform certain privileged critical actions. Each platform contains a permissions file with a set of actions that each user is authorized to perform. Internally, each agent proves its identity by showing an Identity Certificate signed by the Certification Authority (proved in a transparent way to the agent when its registers in the system and provides the login and the password of its owner).

CURRENT SECURITY MECHANISMS FOR AGENT-BASED SYSTEMS

Current security mechanisms for agents such as sandboxing (Borselius 2002), ciphering, or encryption, are security mechanisms applied in other computing paradigms with excellent results, but its application to solve problems in mobile agents must not be straightly applied since initial assumptions change and do not fulfills our security expectations. Obviously, these mechanisms can take part of a tailored solution for a mechanism for a particular security issue addressed.

I claim that security must be considered in every stage of software lifecycle. In fact, several authors have proved that considering security as an additional or orthogonal aspect is an obsolete idea that produces systems with poor security. As a consequence, security of agent-based systems needs to be specifically adapted to these kinds of systems and technologies involved to build them. Evidently, the most relevant feature to consider is the mobility and this impose several restrictions for our assumptions that I deal along this chapter.

As it was pointed out, some of the general software protection mechanisms can be applied to agent protection. However, the particular features of secure agents restrict the use of tailored solutions. Agents are executed on potentially malicious environments. Therefore, it is a common error to simplify the problem assuming the root of trust in a trusted environment, it is required an inspection of trustworthy. In this terms, several mechanisms for secure execution of agents have been proposed in the literature. Most of these were designed with the objective of providing protection for the execution of agents and their environments.

Most of these mechanisms were designed to provide some type of protection or some specific security property. This chapter provides solutions specifically well-suited for agent scenarios. Some protection mechanisms are oriented to the protection of the environments (host) against malicious agents. Among these, you found the Software-Based fault isolation (Guerraoui, 1997) consisting on isolating application modules into distinct fault domains enforced by software, this technique is commonly known as SandBoxing (Jansen, 2000), this is a popular technique that is based on the creation of a secure execution environment for untrusted software. In the agent world a sandbox is a container that limits, or reduces, the level of access its agents have and provides mechanisms to control the interaction among them. The idea behind the Safe Code Interpretation (Borselius, 2002) is that commands considered harmful can be either made safe for or denied to an agent, the best known of the safe interpreters developed for agents is Agent Tcl (Gray, 1996).

A different approach makes use of signing either code or other objects using the digital signature, providing authenticity of that object. A clear example is the Microsoft's Authenticode as a form of code signing that enables Java applets to be signed, ensuring users that the software was has not been tampered with or modified and the identity of the author is verified. Another technique known as state appraisal (Farmer, 1996) is based on ensuring that an agent has not been somehow subverted due to alterations of its state information. Appraisal functions are used to determine what privileges to grant an agent, based on both on conditional factors and whether identified state invariants hold. An agent whose state violates an invariant can be granted no privileges, while an agent whose state fails to meet some conditional factors may be granted a restricted set of privileges. The basic idea behind the Path Histories (Roth, 1998) is to keep an authenticable record of the prior platforms visited by an agent in such a way that a newly visited platform can determine whether to process the agent and what the resource constraints to apply. For this purpose, each agent platform adds a signed entry to the path to indicate its identity and the identity of the next platform to be visited

Necula (1998) technique known as proof-carrying code is a general mechanism for verifying that the agent code can be executed in the host system in a secure way. Proof-carrying code and its variant proof-referencing-code force to the code producer to formally prove that the program possesses safety properties, previously stipulated by the code consumer. It is important to mention the fact that this is a prevention technique. One of the most important problems of these techniques is the difficulty of identifying which operations (or sequences of them) can be permitted without compromising the local security policy. For this purpose, every code fragment includes a detailed proof that can be used to determine whether the security policy of the host is satisfied by the agent. Therefore, hosts just need to verify that the proof is correct (i.e. it corresponds to the code) and that it is compatible with the local security policy. In a variant of this technique, called proof-referencing code, the agents do not contain the proof, but just a reference to it (Wooldridge, 1997). These techniques share some similarities with the constraint programming technique; they are based on explicitly declaring the set of allowed operations. One of the most important problems of these techniques is the difficulty of identifying which operations (or sequences of them) can be permitted without compromising the local security policy.

Other mechanisms are oriented to protect agents against malicious servers. Among these approaches you found the concept of Partial Result Encapsulation, which consist on the encapsulation of the results of an agent's actions, at each platform visited to be verified. A version of this technique is the presented by Yee as Partial Result Authentication Codes (PRAC) (Bennet, 1997) consisting of cryptographic checksums formed using secret key cryptography. However, this technique presents an important draw- back when a malicious platform retains copies of the original keys or key generating functions of an agent. An improvement is that rather than relying on the agent to encapsulate the information, each platform can be required to encapsulate partial results along the way (Muñoz, 2010). However, Bennet (1997)] noted that forward integrity could also be achieved using a trusted third party that performs digital time-stamping. Thus, a timestamp (Roth, 1998) allows one to verify that the contents of a file or document existed, as such, at a particular point in the time. Also Yee raises the concern that the granularity of the timestamps may limit an agent's maximum rate of travel, since it must reside at one platform until the next time period. Another possible concern is the general availability of a trusted time-stamping infrastructure. A variation of this technique is the named Path Histories (Borselius, 2002), which is a general scheme for allowing an agent's itinerary to be recorded and tracked by another cooperating agent and vice versa. Some drawbacks of this technique include the cost of setting up the authenticated channel and the inability of the peer to determine which of the two platforms is responsible if the agent is killed. The Itinerary Recording with Replication and Voting approach is a technique for ensuring that a mobile agent arrives safely at its destination (Sander, 1998). The idea is that rather than a single copy of an agent performing a computation, multiple copies of the agent are used. Although a malicious platform may corrupt a few copies of the agent, enough replicates avoid the encounter to successfully complete the computation. Evidently, this approach is similar to Path Histories, but extended with fault tolerant capabilities. The technique seems appropriate for specialized applications where agents can be duplicated without problems, the task can be formulated as a multi-staged computation, and survivability is a major concern. One obvious drawback is the additional resources consumed by replicate agents. A Sanctuary (Bennet, 1997) consists on an execution environment where a mobile agent can be securely executed. Most of these proposals are built with the assumption that the platform where the sanctuary is implemented is secure. Unfortunately, this assumption is not appropriate in the current situation. Several techniques can be applied to an agent in order to verify self-integrity in order to avoid that the code or the data of the agent is inadvertently manipulated. Anti-tamper techniques, such as encryption, checksumming, anti-debugging, anti-emulation and some others (Collberg, 2000) share the same goal, but they are also oriented towards the prevention of the analysis of the function that the agent implements. There are techniques that combines some of these as (Vigilson, 2012) that proposed a security model based on the protection of both code, data and itinerary of mobile agent using a two level verification. They perform an authentication at first level and the integrity of code is verified at second level, this protect against other malicious mobile agent.

Additionally, some protection schemes are based on self-modifying code, and code obfuscation (Muñoz, 2009a). In the case of agents, these techniques take advantage of the reduced execution time of the agent in each platform.

A detection-based technique is the execution tracing (Vigna, 1997) for detecting unauthorized modifications of an agent through the faithful recording of the agent's behaviour during its execution on each agent platform. Each platform involved has to create and retain a non-repudiation log or trace of the operations performed by the agent while resident there, and to submit a cryptographic hash of the trace upon conclusion as a trace summary or fingerprint. This approach has several drawbacks, the size and number of logs to be retained is the most obvious, and the fact that the detection process is triggered occasionally, based on suspicious results or other factors. The Environmental Key Generation (Borselius, 2002) describes a scheme for allowing an agent or take predefined actions when some environmental condition is satisfied. The main weakness of this approach is that a platform that completely controls the agent could simply modify the agent to print out the executable code upon receipt of the trigger, instead of executing it. Another drawback is that an agent platform typically limits the capability of an agent to execute code created dynamically, since it is considered an unsafe operation. The objective of Computing with Encrypted functions (Borselius, 2002) is to determine a method whereby mobile code can safely compute cryptographic primitives. The approach is to have the agent platform execute a program embodying an enciphered function without being able to discern the original function, even though the idea is straightforward, the trick is to find the appropriate encryption schemes that can transform arbitrary functions as intended. This technique can be very powerful but does not prevent denial of service, replay, experimental extraction, and other forms of attack against the agent. Hohl (1998) proposes the Blackbox technique. The strategy behind this technique is scramble the code in such a way that no one is able to gain a complete understanding of its function, or to modify the resulting code without detection. However, the main drawback is that there is no known algorithm or approach for providing Blackbox protection. Several techniques can be applied to an agent to verify self-integrity and avoid that the code or the data of the agent is inadvertently manipulated. Anti-tamper techniques, such as encryption, checksumming, anti-debugging, anti-emulation and some others share the same goal, but they are also oriented toward the prevention of the analysis of the function that the agent implements. Additionally, some protection schemes are based on self-modifying code, and code obfuscation (Esparza, 2003). Finally, there are techniques that create a two-way protection. Some of these are based on the aforementioned protected computing approach (Maña, 2006, Maña 2006b).

Muñoz (2010) proposed a technique is based on detecting manipulation attacks performed during the agent's execution. This approach also traces the malicious hosts responsible for the manipulation attacks. A combination of this technique with software watermarking (Stern, 1999; Alechina, 2006; Esparza, 2003) exists in order to embed a mark into the agent, then agent's execution creates marked results. When the agent returns to the origin host, these results are examined in order to find the embedded mark whether the mark has changed it means that the executing host has modified the agent, and it is a possible attack. A different approach is represented by software watermarking techniques (Esparza, 2003; Hachez, 2003). In this case the purpose of protection is not to avoid the analysis or modification but to enable the detection of such modification. The relation between all these techniques is strong. In fact, it has been demonstrated that neither perfect obfuscation nor perfect watermark exists (Maña, 2007). Esparza (2003) applied traceability techniques to protect agents against malicious hosts. All of these techniques provide short-term protection; therefore, in general they are not applicable for our purposes. However, in some scenarios, they can represent a suitable solution, especially, when combined with other approaches.

There are many proposals for systems based on checks, in these systems the software includes "checks" to test whether certain conditions are met. You can distinguish solutions based exclusively on software, and other ones that require some hardware components. However, in both types of schemes, the validation function is included software. Therefore, it can be discovered using reverse engineering and other techniques. This is particularly relevant in the case of agents. Theoretic approaches to the formalization of the problem have demonstrated that self-protection of the software is unfeasible (Schwuttke,1993). By extension, all autonomous protection techniques are also insecure.

Esparza (Esparza, 2004) detects manipulation attacks performed during the agent's execution, using software watermarking techniques in order to embed a mark into the agent. The agent's execution creates marked results. When the agent returns to the origin host, these results are examined in order to find the embedded mark. Mobile agent watermarking detects manipulation attacks by embedding the same mark in the results of all the executing hosts. Unfortunately, watermarking schemes are not resilient to collusion attacks. For this reason, mobile agent fingerprinting is presented as the way to detect collusion attacks. A different mark is embedded in the mobile agent in order to detect manipulation and collusion attacks.

An improvement technique to the Mobile Agent Watermarking approach (MAW) (Hachez, 2003) is based on allowing the watermark can change dynamically during execution, this is known as Hora system (Esparza, 2003). Before sending the agent, the origin host embeds a watermark into the agent's code by using software watermarking techniques. During the execution in each host, the agent creates a data container that will be used later to verify the execution integrity and to hide the results. The agent transfers the watermark to the container by putting any kind of available data inside of it in an ordered way. When the execution finishes, the results are also fitted into the container. When the agent returns to the origin host, it applies a set of integrity rules to all the data containers. These rules can be inferred from the modifications performed in the agent´s code during the watermark embedding. If a container does not fulfill the rules, this means that the corresponding host is malicious. The proposal not only detects manipulation attacks performed during the agent´s execution, but it also proves the malicious behavior of the host. Then, in each host, the agent´s code creates a container to transfer the watermark of the code and to hide the results.

In some scenarios, the protection required is limited to some parts of the software (code or data). In this way, the function performed by the software, or the data processed, must be hidden from the host where the software is running. Some of these techniques require an external offline processing step is necessary to obtain the desired results. Among these schemes, function hiding techniques allow the evaluation of encrypted functions (Sandhu, 1996). This technique protects the data processed and the function performed. For this reason, this one of the appropriate techniques for protecting agents. However, it can only be applied to the protection of polynomial functions.

The case of online collaboration schemes is also interesting. In these schemes, part of the functionality of the software is executed in one or more external computers. The security of this approach depends on the impossibility for each part to identify the function performed by the others. This approach is very appropriate for distributed computing architectures such as agent-based systems or grid computing, but has the important disadvantage of the impossibility of its application to off-line environments

Finally, there are techniques that create a dual protection. Some of these are hardware-based, such as the Trusted Computing Platform. With the recent appearance of ubiquitous computing, the need for a secure platform has become more evident. Therefore, this approach adds a trusted component to the computing platform, usually built-in hardware, which is used this to create a foundation of trust for software processes (Maña, 2007; Muñoz 2009b).

In some scenarios, the protection required is limited to some parts of the software (code or data). In this way, the function performed by the software, or the data processed, must be hidden from the host where the software is running. Some of these techniques require an external offline processing step in order to obtain the desired results. Among these schemes, function hiding techniques allow the evaluation of encrypted functions. This technique protects the data processed and the function performed. I consider as an appropriate technique for protecting agents. However, this is limited since it can only be applied to the protection of polynomial functions.

The case of online collaboration schemes is also interesting. In these schemes, part of the functionality of the software is executed in one or more external computers. The security of this approach depends on the impossibility of each part to identify the function performed by others. This approach is very appropriate for distributed computing architectures such as agent-based systems or grid computing, but has the important disadvantage of the impossibility of its application to off-line environments.

I advocate for a technique that creates a dual protection. Some of these are hardware-based, such as the based on Trusted Computing Platform. With the recent appearance of ubiquitous computing, the need for a secure platform has become more evident. Therefore, this approach adds a trusted component to the computing platform, usually built-in hardware used to create a foundation of trust for software processes. Other techniques are software-based, for instance Protected Computing (Muñoz, 2011b) approach, this technique is based on the partitioning of the software elements into two or more dependent parts, then a part of this code will be remotely executed in a different agent.

DUAL PROTECTION MECHANISMS

Two dual protection mechanisms are proposed to provide both protection of the agent against a malicious host and to provide protection to the host against a malicious agent simultaneously.

The first approach is based on the use of cryptographic hardware; our particular solution is based on the use of Trusted Computing to protect Agent Migration (Muñoz, 2009c). The Secure Migration Library (SecMiLiA) (Muñoz, 2009) was designed and developed to provide the secure migration functionality. In order to give a friendly use of the security mechanism provided.

Sander (1998) asked the question: Can a program actively protect itself against its execution environment that tries to divert the intended execution towards a malicious goal. By means of after a little thought this seems to be a problem impossible to solve because it leads to an infinite recourse. The assessment routine that would detect wrong execution of code or tampering of data and that would try to counter them would also be subject to diversion. For mobile code applications, more specifically for mobile software agents which are designed to run on potentially arbitrary computers, this problem is of primordial importance. Without strong guarantees on computation integrity and privacy, mobile programs would always remain vulnerable to hijacking and brainwashing. Pearson (2002) defines a related notion, namely that of a trusted platform as follows: 'A Trusted Platform is a computing platform that has a trusted component, probably in the form of built-in hardware, which it uses to create a foundation of trust for software processes'.

Agent migration mechanism is continuing the execution of an agent on another location, keeping code, execution state and data of the agent and initiated on behalf of the agent and not by the system. The main motivation for this migration is to move the computation to a data server or a communication partner to reduce network load by accessing a data server a communication partner by local communication. Then migration is done from a source agency where agent is running to a destination agency. A secure migration mechanism (Muñoz, 2010b) based on remote attestation functionality provided by TPM is the core of SecMiliA (Muñoz, 2009d). This secure mechanism is based on the testing the trust of destination agency before the migration process actually is performed. This guarantees that agent execution is always performed in a secure environment. This gives a solution to the problem of the malicious hosts. Thus, agent reaches a secure environment where its execution goes on, in such a way that agents cannot modify the host agency.

The second approach is the "protected computing" methodology (Maña, 2006) based on dividing the application code into two or more mutually dependent parts. Some of these parts (which you will call private parts) are executed in a secure processor, while others (public parts) are executed in any processor even if it is not trusted. A complete description of the application of this technology is out of the scope of this chapter, it can be found in (Maña, 2009).

Protected computing model is applied to protect agent societies in a multi-agent setting, where several agents are sent to different (untrusted) agencies in order to perform some collaborative task. Because agents run in potentially malicious hosts, the goal in this scenario is to protect agents from the attacks of malicious hosts. The basic idea is to make agents collaborate, not only in the specific tasks they are designed to perform, but also in the protection of other agents. In this way each agent acts as secure coprocessor for other agents.

This scheme is suitable for protecting a set of several mutually dependent agents. Consequently, in this general case, a conspiracy of all hosts is necessary in order to attack the system. In terms of usability the "Automatic Tool for Code Partitioning" (CPT) was delivered to split the code into parts.

The Protected Computing (Maña, 2009b) scheme can be applied in order to protect a society of collaborating agents by making every agent collaborate with one or more remote agents running in different hosts. These agents act as secure

Table 1. Comparative table with pros and cons of different security mechanisms for agent based systems

	Manipulation of interaction with other Agents	Malicious Network	Spying out Data/code	Code Manipulation	Control Flow Manipulation	Masquerading	Host Collaboration to attack	Denial of Execution	Expertise in Security required	Dual Protection
Sandbox	Protected	Not Protected	Protected	Protected	Protected	Not Protected	Not Protected	Not Protected	Not Required	Not Provided
Software based fault isolation	Protected	Not Protected	Protected	Protected	Protected	Not Protected	Not Protected	Not Protected	Required	Not Provided
Safe code Interpretation	Not Protected	Protected	Protected	Protected	Protected	Protected	Not Protected	Not Protected	Required	Not Provided
Agent TCL	Not Protected	Protected	Protected	Protected	Protected	Protected	Not Protected	Not Protected	Required	Not Provided
Code Signing	Not Protected	Protected	Protected	Protected	Protected	Protected	Not Protected	Not Protected	Required	Not Provided
State Appraisal	Not Protected	Protected	Protected	Protected	Protected	Protected	Not Protected	Not Protected	Required	Not Provided
Path Histories	Not Protected	Can be Detected	Not Protected	Not Protected	Not Protected	Not Protected	Not Protected	Not Protected	Required	Not Provided
Proof Carrying Code	Not Protected	Protected	Protected	Protected	Protected	Protected	Not Protected	Protected	Required	Not Provided
Partial Results Encapsulation	Not Protected	Not Protected	Protected	Protected	Protected	Protected	Not Protected	Not Protected	Required	Not Provided
Sanctuaries	Not Protected	Not Protected	Protected	Protected	Protected	Protected	Not Protected	Protected	Required	Not Provided
Itinerary Recording with replication and/or voting	Not Protected	Protected	Protected	Protected	Protected	Protected	Not Protected	Not Protected	Not Required	Not Provided
Checksumming	Not Protected	Protected	Protected	Protected	Protected	Protected	Not Protected	Not Protected	Not Required	Not Provided
Blackbox	Not Protected	Not Protected	Protected	Protected	Protected	Protected	Not Protected	Protected	Not Required	Not Provided
Detecting manipulation (watermarking)	Not Protected-Detect	Not Protected-Detect	Not Protected	Not Protected-Detect	Not Protected	Not Protected	Not Protected	Not Protected	Not Required	Not Provided
Online collaboration Schemes	Not Protected	Protected	Protected	Protected	Protected	Not Protected	Protected	Protected	Required	Not Provided
Dynamic multi-hop protection	Not Protected	Protected	Protected	Protected	Protected	Protected	Not Protected	Protected	Required	Not Provided
Secure Migration Protocol based on Trusted Computing	Protected	Protected	Protected	Protected	Protected	Protected	Protected	Protected	Not Required	Not Provided
Protected Computing Approach	Not Protected	Not Protected	Protected	Protected	Protected	Protected	Not Protected	Protected	Protected	Provided
SecMiLiA with protected computing enabled	Protected	Protected	Protected	Protected	Protected	Protected	Not Protected	Protected	Not Required	Provided

coprocessors for the first one. This strategy increases the performance by avoiding the transmission of the protected code sections over the network. In contrast, it is only suitable in those scenarios where the set of agents to be protected is static and can be determined before their actual execution.

The Static Mutual Protection strategy (Muñoz, 2011) can be successfully applied to many different scenarios. However, there will be scenarios where will not possible to foresee the possible interactions between the agents, where the agents will be generated by different parts, or that will involve very dynamic multi-hop agents. In these cases, the Static Mutual Protection strategy will be difficult or impossible to apply.

Dynamic Protection is proposed where each agent will be able to execute arbitrary code sections on behalf of other agents in the society. Dynamic Protection Tool (DPT) will be able to allocate into every agent a little virtual machine code. This virtual machine will be able to execute public and private code from other agents on the fly. Doing this, there will be not necessity of fixed assignations between agents, because every agent will be a potential secure processor (Muñoz, 2009) for the rest of the agents in the system. Some ongoing focus on the development of the automatic tools that support the development process. Actually, you count on prototypes of the tools that process the agents. This tools work with a predefined policy. Ongoing work is on the flexibility and adaptability of those tools to different parameters in the policies. This first line also includes the description of such policies.

CONCLUSION

This chapter makes a complete survey of every security mechanism for agent based systems. Table 1 includes a comparison between all security mechanisms for agent based systems. This table describes the kind of protection supported by every mechanism according to the wide variety of possible attacks described along this chapter. At a first glance, most of security mechanisms are traditional solutions applied to a different paradigm. Results are not as valuable as it was expected since those were not tailored solutions. To offer a complete review, we also included tailored security solutions that were deeply analyzed and compared among them. The most promising horizon is not in a perfect solution that covers all aspects but a combination with different approaches can provide a dual protection mechanism. From security engineering perspective, an essential point to address is to facilitate the use of robust security mechanisms to agent system developers. Despite of existing research provides useful solutions for warrant the security in multi agent systems still remains unsolved problems.

REFERENCES

Alechina, N., Alechina, R., Habner, J., Jago, M., & Logan, B. (2006). Belief revision for AgentSpeak agents. Proceedings of Autonomous Agents and Multi Agents Systems 2006, 1288 – 1290. doi:10.1145/1160633.1160868

Ansel, J., Marchenko, P., Erlingsson, Ú., Taylor, E., Chen, B., Schuff, D. L., & Yee, B. (2011). Language-independent sandboxing of just-in-time compilation and self-modifying code. *Proceedings of the 32nd ACM SIGPLAN conference on Programming language design and implementation - PLDI '11.* 10.1145/1993498.1993540

Banks, G., Fattori, A., Kemmerer, C., Kruegel, C., & Vigna, G. (2011). MISHIMA: Multilateration of Internet hosts hidden using malicious fast-flux agents. *Proceedings of Conference on Detection of Intrusions and Malware and Vulnerability Assessment (DIMVA).* 10.1007/978-3-642-22424-9_11

Bennet, S. Y. (1997). *A Sanctuary for Mobile Agents.* Technical Report CS97-537. University of California in San Diego. Available at http://www- cse.ucsd.edu/users/bsy/index.html

Bordini, R. H., Hübner, J. F., & Wooldridge, M. (2007). *Programming Multi-Agent Systems in AgentSpeak using Jason.* doi:10.1002/9780470061848

Bork, D., Pavlidis, M., & Utz, W. (2017). *Modeling Method Conceptualization within OMiLAB: The SecureTropos Case. In RCIS 2017* (pp. 470–475). Brighton: PDF.

Borselius, N. (2002). Mobile agent security. *Electron Commun Eng J, 14*(5), 211–218. doi:10.1049/ecej:20020504

Bresciani, P., Perini, A., Giorgini, P., Giunchiglia, F., & Mylopoulos, J. (2004). Tropos: An agent-oriented software development methodology. *Autonomous Agents and Multi-Agent Systems, 8*(3), 203–236. doi:10.1023/B:AGNT.0000018806.20944.ef

Brooks, R. R. (2004). Mobile code paradigms and security issues. *IEEE Internet Computing, 8*(3), 54–59. doi:10.1109/MIC.2004.1297274

Clements, P., Papaioannou, T., & Edwards, J. (1997). Aglets: Enabling the Virtual Enterprise. Proceedings of Managing Enterprises Stakeholders, Engineering, Logistics and Achievement (ME-SELA'97).

Collberg, C., & Thomborson, C. (2000). *Watermarking, Tamper-Proofing, and Obfuscation Tools for Software Protection.* University of Auckland Technical Report 170.

Esparza, O., Fernández, M., & Soriano, M. (2003a). Protecting mobile agents by using traceability techniques. *IEEE International Conference on Information Technology: Research and Education. ITRE 2003*. 10.1109/ITRE.2003.1270618

Esparza, O., Fernández, M., Soriano, M., Muñoz, L., & Forné, J. (2003). Mobile Agent Watermarking and Fingerprinting: Tracing Malicious Hosts. *Database and Expert Systems Applications (DEXA'03)*.

Esparza, O., Soriano, M., Muñoz, J. L., & Forné, J. (2003b). Host revocation authority: A way of protecting mobile agents from malicious hosts. Lecture Notes in Computer Science, 2722.

Farmer, W., Guttman, J., & Swarup, V. (1996). Security for Mobile Agents: Authentication and State Appraisal. *Proceedings of the 4th European Symposium on Research in Computer Security*, 118-130. 10.1007/3-540-61770-1_31

Gray, R. (1996). Agent Tcl: A Flexible and Secure Mobile-Agent System. *Proceedings of the Fourth Annual Tcl/Tk workshop (TCL 96)*, 9-23.

Gray, R. (2004). Mobile Agents: Overcoming the Early Hype and a Bad Name. *Proceedings of IEEE International Conference on Mobile Data Management (MDM)*, 302.

Guerraoui, R., & Schiper, A. (1997). Software-based replication for fault tolerance. *Computer*, *30*(4), 68–74. doi:10.1109/2.585156

Gunter, C. A., Peter, H., & Scott, N. (1997). Infrastructure for Proof-Referencing Code. *Proceedings, Workshop on Foundations of Secure Mobile Code*.

Hachez, G. (2003). *A Comparative Study of Software Protection Tools Suited for E-Commerce with Contributions to Software Watermarking and Smart Cards* (PhD thesis). Universite Catholique de Louvain. Retrieved from http://www.dice.ucl.ac.be/hachez/thesis gael hachez.pdf

Helsinger, A., Thome, M., & Wright, T. (2004). Cougaar: A Scalable, Distributed Multi-Agent Architecture. *IEEE*, *2*, 1910–1917. doi:10.1109/ICSMC.2004.1399959

Hohl, F. (1998). Time Limited Blackbox Security: Protecting Mobile Agents From Malicious Hosts. In G. Vigna (Ed.), Mobile Agents and Security (pp. 92-113). Springer-Verlag.

Ivanovic, M., & Ninkovic, S. (2017). Personalized HealthCare and Agent Technologies. *Proceedings 11ᵗʰ KES Conference on Agents and Multi-Agent Systems- Technology and Applications*.

Jansen, W. (1998a). *Mobile Agents and Security*. National Institute of Standards and Technology. Retrieved April 8, 2005, from http://www.csrc.nist.gov/staff/jansen/pp-agentsecurityfin.pdf

Jansen, W. (1998b). *Countermeasures for Mobile Agent Security, Computer Communications, Special issue on advanced security techniques for network protection* (Vol. 23). Elsevier Science.

Jansen, W., & Karygiannis, T. (1998). Mobile Agent Security. NIST Special Publication, National Institute of Standards and Technology, 800-19.

Jansen, W. A. (2000). Countermeasure for mobile agent security. *Computer Communications*, *23*(17), 1667–1676. doi:10.1016/S0140-3664(00)00253-X

Johansen, D. (2004). Mobile Agents: Right Concept, Wrong approach. In *Proceedings of the 2004 IEEE International Conference on Mobile Data Management* (pp. 300-301). IEEE Computer Society.

Kotz, D., & Gray, R. (1999). Mobile Agents and the Future of the Internet. *Operating Systems Review*, *33*(3), 7–13. doi:10.1145/311124.311130

Krivic, P., Skocir, P., Kusek, M., & Jezic, G. (2017). Microservices as Agents in IoT Systems. *Proceedings 11th KES Conference on Agents and Multi-Agent Systems-Technology and Applications*.

Lange, D. (1998). Mobile Objects and Mobile Agents: The Future of Distributed Computing? In *Proceedings of the 12th European Conference Object-Oriented Programming (ECOOP)* (vol. 1445, p. 1). Springer-Verlag.

Lange, D., & Oshima, M. (1999). Seven Good Reasons for Mobile Agents. *Communications of the ACM*, *42*(3), 88–89. doi:10.1145/295685.298136

Li, X., Zhang, A., Sun, J., & Yin, J. (2004). The Research of Mobile Agent Security. In *Second International Workshop on Grid and Cooperative Computing (GCC)* (vol. 3033, pp. 187-190). Shanghai, China: Academic Press.

Maña, A., & Muñoz, A. (2006) Protected Computing vs. *Trusted Computing. In International Conference on Communication Systems Software and Middleware (COMSWARE'06)*. New Delhi: IEEE.

Maña, A., & Muñoz, A. (2007b). Trusted Code Execution in Javacard. *International Conference on Trust, Privacy and Security in Digital Business. TrustBus 2007: Trust, Privacy and Security in Digital Business*, 269-279.

Maña, A., Muñoz, A., & Serrano, D. (2007). Towards Secure Agent Computing for Ubiquitous Computing and Ambient Intelligence. *Fourth International Conference, Ubiquitous Intelligence and Computing, Hong Kong (China) 2007.*

Maña, A., Muñoz, A., & Serrano, D. (2009). Protected Computing Approach: Towards the Mutual Protection of Agent Computing. *7th International Conference on Practical Applications of Agents and MultiAgent Systems PAAMS 2009.* 10.1007/978-3-642-00487-2_57

Marrow, P., & Ghanea-Hercock, R. (2000). Mobile Software Agents – Insect-Inspired Computing. *BT Technology Journal, 18*(4), 129–139. doi:10.1023/A:1026771012206

Matulevicius, R., Mouratidis, H., Mayer, N., Dubois, E., & Heymans, P. (2012). Syntactic and Semantic Extensions to Secure Tropos to Support Security Risk Management. *J. UCS, 18*(6), 816–844.

Milojicic, D., LaForge, W., & Chauhan, D. (1998). Mobile Objects and Agents. *Proceedings of the Second USENIX Conference on Object Oriented Technologies and Systems (COOTS).*

Mouratidis, H. (2011). Secure software systems engineering: The Secure Tropos approach. *Journal of Software, 6*(3), 331–339. doi:10.4304/jsw.6.3.331-339

Mouratidis, H., & Giorgini, P. (2009). Enhancing secure tropos to effectively deal with security requirements in the development of multiagent systems. In *Safety and Security in Multiagent Systems* (pp. 8–26). Springer Berlin Heidelberg. doi:10.1007/978-3-642-04879-1_2

Mouratidis, H., Kolp, M., Faulkner, S., & Giorgini, P. (2005). A Secure Architectural Description Language for Agent Systems. *AAMAS, 5,* 25–29.

Muñoz, A., Anton, P., & Maña, A. (2011). Static mutual approach for protecting mobile agent. In Advances in Intelligent and Soft Computing (Vol. 91, pp. 51–58). Academic Press. doi:10.1007/978-3-642-19934-9_7

Muñoz, A., & Maña, A. (2009b). A Hardware Based Infrastructure for Agent Protection. 3rd Symposium of Ubiquitous Computing and Ambient Intelligence 2008. *Advances in Soft Computing, 51,* 39-47.

Muñoz, A., & Maña, A. (2011b). TPM-based protection for mobile agents. *Security and Communication Networks, 4*(1), 45–60. doi:10.1002ec.158

Muñoz, A., Maña, A., & Antón, P. (2010). In the track of the agent protection: A solution based on cryptographic hardware. *Lecture Notes in Computer Science, 6258,* 284–297. doi:10.1007/978-3-642-14706-7_22

Muñoz, A., Maña, A., & Antón, P. (2010b). A solution based on cryptographic hardware to protect agents. In *Proceedings - 13th International Conference on Network-Based Information Systems, NBiS 2010* (pp. 400–407). Academic Press. 10.1109/NBiS.2010.115

Muñoz, A., Maña, A., Harjani, R., & Montenegro, M. (2009a). Agent Protection based on the use of cryptographic hardware. *IEEE 33rd International Computer Software and Applications Conference Ubicación.*

Muñoz, A., Maña, A., & Serrano, D. (2009). SecMiLiA: An approach in the agent protection. In *Proceedings - International Conference on Availability, Reliability and Security, ARES 2009* (pp. 341–348). Academic Press. 10.1109/ARES.2009.50

Muñoz, A., Maña, A., & Serrano, D. (2009c). Trusted Computing: The Cornerstone in the Secure Migration Library for Agents. *7th International Conference on Practical Applications of Agents and Multi-Agent Systems.*

Muñoz, A., Maña, A., & Serrano, D. (2009d). The Role of Trusted Computing in Secure Agent Migration. *3rd International Conference on Research Challenges in Information Science (RCIS 2009).*

Necula, G. C., & Lee, P. (1998). Safe, untrusted agents using proof-carrying code. In G. Vigna (Ed.), *Mobile agents and security, LNCS 1419* (pp. 61–91). Berlin: Springer. doi:10.1007/3-540-68671-1_5

Ordille, J. (1996). When agents Roam, Who can You Trust? *Proceedings of the First Conference on Emerging Technologies and Applications in Communications.* 10.1109/ETACOM.1996.502505

Pavlidis, M., & Islam, S. (2011, June). SecTro: A CASE Tool for Modelling Security in Requirements Engineering using Secure Tropos. In *CAiSE Forum* (pp. 89-96). Academic Press.

Pavlovskaya, M., Gaisin, R., & Dautov, R. (2017). Finding Correlations Between Driver Stress and Traffic Accidents: An Experimental Study. *Proceedings 11th KES Conference on Agents and Multi-Agent Systems- Technology and Applications.*

Pearson, S. (2007). *How Can You Trust the Computer in Front of You? Technical Report Trusted E-Services Laboratory, HP Laboratories Bristol.* HPL-2002-222. Trusted Computing Group. TCG Specification Architecture Overview, Revision 1.4 (2007). Retrieved from https://www.trustedcomputinggroup.org/groups/TCG 1 4 Architecture Overview.pdf

Pham, V., & Karamouch, A. (1998). Mobile Software Agents: An Overview. *IEEE Communications Magazine, 36*(7), 26–37. doi:10.1109/35.689628

Riordan, J., & Scheneider, B. (1998). Environmental Key Generation Towards Clueless Agents. G. Vigna (Ed.), Mobile Agents and Security. Springer-Verlag.

Roth, V. (1998) Secure recording of itineraries through cooperating agents. *Proceedings of 4th workshop on mobile object systems: secure internet mobile computations,* 147–154.

Rothermel, K., Hohl, F., & Radouniklis, N. (1997). Mobile Agent Systems: What is Missing? *Proceedings of the International Working Conference on Distributed Applications and Interoperable Systems (DAIS),* 111-124.

Rul, S., Vandierendonck, H., & De Bosschere, K. (2009). Towards automatic program partitioning. *Conference On Computing Frontiers, 9.* doi:10.1145/1531743.1531759

Sander, T., & Tschudin, C. (1998). Protecting Mobile Agents Against Malicious Hosts. In G. Vigna (Ed.), Lecture Notes in Computer Science: Vol. 1419. *Mobile Agents and Security. Springer-Verlag.* doi:10.1007/3-540-68671-1_4

Sandhu, R., & Samarati, P. (1996). Authentication, access control, and audit. *ACM Computing Surveys, 28*(1), 241–243. doi:10.1145/234313.234412

Schoder, D., & Eymann, T. (2000). The Real Challenges of Mobile Agents. *Communications of the ACM, 43*(6), 111–112. doi:10.1145/336460.336488

Schwuttke, U. M., & Quan, A. G. (1993). Enhancing Performance of Cooperating Agents in Real-Time Diagnostic Systems. In *Proceedings of the Thirteenth International Joint Conference on Artificial Intelligence (IJCAI-93)* (pp. 332-337). Menlo Park, CA: Academic Press.

Shepherdson, D. (2003). The JACK Usage Report. *Proceedings of the Autonomous Agents and Multi Agents Systems 2003 (AAMAS 03).*

Stern, J. P., Hachez, G., Koeune, F., & Quisquater, J. J. (1999). Robust Object Watermarking: Application to Code. In *Proceedings of Info Hiding '99.* Springer-Verlag. Retrieved from http://www.dice.ucl.ac.be/crypto/publications/1999/codemark.pdf

Vigilson Prem, M., & Swamynathan, S. (2012). Securing mobile agent and its platform from passive attack of malicious mobile agents. In *IEEE-International Conference on Advances in Engineering, Science and Management* (pp. 605–609). ICAESM. Retrieved from http://www.scopus.com/inward/record.url?eid=2-s2.0-84863963880&partnerID=40&md5=c70f6cd57f573d678601718e70e13008

Vigna, G. (1997). Protecting mobile agents through tracing. *Proceedings of the 3rd ECOOP workshop on mobile object systems.*

Vigna, G. (2004). Mobile Agents: Ten Reasons for Failure. In *Proceedings of the 2004 IEEE International Conference on Mobile Data Management* (pp. 298-299). IEEE Computer Society.

Wang, H., & Wang, C. (1997). Intelligent Agents in the Nuclear Industry. *IEEE Computer, 30*(11), 28–34. doi:10.1109/2.634838

White, J. (2004). *Mobile Agents White Paper, General Magic.* Retrieved March 17, 2004, from http://www.genmagic.com/agents/Whitepaper/whitepaper.html

Wooldrigde, M. (1997). Agent-based Software Engineering. *IEE Proceedings. Software Engineering, 144*(1), 26–37. doi:10.1049/ip-sen:19971026

ENDNOTES

[1]   JADE (Java Agent DEvelopment Framework) is a software Framework fully implemented in the Java language. It simplifies the implementation of multi-agent systems through a middle-ware that complies with the FIPA specifications and through a set of graphical tools that support the debugging and deployment phases.

[2]   JADE (Java Agent DEvelopment Framework) is a software Framework fully implemented in the Java language. It simplifies the implementation of multi-agent systems through a middle-ware that complies with the FIPA specifications and through a set of graphical tools that support the debugging and deployment phases.

[3]   FIPA:Foundation for Intelligent Physical Agents. Online available at: http://www.fipa.org/Bennet S. Yee, "A Sanctuary for Mobile Agents". Secure Internet Programming 1999.

Chapter 3
Attack Detection in Cloud Networks Based on Artificial Intelligence Approaches

Zuleyha Yiner
Siirt University, Turkey

Nurefsan Sertbas
Istanbul University – Cerrahpaşa, Turkey

Safak Durukan-Odabasi
ⓘ https://orcid.org/0000-0002-9486-666X
Istanbul University – Cerrahpaşa, Turkey

Derya Yiltas-Kaplan
Istanbul University – Cerrahpaşa, Turkey

ABSTRACT

Cloud computing that aims to provide convenient, on-demand, network access to shared software and hardware resources has security as the greatest challenge. Data security is the main security concern followed by intrusion detection and prevention in cloud infrastructure. In this chapter, general information about cloud computing and its security issues are discussed. In order to prevent or avoid many attacks, a number of machine learning algorithms approaches are proposed. However, these approaches do not provide efficient results for identifying unknown types of attacks. Deep learning enables to learning features that are more complex, and thanks to the collection of big data as a training data, deep learning achieves more successful results. Many deep learning algorithms are proposed for attack detection. Deep networks architecture is divided into two categories, and descriptions for each architecture and its related attack detection studies are discussed in the following section of chapter.

DOI: 10.4018/978-1-5225-7353-1.ch003

INTRODUCTION

Cloud networks include virtual data centers that handles the physical or traditional data centers to give the opportunity of storing data or benefiting from the hardware devices to the end users (Bhamare et al., 2016). Several computer application areas such as image processing need very large amount of storage size and processing time (Marwan et al., 2018). This leads to the requirement of spread usage of cloud networks that achieve a gain on operational and physical costs.

Cloud computing covers several branches of computer engineering discipline. These are distributed computing, grid computing, networking, software, and virtualization. The cloud also involves many advantages related with the sides of computer hardware or software, namely data storage solutions, scalability, rapid configuration, security options, lower costs, flexibility in the network access, and so on. Actually cloud computing can be defined with different explanations such as virtualization of on-demand resources and abstraction of services. However, cloud computing can be explained in two general definitions. The first definition says that it is an infrastructure that gives the opportunity to the end-user applications with a payment in return for the software/hardware usage rate. The second definition means that it is a model in which the end-users access the network area involving hardware or software elements such as servers, storage devices, and applications by the help of the service providers. If the stored data is about healthcare and obtained as several images from the patients, the service provider brings profit to the healthcare organizations especially on data management, access, and processing from several different user points (Said et al., 2016, Chonka et al., 2011, Marwan et al., 2018).

The largest technology companies in the world, namely Google, Amazon, and Ebay, make investments for cloud computing. Technology vendors enable the customers to use any hardware or software parts in their computers against payment of a fee. By the time going on, the attacks over the cloud systems gain an increase on their amounts and a robustness in their structures. Because that the cloud infrastructure is a sharing environment, the security becomes vital and vulnerable. The two endpoints of the cloud, namely service provider and the user should be confident that the security problems are solved in the cloud network. Some private data such as patient files should be encrypted before sending to the remote servers (Chonka et al., 2011, Said et al., 2016).

CLOUD ARCHITECTURE AND CLOUD SECURITY ISSUES

There are three different layers in a cloud structure. These are Deployment Models, Service Models, and Essential Characteristics respectively from the bottom to the top.

Figure 1. Delivery models of cloud

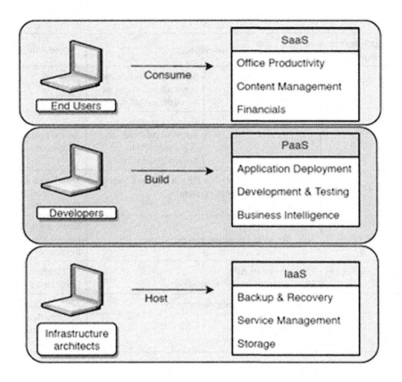

The classes in the Deployment Models are public, private, hybrid, and community. For any class of the deployment models, there are delivery models called Service Models, which involve Infrastructure as a Service (IaaS), Platform as a Service (PaaS), and Software as a Service (SaaS). These models are the core of the cloud network and get several characteristics from the top level of the structure. The characteristics can be exemplified as measured service, on-demand self-service, and rapid elasticity (Said et al., 2016).

The large amounts of data and customers in a cloud environment cause the performance degradation and inaccessibility to the network. To solve any problem and also any security issue, the cloud computing requires specific methods. Because the system and its properties like sharing of the resources are different from the other networking types.

A brief description for security challenges in cloud and candidate solutions for each challenge are given in Table 1.

According to an extensive research on cloud computing, it is obvious that there are different security levels for different service models. The security issues of a service model are different from the others.(Said et al., 2016). Nearby the service

Table 1. Security challenges in cloud computing with its description and candidate solutions

Security Challenges in Cloud Computing	Description		Candidate Solutions
Data Security	Confidentiality & Integrity	Stored data in the cloud is not altered in any way by unauthorized parties	Encryption based solutions
	Privacy	Ensuring that the sensitive information is not revealed to unauthorized users	Access control mechanisms
Access & Identity Management	User that does not satisfies the min required level of trust should not enter the system Account hijacking		Trust based solutions Authentication solutions Use of better credentials
Device Vulnerabilities	U2L attacks to gain super user privileges		Better configurations Firmware updates Regular security patches
Securing communication channel	Use of insecure APIs Eavesdropping of communication		HTTPS/SSL Proxy based solutions
NW wide monitoring	Unauthorized and malicious activity		Artificial intelligence based methods (Anomaly and signature based detection)
Availability	Exhaustion of assets Preventing users from using a service		

models, the security issues also change according to the data privacy stages. For example, a patient database should be encrypted with any robust algorithm. The encryption algorithms in the literature are mentioned as 3DES, AES, RSA DES, and ECC. However, these algorithms are not used in an encrypted domain, so they do not provide data process in a secure way. Some security algorithms on cloud computing give the ability of processing on encrypted data to the service providers without any knowledge on the raw data parts. The processes on the data should be done fast. Because that data amount becomes so large in cloud environments, data can be processed by some schemes that work distributed and parallel. This approach brings performance and reliability even though the file processing operations are done on the encrypted parts of the distributed data (Marwan et al., 2018).

Marwan et al. (2018) remarked that the security level changes with the cloud providers and Service Level Agreement (SLA) involving Quality of Service (QoS) definitions. Security becomes more complex when the processing input is about a sensitive information such as patients' data as mentioned above. Therefore, the protection of such private data from the malicious attacks is very necessary. The basic aim of the attacks in a cloud system is the exhaustion of some assets such as power, storage capacity or bandwidth (Chonka et al., 2011).

There are several types of attack tools in present form. Extensible Markup Language (XML)-based Denial of Service(X-DoS) and Hypertext Transfer Protocol (HTTP)-based Denial of Service (H-DoS) are two of the simple attack tools. In X-DoS, the malicious part can be seen in XML messages sending to a Web server/ service. An X-Dos attack sample (Coercive Parsing) exploits web server CPU by using consecutive open tags and changing message contents on the web. In a new version, Distributed X-DoS (DX-DoS), X-DoS attacks are done with multiple hosts to injure a target computer. On the other hand, H-DoS exploits the communication channels of a web server by sending it huge amount of http requests (Chonka et al., 2011).

ATTACK DETECTION WITH MACHINE LEARNING METHODS

Machine learning has been used in various kinds of applications in cloud computing. These applications have been exemplified as energy efficiency, resource management, and security. These three areas were studied by Fiala (2015) in terms of machine learning algorithms. Fiala (2015) gave the security part by describing the trust level firstly. The system can give or reject the access right to a participant for a cloud network according to the participant's trust level. The value of trust level is computed with a specific algorithm. One sample algorithm obtains a trust value by summing all risk levels. There are two general classes of methods for threat detection in cloud security. These are anomaly detection and signature detection. In anomaly detection, an anomaly (or threat) can be found according to the exceptions that are the deviations from the normal behaviors in the network. Here a normal behavior sometimes can be found as a threat. On the other hand, signature detection uses the agents' signatures. If there are malicious activity in a history of an agent, the system rejects the access. However, this method is useful for only predetermined signatures. Some researchers combine the anomaly and signature detection for finding a hybrid method in which anomaly part is used for dynamic network situations and signature part is for static network conditions. Fiala (2015) made reference to a hybrid method using the combination of Naïve Bayes Tree (NBT) and Random Forest (RF). In this method, the training set concludes a classification pattern which distinguishes the anomalies. Here, each one of the attack classes such as Probe, User to Root (U2R), Remote to Local (R2L), and Denial of Service (DoS) includes some specific attacks obtained from KDD'Cup 99 data set. The method was compared with another one that used RF and K-Nearest Nodes (KNN) together. The method with NBT and RF overcame the RF and KNN method. But the data set is very old and cannot be adapted to any new dynamic network systems like cloud technologies.

Fiala (2015) discussed another framework including the detection rules in a domain specific language (DSL). DSL includes some rules for both anomaly and signature detection. The behaviors were dependent on categorized sub-profiles of service, user, host, and workflow. The classification was also extended with including time tracks like immediate, hourly, or monthly to each sub-profile. This hybrid framework does not have a complete testing and validating parts, so has not been compared with any other concrete method.

Bhamare et al. (2016) mentioned that the data sets were important to get different results from different cloud scenarios in collaboration with machine learning methods. They emphasized that the data sets using for problem solutions on the cloud security were not adequate. This situation causes the artificial intelligence solutions to become ineffective. For example, a solution method working with a data set may not be successful with another data set.

Bhamare et al. (2016) used two different data sets, namely UNSW and ISOT, during the training phase by benefiting from supervised machine learning models. These models are logistic regression, J48 decision tree, Naïve Bayes, and Support Vector Machines (SVM). UNSW data set was generated in Australian Centre for Cyber Security with considering normal and attack traffic activities of the network. The traffic input comes from the tcpdump tool. UNSW data set has nine classes of attacks. These are Analysis, Backdoors, DoS, Exploits, Fuzzers, Generic, Reconnaissance, Shellcode and Worms. On the other hand, ISOT data set got the normal traffic from the Traffic Laboratory at Ericsson Research in Hungary and Lawrence Berkeley National Laboratory and the attack traffic from the Honeynet project. The attack traffic part has very small percentage in overall input data and includes the Storm and Waledac botnets. The logistic regression has the best accuracy with UNSW data set and Weka tool. Also the rates of True-Positive (TP: detection of abnormal packets correctly), False-Negative (FN: detection of abnormal packets like normal), True-Negative (TN: detection of normal packets correctly), and False-Positive (FP: detection of normal packets like abnormal) were analyzed. In this analysis, again the logistic regression has the best TP and FN rates, an SVM class has the best TN and FP rates by having very small difference with logistic regression. So the overall performance is good in logistic regression for UNSW data set. This decision is valid for overall performance values of J48 decision tree and logistic regression respectively with ISOT data set.

Said et al. (2016) proposed another method for security in cloud computing using data mining that could support an information base for the machine learning applications. In this study, the main intrusion detection and data mining algorithm is decision tree. The researchers have also investigated some other machine learning methods such as Naïve Bayes, multilayer perceptron, SVM, and Partial Tree (PART) that had been implemented with Weka in the literature. Said et al. (2016) used the analysis of confusion matrix to get the performance comparison of the methods. By the help of the data mining approach, the records were classified based on the decision sets obtained as the branches of the decision tree. The decision tree C4.5 rule generation for the data classification was used here. The rates of the data categories of secured and unsecured represent the security situation and thus a requirement for the solution. The study proves that a simple decision tree model Chaid algorithm security rating for classifying approach is very strong method. The study covers some measurement metrics, but there is not any value table or assignment on these metrics, namely TP, FP, precision rate, and so on. In other words, the simulation values have not been given in a clear way.

Marwan et al. (2018) proposed three-level system for cloud security. This system involves Client, CloudSec, and Cloud Provider as three main parts. The data encryption and fragmentation are done on CloudSec with using HTTPS/SSL. CloudSec also provides the security of data during its utilization by the cloud part. Each client or consumer has some permission to access the specific data. For this reason, there are some rules about authorization that are defined before in the cloud system. Inside the system, machine learning classification methods are used during the data segmentation. Because that the study handles the medical data as images, the study is relevant to the image segmentation algorithms in the literature. But the main difference here is the proposed method involves data security and protection. SVM is used for classification and Fuzzy C-means (FCM) trains the SVM classifiers to increase the performance. For SVM implementation, the researchers used LIBSVM that is an open source library machine learning tool. They additionally used color feature on the images with FCM algorithm. The proposed method was tried on JPG format pictures with using the pixel colors to partition the Picture into four different areas. Each area was used for image processing in segmentation independently and at the end, the whole image was constructed. The two fundamental functions, namely Gaussian filtering and image enhancement, were applied to support the quality on the images. The study was completed with comparing the original images and the processed ones. The proposed SVM and FCM hybrid method is easy and cost effective.

Chonka et al. (2011) inspired from the idea of Deterministic Packet Marking (DPM) algorithm to store the identity of a message source. Because the obfuscation of an attacker is achieved by himself easily. DPM marks specific parts like ID in the header of the incoming packet entering arriving at the edge ingress router. The marking information does not change during the network tour. In this study, the marking is used in web service messages in the form of Service-Oriented Traceback Mark (SOTM).

In this study, Service-Oriented Traceback Architectural (SOTA) framework has some advantageous properties. First of all, SOTA provides the security of the system even for X-DoS or DX-DoS. The changing version of the packet header in

Table 2. Machine learning approaches used for attack detection

Author	Year	Used Approach	Data set
Fiala	2015	A hybrid method using combination of NBT and RF	KDD'Cup 99
Bhamare et al.	2016	Logistic regression, J48 decision tree, Naïve Bayes and SVM	UNSW and ISOT
Said et al.	2016	Decision tree, Naïve Bayes, multilayer perceptron, SVM and Partial Tree (PART)	No description
Marwan et al.	2018	SVM and Fuzzy C-Means for training SVM classifiers	No description
Chonka et al.	2011	SOTA and WS-Security	StuPot Project (2009)

IPv6 brings with it inadequacy of the current traceback methods. SOTA does not put any information into the IP packet, so it does not change the protocol. SOTA is flexible to be used in any grid system.

The study covers a Cloud TraceBack (CTB) and a Cloud Protector. CTB is located at the edge routers, receives the service requests, and marks the request packet headers. At the same time, CTB removes the address of the service provider as a security step. The identity backup can be performed with CTBM (CTB Mark) tags against any hack. After CTB marking on the request message for identification of the attack source, the SOAP message is sent to the web server. On this way, CTB provides cloud victim to trace the attack back to the source in a matter of seconds.

The Cloud Protector part is responsible from the detection of X-DoS messages with its trained back propagation neural network structure. The main assignment of Cloud Protector is the detection and filtration of X-DoS and H-DoS messages.

The algebraic model of this study represents the idea of the polynomial structure in a literature study (see Dean (2002)). The experimental results of CTB (SOTA on the figures) are compared with that of SOAP authentication and WS-Security. SOAP and WS-Security are popular security mechanisms for cloud systems. The response time of SOTA is more efficient than the others. Similarly, the experiments on Cloud Protector represent the results with training phase and the test dataset as in comparison. It is noted that the results on neural network method may change with the adjustment of some metrics during the setting. These metrics are layer number, momentum, threshold, and learning rate.

In Table 2, machine learning approaches used for attack detection in cloud.

DEEP LEARNING

Most of the cyber attacks are small variants of the previously known attacks. Therefore, traditional machine learning approaches fail to identify such attacks and there should be a mechanism to distinguish novel attacks. Current developments in the computing hardware and efficient algorithms introduces deep learning as a powerful solution. Moreover, the collection of big data as a training data has a great contribution to the success of deep learning. Deep learning has a potential for wide application range due to the automated feature engineering and unsupervised pre-training. Such features increase the accuracy of DL models and shortens the processing time (Vincent et al., 2010)

Classical multi layer neural networks always results local optimum solution and the convergence cannot be guaranteed. Deep learning is proposed in 2006 by solving such problems by two-stage training approach including pre-training and fine-tuning. Pre-training is an unsupervised training phase that establishes an initialization point for the further phase. Fine-tuning is a supervised phase that tries to optimize the parameters for domain by minimizing the error. Thus, effective weight initialization in deep learning avoids the local optima and achieves better convergency than the traditional neural networks (Hinton et al., 2006), (Zhang et al, 2018).

In classical machine learning approaches, determining feature representations of raw data is done manually which is time consuming procedure. Performing automatic feature engineering with no direct human interaction is a breakthrough in machine learning. Deep learning enables learning more complex features automatically which reduces feature-engineering time in classical approaches. Deep learning has a potential for wide application range due to the automated feature engineering and unsupervised pre-training. Such features increase the accuracy of DL models and shortens the processing time (Gao et al., 2014).

Such advancements solve the problems related with the complexity and computing difficulties of neural networks. Therefore, deep learning becomes widely used technology in several fields such as autonomous systems, multimedia analytics, medical diagnostics and economics.

Basically, deep learning is the application of multi-layer neural networks whose general structure is shown in following figure. Deep neural network composed of input layer, at least one hidden layer and output layer. Raw input data is fed into the first layer called input layer. Data is trained at that layer and output is provided to the next layer as a learning data. Neurons are initiated with different weights simultaneously and each neuron updates its weights by using its lost function to obtain best logistic fit to the incoming data (Hatcher et al., 2018). Such iteration continues until the desired number of layers is obtained. The representations obtained from the last layer which is called as output layer, can be in a form of classification values, etc. The number of hidden layers and the connections between layers are varies depending on the application.

Figure 2. Deep neural network structure

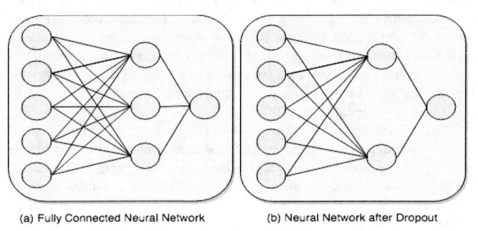

(a) Fully Connected Neural Network   (b) Neural Network after Dropout

In fully connected layer which is shown in Figure 2a, all neurons are connected to all input. In case that some nodes are removed for avoiding overfitting, the structure is called as dropout layer which is shown in Figure 2b.

Main limitations of deep learning approaches are as follows:

- There exist several parameters in deep learning networks and there is not a standardized way to find best values of such parameters. Therefore, learning such parameters is a difficult optimization task.
- Huge volume of data is needed to train deep learning networks. Training such a huge data requires a lot of computational power which is another drawback.
- Moreover, computationally intensive nature of deep learning includes lots of operations and tasks like matrix multiplications on a large scale which requires specialized GPU hardware. Organizations need capital investments to obtain such resources.

DEEP LEARNING ALGORITHMS

In this section, background information about main deep learning architectures and related attack detection studies from the literature are provided. Several number of deep learning methods have been proposed recently, and such methods can be broadly classified into two categories depending on how they are intended to use as generative and discriminative architectures which are illustrated in Figure 3 (Hodo et al., 2017).

Figure 3. Deep networks categorization

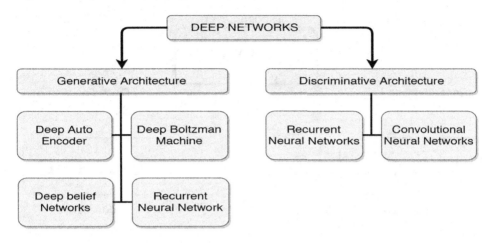

Generative Architecture

Learning the lower layers of the network is a problem in traditional approaches especially in case of limited training data. In 2006, the model proposed by Hinton et al. attracted the attention of researchers. The proposed architecture, deep belief networks, trains one layer at a time greedily and outputs multi-layer probabilistic model (Xu et al., 2015). Therefore, layer by layer learning from bottom up enables fast learning and requires few labeled data. Such architecture is a breakthrough in the development of deep learning.

During the past years, several deep generative models similar to DBN are proposed such as deep neural networks (DNNs), deep autoencoder, DBM, recurrent neural network (RNN), and so on (Deng, 2014). This section briefly introduces most common generative architecture including deep belief network, deep autoencoder, and DBM

Deep Autoencoder

Deep Auto-Encoder (AE) is an energy based deep model that has different forms such as stacked autoencoder and denoising auto encoder (Deng, 2014). The denoising auto encoder aims to reconstruct the input from a corrupted version of it while the stacked auto encoder aims to learn hierarchical features from data and obtain better representations.

A typical problem with deep auto encoder, which has more than one hidden layer, suffers from local minima problem in case training with back propagation. Moreover, back propagation of an error to the first few layers is another problem. Such problem is solved by using initial weights that close to final solution (Deng et al., 2014).

Figure 4. Auto encoder structure

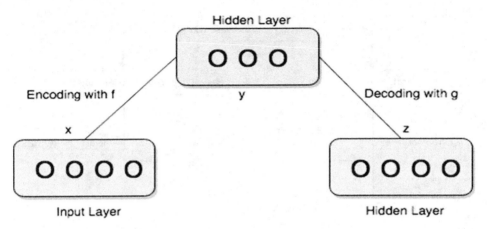

Basic auto encoder structure is given in Figure 4. AE has at least three layers which are input layer, hidden layer and output layer as in neural networks. Input data x is transformed to the y using encoding function f and the hidden representation y is reconstructed using decoding function g. Finally, output is the data input itself.

Zhang et al. (2018) proposes SSAE-XGB method, which uses stacked sparse autoencoder for intrusion detection. Experimental results show that SSAE-XGB performs better than traditional PCA method in dimension reduction. Moreover, they use sparsity constraint and improve the generalization ability. Thus, the proposed approach can deal with imbalanced data efficiently. In (Yousefi-Azar et al., 2017), auto encoders are used to extract semantic similarity between the feature vectors. Thus, better feature representations are obtained and this makes the model more computationally efficient. Proposed scheme is tested considering two types of security tasks, which are network based anomaly intrusion detection and malware classification. Results show that the approach can easily obtain more discriminative features while reducing the dimensions.

Deep Boltzmann Machine

A Deep Boltzmann machine (DBM) has several hidden layers unlike the Restricted Boltzmann Machines (RBMs) which has only one hidden layer. The connections exist only between hidden units in adjacent layers. In other words, there is no connection between the nodes on the same layer such as hidden to hidden and visible to visible. A simple structure of DBM is given in following figure.

Similar to the DBNs, DBMs can be trained on unsupervised data and can be fine- tuned using tagged data for a specific task. Also, DBMs are very powerful for

Figure 5. Deep Boltzman Machine (DBM) structure

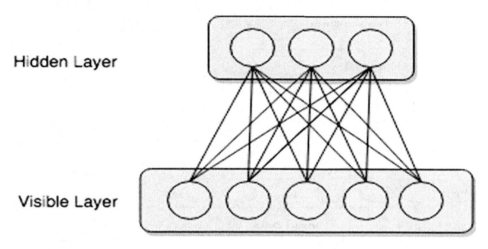

extracting efficient representations of data which is quite useful for classification. Unpredictable nature of network traffic data and continuously evolving anomalies lead researchers to use a self learning mechanism. Thus, Discriminative Restricted Boltzmann Machine based detection is proposed to obtain good classification accuracy in (Fiore et al., 2013). In (Imamverdiyev et al., 2018), multilayer RBM-based DoS attack detection mechanism is proposed by optimizing the deep RBM model. They tested the performance of the proposed model on NSL-KDD dataset and results shows that the proposed model gives more accurate detection than the previously used methods such as SVM, decision tree, Bernoulli-Bernoulli RBM and Gaussian–Bernoulli RBM. The framework introduced by (Nguyen et al., 2018), trains a neural network in offline mode for initializing the weights. They use Gaussian Binary Restricted Boltzmann Machine for pre-training phase. Then, the trained model is used for detecting the cyber-attacks in the cloud in online mode. Proposed framework is able to learn new attacks and detect the previously known ones with high accuracy.

Deep Belief Network

A typical Deep Belief Network (DBN) structure consists of a neural network layer andseveral stacked Restricted Boltzmann Machines (RBMs). RBM is a kind of two layer neural network including visualandhiddenlayer. RBMsaretrainedtofindamodelparameterofDBN.BP neural network is a kind of multi layer neural network which includes forward and back propagation phases.

Figure 6. Deep Blief network structure

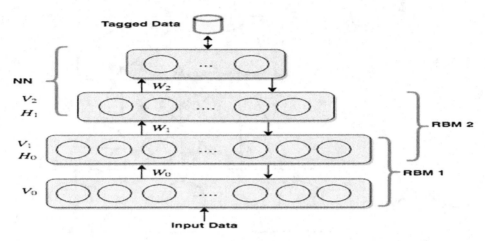

Basic deep belief network structure is given in Figure 6. Such structure has two main phases as unsupervised pre-training and supervised fine tuning. In pre-training phase RBMs are trained layer by layer and weights are updated depending on the relation between v_i and h_i. Such process is useful for initializing the weight parameter of a deep neural network. The output layer of the last RBM is taken as the input vector of the BP neural network. Therefore, training process of multi RBMs determines the initial weights of the BP neural network. The weight initialization process rather than the random initialization, decreases the long training time and overcomes the local optimum problem. Then, unlike the pre-training phase, tagged data will be used to fine-tune the model parameters. BP neural network uses the model parameter, which is an output of RBM training process, and fine tunes the model parameter with iterations. Fine-tuning phase supervises the entire network from top to bottom. At the end of the fine-tuning phase, the optimal DBN training model, which can be used for classification of test data, is obtained. In case that the classification results do not meet the stopping criteria, RBMs are re-trained. Then, the obtained weights are used in fine-tuning phase.

DBNs are widely used as an attack detection approach. In (Gao et al., 2014), NSL-KDD dataset is used for an intrusion detection by building DBN. Experimental results show that the DBN model containing two RBMs and a BP layer, improves the speed of the intrusion detection. In a similar study done by(Gao et al., 2014), the best results are obtained by using four-hidden-layer RBM which approves thatthe depth of the DBN model is determined by experiments and such experiments are lacks of theoretical support. In (Alom et al., 2015), they proposed to use DBN for the detection and classification of the intrusions in network. They use DBN for both a dimension reduction by using only unsupervised training and a classification by associating the class labels with the feature vector. Experimental results show that the proposed model performs better than the existing approaches such as SVM and DBN-SVM in terms of the accuracy and training time.

Discriminative Architecture

Discriminative architecture uses discriminative power for classification. In this model, the output label sequence is associated with input data sequence.

Discriminative architecture is used. This section briefly introduces most common discriminative architecture including recurrent neural network and its types LSTM and Gated Recurrent Unit and convolutional neural networks.

Recurrent Neural Network

A recurrent neural network (RNN) is a class of artificial neural network where connections between nodes form a directed graph along a sequence. RNN is a type of feedforward networks that has a cycle and also it is known as the deepest of all NNs. RNN is a type of generative and discriminative deep networks. When output data is discussed in preceding subsection, namely it is used as predicted input data in the future (Deng et al., 2014).

Recurrent Neural Networks (RNN) are strong, robust and dynamic type of neural networks and they are the only ones with an internal memory. The usage of this memory came up to remove difficulties of learning to store information very long (Bengio et al., 1994). Thanks to this memory, these networks are efficient for understanding a sequence and its context, so they are more preferable for sequential

Figure 7. A recurrent neural network (Lecun et al., 2015)

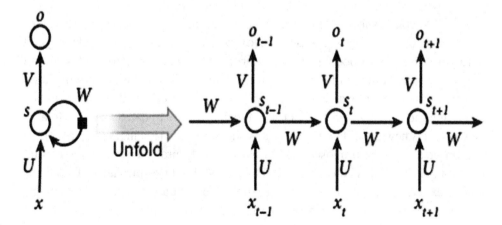

data like time series, video, audio and text. This network is popular in such areas like speech recognition, natural language processing, machine translation, video and much more. Giving efficient predictive results depends on input data and this makes RNN different from other machine learning algorithms.

RNNs consist of input unit, hidden unit and output unit, The artificial neurons used for getting input from neurons at previous time step for each unit grouped as x, s, o respectively. s_t is value of s at time t. U, V, W weights parameters are used in each step and they are same at each state. Figure 7 shows a RNN and its unfolding notation in time which is reprinted from Lecun et al. (2015).

Hidden state at the time t is formulized as s_t and it is a function of input of at the same step x_t. which is modified a U weight matrix added to the hidden state of the previous time step s_{t-1} multiplied by its own hidden-state-to-hidden-state matrix W. (transition matrix) The error they generate will return via backpropagation and be used to adjust their weights until error does not get lower. The sum of weight is transformed by function.

Due to being strong classifier, RNNs are used for many intrusion detection models. Yin et al. (2017) studied on binary classification and multiclass classification and proposed an intrusion detection model based on RNN with using NSL-KDD dataset. They experimented number of neurons and different learning rate effects on their model. They got best detection while learning rate is 0.1 and hidden layer size is 80.

Long Short-Term Memory Units (LSTMs)

The Long Short-Term Memory (LSTM) cell can process data sequentially and keep its hidden state through time and it is unit of recurrent neural network. LSTM network is the type of recurrent neural network with LSTM units.

A common LSTM unit is composed of a cell, an input gate, an output gate and a forget gate. The cell remembers values over arbitrary time intervals and the three gates provide the flow of information into and out of the cell.

A LSTM cell is showed in Figure 8. There are input gate (i), forget gate (f) for passing previous memory h_{t-1}, output gate (o) and cell state (c). The basic idea beyond this algorithm is, firstly deciding which information will be taken from cell state and which new information will be stored in cell state. Secondly, it is step for deciding to output based on cell state. Storing new information step has 2 layer: input gate layer (sigmoid layer) which is about which value will be updated and a tanh layer which creates new candidate values that is added to state (Palangi et al., 2015).

Kim et al. (2016) proposed LSTM Recurrent Neural Network for intrusion detection. In this study, they used KDD Cup 1999 dataset instances. They have done 2 experiments, the first one is finding hyper-parameter value that affects performance. As second experiment, they measure performance of IDS model based

Figure 8. A LSTM cell

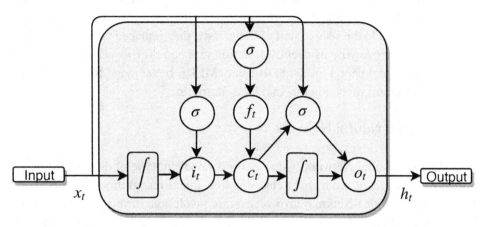

on this hyper-parameter. Many studies show that learning rate (LR) and hidden layer size (HLS) have great effect on performance. In this study, they chose LR as 0.01 and hidden layer size as80. Based on these parameters they got above 95% accuracy. While this IDS model has better detection rate and accuracy than other classification algorithms, False Alarm Rate may be improved.

Gated Recurrent Unit (GRU) Recurrent Neural Network

RNN networks has great success on classification for many network attacks but sometimes it has gradient vanishing problem (Schmidhuber, 2015). Cho et al. (2014) proposed GRU method to overcome gradient descent problem. In this model, hidden layer is replaced with GRU node. Every GRU node has two gates, which are update gate for updating contents of unit and reset gate for forgetting state, which computed previously

Kim et al. (2015) studied on intrusion detection classifier based on GRU RNN. In this study, they used KDD Cup 1999 dataset instances. The result of their approach shows the best detection rate as above 90% and False Alarm Rate as 10% while hidden layer size is 80 and learning rate is 0.01. However, their model does not show good solution for classification of Probe and R2L attacks. This proposed model may be better than some classification algorithms, but it must be tested on another dataset to get right results.

Xu et al. (2018) studied on characteristic of time-related intrusion. They proposed an IDS model based on recurrent neural network with gated recurrent units (GRU). The general difference between LSTM and GRU based recurrent network is about number of gates and parameters. GRU based one has fewer gates due to having no forget gate. For their experiments, they used NSL-KDD and KDD 99 datasets. First part of their study is evaluating performance of GRU and Multilayer Perceptron based IDS model. In the second part of their study, they replaced GRU with LSTM unit. They got above 90% as overall detection rate and 90% as accuracy for both datasets. The experimental result of GRU with MLP is better than LSTM with MLP in term of accuracy, detection rate and false alarm rate.

Convolutional Neural Network

Convolutional Neural Network (ConVNets) is prevalent type of deep learning for computer vision, large-scale image classification, image recognition, segmentation, face recognition. ConVNets may involve several convolutional layer and subsampling. It has 3 layer which are convolutional layer for convolution operation to get the weight sharing, subsampling layer for reducing dimension and fully connected layer. In subsampling layer, average or maximum pooling operation is applied. Local connections, shared weights, pooling and use of many layers make ConVNets providing advantage on natural signals (Lecun et al., 2015). There is no study of directly used ConVNets for intrusion detection or prevention for network.

FUTURE RESEARCH DIRECTIONS

Cloud computing is a model for enabling ubiquitous, convenient, on-demand network access to a shared pool of configurable computing resources (e.g., networks, servers, storage, applications, and services) that can be rapidly provisioned and released with minimal management effort or service provider interaction. Along these features, cloud computing suffers from many attacks. Efficient intrusion detection and prevention systems must be applied to cloud infrastructure to remove or prevent attacks. Deep learning approaches give very effective results for intrusion detection based on an optimal model selection and optimization. It is aimed to propose a deep learning based intrusion detection model for cloud as future study.

CONCLUSION

Cloud computing, which provide end-users to access network hardware and software resources involve many branches of computer engineering. Deployment Models, Service Models and Essential Characteristic are layer of cloud. It can be said that measured service, on-demand self-service, and rapid elasticity are protensity features of cloud.

Cloud computing has been growing for quite some time. Several efforts have been done to provide broad range of services that provides users an ability to scale up and down depending on their requirements. On the other hand, the remote computing concept brings several security vulnerabilities for both consumer and provider side. Therefore, cloud computing should be secure enough to preserve privacy for both sides and to detect intruders.

Existing machine learning solutions based on the detection of previously known attacks. Also, manual feature engineering is needed to represent data in a proper way. Deep learning can be a candidate solution for such kind of problems. There exist several attack detection studies by taking advantage of deep learning and securing the working environment. To the best of our knowledge, there exists only few studies that use deep learning based solutions to detect intruders in the cloud.

In this chapter, general information about cloud computing, security issues of cloud computing, attack detection approaches based on machine learning algorithms is given. Then, an application of neural network deep learning architecture is described. Based on this description, deep learning algorithm is categorized as generative and discriminative which are based on layer by layer training from bottom up and using discriminative power for classification respectively.

REFERENCES

Alom, M. Z., Bontupalli, V., & Taha, T. M. (2015). Intrusion detection using deep belief networks. In *Aerospace and Electronics Conference (NAECON), 2015 National* (pp. 339-344). IEEE. 10.1109/NAECON.2015.7443094

Bengio, Y., Simard, P., & Frasconi, P. (1994). Learning long-term dependencies with gradient descent is difficult. *IEEE Transactions on Neural Networks, 5*(2), 157–166. doi:10.1109/72.279181 PMID:18267787

Bhamare, D., Salman, T., Samaka, M., Erbad, A., & Jain, R. (2016, December). Feasibility of Supervised Machine Learning for Cloud Security. In *Information Science and Security (ICISS), 2016 International Conference on* (pp. 1-5). IEEE.

Chonka, A., Xiang, Y., Zhou, W., & Bonti, A. (2011). Cloud security defence to protect cloud computing against HTTP-DoS and XML-DoS attacks. *Journal of Network and Computer Applications, 34*(4), 1097–1107. doi:10.1016/j.jnca.2010.06.004

Dean, D., Franklin, M., & Stubblefield, A. (2002). An algebraic approach to IP traceback. *ACM Transactions on Information and System Security, 5*(2), 119–137. doi:10.1145/505586.505588

Deng, L. (2014). A tutorial survey of architectures, algorithms, and applications for deep learning. *APSIPA Transactions on Signal and Information Processing, 3.*

Fiala, J. (2015). *A Survey of Machine Learning Applications to Cloud Computing.* Retrieved from http://www.cse.wustl.edu/~jain/cse570-15/ftp/cld_ml/index.html

Fiore, U., Palmieri, F., Castiglione, A., & De Santis, A. (2013). Network anomaly detection with the restricted Boltzmann machine. *Neurocomputing, 122,* 13–23. doi:10.1016/j.neucom.2012.11.050

Gao, N., Gao, L., Gao, Q., & Wang, H. (2014, November). An intrusion detection model based on deep belief networks. In *Advanced Cloud and Big Data (CBD), 2014 Second International Conference on* (pp. 247-252). IEEE.

Hatcher, W. G., & Yu, W. (2018). A Survey of Deep Learning: Platforms, Applications and Emerging Research Trends. *IEEE Access: Practical Innovations, Open Solutions, 6,* 24411–24432. doi:10.1109/ACCESS.2018.2830661

Hinton, G. E., & Salakhutdinov, R. R. (2006). Reducing the dimensionality of data with neural networks. *Science, 313*(5786), 504-507.

Hodo, E., Bellekens, X., Hamilton, A., Tachtatzis, C., & Atkinson, R. (2017). *Shallow and deep networks intrusion detection system: A taxonomy and survey.* arXiv preprint arXiv:1701.02145.

Imamverdiyev, Y., & Abdullayeva, F. (2018). Deep Learning Method for Denial of Service Attack Detection Based on Restricted Boltzmann Machine. *Big Data, 6*(2), 159–169. doi:10.1089/big.2018.0023 PMID:29924649

Kim, J., Kim, J., & Kim, H. (2015). An Approach to Build an Efficient Intrusion Detection Classifier. *Journal of Platform Technology, 3*(4), 43–52.

Kim, J., Kim, J., Thu, H. L. T., & Kim, H. (2016, February). Long short term memory recurrent neural network classifier for intrusion detection. In *Platform Technology and Service (PlatCon), 2016 International Conference on* (pp. 1-5). IEEE.

Marwan, M., Kartit, A., & Ouahmane, H. (2018). Security Enhancement in Healthcare Cloud using Machine Learning. *Procedia Computer Science, 127,* 388–397. doi:10.1016/j.procs.2018.01.136

Nguyen, K. K., Hoang, D. T., Niyato, D., Wang, P., Nguyen, D., & Dutkiewicz, E. (2018, April). Cyberattack detection in mobile cloud computing: A deep learning approach. In *Wireless Communications and Networking Conference (WCNC)* (pp. 1-6). IEEE. 10.1109/WCNC.2018.8376973

Palangi, H., Ward, R. K., & Deng, L. (2016). Distributed Compressive Sensing: A Deep Learning Approach. *IEEE Transactions on Signal Processing*, *64*(17), 4504–4518. doi:10.1109/TSP.2016.2557301

Said, H. M., Alyoubi, B. A., El Emary, I., & Alyoubi, A. A. (2016). Application of Intelligent Data Mining Approach in Securing the Cloud Computing. *International Journal of Advanced Computer Science and Applications*, *7*(9), 151–159.

Schmidhuber, J. (2015). Deep learning in neural networks: An overview. *Neural Networks*, *61*, 85–117. doi:10.1016/j.neunet.2014.09.003 PMID:25462637

Vincent, P., Larochelle, H., Lajoie, I., Bengio, Y., & Manzagol, P. A. (2010). Stacked denoising autoencoders: Learning useful representations in a deep network with a local denoising criterion. *Journal of Machine Learning Research*, *11*(Dec), 3371–3408.

Xu, C., Shen, J., Du, X., & Zhang, F. (2018). An Intrusion Detection System Using a Deep Neural Network with Gated Recurrent Units. *IEEE Access: Practical Innovations, Open Solutions*.

Xu, J., Li, H., & Zhou, S. (2015). An overview of deep generative models. *IETE Technical Review*, *32*(2), 131–139. doi:10.1080/02564602.2014.987328

Yin, C., Zhu, Y., Fei, J., & He, X. (2017). A deep learning approach for intrusion detection using recurrent neural networks. *IEEE Access: Practical Innovations, Open Solutions*, *5*, 21954–21961. doi:10.1109/ACCESS.2017.2762418

Yousefi-Azar, M., Varadharajan, V., Hamey, L., & Tupakula, U. (2017, May). Autoencoder-based feature learning for cyber security applications. In *Neural Networks (IJCNN), 2017 International Joint Conference on* (pp. 3854-3861). IEEE.

Zhang, B., Yu, Y., & Li, J. (2018, May). Network Intrusion Detection Based on Stacked Sparse Autoencoder and Binary Tree Ensemble Method. In *2018 IEEE International Conference on Communications Workshops (ICC Workshops)* (pp. 1-6). IEEE. 10.1109/ICCW.2018.8403759

Zhang, Q., Yang, L. T., Chen, Z., & Li, P. (2018). A survey on deep learning for big data. *Information Fusion*, *42*, 146–157. doi:10.1016/j.inffus.2017.10.006

ADDITIONAL READING

Hinton, G. E., Osindero, S., & Teh, Y. W. (2006). A fast learning algorithm for deep belief nets. *Neural Computation*, *18*(7), 1527–1554. doi:10.1162/neco.2006.18.7.1527 PMID:16764513

Kim, H., Kim, J., Kim, Y., Kim, I., & Kim, K. J. (2018). Design of network threat detection and classification based on machine learning on cloud computing. *Cluster Computing*, 1–10.

Kim, P. (2017). *MATLAB Deep Learning: With Machine Learning, Neural Networks and Artificial Intelligence*.

MartinL. (2010). *White Paper*. Retrieved from http://www.lockheedmartin.com/data/assets/isgs/documents/CloudComputingWhitePaper.pdf

Massachusetts Institute of Technology. (2018). More efficient security for cloud-based machine learning: Novel combination of two encryption techniques protects private data, while keeping neural networks running quickly. Retrieved from www.sciencedaily.com/releases/2018/08/180817125349.htm

KEY TERMS AND DEFINITIONS

Data Center: Large areas or buildings that accommodate computer systems, data warehouse, and servers of the enterprises.

Trust Level: Access degree of end users to the cloud or any other computer infrastructure.

Chapter 4
Network Manipulation Using Network Scanning in SDN

Thangavel M.
Thiagarajar College of Engineering, India

Pavithra V.
Thiagarajar College of Engineering, India

Guru Roja R.
Thiagarajar College of Engineering, India

ABSTRACT

Network scanning commonly implies the use of the computer network to collect information about the target systems. This type of scanning is performed by hackers for attacking the target and also by the system administrators for assessment of security and maintaining the system. Network scanning mainly analyzes the UDP and TCP network services that are running on the target, the operating system that is used by the target, and the security systems that are placed between the user and targeted hosts. Network scanning includes both the network port scanning and vulnerability scanning. Network manipulation is an effort that is made by the user to modify the network or structure of a network and thus using online network tools to achieve the target. Software-defined networking is a term that comprises several network technologies with the aim of making it adapt the features of flexibility. Key terms for SDN implementation include separation of functionality, virtualization in the network, and configuring programmatically. This chapter explores network manipulation using network scanning in SDN.

DOI: 10.4018/978-1-5225-7353-1.ch004

INTRODUCTION

Software-defined networking is a term which includes several network technologies which were aimed at making the network flexible as the server which is virtualized and the storage mechanism of the latest and modern data centres. Software-defined networks can also be defined as the separation of the control plane from the forwarding plane and that control plane consists of multiple devices. The aim of SDN is to allow the network administrators and the engineers to adapt to the changing business requirements. In case of Software-defined networks, the administrator can manage traffic from a central control eliminating the need to operate switches and is also capable of delivering services wherever required without considering to what the server or hardware components are connected to. The key technologies for implementing Software-defined networks are functional separation, network virtualization, and automation through programmability. The major advantages of SDN are that it is dynamic, manageable, cost-effective, adaptable, and ideal for high bandwidth and also it decouples the network control and forwarding functions.

A Software-defined application is a program that is designed to perform in a software-defined environment. SDN applications can replace and add functionalities to the hardware devices of a network implemented through the firmware. SDN architecture has several forms. Following is the SDN architecture which is based on SDN controllers. The first tier is the physical layer which consists of all the hardware devices and cables required. In case of an SDN controller, network control is separated from the hardware and given to the software application. Controllers which are used to start and terminate the traffic make up the second layer of the SDN architecture. The third layer consists of Software-defined applications which control the functions using the SDN controller. Some types of SDN applications consist of programs which can be used for network virtualization, network monitoring, intrusion detection, flow balancing and so on (Ali et al., 2015).

Software-defined network attacks have unfortunately become a reality today and an attacker uses several exploits to breach through the network. Since this technology is not familiar to most of the network engineers and the history of attacks in SDN remains unknown, thousands of vulnerabilities are out there. In traditional networking, the control and data plane tend to exist on each device whereas in SDN the two planes are separated. In order to enhance flexibility, the control plane is placed on an SDN controller and the data plane is located on the physical or virtual switch. Both planes communicate through a protocol named OpenFlow.

Possible vulnerabilities in software-defined networks include

- Connecting to the passive listening ports most software-defined networks switches include for debugging in order to retrieve the flow tables.
- Using information from the flow table such as round-trip time variation.
- Also, the traffic can be sniffed due to limited protection.
- Also, the vulnerabilities in switches and operating systems can be used to exploit those networks.
- Base control OpenFlow errors.
- Making use of malicious controllers to send malicious instructions to the devices in SDN.
- Perform man in the middle attack to modify the instruction sent by the trusted controller to the devices present.

Whenever an attack happens at the target an action is taken to counteract that threat or damage, this is called a Countermeasure. Possible countermeasures for the above-listed attacks are

- Placing the controllers at a secured location with strict access policies.
- A dedicated channel should be established between the controller and SDN devices.
- Have several duplicate entities for an SDN controller and also protect the channel through which the communication takes place using encryption.
- Network elements should also be provided high security with encryption since there are easier possibilities of compromising a network element.
- Update the patches in your servers periodically.
- Use and implement packet dropping techniques at the control plane. Packet drop occurs when a router receives it and specifically decides not to pass it on to the next hop
- Do not use default passwords instead make use of strong passwords and periodically update them in order to avoid brute force attacks.

The attacks possible in SDN include

- **Network Manipulation** which is a critical attack that occurs in the control plane which is performed by compromising the SDN controller and produces fake network data and compromises the entire network.
- **Traffic diversion** which occurs to the network elements in the data plane by compromising a network element which forwards the traffic in a different direction and also allows eavesdropping.

- **Side channel attack** which targets the network elements of the data plane and monitors the timing information and the time taken for the establishment of the network to make the attacker ensure whether a flow rule exists or not.
- **App manipulation** which takes place by means of flaws in the application plane and provides a path for exploit. An exploit of the vulnerability in the application can cause malfunction, disruption of service and eavesdropping of data.
- **Denial-of-Service** which can occur in all parts of SDN causing complete disruption of services.
- **ARP spoofing attack** which can cause man-in-the-middle attack and ARP cache poisoning. This can be used by the attacker to perform filtration of the network, sniff the traffic, modify the traffic and can even block the traffic. This can make changes to the topology of the network and poisoning can be performed using protocols such as LLDP (Link Layer Discovery Protocol) and IGMP (Internet Group Management Protocol).
- **API exploitation** which occurs through the vulnerabilities in the application programming interfaces of the software components and the attacker discloses unauthorized information.
- **Traffic sniffing** which is a popular attack that is used by an attacker to capture and analyze the traffic and also perform eavesdropping data using network elements to steal confidential information. Also, the attacker takes advantage of the unencrypted communications to gain information about network flows and traffic which is allowed in the network.
- **Password guessing or brute force** which happens on a non-SDN element. With this attack, an unauthorized user can gain access to the network easily (Young, 1964).

The most threatening attack is the one which takes place by means of the centralized controller which happens to be a high-value target. This is because emerging network technologies can provide chances for the occurrence of new vulnerabilities or make the previously existing vulnerabilities even worse. Besides the challenges in the traditional networks the controller and the control plane, connections can bring new security challenges that are possible only in SDN. A single vulnerability can cause a huge amount of damage to the network so security should be the basic component of Software-defined networks. The SDN controller is considered to be the most vulnerable one because by compromising the SDN controller the attacker could gain access and control the entire network. By providing centralized control the performance measures of SDN could be improved but the workload of the administrator is doubled and also the security needs to be monitored manually (Ali et al., 2015).

Another feature of SDN which happens to be more vulnerable is the programmability feature. To increase flexibility and to make SDN agile, network programmability has become a nature of Software-defined networks. In case of interconnected systems, where the fundamental operations are programmable the vulnerability factor has also invariably increased. Since programmatic access is provided to the user it is more prone to attacks. Thus if isolation is not properly implemented the control information and network elements have a risk of being exploited.

Network manipulation in SDN is the process of modifying the network and using network manipulating tool to compromise the network. Modification of SDN can be done in terms of changing the contents of the network or altering the infrastructure. The online network manipulating tools typically manage to compromise the search engines and the social media contents. In this case, the attacker compromises the SDN controller to create false network data and starts to perform attacks on the entire system. Network manipulation can be done through network scanning which is the process of identifying hosts, ports, and services in a network. This is a method of intelligence gathering that an attacker uses to gain information about the target network.

NETWORK SCANNING IN SDN

Network Scanning refers to a set of techniques and procedures for identifying hosts, ports, and services on a network. It is one of the mechanisms the attacker uses to gain knowledge and create a profile of the target organization or network. The major objectives of network scanning include the discovery of the live hosts, IP address and also the ports of the live hosts identified. It also provides information about the operating system and architecture, vulnerabilities and possibility of exploits in the live hosts identified.

Network scanning methodology includes the following steps:

- Check for Live Systems
- Check for Open Ports
- Scanning beyond IDS
- Banner Grabbing
- Scan for Vulnerability
- Draw network Diagrams
- Prepare Proxies

Check for Live Systems

Using Ping Scan

The live systems can be identified by ICMP (Internet Control Message Protocol) Scanning. ICMP scanning involves sending ICMP ECHO requests to a host in the target SDN. If the host is alive, it will respond with an ICMP ECHO reply. This type of ping scan is useful in determining active devices in the target network and also to determine the presence of a firewall by checking whether the ICMP passes through the firewall or not. This can be done using the Nmap tool.

Ping scan is performed by sending ICMP echo request from the source to the destination and receiving an echo reply.

The output displays whether the system is live or not after the echo reply is received. The MAC address of the live system is also displayed.

Figure 1. Ping scan

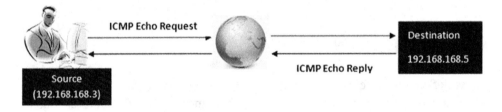

Figure 2. Ping scan using Nmap

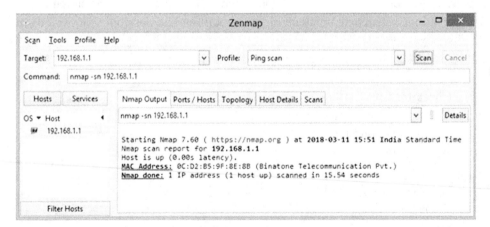

Using Ping Sweep

The method of ping sweep is useful in identifying the live host from a range of IP addresses. This is done by sending ICMP request to multiple hosts on SDN. If the host is alive, an ICMP ECHO reply is received.

Attackers make use of subnet mask calculators to identify the subnet mask and the number of hosts present in the subnet. Attackers make use of this ping sweep method to create an inventory of live systems in the targeted Software-defined network. Ping Sweep can also be performed using Nmap.

Ping sweep sends an ICMP echo request to all the nodes in the network. The system which makes an echo reply is said to be in live mode.

Figure 3. Ping sweep

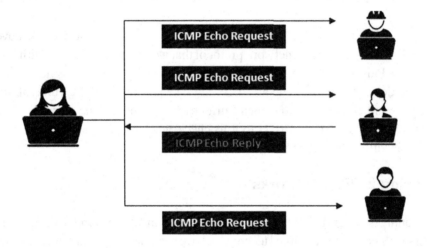

Figure 4. Ping sweep using Nmap

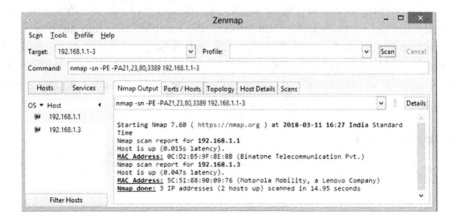

The results display the nodes/systems that are live in the network.

Ping Sweep Tools

- Angry IP Scanner is capable of pinging each IP address in SDN to check whether the host is alive or not and then also displays its hostname, MAC address and scans ports.
- SolarWinds Engineer Toolset's Ping Sweep scans a range of IP addresses to identify which hosts are alive and idle. It is also capable of performing reverse DNS lookup.
- Other tools include Colasoft Ping Tool, Advanced IP Scanner, Ping Sweep, OpUtils, and PingInfoView.

Check for Open Ports

The open ports are identified using SSDP Scanning. The Simple Service Discovery Protocol (SSDP) is a type of network protocol that works in combination with UPnP (Universal Plug and Play) in order to the plug and play devices available in the Software-defined network. The attackers can take advantage of the vulnerabilities in the plug and play devices to launch Buffer overflow and DoS attacks. They make use of UPnP SSDP M-SEARCH tool to check whether the host machine in the network is vulnerable to exploits or not.

Scanning in IPv6 Networks

The IP address size if IPv6 is from 32 bits to 128 bits and thus it supports a number of addressing hierarchy. Traditional techniques have become computationally infeasible due to the size of the search space in a subnet of IPv6. Scanning methodologies in IPv6 networks are more complex when compared to IPv4 and some scanning tools do not support ping sweep in IPv6 networks. Attackers can obtain the IPv6 addresses by analyzing the network traffic, monitoring the recorded logs and analyzing the information in the header lines of unsent mail and messages. Thus scanning an IPv6 networks needs a large number of times since the number of hosts is higher when compared to IPv4 addresses and compromising one host can allow the attacker to probe all the host's link-local multicast address.

Scanning Tools

Some of the scanning tools include

- **Nmap** which can be used for network inventory, managing services and schedules and monitoring host or service options. The attacker can obtain information such as live hosts on SDN, services, and type of packet filters or firewall and type of OS and version of OS used.
- **Hping2 / Hping3** is a command line tool for network scanning and packet crafting tool for TCP/IP protocol. Example: To perform ICMP Ping the command used is **hping3 -1 -10.0.0.25.**

Scanning Techniques

Scanning TCP Network Services include

- Open TCP Scanning Methods
  - TCP Connect or Full Open Scan
- Stealth TCP Scanning Methods
  - Half-open Scan
  - Inverse TCP flag Scanning
  - ACK flag probe Scanning
- Third Party and Spoofed TCP Scanning Methods
  - IDLE/IPID Header Scanning

Scanning UDP Network Services include

- UDP Scanning

TCP Connect / Full Open Scan

TCP Connect scan detects whether a port is open or not by means of the three-way handshake protocol. This scan is capable of establishing a full connection and tears it down by sending RST (reset) packet. This does not require superuser privileges.

Scan Result if the Port is Open and Closed

The scan results from Figure 5 are used to find whether the system is live or not by performing three-way handshake.

Stealth Scan (Half-Open Scan)

Half-open scan resets the TCP connection between the client and the server before the three-way handshake protocol gets completed thus making a half-open connection.

Figure 5. Full open Scan - results

Scan result if the port is open:

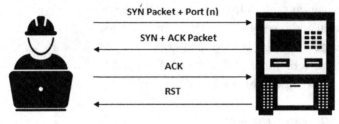

Scan result if the port is closed

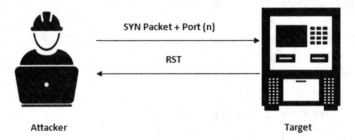

Figure 6. Half scan results

Port is open:

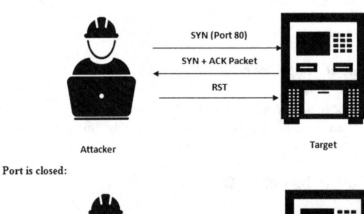

Port is closed:

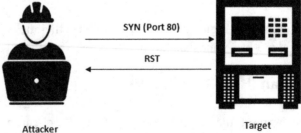

Attackers make use of this type of scanning techniques to bypass firewalls, logging methods and portrait themselves as normal traffic in the SDN.

The client sends an SYN packet to the server in the appropriate port. If the port is open an SYN/ACK packet is received as response. If the server sends an RST packet as a response then the particular port is meant to be closed. The RST packet is sent to close the initiation before a connection is established (Ali et al., 2015).

Port is Open and Closed

The results from Figure 6 show that the system is live if reset packet is not received immediately after a syn packet is sent.

Inverse TCP Flag Scanning

In this type of scanning the attacker sends a TCP probe packet to the target host in SDN. If the port is open, no response is received else the host responds with an RST/ACK packet.

Port is Open and Closed

The scan results from Figure 7 show that the port is closed if reset packet is received in return and port is open if no response is received.

Figure 7. Inverse TCP Scan results

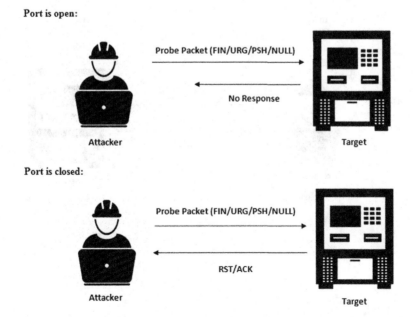

Xmas Scan

In Xmas scan the attacker sends a TCP frame with FIN, URG and PUSH flags set. This will not work any windows operating system. FIN scan works only with Operating systems having RFC-793 based implementation of TCP/IP.

Port Is Open and Closed

The scan results from Figure 8 depict that the port is closed if reset packet is received and port is open if no response is received.

This can also be performed using Nmap tool. The results are as follows (see Figure 9).

The results displays details such as port and protocols used, the state of the system whether it is open or closed, and the service running in the system.

Figure 8. Xmas scan results

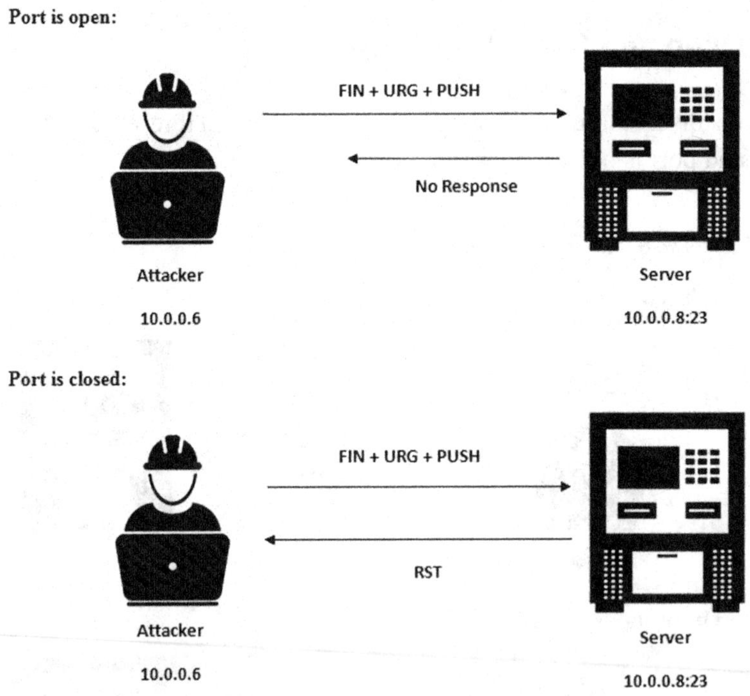

Figure 9. Xmas scan using Nmap

ACK Flag Probe Scanning

The attacker sends TCP probe packets with ACK flag set to a target host in SDN in order to obtain information whether the port is open or not by analyzing the header of the RST packets received.

TTL Based ACK Flag and Windows-Based ACK Flag Probe Scanning

The results from Figure 10 display TTL based ACK flag probe scanning and Windows based ACK flag probe scanning.

- If the Time-to-Live value of RST packet on a port is less than the boundary value 64 then it is known that the port is open.
- If the Windows value of RST packet on a port has a non-zero value then the port is said to be open.

ACK flag probe scanning is also used to gather information about the filtering system present in the target SDN. Attacker sends an ACK probe packet to the target host in SDN. If no response is received then it means that the stateful firewall is

Figure 10. Windows-based ACK flag probe scan results

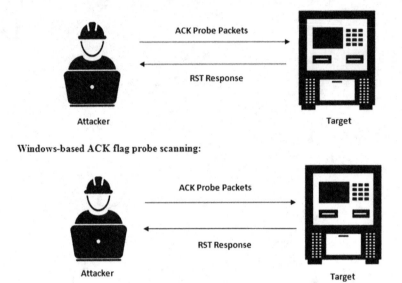

present else if RST response is received then A stateful firewall is not present (Ali et al., 2015).

A Stateful Firewall Is Present

The results from Figure 11 show that the if no response is received then a stateful firewall is present.

Figure 11. Presence of stateful firewall

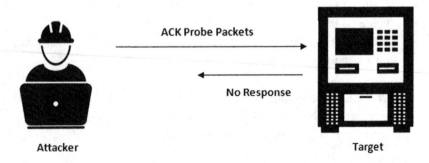

No Firewall

The results from Figure 12 depict that if reset packet is received as response then no firewall is present.

This can also be done using Nmap. The results obtained are shown in Figure 13.

The results from Figure 13 show that all the 1000 nodes are scanned by Nmap and the unfiltered node is displayed.

Figure 12. Absence of firewall

No firewall:

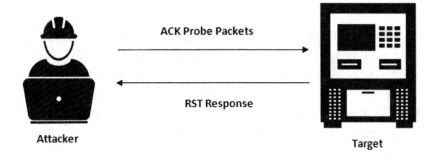

Figure 13. Nmap filtering results

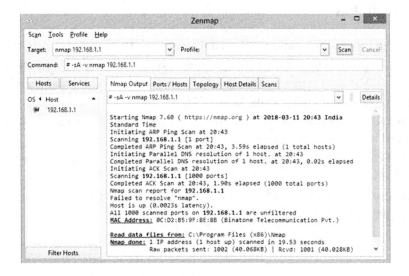

IDLE/IPID Header Scan

Step 1

- The attacker sends SYN + ACK packet to the zombie machine which it has already compromised to probe its fragment identification number (IPID).
- IPID number increases every time an IP packet is sent by the host.
- A Zombie which does not expect an SYN + ACK packet sends an RST packet disclosing the IPID number.
- The attacker analyses the RST packet from zombie to extract the IPID number.

Step 2

- The attacker then sends an SYN packet to the target machine by means of spoofing the IP address of the zombie machine.
- If the port is open, the target host in SDN will send SYN + ACK packet to the zombie and then the zombie responds with an RST packet.
- If the port is closed, the target host will send RST packet to the zombie but the zombie would not respond anything.

Step 3

- The zombie's IPID is probed again by the attacker.

UDP Scanning

There is no three-way handshake for UDP scanning. If the port is open, the host system does not respond with a message. If the port is closed, the system responds with an "ICMP port unreachable message". Spyware, Trojan horses, and other malware make use of UDP to attack an SDN.

Figure 14 shows that the ICMP unreachable message is received if the port is closed and no response is received if the port is open.

UDP Scanning can also be performed using Nmap tool. The results are shown in Figure 15.

The results from Figure 15 display the port, state and service running in the nodes of the network.

Figure 14. UDP scanning

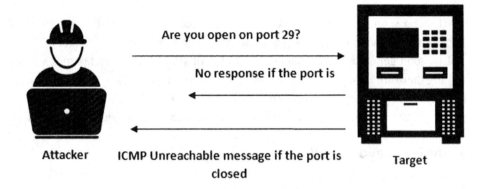

Figure 15. UDP scan Nmap results

ICMP Echo Scanning/List Scan

ICMP echo scanning is used to know whether the ports are up by pinging all of them. The command used in Nmap is **nmap –P <u>cert.org/24</u> 192.168.1.1**

List scan generates and displays all the list of IP addressed and names without pinging them all. Reverse DNS resolution is used for the identification of hostnames. The command used in Nmap is **nmap –sL –v 192.168.1.1**

Scanning tools include NetScan Tools Pro, SuperScan, and MegaPing and so on.

Scanning Beyond IDS

IDS Evasion techniques include

- Using Fragmented IP packets.
- Spoofing IP addresses and Sniff responses from the server.
- Using source routing.
- Using proxy servers or compromised machines to launch attacks in order to remain unidentified.

Banner Grabbing

Banner grabbing also known as OS Footprinting is the process of determining the operating system used by the target system in SDN. They are of two types namely:

- Active Banner Grabbing
- Passive Banner Grabbing

Active Banner Grabbing is that in which specially crafted packets are sent to the system OS and the responses are analyzed. The responses are then compared with the database and the operating system is determined. Changes in response are due to the differences in TCP/IP stack implementation.

Passive Banner Grabbing can be performed using information obtained from error messages, by sniffing network traffic and using page extensions. Example: .aspx which represents the IIS server and Windows platform.

Banner Grabbing Tools include ID Serve, Netcraft, Netcat, and Telnet.

Vulnerability Scanning

Vulnerability Scanning is used to identify vulnerabilities and weaknesses of a system and network in order to find out the ways to exploit SDN. It includes scanning of

- Network vulnerabilities
- Open ports and running services
- Application and services vulnerabilities
- Application and services configuration errors.

Vulnerability Scanning tools include Nessus, GFI LanGuard, and Qualys FreeScan.

Drawing Network Diagrams

Drawing network diagrams would give confidential information to an attacker about the SDN architecture. It also displays the physical or logical path to reach the target (McKeown et al., 2008).

Network Discovery tools include Network topology mapper, OpManager, and NetworkView. The features of these tools include

- Network topology discovery and mapping
- Network mapping for regulatory compliance
- Auto-detect changes to network topology
- Multi-level network discovery

Proxy Servers

Proxy servers serve as an intermediate host for connecting with other computers. Attackers make use of proxy servers for the following reasons:

- To hide the source address so that identification of the attacker remains unknown.
- To mask the original source address by the proxy address so that only the proxy address gets caught.
- For remote access to intranets and websites that have limited access.
- To interrupt the entire request and send it to an attacker through the proxy so that the victim can identify only the proxy address.
- Attackers also make use of **Proxy Chaining** method to avoid their detection.

Proxy Chaining

The steps in proxy chaining include

- A user requests a resource from the target or destination.

Figure 16. Proxy chaining

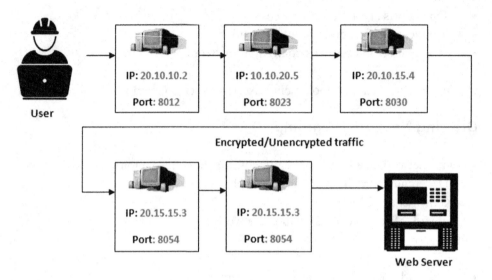

- A proxy client who is present in the user's system redirects the request using the proxy server.
- The proxy server collects the identification number of the user and redirects it to the next proxy server connected to the chain.
- The process is done by all the proxy servers in the chain.
- The proxy server present at the end passes the request to the web server.

Proxy Tools

Some of the proxy tools include

- Proxy Switcher
- Proxy workbench
- TOR and CyberGhost
- SocksChain
- Burp Suite

Anonymizers

An anonymizer is used to remove all the information that is identifiable from the user's computer while surfing. They can be used by the attackers to make their activities untraceable. They also allow us to bypass Internet censors.

Anonymizers are mostly used for

- Privacy and anonymity
- Protection from online attacks
- To access restricted content
- Bypassing IDS and firewall.

Some of the anonymizers include Tails, G-Zapper, Proxify and so on.

Spoofing IP Address

IP Spoofing refers to the process of changing the source IP address so that the attacker becomes untraceable and the attack appears to come from someone else. When a response is received it is received by the spoofed address and not by the attacker original address.

IP Spoofing can be detected using these techniques

- **Using Direct TTL Probes** where the host sends a packet to the suspect that triggers a reply and then the TTL is compared with the packet received from the suspect. If the TTL does not match then the packet is spoofed.
- **Using IP Identification number** where the host sends a probe to the suspect's spoofed traffic that triggers a reply and then the IPID is compared with the suspect traffic. If the IPID's are not in the near value then the suspect traffic is spoofed. This technique is successful even if the suspect is on the same subnet.
- **Using TCP Flow control method** where attacker sending spoofed TCP packets will not receive any response and would not respond to any changes in the congestion window size. Thus if the traffic continues even after the window size is exhausted then the packets are spoofed (Ali et al., 2015).

Countermeasures

Port Scanning

- Configure Firewall and IDS for detecting and blocking probes/probe packets.
- Run Port Scanning tools to ensure whether the firewall properly monitors the port scanning activity.
- Ensure that the firewall could not be bypassed and filtering techniques are implemented.
- Ensure that all the security mechanisms such as IDS, firewall and routers are updated to their latest versions.
- Filter all the incoming ICMP packets and request/response.

- Perform TCP and UDP Scanning to check network configuration.
- Ensure the configuration of anti-scanning and anti-spoofing rules.

Banner Grabbing

- Hiding files extensions from WebPages.
- Use false banners to redirect the attacker and use server mask to change banner information.
- Turn off unnecessary services to avoid unauthorized access to information.

IP Spoofing

- Encrypt the network traffic so that no information can be gained by probing the traffic.
- Using multiple firewalls to provide high-end security.
- Do not rely on single-factor authentication instead use multi-factor authentication.
- Ensure that the firewall does Ingress (incoming packets) and Egress (outgoing packets) filtering.
- Use random sequence number initially to avoid IP spoofing.

Scanning Pen Testing

Pen testing a network for scanning vulnerabilities helps us to determine the live systems, discover open ports and services and grab system banners to launch network manipulation (network hacking) attack.

The Penetration testing attack would provide the following information that helps the network administrators to:

- Close unused ports
- Disable unnecessary services
- Hide or Customize banners
- Calibrate firewall rules
  The steps in Scanning Pen Testing are:
- Start
- Perform host discovery
- Perform port scanning
- Perform Banner grabbing or OS Footprinting
- Scan for vulnerability
- Draw network diagrams

- Prepare proxies
- Document all the findings.

NETWORK MANIPULATION

Network Manipulation is an attempt that is made to change a network and thus attackers make use of tools to influence the network. Each of the technique in network manipulation is implemented by altering the structure or information available in the network.

Software defined networks provide flexibility by separating the control plane and the data plane. In spite of the benefits, this also creates an attack surface for the attacker to gain information about the network. The attacker makes use of the protocols and the devices to attack the target and in case of SDN OpenFlow is one such protocol which can serve as an attack surface. OpenFlow is prone to attacks since it enables communication between the controller and switch. An attacker can eavesdrop and make alterations to the communication thus compromising the network (Ingram Micro Advisor, 2008).

Software defined networks is an emerging architecture that provides more flexibility in managing and programming of networks. The centralized SDN controller is meant to provide deployment and hardening of the network security. However, those SDN controllers are prone to attacks when compared to other conventional networks. For example, an attacker can attempt changing the behavior of the network traffic by compromising the centralized controller. The major issues with the SDN controller are as follows:

- The centralized controller appears to be the central point of attack for the attackers and the primary goal is to provide security to those controllers.
- The OpenFlow protocol is vulnerable to a number of attacks that degrades the performance, availability, and integrity of the network.

In case of attacking a remote system, the first major step is to identify the possible set of attacks that can be made on the network by doing the Footprinting process on the target network.

Footprinting and Reconnaissance

Footprinting is defined as the process of collecting as much as possible information about the target network thus the possible ways of attacking a network could be identified. This is the first foremost step that an attacker does by means of which the attacker could perform social engineering or network attacks that would cause huge damage to economic assets.

The four main steps in Footprinting include

- Know Security Posture
- Reduce Focus Area
- Identify Vulnerabilities
- Draw Network Map

The objectives of Footprinting are

- For collecting network information the following need to be examined
  - Domain area
  - Internal domain names
  - Network blocks
  - IP address of the reachable systems
  - Rogue websites or private websites
  - TCP and UDP services running
  - Access control mechanisms and Access control lists
  - Networking protocols
  - VPN points
  - IDSes running
  - Analog or Digital telephone numbers
  - Authentication mechanisms
  - System Enumeration
- For collecting System information the following need to be examined
  - User and group names
  - System banners
  - Routing tables
  - SNMP information
  - System architecture
  - Remote system type
  - System names
  - Passwords
- For collecting organization's information the following need to be examined
  - Employee details
  - Organization's website
  - Company directory
  - Location details
  - Address and phone numbers

     ◦   Comments in HTML source code
     ◦   Security policies implemented
     ◦   Web server links relevant to the organization
     ◦   News articles
     ◦   Press releases

Footprinting Methodology

The most common Footprinting techniques include

- Footprinting through Search Engines
- Footprinting using advanced Google hacking techniques
- Footprinting through Social Networking Sites
- Website Footprinting
- Email Footprinting
- Competitive Intelligence
- WHOIS Footprinting
- DNS Footprinting
- Network Footprinting
- Footprinting through Social Engineering

Attackers make use of search engines to gather information about a target network. Some of the search engines used for Footprinting include Google, Wikipedia, World Wide Web and so on. This also includes

- Finding company's Public and Restricted Websites
- Determining the Operating System
- Collecting location information
- Collect employee details using Social networking sites
- Gather information from financial services
- Footprinting through job sites
- Monitoring target using alerts
- Information gathering using Groups, Forums, and blogs

Footprinting through advanced Google hacking techniques include

- Analysing the query string
- Identifying vulnerable targets and Google operators

Footprinting Social Networking sites include

- Gathering sensitive information from Facebook, MySpace, LinkedIn, Twitter, Pinterest, and Google+ and so on.
- Through this, the attacker gains information such as
  - Contact Info, location etc
  - Friends list, Friends info
  - The Identity of a family member
  - Interests
  - Activities

Website Footprinting refers to the process of monitoring and analyzing a target organization's to obtain valuable information. This would provide valuable information such as

- Softwares used and its version
- Operating system used
- Sub-directories and parameters
- Filename, path, database field name, or query
- Scripting platform
- Contact details and CMS(Content Management System) details

Email Footprinting is the process of collecting information from the Email header. Some of the E-mail tracking tools include emailTrackPro, PoliteMail, and Email Lookup.

Competitive Intelligence is the process of identifying, gathering, analyzing, verifying and making use of that information to gather information about competitors. The sources of Competitive Intelligence include:

- Websites of Company and Advertisements
- Search engines, Internet, and online database
- Press releases and annual reports
- Social Engineering employees
- Customer and Vendor interviews

WHOIS Footprinting is done by collecting information from WHOIS databases. They contain personal information about domain owners and are maintained by Regional Internet Registries. WHOIS Footprinting can also be done by using tools such as LanWhois, CallerIP, and HotWhois and so on. Information is collected by passing queries into the database and those queries would return information such as

- Domain name details

- Contact details of the domain owner
- Domain name servers
- NetRange
- When a domain has been created
- Expiry records
- Records last updated

DNS Footprinting process includes the process of collecting information about the domain name server. An attacker gathers DNS information to determine the most important hosts in the network and performs Social Engineering attacks on those hosts. Some of the DNS Footprinting tools include DIG, myDNSTools, Professional Toolset and so on.

In order to perform Network Footprinting the following activities need to be performed:

- Locate the network ranges where the attacker needs to create a map of the target network and find out the range of IP addresses and subnet mask used by the target network.
- Traceroute the network which uses the concept of ICMP protocol and makes use of TTL header in the ICMP packets to find the routers present on the way to the target network.
- Traceroute analysis where the Traceroute identified is thoroughly analyzed. The attackers gain information about network topology, trusted routers and firewall locations (McKeown et al., 2008).

Footprinting can also be performed using Social Engineering where human behavior is exploited to extract confidential information. The main aim of Social Engineers would include the following:

- Credit card details and Social security number
- Usernames and passwords
- Security products in use
- Operating system and software versions
- Network input information
- IP address and names of servers

Social Engineering techniques include:

- Eavesdropping
- Shoulder surfing

- Dumpster diving
- Impersonation on social networking sites

Tools for Footprinting

Some of the Footprinting tools include

- Maltego
- Recon-ng
- FOCA
- Prefix Whois
- Tctrace

Countermeasures Against Footprinting

- Restrict the employees from using social networking sites from organization's network.
- Educate and create awareness among employees about Social engineering attacks.
- Web servers need to be configured in order to avoid valuable information being transferred from those servers.
- Use anonymous registration services.
- Avoid sharing valuable information in press releases and financial reports.

Network Manipulation Using Various Attacks

After Footprinting is done and the complete details of the target organization and the network are found, network manipulation attacks can be imposed after the network is completely scanned using scanning techniques which are discussed above.

Attacks on Data Plane

Software defined networks application programming interfaces and various protocols make use of OpenFlow, Open vSwitch, and Simple Network Management protocol. These protocols make use of their own algorithms to provide higher-end security. The communication between the controller and networking devices is vulnerable and attackers could make use of this exploit to make modifications to the flow table.

The flow table can also be spoofed to allow unauthorized traffic along the network. A Man-in-the-middle attack is possible in these cases. The attacker is capable of creating a connection that is independent with the victim's device and exchanges messages between them to make them believe that they are conversing through a private connection even when the whole conversation is controlled by the attacker.

The attacker can also make changes to the messages transferred between the victim's device and his/her friend and also injects new messages. Since the Internet is susceptible to a number of attacks the attacker takes advantage of the vulnerabilities in the open network and tries to steal all the valuable information in the network.

Attacks at Control Plane

The Centralized SDN controller appears to be the main point of attack in case of Software defined networks. SDN controller usually works on a Linux operating system and the attacker takes advantage of the vulnerabilities in the Operating system.

The Attacker can also make an effort to execute DoS attacks to make the controller flooded and to make it idle. In case of network manipulation, the attacker takes control of the centralized controller and sends fake messages to initiate other types of attacks.

Also "Rogue Controller" attack can take place in the Control plane where the attacker can create a rogue controller and can compromise the original controller to forward all the data and requests to the rogue controller. The attacker also makes the victim believe that the responses are from the appropriate controllers and gains all the valuable information about the user.

The attacker can also make use of LLDP (Link Layer Discovery Protocol) and IGMP (Internet Group Management Protocol) which can perform ARP spoofing where the traffic can be sniffed, modified and even stopped from reaching the network (Young, 1964).

Attacks at Application Plane

In software defined networks most of the application running is from other vendors and are not mostly customized. The applications are capable of taking advantage of accessing all the resources since customization is absent.

The main drawback is that there exists no trust relationship between the SDN controller and the application and hence the attacker can make use of the authorized user's information to gain illegal access, inject authorized but illegal entries into the network.

There exist mechanisms where the network is authenticated but the application has no authentication mechanism. There exists absence of two-way authentication. The network-sensitive applications need the cost of traffic characteristic of network specific application. In case of network-specific applications, they provide services like inspection of traffic, access control mechanism and identification of firewalls.

Also there are applications which combine the characteristics of network sensitive, network specific and other application that are capable of recreating an application as a simple virtual element. Hence infected application can bypass the security by using service-specific network applications (Young, 1964).

Solutions for Implementing Security in Data Plane

- An Organization should make use of Transport layer security for authentication and encryption mechanisms.
- Protocols like Simple Network Management Protocol version 3 should be used which is much more secure than SNMP v2 and Secure Shell is much better than Telnet.
- Use OpenFlow protocol which supports encapsulation and encryption.
- Use Flowchecker to verify the consistency of switches and also to provide security to the flow tables.
- The path length between the controller and the switch should be made short to improve the availability of content to applications that provide security and also to enable fast recovery and security analysis.

Solutions for Implementing Security in Control Plane

- Role-based access controls need to be implemented to control unauthorized activity.
- Reduce the response time and error controlling mechanism.
- Adapt to the heterogeneous network to survive against attacks.
- Provide security mechanisms that would improve the integrity of the applications.
- Make use of unsupervised neural networks to extract features.

Solutions for Implementing Security in Application Plane

- Fine-grained access control mechanism needs to be implemented.
- Enable security framework that would provide continuous monitoring and detect threats.
- Dynamically analyze controller program.
- Translate the flow table in such a way that it can detect inconsistency in the application.

FEASIBILITY STUDY ON ATTACKING SOFTWARE-DEFINED NETWORKS

Motivation

In an SDN environment, the control plane can enforce some rules that the data plane requires and thus the network can be controlled efficiently. However, this kind of models can cause problems when the number of requests from the data plane to the control plane is high. When a number of requests to the data planes are high within a short period of time, it can flood the messages to the control plane. Also, the flow table that is present in the data plane can be flooded with rules for handling the requests.

Fingerprinting an SDN Network

If a client sends a packet to an SDN network, the client will continuously monitor the response times because the flow setup time can be added in case of a new flow in comparison with the existing flow (Ingram Micro Advisor, 2008).

Just for better understanding the author would now consider and formalize the response time on the client side. Let us consider the response time for the existing flow as α and the additional flow setup time as β. Also, the author names the response time for the new flow and existing flow as T1 and T2. They can be represented as

$$T1 = \alpha + \beta$$
$$T2 = \alpha$$

Thus an attacker is capable of easily determining the values of T1 and T2 and also can launch fingerprinting attacks on SDN. The attacker may face some problems in this case and they include

- The method by which the values T1 and T2 can be determined.
- How to ensure that the values of T1 and T2 are different in considering the random noises additionally.

The attacker can address the first problem by the common network scanning method which is capable of scanning the changes in the header field. When the SDN scanner acquires the values of T1 and T2 it performs the following steps:

Figure 17. SDN scanner

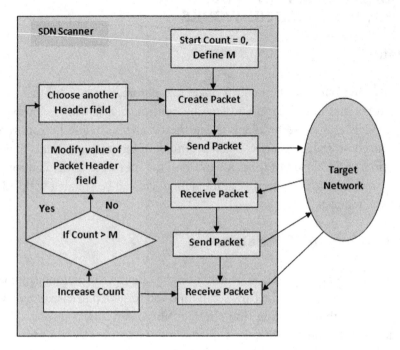

- First, two specially crafted packets are sent to the target network and the response time for each of the packet is noted.
- The SDN scanner that the attacker use assumes that the response time for the first packet as T1 and the response time for the second packet as T2.
- The scanner repeats this process by changing a field in the packet header.
- Then finally SDN scanner collects T1 and T2 for each different header field

The attacker can address the second problem by performing a statistical t-test method. This method is simply used to test whether the two sample T1 and T2 are different from each other. The mean and standard deviation of each sample is obtained easily through this method and the testing methodology is also quite simple. The attacker can also make use of some advanced statistics or machine learning technologies to improve accuracy.

Launching a DoS Attack on SDN

If an attacker makes use of an SDN scanner then he/she could easily identify whether the target network used SDN or not. If the test results confirm that the target network uses SDN then the attacker moves on to conduct the resource consumption attack.

Since the attacker would be aware of the network flow rules used by the target network, he/she would send a network packet to the target network using SDN to consume SDN resources.

Evaluation

In case of a target network using SDN, a major problem exists since the attacker could not gain information from the Internet since SDN is not deployed to many networks. Thus another methodology can be used to estimate T1 and T2 values (Young, 1964).

Estimating T2

The steps include

- 20 ping packets are sent to 28 different networks in order to collect T2 values.
- The response time of the second packets is also collected in order to avoid the addition of flow setup time in an SDN network.
- The ping packet should be sent from the location where the target network is present.

Estimating T1

The steps include

- Estimating the value of T1 is very difficult and thus it is estimated by adding flow setup time with T2 values.
- Using different cases the author can find out the flow setup time for different control planes.

Result

A t-test is applied to the collected values T2 and T1 values that are estimated from samples in order to find out whether T1 and T2 are different. An SDN scanner is capable of fingerprinting 24 networks out of 28 cases which is approximately 85.7%.

Timing SDN Network

A new scanning method is used here which gather much more information about the SDN networks in comparison with the other scanning techniques. This technique can be used by the control plane when the hosts do not evoke a reply even after the packets are injected into the SDN. This measures the control plane's response time with the timing probes. Round trip time depends on the load in the control plane and sending a test packet stream into the target network would increase the round trip time.

By sending different packet streams one could infer whether the control plane process packets with unknown source or destination address also gains information about the rules installed in the forwarding tables of switches. The timing probes may be spoofed ARP requests, OpenFlow Echo message requests and other RTT's that could be used to take charge of the control plane. With the knowledge of the above interface, it is possible to build a communication graph for the hosts in the network and in addition, it is also possible to learn which hosts may be critical in the network and which host is less frequently used.

State Manipulation Attacks in SDN

Manipulation attacks can be done in SDN by exploiting the race conditions that are harmful. A threat model is constructed and the generation of various network events are explained. Vulnerabilities in harmful race conditions can lead to multiple exploits and this can cause disruption and leakage of private information (Ingram Micro Advisor, 2008).

Threat Model

Here the author considers two events - non-adversarial and adversarial. In a non-adversarial case, harmful race conditions rarely occur in the SDN control plane under normal network operation by asynchronous events such as join, leave, up, down and host_config (Young, 1964).

In an adversarial case, the adversary is capable of identifying the harmful race conditions in the source code of the centralized SDN controller and they could trigger them with the help of compromised virtual machines or hosts.

Some of the attacks are mostly possible when the network is configured to use out-of-band control messages. So, it is most probably important to implement SSL or TLS to avoid those attacks.

Pinpointing Harmful Race Conditions

In order to locate dynamic race condition, the first step is to perform dynamic analysis to detect super effective race conditions and then make use of adversarial methods to manifest those race conditions. For example, given an SDN controller, the author first performs dynamic analysis to detect race conditions that perform two or more operations on the shared network state. There are chances of the two operations not having the same locks protecting them but there could be the existence of some similarity between them. Thus it is necessary to re-run the SDN controller to check whether a race condition is harmful or not.

There exist two main challenges in this process:

- How to avoid a race condition that already exists in the false alarms?
- How to investigate and identify harmful race conditions?

To address the first challenge the author needs to model an SDN control plane and for the second challenge to be addressed the author can develop an adversarial testing methodology with a scheduling technique which is called active scheduling to identify harmful race conditions.

Modeling the Control Plane in SDN

For detecting harmful race conditions, a model needs to be developed such that it should be capable of capturing all the critical conditions that take place in the SDN controller. The following need to be monitored to detect race conditions that are harmful:

- Execution Trace
- Application Lifecycle
- Event dispatching
- Sequential event handling
- Port event dispatching

Active Scheduling

Input: A Potentially Harmful Race Condition

The active scheduling technique executes the program that forces two operations to follow a particular order as shown in figure 25. To force the schedule in a control branch, a waypoint is designed to differentiate with other branches. The author makes use of 4 atomic control points(P1, P2, P3 and P4) and one flag(F1) in order to enforce deterministic scheduling between the state reference operation and state update operation with consistent runtime information.

In this algorithm, the author places P1 before operation 1 and P2 before operation 2, P3 after operation 3 and P4 after operation 2. The active Scheduling process is as follows:

- In P1, the waypoint of that control point is marked which indicates that the branch under test is covered and a thread "a" is paused by using a blocking methodology and save the value of runtime parameter if needed.
- Then thread "b" enter control point P2 the author sets flag F1 if the following conditions are satisfied:
  ○ Thread "a" is blocked
  ○ The runtime value of operation 1 is equal to the runtime value of operation 2.
- In P4, the author blocks thread a if the flag F1 is set.

The author implements active scheduling in SDN controller that provide functionalities such as atomic control points and waypoints. For every race operation, all the paths are backtracked to reach the state reference operation. Taking values of the race state operation and its waypoints as an input parameter, the SDN controller is invoked to methods of active scheduling.

DoS Attack Result

The author has to set up a different environment to understand whether the DoS attack that was imposed network was successful or not. The environment would consist of an OpenFlow switch, a controller and two different hosts in which the network communication takes place. The author makes use of a Software-based OpenFlow switch and it is installed on a Linux system. The author sets the maximum flow rule for this switch to 1500 and the values are plotted with time along the Y-axis and bandwidth along the X-axis. The graph would clearly depict the bandwidth and time that is required for launching a Dos attack that would consume resources from the control plane and the data plane (Router Freak, 2017).

Advantages of SDN

Besides multiple attacks such as network manipulation that is possible in SDN, it also has some advantages:

- The major advantage of SDN is that it creates a platform to support data-intensive applications such as Bigdata, Cloud, and Virtualization.

Figure 18. Bandwidth vs time graph

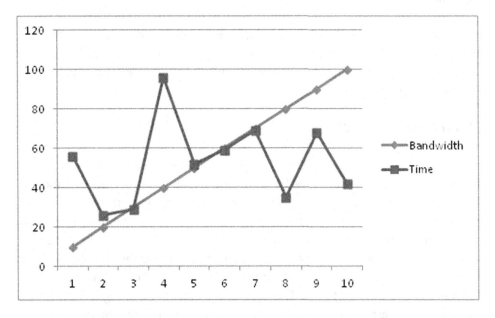

- **Provision for Centralized Network:** Software defined networks are capable of representing the entire network as a centralized view. By means of abstracting the data plane and the control plane, SDN is capable of providing more flexibility in both virtual and physical devices in a centralized location.
- **Managing Enterprise:** Enterprise networks need to set up some more applications and virtual machines to accommodate new requests. SDN allows management of both network switches and devices from a central location. It also allows the network manager to deal efficiently with network configuration.
- **Higher Granular Security:** Virtualization in SDN has made it more challenging. With new firewall going in and out, it is completely difficult to implement firewall policies and filtering policies. Since the SDN controller is centralized, the security policies and information are also centralized. In spite of the disadvantage of the central point of attack, one advantage is that it can effectively be used to security throughout out the entire process.
- **Lower Operating Costs:** SDN is capable of lowering operating system costs and also results in administrative savings since many of the flaws get reduced when the system becomes centralized and automated. In spite of its low costs, it provides administrative efficiency, server utilization improvement, and better virtualization control.

Example of the Attack

It is always better to understand the use cases behind a methodology and the potential of a man-in-the-middle attack to launch network manipulation attacks inside a Software defined network. This case study explains the wide-scale network traffic control (Router Freak, 2017).

China's Great Canon

After the continuous attacks to Github, a git repository which was web-based was designed and a huge amount of traffic was directed towards the servers with most of the initial traffic directed towards the Great Wall of China. Also, the government of China was able to target the exploitation of most of its victims who were innocent by injecting an iframe like JavaScript that would send continuous analytic requests to Baidu in China which is a popular search engine like Google. This has been dubbed as The Great Cannon. The operators made samples of the high volume traffic that was directed towards Baidu. The injected responses containing JavaScript has continuously made requests to the Github thus causing complete Denial-of-Service.

Similar to an SDN environment, the clients within the network need to communicate with an internal component that is also present within the network. Usually, in SDN, a client must pass through a switch that reports to the controller and has the capability of affecting the traffic stream which is much like the operators in Great Cannon. The GC operator has the capability of modifying the HTTP traffic and also injects malicious content into the response. Then the target by making repeated requests to the server a man-in-the-middle attack is launched. The most important thing, in this case, is that the victims were not aware of the fact that their analytic request was not passed to the original server but to the Baidu server in China.

The components of the attack were made into a single man-in-the-middle SDN taxonomy that could efficiently use on a larger scale (Router Freak, 2017).

CONCLUSION

Thus in this book chapter, the author has discussed the scanning and manipulation techniques that are available for posing attacks on a Software defined network. These techniques are not only used by attackers to hack or gain access to a target SDN but could also be used by penetration testing experts to thoroughly check a network to identify the vulnerabilities and make changes so that the network features could not be identified by anyone. Also, countermeasures against scanning and manipulation have been explained that needs to be implemented in organizations where security matters to stop attackers from accessing valuable information. The book chapter explains thoroughly about the attacks possible in SDN and defensive measures the organization needs to implement to avoid such attacks.

Development in SDN is still in process and it is much difficult to find out how attackers would perform an attack on the network. Also, the knowledge of the threats/vulnerabilities and attacks in SDN are limited. To get a fully secured SDN environment it is necessary to overcome the security issues such as network centralized control and programmability features. For now, all that can be done is to prepare a security plan from the past attacks and face the security challenges with better countermeasures.

REFERENCES

9 types of software defined network attacks and how to protect from them. (n.d.). *Router Freak.* Retrieved from: https://www.routerfreak.com/9-types-software-defined-network-attacks-protect/

Ali, S. T., Sivaraman, V., Radford, A., & Jha, S. (2015). A survey of securing networks using software defined networking. *IEEE Transactions on Reliability, 64*(3), 1086–1097. doi:10.1109/TR.2015.2421391

Ingram Micro Advisor. (2008). 7 advantages of software defined networking. *Ingram Micro Advisor.* Retrieved from: http://www.ingrammicroadvisor.com/data-center/7-advantages-of-software-defined-networking

McKeown, N., Anderson, T., Balakrishnan, H., Parulkar, G., Peterson, L., Rexford, J., ... Turner, J. (2008). Openflow: Enabling innovation in campus networks. *Computer Communication Review, 38*(2), 69–74. doi:10.1145/1355734.1355746

Young, G. O. (1964). *Synthetic structure of industrial plastics.* In J. Peters (Ed.), *Plastics* (2nd ed.; Vol. 3, pp. 15–64). New York: McGraw-Hill.

Chapter 5

The Usage Analysis of Machine Learning Methods for Intrusion Detection in Software-Defined Networks

Derya Yiltas-Kaplan
Istanbul University – Cerrahpaşa, Turkey

ABSTRACT

This chapter focuses on the process of the machine learning with considering the architecture of software-defined networks (SDNs) and their security mechanisms. In general, machine learning has been studied widely in traditional network problems, but recently there have been a limited number of studies in the literature that connect SDN security and machine learning approaches. The main reason of this situation is that the structure of SDN has emerged newly and become different from the traditional networks. These structural variances are also summarized and compared in this chapter. After the main properties of the network architectures, several intrusion detection studies on SDN are introduced and analyzed according to their advantages and disadvantages. Upon this schedule, this chapter also aims to be the first organized guide that presents the referenced studies on the SDN security and artificial intelligence together.

INTRODUCTION

Software Defined Network (SDN) architecture is one of the most recently emerging technologies. SDN is described in 2004 by various researchers in the universities of

DOI: 10.4018/978-1-5225-7353-1.ch005

Princeton, Carnegie Mellon, Stanford, and California as its current concept. Its standards have been designed in the last few years.

Inside the traditional computer networks, each device such as router or switch is responsible from the routing and forwarding operations nearby their packet traffic controls. By this way, a traditional network covers the data, control, and management planes in each device. Here the data plane manages the incoming data, the control plane covers the protocols which construct the routing tables, and the management plane follows and changes the functions of the control plane. On the other hand, an SDN diversifies the control and data planes by embedding the control part inside a central element called controller. In this architecture, router/switch devices do not make any process between each other. Instead, each router/switch is connected to the controller and sometimes gets a decision from this controller device. Such centralized structure provides SDN with the advantages of flexibility, high programmability, security, and fast configuration.

The controller in an SDN structure is the main part that manages the network operations. This part is programmable and can be constructed by different software tools. A controller is related with some designations of new services and obtainment of the functions. Some present controller software can be listed as Beacon, Floodlight, NOX, ONOS, POX, and Pyretic. The most widespread one is the Floodlight. The controller software can be implemented for deciding the routes for the packet flows, realizing the network monitoring, managing the flows and other network processes. The researchers say that SDN provides all networking operations by the help of the centralized software part—controller without any requirement of some configurations on other network devices.

Several network operations such as intrusion detection, routing, firewall filtering, and flow forwarding are examples of the tasks of an SDN controller. This chapter is related to the intrusion detection part and analyzes this task based on the studies including machine learning methods. In the literature there is quite limited number of papers that present SDN and machine learning collaborations, of which only some of them give attention to the SDN security issues. The collaboration between SDN and machine learning has only been used for proposing some methods in the security area. This chapter is the first analysis report on the referenced studies with defining the methods by giving their computational success rates as a strong capability.

As a summary of this chapter, the main definitions about SDN structure are given. It is because, without understanding the SDN, one cannot investigate the literature deeply. Nearby SDN, the background about intrusion detection systems and machine learning methods is also explained. After that part, several current studies that give a connection between SDN and machine learning methods are analyzed. The main objective of this chapter is to give a literature review based on comparing the merits and demerits of different methods used in the machine learning phases. At the end, this chapter gives some deficiencies as unsolved problems in the literature of the SDN studies including the machine learning methods.

BACKGROUND

Software Defined Network

SDN is one of the most recent technologies in the area of computer networks. The main parts in an SDN cover the same devices as in traditional networks with a diversity in the functions of the recent devices and an additional controller part inside the new structure. The difference between switch connections on the architecture of a traditional network and that of an SDN can be easily observed from Figures 1-2.

Figure 1 shows that the switches in a traditional network communicate with each other. There are also data and control functions together inside each switch. This means that the switches have several abilities such as giving route directions to the packets and changing some packet transmission rules.

Figure 2 represents that there is not any connection between the switches. The data functions are again inside the switches, but here a switch gets the decision results from the controller. For this reason, the control functions between a switch and the controller is independently of the other switches. The switches and the controller are compatible with the OpenFlow protocol which will be defined below.

Figure 1. Switch connections on traditional network architecture

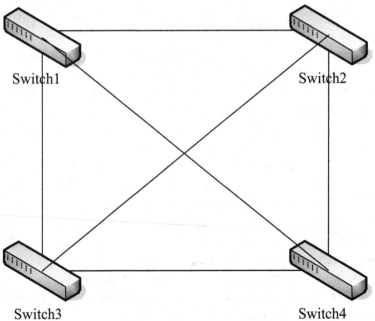

Figure 2. Switch connections on SDN architecture

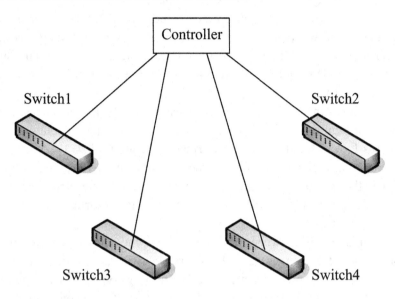

The above-mentioned information gives that the components of an SDN cover four basic properties (Gumus, 2016):

1. The control and data planes become independent based on their functionalities.
2. In contrast to traditional networks, which are based on target address, SDN has flow-based structures.
3. The control plane includes an external element, namely controller as defined above or network operating system.
4. The network is programmable via the network applications working on the controller and interacting with the data plane devices in the lower layers.

The network functions in traditional networks are complicated. As an example, because that the internal structures of today's IP networks, the design of a new routing protocol takes too long for completion of the computation and test phases. It is very significant to mention that this duration may become in between 5-10 years. The protocol update of IPv4 into IPv6 has been continuing for approximately 20 years.

The controller software in SDN is logically centralized and need not be located on a center physically. This requirement is especially important for high security, performance, and scalability. In real applications, SDN consists of physical distributed systems. One of the largest applications for this structure is B4 wide area network of Google that connects its worldwide data centers. This system needs large amount of bandwidth and control on the edge servers and the networks entirely.

Open Networking Foundation has deduced the SDN since 2011. The communication between data and control planes has been standardized as the main assignment of the protocol OpenFlow. OpenFlow is also supported by the large companies such as Google, Microsoft, Facebook, and Verizon. This support indicates that the SDN evolves its environment from academical area into trading one (Gumus, 2016).

An SDN environment with OpenFlow basically includes a controller and several switches as in Figure 2. When a packet arrives at a switch, the routing table on the switch is looked for the routing information of the packet. If there is such a record in the routing table, the routing process starts. Otherwise, the switch sends a message to the controller to find a routing information for the current packet. The response message of the controller contains the routing information as a sending or a dropping event.

The communication between the controller and the switch parts are provided with some types of SDN messages. These are classified as from controller to the switch, asynchronous, and symmetric. The first message type gives the opportunity of checking the status of the switch by the controller. The second message type occurs when there is not available routing information on the routing table inside the switch for a newly incoming packet. Finally the last message type is used to test the connection and send Echo request and reply messages after the connection is set by a controller or a switch.

The most widespread programming environment for an SDN architecture is Mininet. Generally Mininet is set up with Floodlight controller inside a virtual machine and then a network topology is constructed and monitored. Several modules for network operations such as routing or flowing can be managed with these programming items. Selection of the controller takes the leading role here. For example, about Floodlight controller, the programming part is performed with Eclipse or any other Java environment. By this way, the controller functions can be extended and modified based on the goals of the network applications. The flow rules of the controller can also be planned according to the algorithms which take place in the network operations by the help of the programming environments.

The Concept of Intrusion Detection System Related to Machine Learning Methods

The literature studies on main security problems in traditional computer networks are generally related to the firewall structures and intrusion detection systems (IDSs). In particular, IDS is popular and has been studied widespread. An IDS can be defined as a structure that analyzes the network events, detects the intrusions, and notifies the network administrator. The whole system security and data reachability relay on IDS.

There are several IDS classifications in terms of different properties. These properties are the data processing time, architectural structure, information source, and intrusion detection method. This chapter only focuses on intrusion detection method. IDSs can be divided into two groups according to their intrusion detection methods. These are anomaly-based and signature-based groups. The artificial intelligence methods are more suitable for anomaly-based class because of its nature, by which the IDS makes the prediction according to some present network monitoring results such as online network traffic values. These values are compared with some predetermined threshold values. It is noted that anomaly-based IDS is an estimation method, therefore it benefits from some methods such as expert systems and fuzzy logic. As a contrast, in signature-based class, the detection is made according to some predetermined signatures of the network behaviors. In other words, each intrusion is symbolized with a specific signature beforehand (Saruhan Ozdag, 2017).

Machine learning is a subset of artificial intelligence area. Machine learning algorithms are generally divided into two groups: Supervised and unsupervised learning. Some researchers such as Sathya and Abraham (2013) adds reinforcement learning as the third group of this sorting. This chapter addresses only supervised and unsupervised learning because of their extensive usage. In the supervised learning process, the training is achieved through the input-output pairs. The correct results are known before and used inside the input. The training data source is the input and the desired output. An error computation is done by obtaining the difference between the desired and calculated outputs. As a contrast, in unsupervised learning, the correct results and error values are not used. The input data is unlabelled and it is clustered according to some statistical properties (Sathya and Abraham, 2013 and Donalek, 2011). The classification or regression algorithms such as Support Vector Machines (SVMs) and Linear Regression use supervised learning. At the same time, the clustering or association rule learning problems such as k-means and Apriori algorithms require unsupervised learning. Wang and Jones (2017) have observed that clustering is used in both anomaly- and signature-based IDSs. Clustering benefits from the labelled data. On the other hand, as a supervised learning technique, classification is preferable for anomaly detection. However, in general, the supervised learning is not chosen for anomaly detection operations. Since the labelled data for intrusion structures may not be defined, it is mostly available for normal behavioral inputs.

There are lots of studies on intrusion detection that classify the data as intrusion or non-intrusion. These studies generally use supervised learning algorithms such as Decision Trees, Naive Bayes, and SVMs. The computational time of supervised learning is smaller, but the data set and the problem determine which learning type is more applicable for the current situation.

Machine learning is dependent on the data extraction process, which is done on a large data set. Specifically, two data sets are used in a machine learning algorithm on the point of the training and testing phases; and the first one is for training and second one is for testing. The number of data items in each data set can be changed according to the research problem and its solution. After the data organization, training and testing phases, the machine learning algorithms are designed according to some intermediate processes related to the network problem. For example, feature selection and dimensionality reduction processes are implemented by using additional techniques to obtain higher performance values such as accuracy rates of the results.

Some IDSs have been designed by using machine learning techniques. Additionally, the detector generation part can be applied by using different evolutionary methods or other techniques related to artificial intelligence and specifically to the machine learning. Some examples of these techniques are genetic algorithm, evolutionary strategy, and ant colony optimization algorithm. If genetic algorithm is chosen as the main method, its operations such as regeneration, crossover, and mutation are used to get new populations including the individuals that have better properties than before. The properties are chosen according to the network. Here, the population represents the elements of a detector set. Applying genetic algorithm, better results are obtained. Therefore, the additional technique such as genetic algorithm is chosen to improve the machine learning steps, and the performance.

ANALYSIS OF THE PRESENT STUDIES

Machine learning methods use the historical data based on the system security parameters to detect some information about the attack types. One example is the detection of the target host which may be attacked (Nanda et al., 2016). In that study the machine learning algorithms of C4.5 Decision Tree, Bayesian Network, Naive-Bayes, and Decision Table are used to train the model. This training is done for the detection of the host, which may be under attack, by benefiting from the IP address of the attacker. All information about the IP addresses can be obtained from the real-time network data. When SDN is used as the network environment, the controller becomes able to block a subnet entirely instead of the discrete IP addresses of the attackers by using security signatures. The advantage of this strategy is that all IP addresses that used by an attacker inside a single domain can be handled. The success rates of the algorithms are evaluated according to the detection accuracy ratios. The weakness of the study is the usage of Weka machine learning tool. This tool makes the analysis without improving the machine learning algorithm steps. The implementation covers the model training with LongTail public data set which holds the records of SSH brute force attack on the honeypots deployed by Marist

College as an open source project. Three different data sets that used here are 278589 (with Chinese attack data), 187488 (without Chinese attack data), and 91110 (only Chinese attack data). The average prediction accuracy of the algorithms is found as C4.5 Decision Tree = 86.19%, Bayesian Network = 91.68%, Naive-Bayes = 87.78%, and Decision Table = 88.52%.

Jankowski and Amanowicz (2016) presented machine learning algorithms for finding the abnormal activities occurring in the data plane of SDN. Their system has four basic modules that work as the functions of the controller part. These modules are:

1. The Flow bundle module covers information for extracting the traffic statistics and it is located at the OpenDaylight controller. The attributes for flow matching are source and destination IP addresses, source and destination port numbers, and protocol type.

2. The Integrator module gathers the information about the traffic statistics and processes to obtain additional nine features. These features will be used as the input vectors for the next module. These vectors are the packet number in a flow, byte amount in a flow, source port, destination port, duration, flows with different ports from the source host, flows with same ports to the destination host, flow rate to the host, single flow rate to the host.

3. The Classifier module uses the data obtained from the Integrator module and detects the intrusions in SDN data plane. The machine learning algorithms are used in this module. These algorithms are Self-Organizing Maps (SOM), Multi-pass SOM, Learning Vector Quantization (LVQ1), Multi-pass LVQ1, and Hierarchical LVQ1. SOM algorithms are in the type of unsupervised Artificial Neural Network (ANN) and LVQ1 algorithms are in the supervised ANN type.

4. The Controller module supervises the operations of other modules and represents the classification outputs.

The authors used Mininet for SDN network simulation with generating a real traffic and grouping the attack classes as Probe, Remote-to-Local (R2L), DoS, and User-to-Root (U2R) based on the Darpa data set. During the experimental analysis Python scripts were used. The intrusion classifications were done with the algorithms in Weka environment that was commented above as the weakness of aforementioned study done by Nanda et al. (2016). To evaluate the performance of the classification algorithms values True Positive Rate (TPR), False Positive Rates (FPR), and Precision were computed. Hierarchical LVQ1 has the highest TPR of 98.1%, lowest FPR of 1.9%, and Precision of 98%, compared to other training algorithms.

Another SDN environment application detects, classifies, and mitigates the traffic anomaly (da Silva et al., 2016). The system is called ATLANTIC and has two layers, namely Statistical Layer and Classification Layer. ATLANTIC is placed on top of the Network Layer which covers the data and control planes. The communication with the controller is done by REST API. The parts inside the Statistical Layer are Network Driver, Feature Selector, and Statistics Manager. The Network Driver generates traffic snapshot dependent of the current flows of which the information is gathered by the controller. The Feature Selector uses the snapshot to extract the features of duration, packet count, and byte count. The Statistics Manager uses the data obtained from both Network Driver and Feature Selector, and computes the standard deviation, variance, minimum and maximum values, and mean. In the last step, the snapshot and its whole information are sent to the Classification Layer. There are also some parts inside this layer. They are Anomaly Monitor, Flow Classifier, and Flow Manager. In Anomaly Monitor, the snapshot entropy is evaluated, according to the Shannon definition, to make the separation between anomalous and normal types of traffic observable. Because that Anomaly Monitor consumes very low computational resources, it is Lightweight, in opposition to the other parts that are Heavyweight. The second part, Flow Classifier, gets the anomalous snapshots from the Anomaly Monitor and makes the clustering of the similar flows by the help of k-means clustering. The diversification between the malicious and normal flows is done with SVMs. The last part, Flow Manager, notifies the Network Driver about the malicious flows to be blocked and then the Network Driver blocks the incoming packets to the flow by using a firewall rule message in the data plane. The test implementation of the system covers 11 switches and 100 hosts connecting to Floodlight controller in the environment of Mininet. The Lightweight phase needs 0.075 seconds to process 4400 flows with determined topology and Heavyweight phase needs 3 seconds. Furthermore, the SVM finishes the classification with 88.7% of accuracy and 82.3% precision. This system uses machine learning and SDN together but with a lack of attack detection during the state of that the traffic deviations do not differ from normal traffic.

Like ATLANTIC, another anomaly-based approach was presented by Van et al. (2016). In this approach, OpenFlow switch mechanism integrates anomaly-based IDS. The system was implemented with 10G Networked Field-Programmable Gate Array (NetFPGA) hardware and consists of three components as Input, Processing, and Output. Inside Input part, there are Control InPort and Data InPort. While Control InPort processes the packets among controller-switch and stores all packets into the buffer queue, Data InPort processes the data packets. The Processing part covers four elements, namely Incoming Packet Preprocessing, OpenFlow Processing, Security Processing, and Outgoing Packet Processing. Incoming Packet Preprocessing obtains some features from the header and payload fields of the packets. In the OpenFlow

Processing, if the incoming packets come from the control port, then the default OpenFlow instruction is executed and the packets arrived from data ports are forwarded to Security Processing part. The third part is the basic unit of the system for detecting attack packets. This module makes the training phase with KDD Cup 99 Data Set using J48-decision tree algorithm. The J48-decision tree splits the data into 5 decision tree structures from J48_tree 1 to J48_tree 5 specifying the attack categories such as DoS, Probe, U2R, R2L, and Normal of the data set. The last part of the system, Outgoing Packet Processing, gets the packets from the previous two parts and drops the attack packets only. The whole system works with 93.3% accuracy, 91.81% TPR, and 0.55% FPR. The system is successful with respect to early detection of the attacks before affecting the other components of SDN structure. Unfortunately, it is not cost-effective. Because the system should be performed in all of the switches and this utilizes a huge amount of computational resources.

There are also some studies that represent the steps for a specific attack type. For example, Braga et al. (2010) found a method to detect Distributed Denial of Service (DDoS) flooding attack in OpenFlow switches with NOX controller of SDN. Their three modules are stated below:

1.   The Flow Collector module gets the flow entries that stay on the flow tables of OpenFlow switches for specific time durations. The communication link between the controller and a switch is a secure channel. For this purpose, the NOX controller allocates an ID to each authenticated switch. This ID helps the Classifier module to find the related switch that is under the DDoS attack.

2.   The Feature extractor module obtains the flows gathered at Flow Collector to deduce the most important features for attack detection. These features cover the following 6-tuples:

    a.   Average Packets per flow (APf): To compute this feature, at first the flows are sorted in ascending order with respect to their packet numbers and then their median value is calculated.

    b.   Average Bytes per flow (ABf): This is same as APf. The only difference is that the flows are sorted with respect to their byte sizes.

    c.   Average Duration per flows (ADf): The median value of the duration of flows in a Flow Table is calculated. This feature is used to reduce the false-positive rates.

    d.   Percentage of Pair-flows (PPf): Pair-flows have identical communication protocol, where source IP of one flow is the destination IP of other flow and vice-versa. Most normal traffic is in the form of pair-flows. To calculate this feature, the number of flows is multiplied by 2 and then the product is divided by the total number of flows.

e. Growth of Single-flows (GSf): In a DDoS attack, the number of single-flows can grow very high. To calculate this feature, at first the number of all flows – 2*(the number of pair flows) is computed. Then the result is divided by the time interval in which the flow feature was under evaluation.

f. Growth of Different ports (GDp): Since random ports can be generated by a DDoS attack, this feature is calculated as the total number of ports divided by interval.

3. The Classifier module decides if the abovementioned 6-tuples sign an attack or normal traffic. The algorithm used here for traffic classification is SOM as studied by Jankowski and Amanowicz (2016), as mentioned before. The SOM is implemented as a 40 x 40 matrix of neurons with an initial learning-rate of 0.5, an initial neighborhood of 20, and an Epoch limit of 3000.

The system is trained using the first 4-tuples and also all 6-tuples with 3500 attack flows and 5108 normal flows, and tested on 35571 attack flows and 27317 normal flows. The deployment topology consisted of three OpenFlow switches. Detection rate (DR) and the false alarm rate (FAR) are calculated for each switch separately. In switch 3, no attack flows were involved in training the SOM, and therefore it has the lowest DR of 3.52% with 6-tuples and well as FAR of 0.12%. Switch 2 with 6-tuples has highest DR of 99.11% and FAR of 0.46% in comparison to the other two switches. Though, Braga et al. (2010) showed that this system has lower overhead compared to some other detection systems based on the KDD Cup 99 data set.

Another study on DDoS attacks was done by Phan et al. (2016a). This study combines SVM and SOM algorithms for working on control plane. The system covers eight modules: Flow Collector, Feature Extractor, Traffic Classifier, SVM-i, Training Database, SOM, Attack Classifier, and Policy Enforcement. As an initialization step, SVM-i and SOM are trained by using CAIDA (2015 and 2007) data sets that are located in Training Database. After then the Flow Collector aggregates the flows coming in reply to the StatsRequest messages. The Feature Extractor obtains the four attributes as duration, number of packets, protocol, and amount of bytes from the StatsResponse messages. The Traffic Classifier transfers the flow features like duration or packet number to the relevant SVM-i. For example, if the protocol type is TCP, then the relevant SVM called as SVM-TCP. The flows that are in the edges of SVM-hyperplane are thought as suspicious and sent to the SOM to be retrained with respect to the four features. The Attack Classifier module classifies malicious flows as Type-I and Type-II DDoS attacks according to the output of SVM-i and SOM modules. At the end, the Policy Enforcement drops the flows assigned as Type-I attack and deletes the rules of the flows in the set of Type-II attacks. The study of Phan et al. (2016a) differs in the POX controller from most of the studies that use

Floodlight controller. There is only one OpenvSwitch connecting to the internet. The performance was computed as 97.6% accuracy, 98.13% DR, and 3.85% FAR. Additionally, the controller's CPU utilization at the attack time was as low as 25% on average. Even though the better performance of CPU is obtained, the system cannot detect other types of attacks.

Wang and Chen (2017) gave a security mechanism, called SGuard, against DoS attacks. Their system is implemented as an application of NOX controller with capability of stopping spoofing attacks and protecting SDN environment from hazardous network traffic. The modules in the system are Access Control, Classification, and Data Plane Cache. The Access Control is important for tracing the source and location of the attacker. This module collects the information of IP, Port, MAC, and related switch ID inside a table to give the location of the attacker. The switch immediately drops the packets after the system determines the attack source. The Classification module is responsible for the collection of the flow entries within a specific time interval, extraction of six features (i.e., percentage of flows with a small number of packets, percentage of flows with a small average bytes, percentage of flows with short time duration, percentage of reversible flows, the growth rate of irreversible flows, and percentage of flows with short time duration), and using the feature ranking algorithm. In this module, the flows are classified into malicious and normal by using SOM. The SOM is trained with 50x50 node matrix, 20 neighborhood radius, 0.5 learning rate, and 4000 iterations. The last module, Data Plane Cache, is located in between the controller and switches. This module stores table-miss packets when an attacker tries to overwhelm the network resources. This module consists of four components: *Packet Buffer Queue Block* holds table-miss packets migrated at the time of saturation attack and these packets are attended by data plane scheduler using a round-robin algorithm to avoid the resource starvation among the switches and the controller. *NetLog Block* is responsible for caching and maintaining compressed flow tables of SGuard, attaching switches for providing the fault tolerance capability to the network. *Classification Result Block* stores the results generated by the SOM. *Access Control List Block* stores information (Port, MAC, IP) of SGuard authenticated users. The performance of the system was evaluated by calculating the system overhead and detection rate of the classifier. Mininet, Hping3, and iperf were used for simulating the network topology, for generating malicious traffic, and for computing the network performance, respectively. In the experiments, no more than 30% of CPU and 20% of the cache were being consumed at the time of DoS attack and the SGuard's DR reached 99.7%. The experimental results show that SGuard is effective at detecting the DoS attacks and lightweight with reasonably less resource consumption.

Phan et al. (2016b) presented another study in a similar way of their previous study as defined before. The mechanism in this study called OpenFlowSIA provides detection and prevention of SDN against flooding attacks. The algorithms are SVM and the new proposed one is called Idle-timeout Adjustment (IA). The system modules that run in the SDN controller are given in five clauses:

1.   The Flow Collector sends and receives the flow statistics from the switches in a specific time duration.
2.   The Feature Extractor uses the output of Flow Collector and extracts the features of packet number in a flow and duration of a flow.
3.   The SVM-i module is trained by using CAIDA data set by only considering ICMP Flooding (Type-I) with 5000 normal and 5000 attack instances, and TCP SYN Flooding (Type-II) attack with 5000 normal and 5000 attack instances. After this step, the predicted attack flows are sent to the Policy Enforcement module and normal flows are sent to IA Algorithm module.
4.   If the detected attack is of Type-I, the Policy Enforcement module sets the idle-timeout of the flow to 0. This means that it drops all packets that pass through the table of the switch. On the contrary, if the detected attack is in Type-II, the switches delete the related flow entry from their tables.
5.   IA Algorithm module works for tuning the idle-timeout of the flow-based on the results of the SVM-i module. This process keeps the SDN components robust during the attack time.

The system performance is analyzed according to the CPU consumption of the controller and switch. The cases for the evaluation are 1- only for first three modules, 2- only for the first four modules, and 3- for all modules. The CPU consumption was the highest with 52% in the first case and the lowest with 28.5% in the third case, with the initial idle-timeout set to 3 seconds.

Another IDS covering similar modules as in the abovementioned methods is flow-based mechanism (Ajaeiya et al., 2017). The modules of this system are Flow stats Collection, Feature Extraction and Aggregation, and Training and Traffic Classification. All modules are located on the SDN controller. The Flow stats Collection gets some information about the flow statistics with the message of FLOW_STATS. The Feature Extraction and Aggregation obtains the features as Duration, Source_IP, Destination_IP, Source_port, Destination_port, Protocol, Packet_count, and Byte_count. Because that these features are stored randomly they cannot give an accurate result for the classification. Thus another nine features (Current measurement duration, Packet_count, Byte_count, Packet count to duration, Byte count to the duration, Standard deviation (SD) of flow duration, SD of packets, SD of bytes, and SD of byte_count to the duration) are collected for the classification step. The last module, Training and Traffic Classification, uses Bagged Trees algorithm with these nine features. The study compares Bagged Trees algorithm with the Random Forest, SVN, KNN, and Decision Trees algorithms, and proves the efficiency of the former one. Against the other studies in the literature this system works with Ryu controller. The disadvantage of this system is due to the usage of only one switch as in the study of Phan et al. (2016a). This situation represents that the system is not scalable for large-size networks and large amount of packet traffic. The attack types in the system are various such as TCP DoS, HTTP Credential Brute Force, Network SYN Scan, Port Scan, ICMP Flood, SSH Brute Force. The training and testing were executed offline using Matlab 2016b. The performance was evaluated by calculating F1-Score and Bagged Trees obtained the highest F1-Score of 98.34% and the lowest FPR 1.6% in comparison to the other algorithms. Although the system has high performance, it has not been tested in an SDN environment in real-time.

Chen and Yu (2016) proposed a distributed intrusion prevention system, called Collaborative Intrusion Prevention Architecture (CIPA), for large-size networks. CIPA uses ANN algorithm in which the neurons are distributed over the switches operating in the data layer. The switches allocate the computations to one or more neurons. The neurons in the same layer work simultaneously and communicate to each other with logical links. CIPA is trained by using Resilient Backpropagation Algorithm. There are four modules in the system: Input Layer, Hidden Layer, Output Layer, and Mitigation Layer. In the Input Layer, the neurons in the switches collect the features of udp_ratio, icmp_ratio, and the ratio of the difference between syn_num and ack_num, and then send them to the Hidden Layer after some processes. The neurons in the Hidden Layer perform additional computations on the samples and send the results to the next hidden layer or Output Layer. Output Layer neurons decide whether the sample is normal or attack. Another ANN can be used in parallel to this current ANN for finding the attack type and stage. After the intrusion detection, CIPA stimulates all or related switches which play role in Mitigation Layer, and eliminates the intrusions. Like the method of Phan et al. (2016a), this system is designed with POX controller too. The Scapy is used to generate normal and attack (i.e., SYN flood, UDP flood, and IPscan) traffic. Additionally, Low Orbit Ion Cannon is used for generating realistic DDoS attacks. The performance results obtained on average from Scapy attacks are 96.6% DR and 2.88% FPR, and results from DDoS attacks are 95.63% DR and 2.77% FPR. There is also a comparison in this study with the method by Gamer (2012). The simulations from networks size with 50 nodes, 100 nodes, and 200 nodes show that CIPA has higher communication overhead than the latter one.

Goswami (2017) implemented the security model with the parts of the traffic analyzer, reinforcement learning agent, and threat response. The traffic analyzer is responsible for monitoring the network traffic and bringing the information to the agent part. The reinforcement learning agent represents the Q-learning algorithm steps and computes some suitable action lists against the threats. The last part, namely threat response, maintains the flow tables and bandwidth of the switches. This system can be overloaded during the reinforcement learning phase. In this part, there is an available action list in the policy. In real applications, for any state there cannot be any definite action. For this reason, a Reward Signal part is included inside the method and the result of any action during any time t is analyzed whether it is suitable in any time $t+1$. This concludes the need of additional computations for the system.

As the network traffic covers huge amount of packet traffic, the methods related with big data become more practicable in today's applications. Deep learning is a new part of machine learning and it is more suitable for big data implementations. Tang et al. (2016) used this technique as deep neural networks in their IDS relevant to the flow-based anomalies in SDN environment. This model has an input layer with the dimensions equivalent to the feature numbers used for training the model. There are also three hidden layers with twelve, six, and three neurons, and an output layer with two dimensions as anomaly or normal. The batch size of the model is 10 and the epoch number is 100. The learning rates are in the range of [0.1 to 0.0001] for the training phase. The data set in the study is again widespread one, NSL_KDD Dataset, with six traffic-based features of duration, source_bytes, destination_bytes, protocol_type, number of connection to the same host, and number of connections to the same service for training; and there are 41 available features for testing phases. The controller accommodates the IDS application, collects all statistics using *ofp_flow_stats* and *oft_flow_stats_replay* messages through the communication with the switches, and sends these statistics to the IDS to complete the process. The model was trained with various learning rates, and it computed the percentage of Loss and Accuracy in both Train data and Test data. The performance of the model was evaluated using the Test data and resulted in the best accuracy of 75.75 with a learning rate of 0.001. It was concluded that the model with a learning rate of 0.001 generalized better from training samples in comparison to other learning rates, but six features was not adequate for the model to predict intrusions with high accuracy compared to other studies which utilized all NSL-KDD features.

The study of Wang and Jones (2017) is the last example of this section. This study is important about big data and IDS when presenting information without considering an SDN environment. It may also become a guide for such studies about SDN. Wang and Jones (2017) inserted hybrid group into the IDS classification stated before. The disadvantage of signature-based methods is that a small modification inside the attack type cannot be detected by the predetermined rules or signatures. Anomaly-based methods are suitable for network layer attacks such as Denial-of-Service and SYN flood. Anomaly-based methods use the information on the packet header that includes IP addresses, port numbers, and flags. On the other hand, these methods are not acceptable for detecting application layer attacks like R2L or U2R, because a network message also covers some payload except the header during the application process. Hybrid methods eliminate the disadvantages of both signature- and anomaly-based methods.

Table 1. Some properties of the literature studies

Author Name	Year	Machine Learning Method	Computational Rates
Braga et al.	2010	SOM	The lowest DR = 3.52%, the lowest FAR = 0.12%, the highest DR = 99.11%, the highest FAR = 0.46%.
Nanda et al.	2016	C4.5 Decision Tree, Bayesian Network, Naive-Bayes, and Decision Table	Accuracy for C4.5 Decision Tree = 86.19%, Bayesian Network = 91.68%, Naive-Bayes = 87.78%, and Decision Table = 88.52%.
Jankowski and Amanowicz	2016	SOM, Multi-pass SOM, LVQ1, Multi-pass LVQ1, and Hierarchical LVQ1	Hierarchical LVQ1 has the highest TPR of 98.1%, lowest FPR of 1.9%, and Precision of 98% compared to other training algorithms.
da Silva et al.	2016	SVM	Accuracy = 88.7% and precision = 82.3%.
Van et al.	2016	J48-decision tree algorithm	Accuracy = 93.3%, TPR = 91.81%, and FPR = 0.55%.
Phan et al.	2016a	SVM and SOM	Accuracy = 97.6%, DR = 98.13%, FAR = 3.85%, and average CPU utilization = 25%.
Phan et al.	2016b	SVM and IA	The highest CPU consumption = 52% and the lowest CPU consumption = 28.5%.
Chen and Yu	2016	ANN algorithm, Resilient Backpropagation Algorithm	From Scapy attacks: DR = 96.6% and FPR = 2.88%, from DDoS attacks: DR = 95.63% and FPR = 2.77%.
Wang and Chen	2017	SOM	DR = 99.7%, the highest CPU consumption = 30%, and the highest cache consumption = 20%.
Ajaeiya et al.	2017	Bagged Trees, Random Forest, SVN, KNN, and Decision Trees algorithms	Bagged Trees algorithm obtained the highest F1-Score of 98.34% and the lowest FPR 1.6% in comparison to the other algorithms.

Massive on-line analysis covers an evaluation tool set for stream data mining. The data is collected and evaluated based on the machine learning algorithms. Machine learning processes such as classification, clustering, linear regression, and pattern recognition are supported in this set. In general network applications, stream data is constructed from the network message flows. This is also suitable for SDN architecture. In the literature, there are many open source systems to process the stream data, and online machine learning can be relevant here (Wang and Jones, 2017).

Some properties of the above studies are represented in Table 1 in chronological order for simplicity.

OPEN ISSUES AND SUGGESTIONS

Because that SDN has been studied for only several years, there are not much more studies especially on its security part. There are still lots of open issues about security branch in the emerging SDN technology. The most important issue is nonexistence of a data set in SDN environment that represents packet flows. In traditional networks, intrusion detection studies mostly use KDD Cup 99 Data Set that is simulated as a network structure similar to that of USA Air Forces and covers large number of intrusion types. Especially in machine learning studies, a data set should include very large numbers of data. Some aforementioned SDN studies (Van et al., 2016, Braga et al., 2010, and Tang et al., 2016) also use KDD Data Set. These studies can be strenghtened with new data sets.

One important step in machine learning methods is the data collection and feature selection parts. Especially in network applications the data change dynamically, so the evaluations and the training process can be done in an online manner. For big data problems, online feature selection also represents another research area as mentioned by Wang and Jones (2017). It is also explained that big data in the networks cover some redundant data as in the other environments. These redundant or noisy data are also vital for network security issues, because it is extensive in cyber-attacks too. Even though Wang and Jones (2017) gave the comments for traditional networks, the same view is valid for SDN too. Nearby their study, the literature research on this area represents that large amount of unsupervised network data can be analyzed better in deep learning than the machine learning techniques. Deep learning currently has some drawbacks, but it is more suitable in IDS.

As mentioned above, the last member added to the IDS classification based on the intrusion detection method is hybrid group. It is known that anomaly-based group is not suitable for application layer attacks due to the negligence of the packet payloads in its working mechanism. Similarly, signature-based group does not detect an attack with a new structure or change. If the hybrid group is implemented, the process time and resource performance become advantageous.

The software environment is also very important to implement different network scenarios and adapt various algorithms to the SDN backbone. SDN also differs from the traditional network structures at that point. The traditional network operations can be done by using any high-level programming language by handling different types of algorithms or methods. Yet, the software part in SDN is dependent on the controller type for providing some modification requirements in the controller-related module steps. The controller type is also called as the controller software that was mentioned before. As two examples, Floodlight is based on Java and POX is on Python. Nearby with the design of the programming language commands, the machine learning applications on SDN can also be done by the help of some software, such as Weka, which is very easy to use. Weka is widespread in the area of machine learning methods. The algorithms are not modified and are automatically loaded inside the software. This property is a disadvantage for network studies of Nanda et al. (2016), Jankowski and Amanowicz (2016) as explained in the previous section. Instead of using Weka in the machine learning steps, the authors may use the programming language scripts which the controller support.

The software part in the study of da Silva et al. (2016) becomes powerful with the usage of REST API that is a flexible distributed system. However, the study of Silva et al. (2016) is restricted with the situation that the attack detection is only possible with the normal traffic deviation of the system. This study can be extended with various traffic scenarios and network parameters.

The restrictions on the network traffic may be valid for the detected attack types too. For example, the systems of Braga et al. (2010) and Phan et al. (2016a) can only detect DDoS attacks, the system of Wang and Chen (2017) only detects DoS attacks. On the other hand, Jankowski and Amanowicz (2016), Van et al. (2016), Ajaeiya et al. (2017), and Chen and Yu (2016) planned their systems based on various types of network attacks such as U2R, Probe, SYN flood, ICMP flood, and R2L.

The last issue is the network architectures of the proposed studies. The systems with the small number of nodes or switches, namely small-size networks, do not become a guide for the real security solutions. This situation occurs in the studies of Phan et al. (2016a) and Ajaeiya et al. (2017) as each one covers only one OpenvSwitch. If the structures are enlarged as in the real architectures, they can also achieve different traffic characteristics. Thus the computations become more realistic.

CONCLUSION

This chapter reports the studies in the literature, which are based on a collaboration of the areas of machine learning, IDS, and SDN. Some studies are effective for a single attack type, or use the machine learning process for only similar steps such as in the parts of flow collector and feature extractor. In the meantime, most of the network security problems are tackled through the general data sets.

For a security problem in an SDN system, the network conditions should be considered deeply to decide on the choice of machine learning methods. This means that some elements such as the attack type, relevant protocol layer, network size, or packet traffic density affect the conceiving of a machine learning method. The resource utilization like CPU should be lower during the intrusion detection or prevention in an SDN, because the processes are planned at the controller modules. In other words, the workload about the decisions on the network operations in SDN is not distributed over the network devices as in traditional networks. Thus, the central point of controller should include the security modules with eliminating additional burden. On the other hand, a huge amount of flow data is present and required for machine learning steps. This conflict state can be solved by using rational machine learning steps with a reasonable data set. Further suggestions and the analysis in this chapter can be a scientific guide for the researchers.

ACKNOWLEDGMENT

The author would like to sincerely thank Savio S. H. Tse for proofreading this chapter.

REFERENCES

Ajaeiya, G. A., Adalian, N., Elhajj, I. H., Kayssi, A., & Chehab, A. (2017). Flow-based intrusion detection system for SDN. In *IEEE Symposium on Computers and Communications (ISCC)*. IEEE.

Braga, R., Mota, E., & Passito, A. (2010). Lightweight DDoS flooding attack detection using NOX/OpenFlow. In *IEEE 35th Conference on Local Computer Networks (LCN)* (pp. 408-415). IEEE.

Chen, X.-F., & Yu, S.-Z. (2016). CIPA: A collaborative intrusion prevention architecture for programmable network and SDN. *Computers & Security, 58*, 1–19. doi:10.1016/j.cose.2015.11.008

da Silva, A. S., Wickboldt, J. A., Granville, L. Z., & Schaeffer-Filho, A. (2016). *ATLANTIC: A framework for anomaly traffic detection, classification, and mitigation in SDN.* In *IEEE/IFIP Network Operations and Management Symposium (NOMS)*, (pp. 27-35). IEEE.

Donalek, C. (2011). *Supervised and Unsupervised Learning.* Retrieved from http://www.astro.caltech.edu/~george/aybi199/Donalek_Classif.pdf

Gamer, T. (2012). Collaborative anomaly-based detection of large-scale internet attacks. *Computer Networks*, *56*(1), 169–185. doi:10.1016/j.comnet.2011.08.015

Goswami, K. K. (2017). *Intelligent threat-aware response system in software-defined networks* (Unpublished master's thesis). San José State University, San Jose, CA.

Gumus, F. (2016). *Congestion control in software defined networks with machine learning algorithms* (Unpublished master's thesis). Istanbul University, Istanbul, Turkey.

Jankowski, D., & Amanowicz, M. (2016). On efficiency of selected machine learning algorithms for intrusion detection in software defined networks. *International Journal of Electronics and Telecommunications*, *62*(3), 247–252. doi:10.1515/eletel-2016-0033

Nanda, S., Zafari, F., DeCusatis, C., Wedaa, E., & Yang, B. (2016). Predicting network attack patterns in SDN using machine learning approach. In *IEEE Conference on Network Function Virtualization and Software Defined Networks (NFV-SDN)*. IEEE. 10.1109/NFV-SDN.2016.7919493

Phan, T. V., Bao, N. K., & Park, M. (2016a). A novel hybrid flow-based handler with DDoS attacks in software-defined networking. In *Ubiquitous Intelligence & Computing, Advanced and Trusted Computing, Scalable Computing and Communications, Cloud and Big Data Computing, Internet of People, and Smart World Congress (UIC/ATC/ScalCom/CBDCom/IoP/SmartWorld), 2016 Intl IEEE Conferences* (pp. 350-357). IEEE.

Phan, T. V., Toan, T. V., Tuyen, D. V., Huong, T. T., & Thanh, N. H. (2016b). OpenFlowSIA: An optimized protection scheme for software-defined networks from flooding attacks. In *IEEE Sixth International Conference on Communications and Electronics (ICCE)* (pp. 13-18). IEEE. 10.1109/CCE.2016.7562606

Saruhan Ozdag, F. (2017). *Detection of network attacks with machine learning method* (Unpublished master's thesis). Istanbul University, Istanbul, Turkey.

Sathya, R., & Abraham, A. (2013). Comparison of Supervised and Unsupervised Learning Algorithms for Pattern Classification. *International Journal of Advanced Research in Artificial Intelligence, 2*(2), 34–38. doi:10.14569/IJARAI.2013.020206

Tang, T. A., Mhamdi, L., McLernon, D., Zaidi, S. A. R., & Ghogho, M. (2016). Deep learning approach for network intrusion detection in software defined networking. In *International Conference on Wireless Networks and Mobile Communications (WINCOM)*. IEEE. 10.1109/WINCOM.2016.7777224

Van, N. T., Bao, H., & Thinh, T. N. (2016). An Anomaly-based Intrusion Detection Architecture Integrated on OpenFlow Switch. In *Proceedings of the 6th International Conference on Communication and Network Security (ICCNS)* (pp. 99-103). ACM. 10.1145/3017971.3017982

Wang, L., & Jones, R. (2017). Big data analytics for network intrusion detection: A survey. *International Journal of Networks and Communications, 7*(1), 24–31.

Wang, T., & Chen, H. (2017). SGuard: A lightweight SDN safe-guard architecture for DoS attacks. *China Communications, 14*(6), 113–125. doi:10.1109/CC.2017.7961368

ADDITIONAL READING

Abubakar, A., & Pranggono, B. (2017). Machine learning based intrusion detection system for software defined networks. In *2017 Seventh International Conference on Emerging Security Technologies (EST)* (pp. 138-143). IEEE. 10.1109/EST.2017.8090413

Bakker, J. N. (2017). Intelligent traffic classification for detecting DDoS attacks using SDN/OpenFlow (Master's thesis). Victoria University of Wellington, Wellington, New Zealand.

Boero, L., Marchese, M., & Zappatore, S. (2017). Support vector machine meets software defined networking in IDS domain. In *2017 29th International Teletraffic Congress (ITC)* (pp. 25-30). IEEE and ACM SIGCOMM.

Cusack, G., Michel, O., & Keller, E. (2018). Machine learning-based detection of ransomware using SDN. In *Proceedings of the 2018 ACM International Workshop on Security in Software Defined Networks & Network Function Virtualization (SDN-NFV Sec'18)* (pp. 1-6). ACM. 10.1145/3180465.3180467

Li, J., Zhao, Z., & Li, R. (2015). A machine learning based intrusion detection system for software defined 5G network. *IET Research Journals,* 1-8.

Sultana, N., Chilamkurti, N., Peng, W., & Alhadad, R. (2018). Survey on SDN based network intrusion detection system using machine learning approaches. *Peer-to-Peer Networking and Applications*, 1–9. doi:10.100712083-017-0630-0

Wang, P., Chao, K.-M., Lin, H.-C., Lin, W.-H., & Lo, C.-C. (2016). An efficient flow control approach for SDN-based network threat detection and migration using support vector machine. In *The Thirteenth IEEE International Conference on e-Business Engineering (ICEBE)* (pp. 56-63). IEEE. 10.1109/ICEBE.2016.020

KEY TERMS AND DEFINITIONS

Controller: The central element of a software defined network that is responsible from any process management and constructed from software modules.

Data Plane: A part in the software defined network including the switches that provides the flows of the packets through the ports.

Data Set: The input set of an application involving several features.

Intrusion: An attack to a remote computer with a malicious purpose and constraining.

Learning: A phase in the machine learning methods that aggregates some information about the state actions for using in the future predictions of the events.

OpenFlow: Protocol name through the connection in between controller and switch in a software-defined network.

Software-Defined Network: New network platform that migrates several functions from the network devices to a controller software.

Chapter 6
Toward Formal Verification of SDN Access–Control Misconfigurations

Amina Saadaoui
University of Carthage, Tunisia

ABSTRACT

Software-defined networking (SDN) allows centralizing and simplifying network management control. It brings a significant flexibility and visibility to networking, but at the same time creates new security challenges. The promise of SDN is the ability to allow networks to keep pace with the speed of change. It allows frequent modifications to the network configuration. However, these changes may introduce misconfigurations by writing inconsistent rules for single flow table or within a multiple open flow switches that need multiple FlowTables to be maintained at the same time. Misconfigurations can arise also between firewalls and FlowTables in OpenFlow-based networks. Problems arising from these misconfigurations are common and have dramatic consequences for networks operations. To avoid such scenarios, mechanisms to prevent these anomalies and inconsistencies are of paramount importance. To address these challenges, the authors present a new method that allows the automatic identification of inter and inter Flowtables anomalies. They also use the Firewall to bring out real misconfigurations.

INTRODUCTION

In SDN Network devices can be programmed via different communication protocols, such as OpenFlow. In fact, an openFlow network consists of a distributed collection

DOI: 10.4018/978-1-5225-7353-1.ch006

of switches managed by a program running on a logically-centralized controller. Each switch has a flow table that stores a list of rules for processing packets. Each rule consists of a pattern (matching on packet header fields) and actions (such as forwarding, dropping, modifying the packets, or sending them to the controller). The OpenFlow controller installs or uninstalls rules in the switches, reads traffic statistics, and responds to events. For each event, the controller program defines a handler, which may install rules or issue requests for traffic statistics. Therefore, Open flow and Software-Defined Networking (SDN) can simplify network management by offering programmers network-wide visibility and direct control over the underlying switches from a logically-centralized controller, but at the same time brings new security challenges by raising risks of software faults (or bugs), especially switches misconfigurations. Since companies rely only on the availability of their networks, such misconfigurations are costly. Due to the magnitude of this problem, our goal is to develop a method that allows to automatically identify configuration errors among the set of switches rules which should be well configured with respect to the firewall configuration. Finding the correct flow rules is challenging due to a number of reasons. First of all, an openflow switch generally comprises thousands of flow rules that are dependent and second flow rules do not always exactly match firewall rules.

In this paper, we propose a new approach to discover misconfigurations in real-case openFlow switches configurations already designed, our proposed method could be used also before updates occurred by the controller to verify if changes will induce further misconfigurations. This paper is organized as follows: Section 2 presents a summary of related work. Section 3 overviews the formal representation of firewall configurations and security policies and details FDD structure. In Section 4, we present our 65 method to discover and remove superfluous rules. In Section 5, we present our approach to discover simple and distributed firewalls misconfigurations. In Section 6, we articulate our approach to resolve simple firewall misconfigurations. In Section 7, we present first a study of the complexity of our inference systems, and then we address the implementation and evaluations of our tool. Finally, we present our conclusions and discuss our plans for future work.

RELATED WORK

Recently, there have been many verification tools proposed for SDN. Some tools debug controller softwares or applications, while others check the correctness of network policies.

Controller Softwares or Applications Verification

In Canini et al. (2012), the authors propose a tool named NICE which automates the testing of OpenFlow Apps. In fact, it allows to find bugs in real applications and to test the atomic execution of system events. But this tool does not guarantee the errors absence and does not allow to check safety properties. Ball et al. (2014) propose another tool in named vericon that allows to verify the correctness of SDN applications on a large rang of topologies and sequences of network events. The limitation of this work is that authors focus on safety properties without verifying the liveness properties of packets (packets must eventually reach their destinations) and also, they assume that events are executed atomically ignoring out-of order rule installations.

Network Policies Verification

Frenetic (Foster et al., 2011) is a domain-specific language for OpenFlow that aims to eradicate a large class of programming faults. Using Frenetic requires the network programmer to learn extensions to Python to support the higher-layer abstractions. OFRewind (Wundsam et al., 2011) enables recording and replay of events for troubleshooting problems in production networks due to closed-source network devices. However, it does not automate the testing of OpenFlow controller programs. Kazemian, et al. (2013) proposed a method tha allows to verify network properties like reachability, by using Header Space Analysis HAS but their work does not allow to check in real-time if network policy still not violated after rules update for example. Netplumber presented in Kazemian et al. (2013) uses a set of policies and invariants to do real time cheking. It leverages header space analysis and keeps a dependacy graph between rules but it does not allow to model dynamic network behaviors. Hu et al. (2014) introduced in flowgard a new tool that allows to verify the network policy by providing methods to detect and correct firewall policy violations in OpenFlow based networks. FlowChecker (Al-Shaer & Al-Haj, 2010) applies symbolic model checking techniques on a manually-constructed network model based on binary decision diagrams to detect misconfigurations in OpenFlow forwarding tables.

FORMAL SPECIFICATION

In what follows, we define, formally, some key notions.

Open Flow Switch Rules

An OpenFlow Switch configuration consists of a flow table, which perform packet lookups and forwarding, and an OpenFlow channel to an external controller. The switch communicates with the controller and the controller manages the switch via the OpenFlow protocol. A flow table contains a set of flow entries of the form $FL = \{fe_i => a_i; 1 = <i <= n\}$; each flow entry consists of match fields fe_i, and a set of instructions to apply to matching packets $a_i = \{$Forwad, send to Firewall, set (field1, field2 and forward), drop$\}$.

Firewall Configuration

A simple firewall configuration is a finite sequence of filtering rules of the form $FR = \{ri => ai, 1 = <i <= n\}$. These rules are tried in order, up to the first matching one. A filtering rule consists of a precondition ri which is a region of the packet's space P, usually, consisting of source address, destination address, protocol and destination port. Each right member Ai of a rule of F R is an action defining the behavior of the firewall on filtered packets: Ai $= \{$accept, deny$\}$.

In-Switches

For each possible source address we define a couple of these addresses and the set of input-Switches(Sin,I)from which flow income.

FeDD (Flow Entries Decision Diagram) of a Path in a Distributed Environment

A flow entries decision diagram of our network, which is consisting of tens of switches, is constructed using the collection of rules of different flow tables of these switches. Therefore, the FeDD of our network could be represented as follows:

FeDD $= \{$dpj ; $1 <= j <= m\}$, which is an acyclic and directed graph that has the following properties: There is exactly one node in feddi that has no incoming edges. This node is called the root of feddi. The nodes in feddi that have no outgoing edges are called terminal nodes. feddi is the union of direct paths dpi . The algorithm used to construct an feddi is detailed in Liu (2008) and Gouda and Liu (2006). Each direct path is represented as follows:

dpj= dpj.srce & dpj.protocol & dpj.dest & dpj.flowEntries & dpj.action

- dpj.src is the range of source address represented by the direct path dpj .
- dpj .dst is the range of destination address represented by the direct path dpj .

- dpj.protocol is the range of protocols represented by the direct path dpj
- dpj.flowEntries is the set of flow entries from the flow table configuration that match the domain of packets represented by this direct path. But we have to precise for each rule the flow table that belongs to it.
- dpj.action= the action of this direct path dpj. The action of each direct path depends on the actions of each flow entry handled by this direct path from each switches in this path, so we have:
- dpj .action = accept if all flow entries applied the action forward from the source to the destination.
- dpj .action = drop if at least one rule applies the action drop to the packets handled by this direct path.
- dpj .action = set-Field(field1,field2) and Fwd(S_k) if in this direct path we have a flow entry that apply this action.
- dpj .action = Loop, id the flow handled by this direct path is returned to a switch already exists in the set dpj.flowEntries.
- dpj.action= FwdFirewall if at least one rule applies this action to the packets handled by this direct path.

OUR METHOD

In this work, our goal is to propose an automatic method that supports OpenFlow controller by effectively managing flow-tables entries in dynamic OpenFlow-based networks. To achieve our goal and address this challenge, we seek a solution based of inference systems.

Inference System for Constructing FeDD

The first step is to define a set In-switches composed by couples (S_{in}, I) switches from which the traffic flow first. Where I is source addresses that are linked to the switch S_{in}. The verification in our work is based on firewall requirements; therefore, we use the firewall rules and the network topology to define this set I.

Our goal is to construct the FeDD. To achieve this goal we propose in Figure.1 an inference system that presents steps to construct this FeDD.

The rules of this inference system apply to quadruple (fedd, S_{in}, $Rules_m$, F) where fedd is the Flow entries decision diagram of the couple (S_{in}, I), $Rules_m$ is a temporary variable contains a set of rules from different switches in our network that we should parse to get the real path from which packets from sources in the set I passed. F is a temporary variable contains the set of packet matched by rules already parsed. The inference rule start allows to parse rules from the switch S_{in} that match the set I, this

Figure 1. Inference system for constructing FeDD

$$Init \; \frac{}{\varnothing, S_{in}, \varnothing, \varnothing}$$

$$Start \; \frac{FDD, \{r\} \cup S, \varnothing, \varnothing}{construct_{FDD}(FDD, \{r\} \cap I), S, Rules_m, \varnothing} \quad if(\{r\} \cap I \neq \varnothing \; and \; r.action = Fwd(prt, S_j))$$
$$where \; Rules_m = \{(r_m, dp) \; where \; (\{r_m\} \in S_j \; and \; dp = \{r_m\} \cap \{r\} \cap I) \; if \; \{r_m\} \cap \{r\} \cap I \neq \varnothing\}$$

$$Pass \; \frac{FDD, \{r\} \cup S, \varnothing, \varnothing,}{FDD, S, \varnothing, \varnothing} \quad if \; no \; other \; rule \; applies$$

$$Apply \; \frac{FDD, S, (r_m, dp) \cup Rules_m, F}{construct_{FDD}(FDD, dp), S, Rules'_m, F'} \quad if(dp \setminus F \neq \varnothing)$$
$$where \; \begin{cases} F' = \{r_m\} \cup F \; if(verify\_Sw(r_m, F)) \wedge F' = \varnothing \; otherwise \wedge \\ Rules'_m = Rules_m \cup \{(r_n, r_n \cap dp) \; where \; condition\_add\} \end{cases}$$

$$Stop \; \frac{FDD, \varnothing, \varnothing, \varnothing}{FDD}$$

inference rule allows also to define the set Rules$_m$ if the action of the parsed rule r is forward to another switch S$_j$, therefore this set contains rules from the switch S$_j$ that match the set of packets matched by previous traffic. The rule apply allows to route all traffic according to rules matched and actions FORWARD. So the idea implemented by this inference system is as follows: For each flow entry from the switch S$_{in}$, we verify if its action is to forward to another switch, in this case, we parse flow entries of the new switch until we obtain a flow entry with an action drop, FwdFirewall or a forward to another switch already parsed. Therefore, the condition to add a flow entry to the set of rules to be parsed is described, as follows:

$$condition\_add = \left\{ r_n.action = Fwd(prt, S_k) \wedge \{r_n\} \in S_k \wedge (r_n \cap dp \neq \varnothing) \wedge S_k \notin switches(dp) \right\}$$

The flow entries decision diagram of all sets Sin is defined as follows:

$$FeDD = \cup FDD$$

Inference System for Dealing With Set Rules

For a flow rule, we must consider various Set-Field actions, which can rewrite the values of respective header fields in packets that can affect the process of verification. Therefore, before constructing FeDD we have to analyze the impact of these modifications on the flow rules.

The inference system shown in Figure 2 allows to find and assign effective actions to direct paths that have the action set-field. In our work we are interested in discovering switches misconfigurations, therefore, knowing the effective action applied on each direct path is an unavoidable step.

Figure 2. Inference system for dealing with set rules

$$Init \overline{DP - Set, FeDD, \varnothing, \varnothing}$$

$$Parse \frac{\{dp - set\} \cup DP - Set, FeDD, \varnothing, \varnothing}{DP - Set, FeDD, dp_s el, DP - match} \qquad where \quad DP - match = \{dp \in FeDD, dp - set \cap modify - Field(dp - set) \neq \varnothing \wedge S_k \in dp.flowEntries\}$$

$$Update - FeDD \frac{DP - Set, FeDD, dp - set, DP - match}{DP - Set, FeDD', \varnothing, \varnothing} \quad if(\forall dp \in DP - match \; dp.action \neq set - Field(f1, f2))$$
$$where \quad FeDD' = set - action(FeDD, dp - set, Action(DP - match))$$

$$Pass \frac{DP - Set, FeDD, dp - set, DP - match}{DP - Set, FeDD, \varnothing, \varnothing} \quad if \; no \; other \; rule \; applies$$

$$Success \frac{DP - Set, FeDD, \varnothing, \varnothing}{FeDD} \quad if(\forall dp \in FeDD, dp.action \neq undefined)$$

$$Failure \frac{DP - Set, FeDD, \varnothing, \varnothing}{Failure} \quad if \; success \; is \; not \; applied$$

Our inference system is applied on four variables, The first one is the set **DP-Set** which contains all direct paths in our FeDD where actions of these direct paths is equal to "Set-Field(Field1, Field2) and Forward(S_k)".

$$DP - Set = \{dp \in FeDD, dp.action = Set - Field(Field1, Field2) \wedge Fwd(Sk)\}$$

We should find the real action applied by these direct paths.

The second one is our FeDD constructed using the inference system defined in the previous section. The Third component dp_match contains all direct paths from FeDD that match the same packets as a given direct path.

The main inference rule in this inference system is update_FeDD, it allows to update Fedd by assigning the effective action applied a given direct path. In fact, for each direct path from the set DP-Set we try to find this action by verifying if direct path that match the modified direct path (i.e., we modify field1 by field2) and have the switch S_k in their path (dp.flowEntries contains a flow entry from the switch S_k) have all the same action, if it is the case we assign this effective action to the direct path otherwise we consider the action as undefined (This indicative will help us to find misconfigurations in the next steps of our work).

We have to precise that the new direct paths of our set Dp-match could contain other direct paths that have the action set-field, therefore in this case we will re-add the direct path dp-set to the set DP-Set and we will find all applied actions recursively.

The rule Success will be applied if after updating FeDD all actions are defined and the inference rule Failure will be applied otherwise.

We used two functions in this inference system:

Figure 3. Inference system for discovering misconfigurations

$Init$ $\dfrac{}{FeDD, \varnothing, \varnothing, \varnothing}$

$Parse$ $\dfrac{\{dp_i\} \in FeDD, TMC, PMC, \varnothing}{FeDD, TMC, PMC, dp_v}$ $where$ $\begin{cases} dp_v = Modify - Field(dp_i) & if(dp_i.action = set - destinationAddress(f1, d2) \wedge Fwd(S_k)) \\ dp_v = dp_i & otherwise \end{cases}$

$Detec_{misc}$ $\dfrac{FeDD, TMC, PMC, dp_v}{FeDD, fedd, TMC', PMC', \varnothing}$ $if(((dp_v.act \neq FwdFirewall) \vee !Looped(dp_v)) \wedge dom(dp_v) \nsubseteq FR^{dp_v.act})$

$where$ $\begin{cases} TMC' = \{dp_v\} \cup TMC & if(dp_v.act! = undefined \wedge (dom(dp_v) \cap FR^{dp_v.act} = \varnothing)) \wedge \\ PMC' = \{dp_v\} \cup PMC & if(dp_v.act = undefined \vee (dom(dp_v) \cap FR^{dp_v.act} \neq \varnothing)) \end{cases}$

$Pass$ $\dfrac{FeDD, TMC, PMC, dp_v}{FeDD, TMC, PMC, \varnothing}$ $if\ no\ other\ rules\ applies$

$Success$ $\dfrac{\varnothing, \varnothing, \varnothing, \varnothing}{Success}$

$Failure$ $\dfrac{\varnothing, TMC, PMC, \varnothing}{(TMC, PMC)}$ $if\ (TMC \neq \varnothing \vee PMC \neq \varnothing)$

modify-Field(dp-set) which allows to modify fields of the direct path dp-set by replacing field1 by field2.

Action(DP-match): This function returns the action applied by direct paths in the set Dp-match, if all the direct paths apply the same action, otherwise, it returns undefined.

Set-action(FeDD, dp-set,act), this function allows to update FeDD by assigning the action act to the direct path dp-set.

Inference System for Discovering Misconfigurations

In Figure 3, we propose an inference system to discover total and partial misconfigurations. Inference rules are applied on quadruple (FeDD, fedd, TMC, PMC), where FeDD is the set of all flow entries decision diagrams of all paths in our network. fedd is a temporary variable, we use it to parse direct paths of each fedd, TMC and PMC are the sets of total and partial misconfigurations respectively.

The inference rule parse allows to define the direct path to be verified. In most cases is the direct path dpi but in some cases when the dpi.path contains a flow entry that have the action set-Field where field is a destination address, the direct path to be verified is the direct path modified by replacing the destination address with the new one.

The main inference rule in this system is Detect misc, it deals with each direct path and compares the domain of this direct path with the set of packets of the firewall configuration that applies the same action as this direct path. If it is partially or not included by this set then we have a partial or a total misconfiguration. And if the action of the direct path is undefined then we consider this direct path partially misconfigured.

Figure 4. Inference system for Extracting accepted denied

Init	$$(FR, \varnothing, \varnothing)$$
Add_Deny	$$\dfrac{(\{r \Rightarrow deny\} \cup FR, FR^{accept}, FR^{deny})}{(FR, FR^{accept}, FR^{deny} \cup (dom(r) \smallsetminus FR^{accept}))}$$
Add_Accept	$$\dfrac{(\{r \Rightarrow accept\} \cup FR, FR^{accept}, FR^{deny})}{(FR, FR^{accept} \cup (dom(r) \smallsetminus FR^{deny}), FR^{deny})}$$
Stop	$$\dfrac{(\varnothing, FR^{accept}, FR^{deny})}{Stop}$$

The Success rule is applied when we parse all direct paths of all fedd in our network without identifying a misconfiguration (total or partial). Failure is applied when at least one configuration error is identified.

Inference System for Extracting Accepted and Denied Packets

In Figure 4, we propose an Inference system that presents necessary and sufficient steps for extracting accepted and denied packets from a firewall configuration FR.

We extract the accepted and denied packets before and after removing each rule from the firewall configuration, two cases can be faced:

- **Case 1:** FR^{accept} (before removing $r_{\{i\}}$) is equal to FR^{accept} (after removing r_i}) and FR^{deny} (before removing r_i) is equal to FR^{deny} (after removing r_i): In this case, we can remove r_i safely without altering the firewall behavior.
- **Case 2:** FR^{accept} (before removing r_i) is different from FR^{accept} (after removing r_i) and/or FR^{deny} (before removing r_i) is different from FR^{deny} (after removing r_i): in this case we should maintain r_i in the configuration file.

CASE STUDY

We have chosen to apply our approach on a case study of the network topology shown in Figure 5.

The firewall configuration that should be implemented is shown in Table 1. Configurations of three switches are depicted in Tables 2, 3 and 4 respectively. As

Figure 5. Network topology

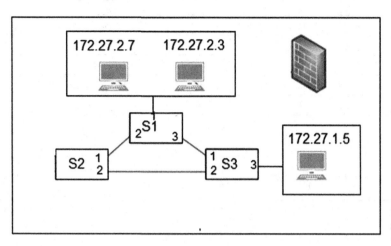

Table 1. Firewall Configuration

Rule N°	Source	Destination	Port	Action
1	172.27.2.7	172.27.1.5	*	drop
2	172.27.2.7	*	22	accept
3	172.27.2.3	*	*	accept
4	172.27.1.5	*	*	accept
5	172.27.2.0/24	*	*	accept
6	*	*	*	drop

Table 2. Switch1 configuration

FE N°	Source	Destination	Port	Action
1	*	172.27.1.5	*	Fwd(S3)
2	172.27.2.3	*	*	Fwd(S2)
3	172.27.2.7	*	*	Fwd(S2)
4	172.2.3.7	*	*	Fwd(S3)
5	*	*	*	drop

defined in the previous section, the first step is to construct FeDD and find paths of packets using configurations of our three switches.

First and before that we should define possible inputs. We have three sets of possible input addresses:

Table 3. Switch2 configuration

FE N°	Source	Destination	Port	Action
1	172.27.2.7	172.27.1.5	*	Fwd(S3)
2	172.2.2.0/24	*	*	Fwd(S3)
3	172.27.2.7	172.27.1.5	22	Set-Srce(172.27.2.7,172.27.2.3) && Fwd(S3)
4	172.27.1.5	*	*	Fwd(S3)
5	*	*	*	drop

Table 4. Switch3 configuration

FE N°	Source	Destination	Port	Action
1	172.27.2.7	172.27.1.5	*	Fwd(port 3)
2	172.27.1.5	172.27.2.7	*	Fwd-Firewall
3	172.27.1.5	*	*	Fwd(S2)
4	172.27.2.3	172.27.1.5	*	drop
5	*	*	*	drop

I1={172.27.2.7, 172.27.2.3} which is linked to switch S1.

I2={172.27.1.5} which is linked to switch S3.

I3 = {* / I1 U I2} which is the set of possible input address sources that could income to switch S2.

Constructing Flow Entries Decision Diagram

As we explained in previous section: FeDD= U FDD. We have three sets of possible input address sources. By applying inference system shown in Figure 6. we will obtain FDD shown on Figures 6, 7 and 8 respectively.

Dealing With Set Flow Entries

After constructing FeDD and defining different actions that could be applied on different packets of our network. We should find actions of different direct paths that have the action (set-Field, Fwd(S_k)). In our case we have one direct path:

Dp2 in FDD1 Shown in Figure 6

Figure 6. fedd1

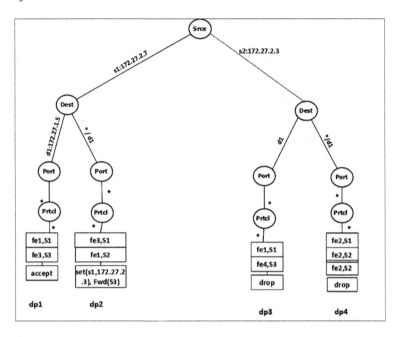

Figure 7. fedd2

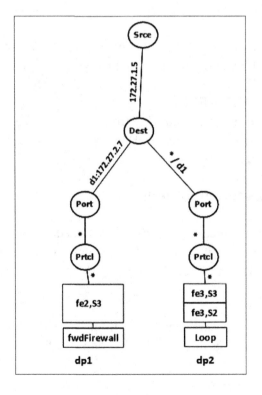

Figure 8. fedd3

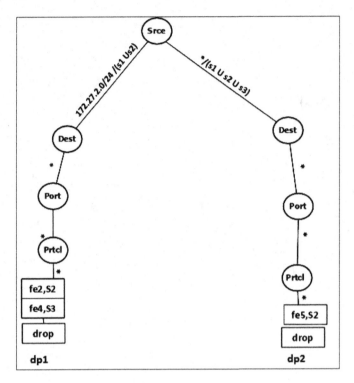

By applying the inference system shown in Figure 6, we should find different direct paths in FeDD that match the modified direct path dp2 (i.e., by replacing 172.27.2.7 by 172.27.2.3 in the field source address) and have a flow entry applied by S3 in their field dp.FlowEntries.

In our case we have direct paths dp3 from FDD1 and the action of this direct path is **drop** therefore we update our FDD by assigning the action drop to the direct path dp2 from FDD1.

Discovering Misconfigurations

Once ensured that all direct paths have an assigned action, we proceed to the discovering of misconfigurations using the inference system previously described in section. We parse all paths of FeDD, for each path we verify if we have an effective misconfiguration:

- **For FDD1:** For packets incoming from the set I1, we have two total misconfigurations, in direct paths dp1 and dp2(the action assigned to the direct path dp2 is drop and the action applied by the firewall is accept). Also we have two partial misconfigurations on direct paths dp3 and dp4.

- **For FDD2**: In this FeDD no misconfiguration are discovered. For dp1, the action applied is redirect to the firewall which is perforce with respect to the firewall. And for the direct path dp2, we cannot make a decision because packet passed by this direct path will be forwarded from S3 to S2 which will by his turn forward it again to S3, therefore this direct path contains a LOOP and no final decision is made.

- **For FDD3**: The direct path dp1 is totally misconfigured, all packets matched by this direct path have a different action as applied in the firewall. The direct path dp2 is partially misconfigured.

DISCUSSION

One of the most intriguing finding from IBM's "2014 Cyber Security Intelligence Index" is that over 95% of all security incidents investigated involve human error, and one of the most commonly recorded form of human errors includes network system misconfiguration. Therefore, it is clear that manual management of SDN switches misconfiguration is the cause of security risk posed to the enterprise. In fact, a typical organization may need to make switches configurations modifications hundreds of times in a month, where each configuration change requires a lot of evaluation time. Therefore, having an effective SDN switches configuration change management tool that allows detecting and correcting automatically misconfigurations arising after these changes is a key. In our work and by using the firewall configuration we facilitate this task to these organizations, because a firewall configuration change may impact several switches and managing this impact by understanding which one of SDN switches configurations need to be modified is not a non-trivial task. By inspecting all paths of switches and all relations between all flow entries we can help the network administrator to automatically discover and correct these misconfigurations..

CONCLUSION

We presented in this paper a set of inference systems for the management of misconfigurations of OpenFlow switches rule sets. More precisely, our proposal is intended for discovering these misconfigurations by using a formal method and a data structure (FeDD). The advantages of our proposal are the following: First, the detection approach is optimal, using the minimum number of operations. Second, we considered all rules, all actions and all modifications using the action set-Field that can be used and not considered by all previous work. While the current approach primarily focuses on discovering switches misconfigurations, in our future work, we plan to resolve these misconfigurations. We are also interested in developing a tool that allows to perform automatically all proposed techniques and test this tool on Cisco Open Network Environment for Government (Cisco, n.d.) which is a comprehensive solution designed to help government network infrastructures become more open, programmable, and application-aware.

REFERENCES

Al-Shaer, E., & Al-Haj, S. (2010). FlowChecker: configuration analysis and verification of federated openflow infrastructures. *3rd ACM Workshop on Assurable and Usable Security Configuration, SafeConfig 2010*, 37-44.

Ball, T., Bjørner, N., Gember, A., Itzhaky, S., Karbyshev, A., Sagiv, M., . . . Valadarsky, A. (2014). VeriCon: towards verifying controller programs in software-defined networks. *SIGPLAN Conference on Programming Language Design and Implementation*, 282-293.

Canini, M., Venzano, D., Peresíni, P., Kostic, D., & Rexford, J. (2012), A NICE Way to Test OpenFlow Applications. *Proceedings of the 9th {USENIX} Symposium on Networked Systems Design and Implementation*, 127-140.

Cisco. (n.d.). Cisco open network environment for government. *Cisco*. Retrieved from: https://www.cisco.com/c/en/us/solutions/industries/government/us-government-solutions-services/software-defined-networking.html

Foster, N., Harrison, R., Freedman, M. J., Monsanto, C., Rexford, J., Story, A., & Walker, D. (2011) Frenetic: a network programming language. ICFP 2011, Tokyo, Japan. doi:10.1145/2034773.2034812

Gouda, M.G. & Liu, A.X. (2006). Structured firewall design. *Computer Networks*. doi:10.1016/j.comnet.2006.06.015

Hu, H., Han, W., Ahn, G-J & Zhao, Z. (2014) FLOWGUARD: building robust firewalls for software-defined networks. *Proceedings of the workshop on Hot topics in software defined networking*, 97-102.

Kazemian, P., Chan, M., Zeng, H., Varghese, G., McKeown, N., & Whyte, S. (2013). Real Time Network Policy Checking Using Header Space Analysis. *Proceedings of the 10th USENIX Symposium on Networked Systems Design and Implementation*, 99—111.

Liu, A. X. (2008). Formal Verification of Firewall Policies. *IEEE International Conference on Communications*, 1494-1498.

Chapter 7
A Review of Dynamic Verification of Security and Dependability Properties

Antonio Muñoz
University of Málaga, Spain

Jamal Toutouh
University of Málaga, Spain

Francisco Jaime
University of Málaga, Spain

ABSTRACT

This chapter reviews the notions of security and dependability properties from the perspective of software engineering, providing the reader with a technical background on dynamic verification and runtime monitoring techniques. The chapter covers the technical background on security and dependability properties with system verification through dynamic verification or monitoring. The authors initially provide a short overview of the security and dependability properties themselves. Once definitions of security and dependability properties are introduced, they present a critical analysis of current research on dynamic verification by presenting general purpose and security oriented dynamic verification approaches.

DOI: 10.4018/978-1-5225-7353-1.ch007

INTRODUCTION

This chapter is a survey that covers the technical background on security and dependability properties, with system verification through dynamic verification or monitoring. We initially provide a short overview of the security and dependability properties themselves. Once definitions of security and dependability properties are introduced, we present a critical analysis of current research on dynamic verification by presenting general purpose and security oriented dynamic verification approaches. We clarify that a security property is the preservation of confidentiality, integrity, accountability, non-repudiation and availability of information.

We also provide a comparative discussion on the presented security and dependability dynamic verification lines of research. For our purposes, dynamic verification are methods that aim to show that desired properties are hold based on observation of the run-time behavior of a system and its interaction with its operational environment.

Additionally, the chapter gives an overview of the research in the area of abductive reasoning, which is a characteristic key of the main approach of this work. Therefore, we highlight the basic aspects of abductive reasoning, together with some recent relevant research approaches.

DYNAMIC VERIFICATION OF SECURITY PROPERTIES

In first place, a review of security properties is given, and then the most relevant dynamic verification mechanisms are described. We distinguish between languages for expressing security properties for dynamic verification and languages for expressing all types of properties for dynamic verification.

Most of the approaches deploy languages based on some sort of temporal logic, as these languages provide the necessary operators for expressing conditions about the temporal ordering and boundaries of occurrence of events, which is required for the expression of most of the properties that need to be verified at runtime. The most popular formal notation for expressing security properties is Linear Temporal Logic (LTL), or extensions of it, and languages with similar expressive power such as Event Calculus.

Some dynamic verification techniques reason about systems at both, low and high level of abstraction, such as Primitive Event Definition Language (PEDL) and Meta Event Definition Language (MEDL) in Java Monitoring and Checking (JavaMaC) framework (Lee, 1999). PEDL is used for writing low-level specifications and is tightly related to the programming language, while MEDL specification makes use of primitive events and conditions in order to state high-level requirements.

Security

Security requirements cover issues related to integrity, confidentiality, availability, non-repudiation, authentication, authorization and privacy (Sun Microsystems, 2003; Verisign, 2005). A complete revision of this topic is out of the scope of this chapter, however (Avizienis, 2000) includes some approaches related to dependability properties. Avizienis defined dependability as "the ability of a (computer) system to avoid failures that are more frequent or more sever, and outage durations that are longer, than is acceptable to the user(s)" and "deliver service that can be justifiably trusted". We defend that security properties can be considered as a subset of the dependability properties set, as the security properties of a system aim to prevent unaccepted leak of private information, a man in the middle attack (Lowe, 1995), and/or unaccepted delays in the delivery of the provided services (denial of service attack (Alvarez, 2003).

A key element is the notion of "justifiable trust" based on the ability to verify in an objective way that the delivered system does not deviate from the required system behavior. Thus the development of system verification capabilities has been the focus of significant research over the last decades, giving as a result the development of a wide spectrum of methods offering such capabilities, which are classified into static and dynamic.

On the one hand, static verification methods are based on one fact: the desired properties of a system will always hold solely based on the specification of the system, without considering its actual run-time behavior.

On the other hand, dynamic verification methods aim to show that desired properties are hold based on observation of the run-time behavior of a system and its interaction with its operational environment.

Static verification is not the focus of this work, we do not provide an overview of methods that fall in this category. However, a brief overview of dynamic verification of systems follows in the next sections of this work.

Dynamic Verification

Dynamic verification enables a software system to improve its security (and therefore dependability), by checking whether its behavior satisfies specific dependability and security properties while it is running. The traditional way of carrying this out, is by means of the monitoring of the execution of a system and the checking of its conformity with the specification of previously set rules.

The arrival of emerging ambient intelligent and ubiquitous environments is making software systems more reliable on technologies such as mobile code and components off the shelf (COTS). One relevant statement is that the static verification and testing of dynamically adapted entities cannot provide adequate results, each one for different reasons. Static verification is a formal method and can prove that a system (or to be more accurate its model) is correct, but it is very time consuming and demands a substantial education and experience from practitioners. On the other hand, testing (Lee, 1996) is an informal method that cannot prove the correctness of a system, since it can never offer a complete coverage of all its possible executions. However this method presents an interesting appeal because it can be easily applied even from inexperienced practitioners. An alternative to these two methods lies in the dynamic verification, which aims to achieve the benefits of both approaches. These methods are based on merging testing and formal specification. Some authors consider dynamic verification as formal methods applied to the implementation of a system, avoiding the pitfalls of ad hoc testing and the complexity of full blown static verification techniques. The dynamic verification of systems has been an active topic for research in several areas, including requirements engineering, program verification, safety critical systems and service centric systems (Pino, 2017).

Several stages set up the dynamic verification (Barringer, 2004; d'Amorim, 2005; Havelund, 2004; Spanoudakis, 2006; Muñoz, 2011; Comuzzi, 2010; Koulouris, 2007; Muñoz, 2013), which are (i) the specification of a formal specification of a system, including safety and security properties, (ii) the application of methods for capturing events of interest and (iii) checking for violations by a monitor, which can verify whether the observed behavior of a system satisfies the required properties or not.

Nevertheless, there are cases such as Aspect Oriented Programming (Kiczales,1997) and Monitoring Oriented Programming (Chen,2003) in which a monitor is automatically generated and the code is instrumented. The monitor is inserted into the code to be monitored. Thus, in such cases, the second stage includes the monitor generation as well. In all other cases, monitors are considered to be software modules separately implemented (Artho, 2004; Havelund,2004) from the monitored system. In these cases, the monitor inputs are the formal specification of the system (products of first stage) and the flow of events generated during the execution of the system. Then, the monitor can check the conformance of the captured runtime behavior of the system (events flows) against the intended system behavior (formal specification).

In a conceptual model, the subject of dynamic verification signified by the class *MonitorableEntity* can be either a System or a System's Environment. Dynamic verification is carried out by a Monitor which observes the Runtime Behavior of a system or its environment. The Runtime Behavior is a set of events generated during the operation of the monitorable entities. These events are generated by one or more Event Generator according to different Event Emission Specifications. An event emission specification describes the particular Event Emission Method to be used and one or more Event Emission Descriptions, which describe the exact types of events that should be generated. The observation of the events in a Runtime Behavior by the Monitor is carried out according to a specific Monitoring Policy, which specifies the Monitoring Properties that should be verified at runtime and the set of Monitoring Actions the Monitor should perform to enable the system control and/or recover violations of the monitoring properties.

GENERAL PURPOSE SYSTEMS DYNAMIC VERIFICATION

In most cases, formal specification of the requirements that are to be dynamically verified is based on Linear Temporal Logic (LTL) (Pnuelli,1977) and variations of it including past and future time LTL (ptLTL and ftLTL respectively). Past and future time Linear Temporal Logics are modal logics for specifying properties of concurrent reactive systems and are used for analysing traces of execution of such systems. ptLTL provides temporal operators that refer to the past states of an execution trace, while ftLTL provides temporal operators that refer to the future/ remaining part of an execution trace. In particular, the Temporal Rover (TR) tool (Pnuelli,1977) supports a future and past time Metric Temporal Logic (MTL). MTL (Chang,1994) extends LTL with relative time and real time constraints.

Havelund et al. (2001,2008) have developed several algorithms, which are relative to temporal logic generation and monitoring. For instance, they propose algorithms for past time logic generation by using dynamic programming (Havelund,2002). They have also used the MAUDE rewriting engine (Robinson,2002), for monitoring future time logic (Havelund,2008) and have proposed algorithms that generate Büchi automata adapted to finite trace LTL (Giannakopoulou,2001).

Other logic/languages used for properties formalization are EAGLE (Barringer,2004) and HAWK (d'Amorim,2005). EAGLE is a rule-based language, which essentially extends the μ-calculus with data parameterization and past time logic. HAWK can be viewed as a specialization of EAGLE for JAVA, as it supports data binding and object reasoning. HAWK further extends EAGLE with event expressions, where events are restricted to method calls and returns. The integration of programming and logic as well as the notation and semantics of event expressions are similar to those used in modal logics like the π-calculus. HAWK also supports extended regular expressions.

According to the concept of Design by Contract (DBC) technique, introduced by Meyer (2000) as a built-in feature of the Eiffel programming language, specifications of pre-conditions and post-conditions can be associated with a class in the form of assertions and invariants and subsequently be compiled into runtime checks. Jass (Moller,2001) and jContractor(Abercrombie,2002) are two java-based DBC systems. Jass is a pre-compiler, which turns the assertion comments into Java code. The JASS sub-language for specifying trace assertions is similar to CSP (Hoare,1985), and its syntax is more like a programming language. jContractor is implemented as a Java library, which allows programmers to associate contracts, consisting of pre/ post- conditions and invariants, with any Java class or interface.

The Monitoring and Checking (MaC) framework (Lee,1999) is based on a logic that combines a form of past time LTL and models real-time via explicit clock variables. JAVA MAC (Kim,2001), a prototype implementation of the MaC framework for monitoring and controlling applications written in Java, defines an event-based language to describe monitors. Note that, in the context of the Java MaC framework, events refer to information that holds instantly during the system runtime, while conditions are defined to illustrate information that holds for a time period. The Java MaC framework is composed of two specification event-based languages: the Primitive Event Definition Language (PEDL) and the Meta Event Definition Language (MEDL). PEDL is used for writing low-level specifications and is tightly related to the programming language. As such, it deals with primitive events and conditions that might occur during the program execution, which are defined using program entities such as variables and methods. The operations on events and conditions can be used to construct more complex events and conditions from the primitive ones. A MEDL specification then makes use of these primitive events and conditions in order to state high-level requirements. Using MEDL, a user can specify the correctness requirements declaratively, without worrying about declaration of variables of primitive types which can be updated by user-defined assignment statements upon arrival of new events. These variables can be referred to in formulas.

Mahbub (2004) developed a framework for monitoring the behavior of service centric systems, which is used to specify formulas describing behavioral and quality properties of service centric systems. In the area of component based programming, Barnett and Schulte (2001) have proposed a framework that uses executable interface specifications and a monitor to check behavioral equivalence between a component and its interface specification. In this framework, there is no need for recompiling, re-linking, or any sort of invasive instrumentation at all, due to the fact that a proxy module is used for event emission. The component's interface specifications are written in the Abstract State Machine Language (AsmL) (Gurevich,2001), which is based on Abstract State Machines (ASM) (Gurevich,1993). This language is executable and supports non-deterministic specifications. Having native COM connectivity, one can not only specify and simulate components in AsmL but also a substitute low-level implementation by high-level specifications. Specifications written in AsmL are operational specifications of the behavior expected of any implementation. They provide a minimal model by constraining implementations as little as possible.

Robinson (2002) proposed a framework for requirements monitoring based on code instrumentation, in which the high-level requirements to be monitored are expressed in KAOS. KAOS (Shanahan,1999) is a framework for goal oriented requirements specification which is based on temporal logic. The KAOS modelling language can support all the phases of requirements acquisition and modelling, starting from initial functional and non-functional goals, formalizing the meaning of such goals using temporal logic formulas and assigning the responsibility for the achievement of these goals to potential agents, which may signify the system in question systems that interoperate with it, and human actors interacting with the system. KAOS has also been used by Feather et al (1998) in a framework they developed to monitor system requirements at runtime, incorporating some capabilities regarding the reconciliation of requirements with the runtime system behavior.

SOFTWARE SYSTEMS MONITORING

In this context, diagnosis focuses on the detection of system failures. Diagnosis typically involves the identification of trajectories of system observations, which have led to a failure. By using automata that recognizes faulty behavior (Bouyer,2005; Grastien, 2005; Pencolé, 2005; Tripakis, 2002), diagnosis is carried through the synchronization of automata modelling the expected behavior of a monitored system and the events captured from it. Pencolé and Cordier (2005) propose a similar but decentralized approach where synchronization is performed for individual system components and then aggregated for the global system.

The problem of fault diagnosis, concerning time, has been studied and analyzed by Tripakis (2002) and Bouyer et al (2005), where the system is modelled as a timed automaton. Timed automata extend the finite state machine model with real time clocks (Alur,1994). In both (Tripakis, 2002; Bouyer,2005), the goals is the devising of algorithms (diagnosis) that would function as efficient online fault detectors of internal faults for any given sequence of observable events generated by the system. Tripakis has worked on the diagnosability of a timed system (plan). In particular, Tripakis has shown that the problem of checking whether a given timed system is diagnosable or not, is a decidable problem and a diagnoser can be constructed as an online algorithm in case that the system is indeed diagnosable. The Δ-diagnosibility diagnosis algorithm proposed by Tripakis is based on state estimation in order to decide whether a fault has occurred and report the fault almost Δ time units after its occurrence, for a given set of observations. In particular, the Δ-diagnosability algorithm keeps track of several possible control states and time ranges (zones) where the clock values can be in. The Δ-diagnosibility problem for timed automata is PSPACE-complete. The complexity to diagnose faults from an observation is doubly exponential with respect to the final states of the system and to the size of the observations.

Due to the high complexity of the Δ-diagnosibility algorithm by Tripakis(2002), Boyer et al. (2005) describe a diagnose, with lower complexity, more appropriate for online diagnosis. Bouyer et al. suggest two deterministic timed automata for realizing an efficient online diagnose. On one hand, Bouyer et al. consider general deterministic timed automata (DTA) for realizing efficient online diagnosers. Bouyer et al. have proved that the problem of checking whether there is a realizable DTA diagnose for a given timed system, provided that the number of clocks and the set of constants are well defined and available to the diagnose, is a decidable problem and is 2EXPTIME-complete. On the other hand, Bouyer et al. study the fault diagnosis problem considering a subclass of DTAs called Event Recording Automata (ERA) (Alur,1994). In the context of ERA, there is an implicit clock attached to each action. The problem of checking whether there is a diagnose realizable as an ERA, provided that the number of clocks and the set of constants are well defined and available to the diagnoser, is decidable and PSPACE-complete.

In (Pencolé,2005), a decentralized model-based approach for diagnosing discrete event systems was proposed. In particular, the proposed formal framework is based on communicating automata for computing online diagnosis of large discrete event systems. According to the authors, the diagnosis is defined as the identification of failure events and their propagations, which can explain the system observations. The system observations are split into temporal windows. For each temporal window, diagnosis (subsystem diagnosis) is performed for each well-defined subsystem of the system. The subsystem diagnoses are, then, merged to build the overall diagnosis for the system (global diagnosis). Each subsystem is modelled as a communicating finite state machine. The explicit behavior of each subsystem can be computed by using a synchronization operation, which is based on a transition system product (Arnold, 1987) and applied to the component models of the subsystem.

SECURITY ORIENTED SYSTEMS

Some of the logics and languages reviewed in the previous sections have also been used either as they were initially proposed or with some semantic modifications and extensions for the formalization of security properties. Naldurg et al (2004), for instance, have proposed a framework for intrusion detection which takes advantage of a system. EAGLE is suitable for expressing temporal patterns that involve reasoning about the data values observed in individual events and thus it allows the description of attacks whose signatures appear to have statistical properties e.g., password guessing or denial of service attacks.

In the area of intrusion detection, (Lazarevic,2005) presents a complete survey. Ko et al (1997) have proposed a specification-based approach, which uses dynamic verification techniques to detect exploitations of vulnerabilities in security-critical programs. According to this framework, one has to specify a trace policy which describes the intended behavior of programs with regards to security properties. A trace policy determines security-valid operation sequences of the execution of one or more programs. For specifying such trace policies, Ko et al. (1997) have developed a grammar, called "parallel environment grammar (PE-grammar)" whose alphabet consists of system operations. A PE-grammar can express various classes of security trace policies, including behavior related access to system objects, synchronization, and operation sequencing and race conditions in concurrent or distributed programs.

Schneider (1998) developed a system called Execution Monitoring (EM), which can monitor violations of security policies by monitoring the execution steps of a system. This system is based on the security automata of Alpern and Schneider (1987), which are a special type of Büchi automata. EM also incorporate mechanisms that can terminate the system execution if it is about to violate its security policy. Following the same automata-based formalism, Ligatti et al (2005) extended the control capabilities of security automata by proposing edit automata, which can remove and add letters (i.e., system actions) to the words (i.e. execution traces) they recognize. On their part Bandara et al. (2003) specified a language based on Event Calculus to model the system behavior and write security policy specifications. The form of EC, which is used in this work, was presented in (Russo,2002). Janicke et al (2005) proposed a security model that allows expressing dynamic access control policies, which can be either time or event-driven. A system's overall security policy can then be composed out of smaller policies which capture specific requirements and which can be individually verified. The advantage of the access control model used in this work is that it allows expressing both parallel and sequential composition. Janicke based their security model on Interval Temporal Logic (ITL), a flexible notation for both propositional and first order reasoning about intervals of time. An important reason of choosing ITL was the availability of an executable subset of the logic, known as Tempura (Moszkowski,1996).

Brisset (2000) worked on establishing and ensuring the correct operation of a Java platform security mechanism for runtime authorization of not trusted applications in remote hosts. The resulting Java security mechanism, which is called *SecurityManager* and belongs to the JAVA runtime library. Sekar (2003) presented an approach called model-carrying code (MCC) for mobile code security. The main components of MCC are: (a) a policy language for specifying security policies and a compiler for this language, (b) a language for specifying program behavior models and techniques for extracting them, and (c) a policy refinement component which is based on model-checking techniques. Their language for policies and behavior models is called Behavior Monitoring Specification Language (BMSL) and it is compiled into extended finite state automata (EFSA). For thoroughness we shall also mention certain high-level languages and frameworks, which have been proposed for security requirements and policies. The KAOS framework, which we have already examined in a previous section on general-purpose formalism, has been extended for modelling, specifying and analyzing security requirements (van Lamsweerde,2006) by including classical security concepts as Adversaries/ attackers, threats and assets. The Confidentiality, Integrity, Availability, Privacy, Authentication and Non-repudiation requirements are sub-classes of the meta-class SecurityGoal in KAOS. Finally, the formal first-order, real-time, linear temporal logic of KAOS has been augmented with epistemic operators (Knows, Belief), which are needed in security-related properties (e.g. Authorizes, UnderControl, Integrity or Using predicates).

Damianou (2001) have defined Ponder as a declarative, object-oriented language to specify security policies to be monitored and applied at runtime. Ponder can be used to specify security policies regarding role-based access control to system resources, and general-purpose system management policies. Ponder was designed with the intention to be an extensible security policy specification language that would be able to cater for future types of policies and, rather than assuming a particular implementation platform, it could map to, and co-exist with, different underlying platforms.

In Service Oriented Computing, Baresi and Guinea (2005) have proposed a framework for runtime monitoring on WS-BPEL processes. Monitoring rules are weaved at runtime into the process they must monitor and a proxy module supports their dynamic selection and execution (Baresi,2005). Finally, they proposed a user-oriented language to integrate data acquisition and analysis into monitoring rules. Their monitoring rules define runtime constraints on WS-BPEL process executions and are expressed using the WSCoL language (Web Service Constraint Language). The development of this language has been inspired by the Java Modelling Language (JML) (Leavens, 2003). WS-CoL is a domain-independent policy assertion language for specifying user requirements (constraints) on the execution of Web services, which can be used within the framework of WS-Policy (Schlimmer,2006) and WS-Security (Kaler,2005). WS-CoL is an assertion language augmented with features for allowing one to retrieve information that originates outside the process. It distinguishes between data collection and data analysis to differentiate the phase in which information is collected (data collection), from the phase in which this data is analyzed (data analysis). Data can be collected from the process directly (e.g., values of internal variables) but they can also come from external sources (e.g., exchanged SOAP messages). An example of a monitoring rule in this language could specify that all exchanged messages must be encrypted using the 3DES encryption algorithm.

THE SECOND STAGE IN DYNAMIC VERIFICATION PROCESS. CAPTURING EVENTS

In the second stage of the general dynamic verification process, the goal is to apply techniques so as to capture the real behavior of the system during its execution. Current event emission methods can be divided into code modifying ones. Code modifying event emission methods require direct access to the source or binary code of a system in order to insert code statements that will generate events of interest. Code instrumentation is an example of a code modifying event emission method in which event generation statements are manually inserted into the code of a system. On its part Aspect Oriented Programming (AOP) has also been used to generate events (through the weaving of aspects into binary or source system code). AOP is a code modifying event emission method, which can be considered as a subcategory of code instrumentation. Monitoring Oriented Programming (Chen,2003) and Design by Contract (Meyer,2000) are also code modifying event emission methods which can be regarded as subcategories of Aspect Oriented Programming (Kiczales, 1997).

Non code modifying event emission methods generate events without altering the code of a system. Such methods access, modify and/or take advantage of capabilities of the general computational environment in which a system is executed, in order to generate the events flow. Reflective middleware approaches (Capra, 2001; Capra, 2003; Mascolo, 2002), proxy-based architectures (Barnett, 2001) and the use of application programming interfaces (APIs) (Artho, 2004; Brörkens, 2002; Mahub, 2004) are examples of event emission methods that belong to this category.

Code-Modifying Event Capture Methods

Code Instrumentation

The technique of code instrumentation (Robinson, 2002) is described as the insertion of statements into the system's code (source or binary code) for monitoring purposes. Instrumentation can be done manually or automatically, e.g. by using Jtrek-JSpy (Goldberg, 2003) or Joie (Cohen, 1998), which automatically instrument Java byte code. During the execution of the instrumented code, an event stream is generated. The generated events can then be directly passed to external monitors or pre-processed before they reach the verification stage.

A tool using code instrumentation for capturing events in Java-based systems is RMon (Robinson, 2002). In RMon, requirements are initially expressed in the KAOS framework, which provides a goal-oriented formal specification language based on temporal logic. Requirements are thus specified as high level goals which must be achieved by the system. These goals must then be mapped onto low-level events which can be monitored at runtime. The system's code is then instrumented in order to capture these low level events, using the Joie framework (Cohen,1998).

In the initial phase of the Java MaC architecture (Kim, 2001), low-level specifications (written in PEDL) are inserted into the byte code of the monitored program through an automatic instrumentation procedure. Furthermore, in the MONID tool (Naldurg,2004) system-level events are generated by appropriately instrumented source code.

Aspect Oriented Programming

Aspect Oriented Programming (AOP) (Kiczales, 1997), also called Aspect Software Development (AOSD), was proposed to support the advanced identification, illustration and separation of non-functional concerns, which crosscut the system's main functionality. Complex programs include various crosscutting concerns (properties of interest such as QoS, energy consumption, fault tolerance, and security). AOP enables the separation of crosscutting concerns during the development of the software. Specifically, the code implementing crosscutting concerns of the system, called aspects, is developed separately from other parts of the system. In AOP, locations in the program where aspect code can be woven, called pointcuts, are typically identified during development. Among others, some examples of AOP approaches are AspectJ (Kiczales, 2001) and Hyper/J (Tarr, 1999).

AOP supports dynamic re-composition in three major ways. First, most adaptions are relative to some crosscutting concern, such as quality-of-service or fault tolerance. AOP enables the code associated with these aspects to be written and managed independently of the application code as well as other parts of the system, such as traditional middleware platforms. Such a separation is needed in order to dynamically replace one instantiation of a particular solution for a concern with another. Second, although compile-time aspect weaving produces a tangled executable that cannot easily be reconfigured, delaying the weaving process until runtime provides a systematic way to realize dynamic re-composition (Hirschfeld, 2004; Wagelaar, 2004). Finally, if adaptability itself is considered as a "generic" aspect (David, 2001; Yang, 2002), then runtime weaving can be used to enhance the program with adaptive behavior, not necessarily anticipated during the original development (e.g. to tolerate newly discovered faults or to detect and respond to new security attacks). This kind of upgrading is especially important in situations where the application is required to run continuously and cannot be easily halted for upgrade. However, there is a need of a formal aspect specification written in a domain-specific knowledge language or using logic, rather than the host programming language itself (Chen,2003). The mapping from specification to implementation, with the support of automatic code generation can then be formally verified.

In particular, AspectJ (Kiczales, 2001) provides an approach to implement cross-cutting features in Java. AspectJ provides a pattern mechanism, called pointcuts, for capturing groups of events, called joinpoints, that may occur during a program's operation (such as method call/receptions, constructor calls, field accesses, and exception events). The pattern matching mechanism includes regular expression matching, with wild-carding over fragments of method names, argument names, types, etc. Extra code, called advices, can be associated with pointcuts, and is inserted by the AspectJ compiler into the joinpoints. Advices can inspect and modify data that are available at joinpoint event (e.g. method-call arguments and return values), and can dynamically create new data, which is only shared with other advice.

For instance, Dingwall-Smith (2002) have developed an aspect oriented approach, in which system providers specify instrumentation code in separate classes, and define composition rules that determine how this code is to be merged with the application code, by using Hyper/J. Also, Baresi (2005) proposed a framework for runtime monitoring of WS-BPEL processes, in which monitoring rules are specified and dynamically weaved into the process they belong to. Furthermore, the instrumentation module of the JpaX framework performs a script-driven automated instrumentation of the program to be verified. JSpy (Goldberg, 2003) is the automated AOP environment package, which is used in JPaX (Havelund, 2002).

Design by Contract

Design by Contract (DBC), as proposed by Meyer (2000) for the object-oriented language Eiffel, is a practical approach to runtime checking in applications. DBC is a lightweight formal technique, which allows one to add semantic information to a program by specifying assertions regarding the program's runtime state. Then, checks for specification violations carried out at runtime. Such a technique stresses the importance of explicitly specifying the constraints that hold before (pre-conditions) and after a program is executed (post-conditions). In the context of the Eiffel object-oriented language, specification of pre/post conditions can be associated with a class in the form of assertions and invariants.

Subsequently, inserted specifications can be compiled into monitoring code. In the Java language, there are two approaches which are based on DBC. Jass (Bartetzko, 2001) is a pre-compiler which turns the assertion comments intro Java code. Properties in Jass are called trace assertions and they specify permissible sequences of method calls in a CSP-like notation. Thus, processes, parallelism, conditionals and data exchange among processes can also be expressed. However, the trace assertions are loosely interpreted; no formal semantic is provided. The Jass pre-compiler translates the trace assertions into runtime checks.

Monitoring Oriented Programming

Monitoring Oriented Programming (MOP) is a paradigm which combines a formal specification with an implementation in order to form a system. In particular, it provides a light-weight formal method for runtime specification checks against the behavior of the implementation. The general MoP paradigm is language specification formalism independent. According to Chen (2003) a MoP environment should provide the capability of adding any logic framework on top of any target programming language via logic plugins, which can be publicly accessed. A logic plug-in consists of two modules, namely the logic engine and the target language shell. Logic engine translate formulae into monitors, encoded in an abstract representation (pseudocode). Then the language shell transforms the monitor pseudocode into the target language code. Thus, the logic plug-in can be considered as the code generator of the monitor.

Non Code Modifying Event Capture Methods

Reflective Middleware

Middleware technologies (Emmerich, 2000) have been designed to support the development of distributed systems. Completely hiding implementation details from the application is very difficult in a mobile setting and not even always desirable, since mobile systems need to quickly detect and allow application designer to inspect the execution context and adapt the behavior of the middleware accordingly.

Reflection and metadata can be successfully exploited to develop middleware targeted to mobile settings. By using metadata, we separate the middleware in two parts: what the middleware does and how the middleware does it. Reflection allows applications to inspect and adapt their metadata. In this way, applications can influence the way their middleware behaves, according to their current context of execution.

Capra (2003) proposed a framework designed to ease the adaption of applications to changing execution conditions, they called it CARISMA. The model considers different layers (operating system, middleware, application and user), each of which is described using metadata in order to ease their interaction. When the application invokes a service, the middleware uses both the application metadata and the metadata reflecting the current execution conditions to decide how to offer the requested service.

Applications can also ask the middleware to be notified when specific execution conditions occur. This system allows for a fine adaption of applications, but it requires that service calls be explicitly coded in the applications. However, a complete transparency is not possible if adaption (which requires awareness) is desired.

CARISMA (Capra, 2003) is a context-awareness based reflective middleware. It includes a reflective API, which allows applications to dynamically inspect their current configuration and alter it to best suit the current environment. CARISMA maintains a representation of the execution context by interacting with the underlying network operating system. Based upon this representation, the application may behave in different ways.

XMIDDLE (Mascolo, 2002) is a middleware for mobile that focuses on the synchronization of replicated XML documents. In order to enable application-driven conflict detection and resolution, XMIDDLE supports the specification of conflict resolution policies through meta-data definitions using an XML schema.

Proxy Architecture

A proxy module acts as an intermediate between the monitored system and its environment, capturing their interaction and emitting the corresponding events. Thus, there is no need for code recompiling, re-linking or any other sort of invasive instrumentation at all. For component based programming, Barnett (2001) proposed a framework that uses executable interface specifications and a monitor to check for behavioral equivalence between a component and its interface specification. Let us assume that a client-server architecture is used.

A component P, which essentially operates as a proxy, is inserted between the client C and the server S. Using a proxy allows the interaction of the client C and the server S to be observed without having to modify either component. P can be created automatically from the definition of the interfaces, which C and S use in order to interact. The proxy forks all of the calls made from C to S so that they are concurrent execution of M and D. Then P compares the results from components M and S. P checks at each interface whether the results agree in terms of their success/failure codes as well as any return values. As long as the results are the same, they are sent to C. In any other case, S and M are deemed not to be behaviorally equivalent.

API-Based Event Capturing

In the last non code modifying event emission subcategory, one finds approaches that make use of specific APIs for capturing and emitting events. For instance, the JNuke tool takes advantage of its virtual machine's (VM) specific API in order to observe the runtime behavior of the monitored system. In particular, the event-based runtime verification API of JNuke's VM serves as a platform for various runtime algorithms. This API provides access to events occurring during program execution. Event listeners can then query the VM for detailed data about its internal state and thus implement any runtime verification algorithm, including detection of high-level data races (Artho, 2003) or state-value errors (Artho, 2004).

In the same family of event capturing methods is the prototype implementation of the specification based intrusion detection system, proposed by (Ko,1997), which takes advantage of audit trails provided by the operating system. The prototype runs under the Solaris 2.4 operating system and uses the auditing services of the Sun BSM audit subsystem. The BSM audit subsystem provides a log of the activities that occur in the system. A BSM audit record contains information such as the process ID and the user IP of the process involved, as well as the path name and the permission mode of the files being accessed. However, it does not contain information about the program the process is running. Therefore, an audit record pre-processor is used to associate the program identification with each audit record. The audit record pre-processor actually filters audit records that are irrelevant to the monitoring system and translates the BMS audit records into the format required by the monitoring system.

CHECKING FOR VIOLATIONS

The third stage of dynamic verification is concerned with the checks that a monitor carries out to identify whether the runtime behavior of a system conforms to certain properties or not. The check is carried out while the system is halted, waiting for the monitor's reply. Once the monitor assures that the monitored properties hold, it allows the system to continue with its normal execution. However, if a violation is reported, the monitor can force the system to execute some other action to remedy the current violation.

A widely used type of runtime checks is the check for admission. In this check a monitor checks an incoming request/application for admission, before actually honouring/executing it. In the following we shall examine some of the solutions for performing admission checks.

Another technique for protecting a system, which is allowed to host mobile code, is signing code with a digital signature. Using digital signatures, one can confirm the authenticity of code, its origin, and its integrity. Typically, the code signer is either the code producer or a trusted entity that has reviewed the code. Especially in mobile agents systems, where an agent can operate on behalf of an end-user organization (Tardo,1996), the signature of an agent is used as an indication of the authority under which the agent operates.

Code signing is tightly bound with public key cryptography, which relies on a pair of keys (private and public) associated with an entity. One key is kept private by the entity and the other is made publicly available. Digital signatures greatly benefit from the existence of a public key infrastructure (PKI), since certificates containing the identity of an entity and its public key (i.e., a public key certificate) can be readily located and verified. The code signer applies an irreversible hash function to the code. The result of this function is a unique message digest of the code, which the code producer encrypts with his private key, thus forming a digital signature of the code. The code consumer can easily verify the source and authenticity of the code by using the same hash function and the appropriate decrypting mechanism, which the code producer used to sign the code. If the signature verification succeeds, the code consumer can execute the code.

Microsoft's Authenticode (Grimes,2004), enables Java applets or Active X controls to be signed, ensuring consumers that the software has not been tampered with and that the identity of the code producer is verified.

Proof Carrying Code (PCC) (Necula,1996) can be used to increase security in systems executing non-trusted, mobile code. With PCC, a program is supplied along with a proof of its correctness and this proof is in a form that can be easily verified mechanically before the program's execution. Therefore, it is now the code producer's responsibility to formally prove that the program will assure the safety properties specified by the code consumer, honoring the security policy of the underlying platform/system. For expressing safety policies, PCC used first-order predicate logic, extended with predicates for type-safety and memory-safety. The non-trusted code is in the form of machine code. For relating machine code to specifications they used a form of Floyd's verification-condition generator. Such a generator extracts the safety properties of a machine code program as a predicate in first-order logic.

Comparing PCC to signed code, PCC is a prevention technique, while code signing is an authentication and identification technique used to deter the execution of unsafe code. Furthermore, the proof is structured in such a way that simplifies its verification, since it must be carried out efficiently without any external assistance.

Model Carrying Code (MCC) is an approach for supporting the safe execution of not-trusted mobile code (Sekar, 2003). The central idea of MCC is that the code producer sends the code along with a high-level model, which describes the code's security-relevant behavior. It should be noted that the generated model has to be usable by all code consumers. The automated model generation is based on model extraction via machine learning from execution traces. In the consumer's side, the model is checked for compliance with the consumer's security policy. If the security policy is satisfied, the code can be executed. In case there are conflicts, the consumer's policy can be refined, taking into consideration the code's functionality. When the code is executed, runtime verification methods are used to guarantee that the consumer's (refined) policy is not violated by the code.

By these means, the model bridges the semantic gap between the low-level binary code and the high-level security policies of the consumer. Moreover, the code producer does not have to know the consumer's security policies (as in PCC). Assuming that a model can be much less complex than the corresponding program, it is feasible for a consumer to automatically determine whether a model conforms to its security policies.

The basic Java Virtual Machine (JVM) security model provides the capability of carrying out checks for admission for not trusted code, via a byte-code verifier (Lindholm,1996). In general, the basic JVM security model comprises three related parts, namely the byte-code verifier, the class loader and the security manager. The JVM verifies all byte-code before execution.

Monitors which can only observe the runtime behavior of a system ("O, pre, A", and "O, post, A") perform post-mortem checks. Post-mortem checks deal with properties which might not be of high importance. Proposed monitoring architectures for this category of monitors, like AMOS (Cohen, 1997) and FLEA (Feather, 1995) maintain event logs and offer proprietary event pattern specification languages or store events in relational databases and deploy standard SQL querying for detecting requirement violations (Robinson, 2002).

CONCLUSION

It has been outlined that run-time monitoring has become an essential element whenever high levels of assurance are required, together with the challenges of runtime monitoring of security and dependability properties in new systems. This has revealed that online monitoring is a promising technique for making safety-critical real-time distributed systems more secure and its increasing importance in these systems. The most relevant dynamic approaches for monitoring, surveillance, and other forms of runtime analyses for security properties have been described in this article. A complete monitor taxonomy based on three criteria: controlling capabilities, timeline of event occurrence, and monitor-system communication kind of communication is overviewed. A wide collection of methods for capturing events according to the dynamic verification process has been studied, which includes: the code-modifying event capture methods, and non-code modifying event capture methods.

We claim that monitoring can be useful for different purposes such as prevention of harm when a strange behavior is detected, then a collection of information from both the application and the environment where it is launched, etc. However, the current concept of monitoring focuses on the runtime supervision and control of applications, allowing the early detection of operation problems of individual application instances and supporting the automated reconfiguration of these applications. Although, no appropriate pre-deployment controls for the services running on a paradigm system as cloud computing exist. Nevertheless, a runtime analysis and control becomes an essential tool for the comprehensive support of the security of cloud software.

The current ongoing work on this field is based on the concept of evolution-oriented monitoring, in which systems are monitor to gather data to inform the evolution process (Toutouh, 2018). These processes are themselves subject to security requirements and need to ensure that the privacy of different stakeholders is preserved whilst sufficient information is communicated to developers to guide evolution. Additionally, the design and development of tailored solutions for monitoring cloud computing and ambient intelligence systems is exposed as a field for researching.

REFERENCES

Abercrombie, P., & Karaorman, M. (2002). jContractor: Bytecode instrumentation techniques for implementing design by contract in java. Electronic Notes in Theoretical Computer Science, 70.

Alpern, B., & Schneider, F. B. (1987). Recognizing safety and liveness. *Distributed Computing, 2*(3), 117–126. doi:10.1007/BF01782772

Alur, R., Fix, L., & Henziger, T. A. (1994). A determinizable class of timed automata. In *Proceedings of 6th Conference on Computer Aided Verification (CAV'94)*. Springer. 10.1007/3-540-58179-0_39

Alvarez, G., & Petrovic, S. (2003). A new taxonomy of web attacks suitable for efficient encoding. *Computers & Security, 22*(5), 435–449. doi:10.1016/S0167-4048(03)00512-1

Arnold, A. (1987). Transition systems and concurrent processes. In *Mathematical Problems in Computation Theory* (pp. 9–21). Warsaw: Banach Center.

Artho, C., & Biere, A. (2005). Combined Static and Dynamic Analysis. *Proceedings of AIOOL '05.*

Artho, C., Biere, A., & Havelund, K. (2004). Using block-local atomicity to detect stale value concurrency errors. In *Proceedings of ATVA'04*. Springer. 10.1007/978-3-540-30476-0_16

Artho, C., Havelund, K., & Biere, A. (2003). High-level data races. *Journal on Software Testing, Verification and Reliability, 13*(4).

Artho, C., Schuppan, V., Biere, A., Eugster, P., Baur, M., & Zweimuller, B. (2004). JNuke: Efficient Dynamic Analysis for Java. *Proceedings of 16th International Conference on Computer Aided Verification (CAV 2004)*, 462-465.

Avizienis, A., Larpie, J. C., & Randell, B. (2000). Fundamental Concepts of Dependability. *Information Survivability Workshop.*

Bandara, A. K., Lupu, E. C., & Russo, A. (2003). *Using event calculus to formalise policy specification and analysis. In Proceedings of Policies for Distributed Systems and Networks* (pp. 26–39). Policy.

Baresi, K., & Guinea, S. (2005). *Dynamo: Dynamic Monitoring of WS-BPEL Processes.* ICSOC 05, *3rd International Conference On Service Oriented Computing,* Amsterdam, The Netherlands.

Baresi, K., Guinea, S., & Plembani, P. (2005). *Using WS-Policy in Service Monitoring.* TES 05, *6th VLDB Workshop on Technologies for E-Services,* Trodheim, Norway.

Barnett, M., & Schulte, W. (2001). Spying on Components: A Runtime Verification Technique. *Proceedings of OOPSLA 2001, Workshop on Specification and Verification of Component Based Systems.*

Barringer, H., Goldberg, A., Havelund, K., & Sen, K. (2004). Rule-Based Runtime Verification. 5th *International Conference on Verification, Model Checking and Abstract Interpretation (VMCAI 04),* 44-57.

Bartetzko, D., Fischer, C., Moller, M., & Wehrheim, H. (2001). Jass -Java with assertions. *Electronic Notes in Theoretical Computer Science, 55*(2).

Bouyer, P., Chevalier, F., & D'Souza, D. (2005). Fault Diagnosis using Timed Automata. *Proceedings of 8th Intern. Conf. on Foundations of Software Science and Computations Structures (FoSSaCS'05),* 219-233. 10.1007/978-3-540-31982-5_14

Brisset, P. (2000). *A Case Study in Java Software Verification.* Appeared in Workshop on Security, Middleware, and Languages, Stockholm, Sweden.

Brörkens, M., & Möller, M. (2002). Dynamic event generation for runtime checking using the JDI. *Electronic Notes in Theoretical Computer Science, 70*(4).

Capra, L., Emmerich, W., & Mascolo, C. (2001). Reflective middleware solutions for context-aware applications. In *Proc. of Reflection. The 3rd Int. Conf. on Meta-level Architectures and Separation of Crosscutting Concerns.* Kyoto, Japan: Springer-Verlag. 10.1007/3-540-45429-2_10

Capra, L., Emmerich, W., & Mascolo, C. (2003). CARISMA: Context Aware Reflective Middleware System for Mobile Applications. *IEEE Transactions on Software Engineering, 29*(10), 929–945. doi:10.1109/TSE.2003.1237173

Chang, E., Pnueli, A., & Manna, Z. (1994). Compositional Verification of Real-Time Systems. *Proc. 9th IEEE Symposium On Logic In Computer Science*, 458-465. 10.1109/LICS.1994.316045

Chen, F., & Rosu. (2003). *Towards Monitoring-Oriented Programming: A Paradigm Combining Specification and Implementation.* Academic Press.

Clavel, M., Durn, F. J., Eker, S., Lincoln Martí-Oliet, N., Meseguer, J., & Quesada, K. F. (1999). The Maude System. *Proc. of the 10th Inter. Conf. on Rewriting Techniques.*

Cohen, D., Feather, M., Narayanswamy, K., & Fickas, S. (1997). Automatic Monitoring of Software Requirements. *Proc. of the 19th Int. Conf. on Software Engineering.* 10.1145/253228.253493

Cohen, G., Chase, J., & Kaminsky, D. (1998). Automatic Program Transformation with JOIE. *Proc. of USENIX Annual Technical Symposium.*

Comuzzi, M., & Spanoudakis, G. (2010). Dynamic set-up of monitoring infrastructures for service based systems. *Proceedings of the ACM Symposium on Applied Computing*, 2414–2421. 10.1145/1774088.1774591

d'Amorim, M., & Havelund, K. (2005). Event-based runtime verification of Java Programs. In *Proc. of the 3rd Int. Workshop on Dynamic Analysis, WODA '05*. St. Louis, MO: ACM Press.

Damianou, N., Dulay, N., Lupu, E. C., & Sloman, M. S. (2001). *The Ponder Policy Specification Language.* Presented at Policy, in *Workshop on Policies for Distributed Systems and Networks*, Bristol, UK. 10.1007/3-540-44569-2_2

David, P. C., Ledoux, T., & Bouraqadi-Saadani, N. M. N. (2001). Two-step weaving with reflection using AspectJ. *OOPSLA 2001 Workshop on Advanced Separation of Concerns in Object- Oriented Systems.*

Dingwall-Smith, A., & Finkelstein, A. (2002). From Requirements to Monitors by Way of Aspects. *Proc. of 1st Int. Conf. on Aspect-Oriented Software Development.*

Emmerich, W. (2000). Software Engineering and Middleware. A Roadmap. In *The Future of Software Engineering - 22nd Int. Conference on Software Engineering (ICSE)* (pp 117-129). ACM Press.

Feather, M., & Fickas, S. (1995). Requirements Monitoring in Dynamic Environments. *Proc. of Int. Conf. on Requirements Engineering.*

Feather, M.S., Fickas, S., van Lamsweerde, A., & Ponsard, C. (1998). Reconciling System Requirements and Runtime Behavior. *Proc. of 9th Int. Work. on Software Specification & Design.*

Giannakopoulou, D., & Havelund, K. (2001). Automata-Based Verification of Temporal Properties on Running Programs. In *Proc. of Inter. Conf. on Automated Software Engineering (ASE'01)* (pp. 412-416). ENTCS. 10.1109/ASE.2001.989841

Goldberg, A., & Havelund, K. (2003). Instrumentation of Java Bytecode for Runtime Analysis. In Proc. Formal Techniques for Java-like Programs. In *Technical Reports from ETH Zurich* (Vol. 408). ETH Zurich.

Grastien, A., Cordier, M., & Largout, C. (2005). Incremental Diagnosis of Discrete-Event Systems. *15th Int. Work. On Principles of Diagnosis (DX05).*

Grimes, R. (2004). *Authenticode.* Microsoft Corporation TechNet, Microsoft Authenticode Reference Guide.

Gurevich, Y. (1993). Evolving Algebras: An attempt to discover semantics. In G. Rozenberg & A. Saloma (Eds.), *Current Trends in Theoretical Computer Science* (pp. 266–292). World Scientific. doi:10.1142/9789812794499_0021

Gurevich, Y., Schulte, W., Campbell, C., & Grieskamp, W. (2001). *The Abstract State Machine Language.* Microsoft Corporation.

Hatcli, J., & Dwyer, M. (2001). Using the Bandera tool set to model-check properties of concurrent Java software. *LNCS, 2154,* 39–58.

Havelund, K. (2008). Runtime verification of C programs. In *TestCom/FATES.* Springer-Verlag. doi:10.1007/978-3-540-68524-1_3

Havelund, K., & Rosu, G. (2001). Monitoring Java Programs with Java PathExplorer. *Proc. of the 1st International Workshop on Runtime Verification (RV'01),* 1, 97-114.

Havelund, K., & Rosu, G. (2001). Monitoring Programs using Rewriting. In *Proc. Int. Conference on Automated Software Engineering (ASE'01)* (pp. 135-143). Institute of Electrical and Electronics Engineers. 10.1109/ASE.2001.989799

Havelund, K., & Rosu, G. (2002). Synthesizing Monitors for Safety Properties. Tools and Algorithm for Construction and Analysis of Systems (TACAS), 342-356. doi:10.1007/3-540-46002-0_24

Havelund, K., & Rosu, G. (2004). An Overview of the Runtime Verification Tool Java PathExplorer. *Methods Syst. Des., 24*(2), 189–215. doi:10.1023/B:FORM.0000017721.39909.4b

Hirschfeld, R., & Kawamura, K. (2004). Dynamic service adaption. *Proceedings of the Fourth IEEE International Workshop on Distributed Auto-adaptive and Reconfigurable Systems (with ICDCS'04)*.

Hoare, C. (2004). *Communicating Sequential Processes*. Retrieved from http://www.usingcsp.com/cspbook.pdf

Janicke, H., Siewe, K., Jones, F., Cau, A., & Zedan, H. (2005). Analysis and Runtime Verification of Dynamic Security Policies. AAMAS 05 workshop on Defence Applications of Multi-Agent Systems, Utrecht, The Netherlands.

Kaler, C., & Nadalin, A. (Eds.). (2005). *Web Services Security Policy Language (WSSecurityPolicy)*. Retrieved from http://www-128.ibm.com/developerworks/library/speci_cation/ws-secpol/

Kiczales, G., Hilsdale, E., Hugunin, J., Kersten, M., Palm, J., & Griswold, W. G. (2001). An Overview of AspectJ. In *Proceedings of the 15th European Conference on Object-Oriented Programming* (pp. 327-353). Springer-Verlag.

Kiczales, G., & Lampig, J. (1997). Aspect-oriented Programming. LNCS, 1241, 220-242. doi:10.1007/BFb0053381

Kim, M., Kannan, S., Lee, I., Sokolsky, O., & Viswanathan, M. (2001). Java-mac: A Runtime Assurance Tool for for Java Programs. Electronic Notes in Theoretical Computer Science, 55.

Ko, C., Ruschitzka, M., & Levitt, K. (1997). Execution Monitoring of Security-Critical Programs in Distributed Systems: A Specification-Based Approach. *Proc. of the IEEE Symp. on Security and Privacy*, 175-187.

Koulouris, T., Spanoudakis, G., & Tsigkritis, T. (2007). Towards a framework for dynamic verification of peer-to-peer systems. *Second International Conference on Internet and Web Applications and Services, ICIW'07*. 10.1109/ICIW.2007.63

Lazarevic, A., Kumar, V., & Srivastava, J. (2005). Intrusion Detection: A Survey. In *Managing cyber-threats: issues approaches & challenges*. Springer. doi:10.1007/0-387-24230-9_2

Leavens, G., Baker, A., & Ruby, C. (2003). *Preliminary Design of JML: A Behavioural Interface Specification Language for Java*. Technical Report 9806u. Iowa State University, Department of Computer Science. Retrieved from http://www.jmlspecs.org/

Lee, D., & Yannakakis, M. (1996). Principles and Methods of Testing Finite State Machines – A Survey. *Proceedings of the IEEE, 84*(8), 1090–1123. doi:10.1109/5.533956

Lee, I., Kannan, S., Kim, M., Sokolsky, O., & Viswanathan, M. (1999). Runtime Assurance Based on Formal Specifications. *Proc. of the Int. Conf. on Parallel and Distributed Processing Techniques and Applications.*

Ligatti, J., Bauer, L., & Walker, D. (2005). Edit Automata: Enforcement Mechanisms for Runtime Security Policies. *International Journal of Information Security, 4*(1-2), 2–16. doi:10.100710207-004-0046-8

Lindholm, T., & Yellin, F. (1996). *The Java Virtual Machine specification.* Retrieved from http://www.javasoft.com/docs/books/vmspec/html/VMSpecTOC.doc.html

Lowe, G. (1995). An Attack on the Needham-Schroeder public-key authentication protocol. *Information Processing Letters, 56*(3), 131–133. doi:10.1016/0020-0190(95)00144-2

Mahub, K., & Spanoudakis, G. (2004). A Framework for Requirements Monitoring of Service Based Systems. *Proc. of the 2nd Int. Conf on Service Oriented Computing.*

Mascolo, C., Capra, L., Zachariadis, S., & Emmerich, W. (2002). XMIDDLE: A Data-Sharing Middleware for Mobile Computing. *Journal on Wireless Personal Communications, 21*(1), 77–103. doi:10.1023/A:1015584805733

Meyer, B. (2000). *Object-Oriented Software Construction* (2nd ed.). Upper Saddle River, NJ: Prentice Hall.

Möller, M., Bartetzko, D., Fisher, C., & Wehrheim, H. (2001). Jass-java with assertions. In *Electronic Notes in Theoretical Computer Science* (Vol. 55). Elsevier Science Publisher.

Moszkowski, B. (1996). The programming language Tempura. *Journal of Symbolic Computation, 22*(5/6), 730–733.

Muñoz, A., Gonzalez, J., & Maña, A. (2013). A Performance-Oriented Monitoring System for Security Properties in Cloud Computing Applications. *The Computer Journal, 55*(8), 979–994. doi:10.1093/comjnl/bxs042

Munoz, A., Harjani, R., & Mana, A. (2011). Dynamic Security Monitoring and Accounting for Virtualized Environments. In *Int Workshop on Convergence Security in Pervasive Environments/Int Workshop on Security on Security and Trust for Applications in Virtualized Environments.* Ubicación.

Munoz, A., Mana, A., & Gonzalez, J. (2013). Dynamic Security Properties Monitoring Architecture for Cloud Computing. Security Engineering for Cloud Computing: Approaches and Tools, 1-18.

Naldurg, P., Sen, K., & Thati, P. (2004). A Temporal Logic Based Framework to Intrusion Detection. *Proc. of the Int. Conf. on Formal Techniques for Networked and Distributed Systems (FORTE).*

Necula & Lee. (1996). *Proof-Carrying Code.* Technical Report CMU-CS-96-165. Carnegie Mellon University.

Pencolé, Y., & Cordier, M. (2005). A Formal Framework for the Decentralised Diagnosis of Large Scale Discrete Event Systems & its Application to Telecommunication Networks. *Artificial Intelligence, 164*(1-2), 121–180. doi:10.1016/j.artint.2005.01.002

Pino, L., Spanoudakis, G., Krotsiani, M., & Mahbub, K. (2017). Pattern Based Design and Verification of Secure Service Compositions. *IEEE Transactions on Services Computing*, 1–1. doi:10.1109/TSC.2017.2690430

Pnueli, A. (1977). The Temporal Logic of Programs. *Proc. of the 18th IEEE Symposium on Foundations of Computer Science*, 46-77.

Robinson, W. (2002). Monitoring Software Requirements using Instrumented Code. *Proc. of the Hawaii Int. Conference on Systems Sciences.*

Russo, A., Miller, A., Nuseibeh, B., & Kramer, J. (2002). An Abductive Approach for Analysing Event-Based Requirements Specifications. Presented at *18th Int. Conf. on Logic Programming (ICLP)*, Copenhagen, Denmark. 10.1007/3-540-45619-8_3

Schlimmer, J. (Ed.). (2006). *Web Services Policy Framework (WS-Policy Framework).* Retrieved from http://www.ibm.com/developerworks/library/speci_cation/ws-polfram/

Schneider, F. B. (1998). *Enforceable Security Policies.* Cornell University Technical Report TR98- 1664.

Sekar, R., Venkatakrishnan, V. N., Basu, S., Bhatkar, S., & Du Varney, D. (2003). Model-Carrying Code: A Practical Approach for Safe Execution of Untrusted Applications. *ACM Symposium on Operating Systems Principles.*

Shanahan, M. (1999). The Event Calculus Explained. Artificial Intelligence Today, 409-430. doi:10.1007/3-540-48317-9_17

Spanoudakis, G., & Mahub, K. (2006). Non Intrusive Monitoring of Service Based Systems. *Int. Journal of Cooperative Inform. Systems*, *15*(3), 325–358.

Tardo, J., & Valente, K. (1996) Mobile Agent Security Telescript. In *Proceedings of IEEE COMPCON '96* (pp. 58-63). IEEE Computer Society Press.

Tarr, P. L., Ossher, H., Harrison, W. H., & Sutton, S. M. Jr. (1999). N degrees of separation: Multidimensional separation concerns. *International Conference on Software Engineering*, 107-119.

Toutouh, J., Muñoz, A., & Nesmachnow, S. (2018). Evolution Oriented Monitoring oriented to Security Properties for Cloud Applications. In *Proceeding of ARES 2018 Proceedings of the 13th International Conference on Availability, Reliability and Security*. ACM.

Tripakis, S. (2002). Fault Diagnosis for timed automata. *Proc. 7th Int. Symp. Formal Techniques in Real-Time and Fault Tolerant Systems*, 205-224. 10.1007/3-540-45739-9_14

van Lamsweerde, A. (2006). Elaborating Security Requirements by Construction of Intentional Anti-Models. In *Proceedings of ICSE'04, 26th International Conference on Software Engineering*. ACM-IEEE.

Wagelaar, D. (2004). Towards a context-driven development framework for ambient intelligence. *Proceedings of the Fourth IEEE International Workshop on Distributed Auto-adaptive and Reconfigurable Systems (with ICDCS'04)*.

Yang, Z., Cheng, B. H., Stirewalt, R. E., Sowell, J., Sadjadi, S. M., & McKinley, P. K. (2002) An aspect oriented approach to dynamic adaptation. *Proceedings of the ACM SIGSOFT Workshop On Self-healing Software (WOSS'02)*. 10.1145/582128.582144

Yellin, F. (1996). *Low-level security in Java*. Retrieved from http://www.javasoft.com/sfaq/veri_er.html

Chapter 8

A Formal Ticket-Based Authentication Scheme for VANETs

Ons Chikhaoui
SUPCOM, Tunisia

Aida Ben Chehida
SUPCOM, Tunisia

Ryma Abassi
SUPCOM, Tunisia

Sihem Guemara El Fatmi
SUPCOM, Tunisia

ABSTRACT

Vehicular ad hoc networks (VANETs) enable vehicles to exchange safety-related messages in order to raise drivers' awareness about surrounding traffic and roads conditions. Nevertheless, since these messages have a crucial effect on people's lives and as we cannot disregard the probability of attackers intending to subvert the proper operation of these networks, stringent security support should be applied on these messages before they can be relied on. Authenticating these messages before considering them is one of the key security requirements since it enables the receiver to make sure of the received message's integrity and the genuineness of its originator. This chapter presents a conditional privacy-preserving authentication scheme for VANETs.

DOI: 10.4018/978-1-5225-7353-1.ch008

INTRODUCTION

Vehicular Ad hoc NETworks (VANETs) are advanced instances of Mobile Ad hoc NETworks (MANETs) with the intention of providing a wide variety of services, ranging from safety-related warning systems to improved navigation mechanisms as well as information and entertainment applications (Tripathi & Venkaeswari, 2015). Communications between vehicles, V2V, and between vehicles and installed Road Side Units (RSUs), V2I, helped designing these applications (Younes & Boukerche, 2015). Both types of communications are controlled by a short-range wireless communication protocol, called the Dedicated Short-Range Communication (DSRC) protocol (He et al., 2015). Using VANETs, vehicles become able to exchange safety related messages in order to raise drivers' awareness. These messages include safety beaconing and warning messages. Beacon messages are periodically broadcasted by vehicles: they contain the current speed, heading, breaking use, etc. of the sender vehicle (De Fuentes, Gonzalez-Tablas & Ribagorda, 2011). Warning messages are sent to alert vehicles about critical situations such as accidents, traffic congestions, etc. Since it is clear that these messages are of a perilous nature due to their direct impact on people's lives and as it is not realistic to neglect the possibility of the existence of attackers aiming at abusing the network, securing these messages becomes a mandatory requirement. One of the essential security requirements is message authentication as it enables the receiver to make sure of the integrity of a received message as well as the genuineness of its originator. However, in VANETs context, this should be done while preserving the privacy of the real identity of the sending vehicle to protect this latter from several attacks: for instance the illegal tracking attack. In addition, in liability-related cases, legal authorities should be able to identify misbehaving vehicles. These latter should then be evicted from the network to prevent them from causing further damages.

To cope with the security needs mentioned above, we propose a scheme that uses temporary tickets to enable vehicles to communicate with each other while conditionally maintaining their privacy. An identity-based signature technique that does not include the time-consuming bilinear pairing and map-to-point hash functions is used for authentication. The proposal is built upon five phases. The first phase is the network initialization phase during which the Trusted Authority (TA) initializes the network. The second phase is the authentication phase during which a mutual authentication takes place between a vehicle and its current RSU whenever the vehicle enters into a new domain and/or the validity period of the present ticket of the vehicle expires. The third phase is the signature generation and verification phase in which vehicles sign their outgoing safety related messages and authenticate received ones. The fourth phase, the traceability phase, is conducted in order to recover, by the TA, the real identity of a misbehaving vehicle. And the final phase is the revocation phase which is performed to isolate, by RSUs, misbehaving vehicles from the network. An in-depth security analysis is provided to prove the efficiency of our scheme in terms of message authentication, non-repudiation, identity privacy preservation, short-term linkability, long-term unlinkability, traceability, identity revocation and resistance to multiple types of attacks. A formal validation using the Automated Validation of Internet Security Protocols and Applications (AVISPA) tool (Armando et al., 2005) is also achieved in order to confirm more the fulfillment of security goals. In fact, our proposal is validated based on two cases: the first one is the mutual authentication between an RSU and a vehicle during the authentication phase, while the second one is the authentication of a sending vehicle by a receiving vehicle during the signature generation and verification phase.

The remainder of the paper is organized as follows: Section 2 reviews some related works. In section 3, the scheme overview is presented. Section 4 describes the proposed scheme. In section 5, the security analysis is fulfilled. Section 6 illustrates the formal validation using AVISPA tool. Finally, section 7 concludes the chapter.

RELATED WORK

In this section, we present some existing schemes that were conducted in order to achieve anonymous authentication in VANETs. According to the methods used in the works, we can categorize them into three classes: works based on asymmetric key cryptography, works based on symmetric key cryptography and works based on hybrid methods (i.e., they combine asymmetric key cryptography with symmetric key cryptography).

Works Based on Asymmetric Key Cryptography

Fan *et al.* (2014) used blind signature technique to deal with anonymous authentication in VANETs. RSUs blindly sign the safety messages of vehicles that exist in their coverage areas. However, a receiving vehicle must be in the coverage area of the signing RSU to be able to verify the validity of a received signature. In Liu, Wang, and Chen (2015), vehicles use pseudonyms instead of their real identities to maintain their privacy when communicating with other vehicles and RSUs in the network. Vehicles autonomously generate their own pseudonyms. An identity-based signature method using bilinear pairing is utilized. A proxy vehicle verifies, in batch, the validity of signatures on messages of other vehicles. RSU checks, in batch, the verification results of proxy vehicles. A drawback of this scheme is its vulnerability to the Sybil attack as vehicles self-generate their own pseudonyms. In addition, a concern about batch verification technology is the fact that the batch verification fails if at least one invalid signature exists in the verified batch. In reality, it is infeasible to assume that all signatures are valid. Adversaries can attempt to negate the advantages of batch verification by polluting signatures within a batch (Chen et al., 2015). In He et al. (2015), vehicles also use pseudonyms instead of their real identities to anonymously communicate with other vehicles and RSUs in the network. Vehicles generate their own pseudonyms themselves. The scheme uses an identity-based signature method without bilinear pairing to decrease the computational complexity of the bilinear pairing function. The batch verification of signatures is also possible. However, the scheme is vulnerable to the Sybil attack because of the self-generation of pseudonyms by vehicles. It is also vulnerable to the Global Positioning System (GPS) spoofing attack as no information is provided to prove the trustworthiness of a position supplied by a vehicle. The concern about bad batches exists as well. In Mrabet, El Bouanani, and Ben-Azza (2015), attribute-based signature is used to achieve anonymous authentication in VANETs. A vehicle is able to generate a valid signature on a message if and only if its set of attributes satisfies the signing predicate of that message. The proposed scheme is vulnerable to the Sybil attack as when a vehicle receives the same message multiple times, it cannot verify if the message was sent by different vehicles or repeatedly transmitted by the same vehicle. The scheme is also vulnerable to the GPS spoofing attack as no proof is provided to confirm a location presented by a vehicle. In Shao et al. (2016), group signature is used to ensure anonymous authentication among vehicles. Vehicles within the communication range of a same RSU form a group. Each group member receives a group certificate from its current RSU. The scheme presented a method to thwart the Sybil attack and hence to enable a receiving vehicle to accept a message only if it was confirmed by a certain threshold number of vehicles. The batch verification of group signatures is possible in this scheme. However, a vehicle must provide its real identity to RSUs in order to get its group certificates. Besides, a misbehaving vehicle is only denied from obtaining new group certificates; however, its present group certificate could still be valid. The concern about bad batches is also existent.

Works Based on Symmetric Key Cryptography

In Mejri, Achir, and Hamdi (2016), vehicles of a same platoon generate a symmetric group key to anonymously authenticate each other. The symmetric group key is established using a proposed Group Diffie-Hellman algorithm and a pre-shared secret between the members of the platoon. Although this scheme reduces the computation overhead by using symmetric key cryptography instead of asymmetric key cryptography, it is vulnerable to the repudiation attack as symmetric key cryptography does not satisfy the non-repudiation requirement. This scheme is also vulnerable to the Sybil attack as when a vehicle receives the same message multiple times, it cannot distinguish whether the message was sent by different vehicles or resent many times by the same vehicle.

Works Based on Hybrid Methods

In Buttner, Bartels, and Huss (2015), vehicles use ring signatures to anonymously establish symmetric keys between each other. This scheme is vulnerable to the repudiation attack as symmetric key cryptography does not meet the non-repudiation requirement.

To the best of our knowledge, there is no existing work that satisfies several security requirements at the same time.

As for our proposal, it satisfies message authentication, non-repudiation, identity privacy preservation, short- term linkability, long-term unlinkability, traceability, identity revocation and it resists to the identity resolution attack, the impersonation attack, the Sybil attack, the modification attack, the Global Positioning System (GPS) spoofing attack, the replay attack and the repudiation attack.

SCHEME OVERVIEW

In this section, we present the network model, the used assumptions, the security goals and the preliminaries of the proposed scheme.

Network Modeling

As depicted in Figure 1, the network modeling in our scheme is based on three entities:

- **The Trusted Authority:** The TA divides its territory into different domains containing a given number of RSUs and assigns to each domain a sequence number. Moreover, the TA divides the time domain into equal serial time slots, registers vehicles and provides them with credentials and their corresponding private keys. With each set of credentials and private keys, the TA supplies the related vehicle with a public key certificate containing a vehicle's pseudonym that can be used latter to request, from the TA, a new set of credentials and the corresponding private keys. Furthermore, the TA registers RSUs and provides each one of them with an identity and a corresponding private key. Finally, the TA is in charge of resolving disputes, recovering the real identity of a misbehaving vehicle and deciding its penalty.
- **RSUs:** They communicate with the TA via wired links and communicate with vehicles (OBUs) via wireless links by using the DSRC protocol. Moreover, they receive the revocation lists from the TA and verify the revocation status

Figure 1. considered network modeling

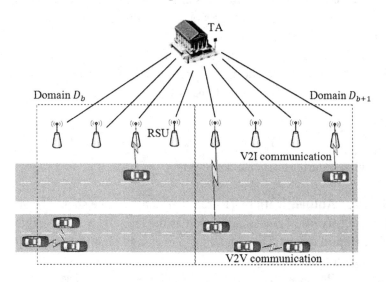

of vehicles as well as signing credentials of legitimate ones in order to relieve vehicles of downloading and checking the revocation lists.

- **Vehicles:** Vehicles are mobile nodes equipped with OBUs enabling them to wirelessly communicate with other vehicles and RSUs based on the DSRC protocol and use Tamper Proof Devices (TPDs) to store their sensitive information. Moreover, they request, from the TA, credentials and the corresponding private keys whereas they request, from RSUs, to sign their credentials. They form their tickets from their signed credentials and use them to communicate with each other while protecting their privacy. They exchange safety related messages, authenticate received ones, and report to the TA any misbehavior.

Scheme Assumptions

Our scheme is based on the following assumptions:

1. The TA is totally trusted by all the vehicles and the RSUs and cannot be compromised. The TA has also high storage and computation capabilities.
2. RSUs are densely deployed along the roads.
3. Before the installation of each registered RSU, the TA assigns it with a public key certificate (that contains an RSU's unique identifier) and the corresponding private key. This certificate will be used for the secure communication between the TA and the related RSU.

4. The division of the time domain is known by all RSUs in the network. Before the beginning of each new time slot, the TA broadcasts a reminder of the new time slot (i.e., the start and end time).
5. Each vehicle is equipped with a clock used for time indication and check.
6. The network can provide time synchronization and the Global Time (i.e., Greenwich Means Time: GMT) is used.

Security Goals

The following security goals are achieved:

- **Message Authentication**: The receiver of a message should be able to verify the integrity of this message as well as the legitimacy of its originator.
- **Non-Repudiation**: The sender of a message should not be able to deny having sent that message.
- **Identity Privacy Preservation**: The TA should be the only one able to disclose the real identity of a vehicle.
- **Short-Term Linkability**: When a same vehicle sends two or more safety messages in the same time slot, the receiver should be able to verify that these messages are generated by the same vehicle.
- **Long-Term Unlinkability**: Apart from the TA, none should be able to link the relationship among two or more different tickets of the same vehicle.
- **Traceability**: The TA should be able to recover the real identity of a misbehaving vehicle from its tickets.
- **Identity Revocation**: Misbehaving vehicles should be evicted from the network.
- **Defense Against Several Types of Attacks**: The scheme should be able to resist multiple attacks namely the identity resolution attack, the impersonation attack, the Sybil attack, the modification attack, the GPS spoofing attack, the replay attack and the repudiation attack.

Preliminaries

We adopt the identity-based signature technique for its computational and communicational efficiency. In identity-based signature schemes, the identity of an entity serves as the public key of that entity. The related private key is extracted from the identity by a trusted third party, called Private Key Generator (PKG). The entity uses the extracted private key to sign its outgoing messages. Receivers use the identity of the sender to verify the validity of received signatures.

To instantiate our scheme, we decided to use the identity-based signature scheme proposed in Bellare, Namprempre, and Neven (2004), called the BNN-IBS scheme. The BNN-IBS scheme possesses the following properties:

- It is based on elliptic curve cryptography.
- It does not use the time-consuming bilinear pairing and map-to-point hash functions.
- It has been proved to be existentially unforgeable against the chosen message and ID attacks (i.e., euf-cma-ida secure) in Bellare, Namprempre, and Neven (2004) under the discrete logarithm problem.

It is worth noting that an important advantage of our proposal is its re-usability, i.e., it can also be reutilized with other new identity-based signature schemes for security and performance improvements.

For the description of the BNN-IBS scheme, we take the one provided in Yasmin, Ritter, and Wang (2014), (*Remark*: in the Key Extract algorithm, we have $s_u = r_u + c_u s$).

PROPOSED SCHEME

This scheme is built upon five phases: network initialization phase, authentication phase, signature generation and verification phase, traceability phase and revocation phase. The notations used in our scheme are listed in Table 1.

Table 1. Notations

Notation	Meaning
TA	The Trusted Authority
E / F_q	An elliptic curve E over a finite field F_q
q	The field size
p	A large prime number
P	A point of order p on the curve E
G	A cyclic group of order p under the point addition "+" generated by P
s / P_{TA}	The secret/public key of TA

continued on following page

Table 1. Continued

Notation	Meaning
H_i	Secure and collision resistance one-way hash function, $i = 1,\ 2$
D_b	The b th domain
$RSU_{a,b}$	The a th RSU of D_b
$ID_{RSU_{a,b}}$	The identity of $RSU_{a,b}$
$GC_{RSU_{a,b}}$	The geographical coordinates of $RSU_{a,b}$
$s_{RSU_{a,b}}$	The private key of $RSU_{a,b}$ that corresponds to $ID_{RSU_{a,b}}$
ΔT	The length of a time slot
CP	A certain period chosen by TA
TS_x	The x th time slot
V_i	The i th vehicle
RID_{V_i}	The real identity of V_i
$Cred_{V_i,TS_x}$	The credential of V_i for TS_x
s_{V_i,TS_x}	The private key of V_i that corresponds to $Cred_{V_i,TS_x}$
TK_{V_i,TS_x}	The ticket of V_i in TS_x
PID_{V_i}	A pseudo-identity of V_i
$Cert_{V_i}$	A certificate of V_i that includes PID_{V_i}
$priv_{V_i}$	The private key of V_i that corresponds to $Cert_{V_i}$
$\sigma_{RSU_{a,b}}(\alpha)$	The signature on message α for $ID_{RSU_{a,b}}$
$\sigma_{V_i,TS_x}(\alpha)$	The signature on message α for $Cred_{V_i,TS_x}$
RL_{TS_x}	The revocation list that corresponds to TS_x
m	A safety message content
M_{V_i,TS_x}	A safety message of V_i in TS_x
$\|$	Message concatenation

A general description of the method is presented in Figure 2.

Figure 2. Different phases of the proposed scheme

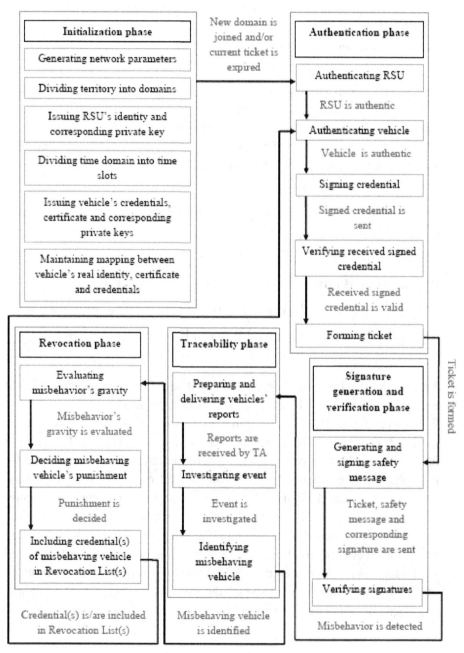

Network Initialization Phase

The TA plays the role of PKG and it initializes the network by performing the following steps:

1. The TA sets up the network parameters by performing the Setup algorithm of the BNN-IBS scheme.
2. The TA publishes the network parameters $\{ E \: / \: F_q, \: G, \: P, \: q, \: p, \: P_{TA}, \: H_1, \: H_2 \}$ and keeps s secret.
3. The TA divides its territory into different domains according to the number of RSUs and the direction of the road.
4. The TA assigns to each domain a sequence number.
5. The TA sets the identity of the RSU as its geographical coordinates concatenated with the sequence number of the domain to which it belongs. The identity of $RSU_{a,b}$ is: $ID_{RSU_{a,b}} = GC_{RSU_{a,b}} \parallel D_b$.
6. The TA extracts the private key $s_{RSU_{a,b}}$ that corresponds to $ID_{RSU_{a,b}}$ by performing the Key Extract algorithm of the BNN-IBS scheme.
7. The TA securely sends $< ID_{RSU_{a,b}}, \: R_{RSU_{a,b}}, \: s_{RSU_{a,b}} >$ to $RSU_{a,b}$. $RSU_{a,b}$ verifies the validity of its private key $s_{RSU_{a,b}}$ by checking whether $R_{RSU_{a,b}} + c_{RSU_{a,b}} P_{TA}$ $= s_{RSU_{a,b}} P$ holds. The demonstration is provided in Islam and Khan (2016), (*Remark:* see Yasmin, Ritter, and Wang (2014) for the definition of $R_{RSU_{a,b}}$ and $c_{RSU_{a,b}}$).
8. The TA divides the time domain into equal serial time slots. The length of each time slot is ΔT. Hence, one CP contains w time slots.
9. 9. Each vehicle must register itself in the TA to request its credentials required for tickets generation. The vehicle provides its real identity to the TA. The real identity of a vehicle corresponds to its serial number. The TA generates for the vehicle one credential for each time slot of one CP. Each credential contains two fields. The first field is the hash value, using a secure hash function such as SHA3-224 (Sha3-224, n.d.), of the timestamp of the generation of the credential concatenated with a nonce. The nonce is added in order to more secure the scheme against the preimage attack on the hash function. The second field is the validity period of the credential which corresponds to the boundaries of the interval of the time slot to which the credential is dedicated. An example of a credential dedicated to the time slot TS_x is as follows:

H(timestamp ∥ nonce)[time of start of TS_x, time of end of TS_x]

For a registered vehicle V_i with a set of credentials that starts from the time slot TS_x, the set of credentials of V_i is { $Cred_{V_i,TS_x}$, $Cred_{V_i,TS_{x+1}}$,..., $Cred_{V_i,TS_{x+w-1}}$ }.

10. The TA extracts the private key that corresponds to each one of V_i's credentials. For each credential $Cred_{V_i,TS_{x+k}}$ (where $0 \leq k \leq w-1$), the TA extracts the corresponding private key $s_{V_i,TS_{x+k}}$ by performing the Key Extract algorithm of the BNN-IBS scheme.

11. The TA also generates, for V_i, a public key certificate $Cert_{V_i}$ and the corresponding private key $priv_{V_i}$. $Cert_{V_i}$ contains a pseudo-identity PID_{V_i} of V_i. PID_{V_i} is the hash value of the timestamp of the generation of $Cert_{V_i}$ concatenated with a nonce. $Cert_{V_i}$ also includes a validity period that corresponds to the boundaries of the interval of the CP to which the set of V_i's credentials is dedicated. V_i will use $Cert_{V_i}$ to securely request and obtain, from the TA, a new set of credentials and the corresponding private keys before the expiration of the last credential of its current set.

12. The TA retains the mapping between RID_{V_i}, $Cert_{V_i}$ and all the credentials $Cred_{V_i,TS_{x+k}}$, (*Remark*: The TA classifies the retained credentials, of the registered vehicles, according to their corresponding time slots in order to facilitate the traceability of misbehaving vehicles later on).

13. The TA securely sends, to V_i, $< Cred_{V_i,TS_{x+k}}$, $R_{V_i,TS_{x+k}}$, $s_{V_i,TS_{x+k}} >$ and $< Cert_{V_i}$, $priv_{V_i} >$. V_i can verify the validity of its private key $s_{V_i,TS_{x+k}}$ by checking whether $R_{V_i,TS_{x+k}} + c_{V_i,TS_{x+k}} P_{TA} = s_{V_i,TS_{x+k}} P$ holds.

Authentication Phase

The mutual authentication between vehicles and RSUs should occur in these two cases:

Case 1: Whenever a vehicle enters into a new domain, so the vehicle should update its current ticket.

Case 2: Whenever the current ticket of a vehicle expires (i.e., the ticket's corresponding time slot ends), so the vehicle should change its current ticket.

The Mutual Authentication in Case 1

1. Each $RSU_{a,b}$ must periodically announce itself to the vehicles as follows:

    a. $RSU_{a,b}$ selects a timestamp t used for freshness and generates $\sigma_{RSU_{a,b}}(t)$ by performing the Sign algorithm of the BNN-IBS scheme.

    b. $RSU_{a,b}$ broadcasts $< ID_{RSU_{a,b}} , t , \sigma_{RSU_{a,b}}(t) >$ within its coverage area.

2. Once a vehicle V_i receives $< ID_{RSU_{a,b}} , t , \sigma_{RSU_{a,b}}(t) >$, it performs the following steps:

    a. V_i checks t.

    b. If t is fresh then V_i verifies $GC_{RSU_{a,b}}$ in $ID_{RSU_{a,b}}$ by using the GPS. Else V_i drops the message and exits.

    c. If $GC_{RSU_{a,b}}$ in $ID_{RSU_{a,b}}$ are correct then V_i verifies D_b in $ID_{RSU_{a,b}}$. Else V_i drops the message and exits.

    d. If D_b is a new domain for V_i then V_i verifies the validity of $\sigma_{RSU_{a,b}}(t)$ by performing the Verify algorithm of the BNN-IBS scheme. Else V_i drops the message and exits.

    e. If $\sigma_{RSU_{a,b}}(t)$ is valid then V_i uses its tuple $< Cred_{V_i,TS_{x+k}} , R_{V_i,TS_{x+k}} , s_{V_i,TS_{x+k}} >$ that corresponds to the current time slot TS_{x+k} in order to authenticate itself to $RSU_{a,b}$: V_i selects a timestamp t used for freshness and generates $\sigma_{V_i,TS_{x+k}}(t)$ by performing the Sign algorithm of the BNN-IBS scheme. Then, V_i sends $< Cred_{V_i,TS_{x+k}} , t , \sigma_{V_i,TS_{x+k}}(t) >$ to $RSU_{a,b}$. Else V_i drops the message and exits.

3. Once $RSU_{a,b}$ receives $< Cred_{V_i,TS_{x+k}} , t , \sigma_{V_i,TS_{x+k}}(t) >$, it performs the following steps:

    a. $RSU_{a,b}$ checks t.

    b. If t is fresh then $RSU_{a,b}$ checks if the validity period indicated in $Cred_{V_i,TS_{x+k}}$ corresponds to the current time slot (i.e., TS_{x+k}). Else $RSU_{a,b}$ drops the message and exits.

    c. If the indicated validity period corresponds to the current time slot then $RSU_{a,b}$ checks $Cred_{V_i,TS_{x+k}}$ against $RL_{TS_{x+k}}$. Else $RSU_{a,b}$ drops the message and exits.

d. If $Cred_{V_i,TS_{x+k}}$ is not in $RL_{TS_{x+k}}$ then $RSU_{a,b}$ verifies the validity of $\sigma_{V_i,TS_{x+k}}(t)$ by performing the Verify algorithm of the BNN-IBS scheme. Else $RSU_{a,b}$ drops the message and exits.

e. If $\sigma_{V_i,TS_{x+k}}(t)$ is valid then $RSU_{a,b}$ generates $\sigma_{RSU_{a,b}}\left(Cred_{V_i,TS_{x+k}}\right)$ by performing the Sign algorithm of the BNN-IBS scheme. Else $RSU_{a,b}$ drops the message and exits.

f. $RSU_{a,b}$ sends $<ID_{RSU_{a,b}}, Cred_{V_i,TS_{x+k}}, \sigma_{RSU_{a,b}}\left(Cred_{V_i,TS_{x+k}}\right)>$ to V_i.

4. Once V_i receives $<ID_{RSU_{a,b}}, Cred_{V_i,TS_{x+k}}, \sigma_{RSU_{a,b}}\left(Cred_{V_i,TS_{x+k}}\right)>$, it performs the following steps:

a. V_i verifies the validity of $\sigma_{RSU_{a,b}}\left(Cred_{V_i,TS_{x+k}}\right)$ by performing the Verify algorithm of the BNN-IBS scheme.

b. If $\sigma_{RSU_{a,b}}\left(Cred_{V_i,TS_{x+k}}\right)$ is valid then V_i sets its ticket $TK_{V_i,TS_{x+k}}$ as the concatenation of $ID_{RSU_{a,b}}$, $Cred_{V_i,TS_{x+k}}$ and $\sigma_{RSU_{a,b}}\left(Cred_{V_i,TS_{x+k}}\right)$. Else V_i drops the message and exits.

Supposing that V_i was in D_{b-1}, its ticket $TK_{V_i,TS_{x+k}}$ will be updated from

$$ID_{RSU_{f,b-1}} \ Cred_{V_i,TS_{x+k}} \ \sigma_{RSU_{f,b-1}}\left(Cred_{V_i,TS_{x+k}}\right)$$

to

$$ID_{RSU_{a,b}} \ Cred_{V_i,TS_{x+k}} \ \sigma_{RSU_{a,b}}\left(Cred_{V_i,TS_{x+k}}\right)$$

The Mutual Authentication in Case 2

In this case, the same steps are performed as in *case 1* except that V_i omits the verification of D_b in $ID_{RSU_{a,b}}$, and it directly moves from verifying $GC_{RSU_{a,b}}$ in $ID_{RSU_{a,b}}$ to verifying the validity of $\sigma_{RSU_{a,b}}(t)$.

Supposing that V_i was using, in TS_{x+k-1}, the ticket $TK_{V_i,TS_{x+k-1}}$:

$$ID_{RSU_{d,g}} \quad Cred_{V_i,TS_{x+k-1}} \quad \sigma_{RSU_{d,g}}\left(Cred_{V_i,TS_{x+k-1}}\right)$$

The new ticket $TK_{V_i,TS_{x+k}}$ of V_i in TS_{x+k} is:

$$ID_{RSU_{a,b}} \quad Cred_{V_i,TS_{x+k}} \quad \sigma_{RSU_{a,b}}\left(Cred_{V_i,TS_{x+k}}\right)$$

Signature Generation and Verification Phase

In this phase, vehicles sign their outgoing safety messages and authenticate received ones (i.e., safety messages) as follows:

1. After forming $TK_{V_i,TS_{x+k}}$, V_i uses $< Cred_{V_i,TS_{x+k}}, R_{V_i,TS_{x+k}}, s_{V_i,TS_{x+k}} >$ to sign its safety messages, in TS_{x+k}, by performing the following steps:

   a. V_i selects a timestamp t used for freshness, calculates $M_{V_i,TS_{x+k}} = (m \parallel t)$ and generates $\sigma_{V_i,TS_{x+k}}\left(M_{V_i,TS_{x+k}}\right)$ by performing the Sign algorithm of the BNN-IBS scheme.

2. V_i sends $< TK_{V_i,TS_{x+k}}, M_{V_i,TS_{x+k}}, \sigma_{V_i,TS_{x+k}}\left(M_{V_i,TS_{x+k}}\right) >$ to other vehicles.

3. Once a receiver V_j receives $< TK_{V_i,TS_{x+k}}, M_{V_i,TS_{x+k}}, \sigma_{V_i,TS_{x+k}}\left(M_{V_i,TS_{x+k}}\right) >$, it should perform the following steps in order to authenticate $M_{V_i,TS_{x+k}}$:

   a. V_j checks t.

   b. If t is fresh then V_j checks the validity period indicated in $TK_{V_i,TS_{x+k}}$. Else V_j drops the message and exits.

   c. If $TK_{V_i,TS_{x+k}}$ is still valid then V_j verifies the validity of $\sigma_{RSU_{a,b}}\left(Cred_{V_i,TS_{x+k}}\right)$ by performing the Verify algorithm of the BNN-IBS scheme, (*Remark*: V_j gets $ID_{RSU_{a,b}}$ from $TK_{V_i,TS_{x+k}}$). Else V_j drops the message and exits.

   d. If $\sigma_{RSU_{a,b}}\left(Cred_{V_i,TS_{x+k}}\right)$ is valid then V_j verifies the validity of $\sigma_{V_i,TS_{x+k}}\left(M_{V_i,TS_{x+k}}\right)$ by performing the Verify algorithm of the BNN-IBS scheme, (*Remark*: V_j gets $Cred_{V_i,TS_{x+k}}$ from $TK_{V_i,TS_{x+k}}$). Else V_j drops the message and exits.

e. If $\sigma_{V_i,TS_{x+k}}\left(M_{V_i,TS_{x+k}}\right)$ is valid then V_j accepts the message. Else V_j drops the message and exits.

Traceability Phase

In cases of misbehaviors (i.e., a misbehaving vehicle V_i sends a bogus and misleading message $M_{V_i,TS_{x+k}}$ to other vehicles), the TA recovers the real identity of V_i as follows:

1. The TA receives from vehicles reports that contain $< TK_{V_i,TS_{x+k}}$, $M_{V_i,TS_{x+k}}$, $\sigma_{V_i,TS_{x+k}}\left(M_{V_i,TS_{x+k}}\right) >$.
2. The TA investigates the event.
3. The TA retrieves $Cred_{V_i,TS_{x+k}}$ from $TK_{V_i,TS_{x+k}}$.
4. The TA determines TS_{x+k} from $Cred_{V_i,TS_{x+k}}$.
5. The TA scans the retained credentials, that correspond to TS_{x+k}, of all the registered vehicles until finding $Cred_{V_i,TS_{x+k}}$.
6. The TA recovers RID_{V_i} from the retained mapping between the real identity of each registered vehicle and all its credentials.

Revocation Phase

According to the level of gravity of the misbehavior, the TA decides whether to temporarily or permanently revoke V_i.

In the temporary revocation:

1. The TA chooses the number of time slots of the revocation.
2. The TA includes the credential(s) of V_i that correspond(s) to the time slot(s) of the revocation in the related revocation list(s).

In the permanent revocation:

1. The TA includes all the remaining credentials of V_i in the revocation lists that correspond to their time slots.
2. The TA will also deny V_i from getting new credentials in the next credentials' refill.

The revocation process is as follows:

1. In the beginning of each time slot, the TA broadcasts to the RSUs in the network, the revocation list that corresponds to that time slot.
2. When V_i requests for a signed credential while this credential is included in the revocation list, its request will be denied by all RSUs.

SECURITY ANALYSIS

In this section, a security analysis of our scheme is provided:

*   **Message Authentication:** Each node (an RSU/a vehicle) has to sign its outgoing messages. The validity of the identity-based signature of an RSU $RSU_{a,b}$/a vehicle V_i on a message ensures to a receiver that the signing RSU $RSU_{a,b}$/vehicle V_i, using an identity $ID_{RSU_{a,b}}$/a credential $Cred_{V_i, TS_{x+k}}$, has the private key that corresponds to $ID_{RSU_{a,b}}$/$Cred_{V_i, TS_{x+k}}$. When dealing with safety messages, a receiving vehicle V_j has also to verify the validity of the identity-based signature of an RSU on the credential of the sending vehicle in order to check the legitimacy of this latter since RSUs sign only credentials that are not included in revocation lists. For the integrity requirement, the validity of an identity-based signature on a message guarantees to a receiver the integrity of the signed message.
*   **Non-Repudiation:** In our scheme, digital signature (identity-based signature) is used in order to fulfill non-repudiation since a sender cannot deny having sent a certain message if it has signed and transmitted that message.
*   **Identity-Privacy Preservation:** In our scheme, vehicles use credentials to authenticate themselves to RSUs. A credential does not contain any identifying information and it is regularly changed with each new time slot (i.e., whenever its validity period expires). Vehicles also use tickets to send their safety messages. A ticket is formed by appending, to a verified credential, the identity of the verifying RSU and its identity-based signature on the credential. Hence, the obtained ticket does not include the real identity of its owner vehicle. Besides, a ticket is regularly changed with the expiration of its related credential. Thus, our scheme maintains the identity privacy preservation.
*   **Short-Term Linkability:** A required property in some applications of VANETs is that in the short-term, a receiver be capable to link messages

generated by the same vehicle. In our scheme, a vehicle uses the same credential over one time slot. Hence, its messages signed by the private key that corresponds to that credential can be linked to each other.

- **Long-Term Unlinkability:** In our scheme, the credentials of a vehicle do not include any connecting information to each other or to the vehicle's real identity. Besides, each credential of a vehicle expires with the end of the corresponding time slot. Hence, in each time slot, the related credentials of all the vehicles expire simultaneously. Thus, all the vehicles change their tickets in the beginning of each new time slot. In view of this reasoning, except for the TA, no other third party can reveal the relation among two or more tickets of the same vehicle.
- **Traceability:** In our scheme, the TA retains the mapping between the real identity of each registered vehicle, its public key certificate and the set of all its credentials. Hence, the TA can recover the real identity of a misbehaving vehicle given its ticket.
- **Identity Revocation:** The TA includes credentials of misbehaving vehicles in revocation lists. RSUs do not sign credentials included in revocation lists. Hence misbehaving vehicles are evicted from the network.

Defense Against Several Types of Attacks

Our scheme can resist several types of attacks as follows:

- **Identity Resolution Attack**: Our scheme can resist the identity resolution attack, according to the abovementioned analysis about identity privacy preservation and long-term unlinkability.
- **Impersonation Attack**: Each vehicle and RSU in the network has to sign its outgoing messages. Hence, an adversary cannot assume the identity of another vehicle or RSU as it will not be able to utilize the convenient private key.
- **Sybil Attack**: A malicious vehicle may intend to appear as many vehicles by simultaneously using different tickets. However, in our scheme each vehicle has in its set of credentials only one credential (hence only one ticket) for each time slot. Whenever a time slot ends, the corresponding credential (hence the corresponding ticket) of the vehicle expires and can no longer be used. Besides, RSUs do not sign, for vehicles, credentials of upcoming timeslots. In this situation, a malicious vehicle might attempt to get multiple sets of credentials from the TA in only one CP in order to have multiple credentials related to the same time slot and hence to be able to execute a Sybil attack. However, in our scheme the TA maintains the mapping between

the real identity of each registered vehicle, its public key certificate and the set of all its credentials. Whenever a vehicle contacts the TA for a new set of credentials, the vehicle must provide its real identity. The TA will check the identity of the requesting vehicle against the table of real identity, public key certificate and credentials mappings. If the requesting vehicle has a set of credentials that still contain non-expired credentials, the TA will revoke them (i.e., each one of them will be included in the revocation list of its corresponding time slot) before giving a new set of credentials to the requesting vehicle. Thus, our scheme can thwart the Sybil attack.

- **Modification Attack**: All vehicles and RSUs in the network sign their messages before sending them. Receivers can detect the modification of received messages by verifying whether the corresponding identity based signature is valid.
- **Global Positioning System (GPS) Spoofing Attack**: A malicious vehicle may try to misguide other nodes in the network by faking its actual location. In our scheme, each ticket of a vehicle includes the identity of the RSU that signed the related credential. A credential should be signed whenever its corresponding time slot starts or the vehicle enters into a new domain. The validity period of a credential (hence the related ticket) is limited (only one time slot). Hence, a vehicle cannot escape the step of signing credentials by RSUs. Otherwise, receivers will not accept the vehicle's safety messages. The identity of an RSU is composed of its geographical coordinates concatenated with the sequence number of the domain to which it belongs. Thus, the receiver can have an idea about the vicinity of the sending vehicle.
- **Replay Attack**: Each vehicle/RSU in the network includes a timestamp in each message it sends. Receivers can detect the replay of a message by verifying the freshness of the incorporated timestamp.
- **Repudiation Attack**: Our scheme can resist the repudiation attack, according to the abovementioned analysis about non-repudiation.

FORMAL VALIDATION

In order to verify more the robustness of our proposal, a formal security analysis is conducted using AVISPA tool. AVISPA tool uses a High Level Protocol Specification Language (HLPSL) to describe security protocols and to specify which security goals are expected to be achieved by a given one (Armando et al., 2005). HLPSL is based on two types of roles: the first type is the basic roles which describe the actions of agents at the time of the execution of the protocol. The second type is the composed roles which instantiate several basic roles in order to model the execution of the entire protocol. To validate the safety of a particular protocol, the security properties that need to be satisfied are modeled as security goals in HLPSL. In fact, to make AVISPA tool search for an attack, one should introduce a goals section to define security goals (Abdelnur, Avanesov & Rusinowitch, 2009). Let us note that AVISPA incorporates four different back-ends: On-the-fly Model-Checker (OFMC), Constraint-Logic-based Attack Searcher (CL-AtSe), SAT-based Model-Checker (SATMC) and Tree Automata based on Automatic Approximations for the Analysis of Security Protocols (TA4SP) (Armando et al., 2005). The AVISPA tool takes as input an HLPSL specification, translates it to the Intermediate Format (IF) and analyzes the result by invoking back-ends, which return attacks (if any) to the user (Gotsman, Massacci & Pistore, 2005).

Our proposal was validated based on two cases:

Case 1: The mutual authentication between an RSU and a vehicle during the authentication phase.

Case 2: The authentication of a sending vehicle by a receiving vehicle during the signature generation and verification phase.

Case 1: The Mutual Authentication Between an RSU and a Vehicle

Two sub-cases are modeled. The first sub-case is used to verify that a vehicle authenticates an RSU, and the second sub-case is used to verify that an RSU authenticates a vehicle.

Sub-Case 1: A Vehicle Authenticates an RSU

Two basic roles are specified: the role rsu and the role vehiclei. The specifications of the role rsu, the role vehiclei, the role session, the role environment and the goal section are presented in Figure 3, Figure 4, Figure 5, Figure 6 and Figure 7.

As shown in Figure 3, the specification of the rsu role starts with a list of role parameters: the name of the agent that plays the rsu role (R), the name of the agent that plays the vehiclei role (Vi), the public key of R (IDr), the public key of Vi (Credvi) and two variables of type Dolev-Yao channel (Dolev & Yao, 1983) (denoted by channel(dy) in the roles) i.e., public channel (SND and RCV) to send and receive messages. Next, we have the list of local variables of the rsu role (keyword local) such as the timestamps of R and Vi (Tr and Tvi). What follows are the transitions. In the first transition, R uses the HLPSL function new(), that enables the generation of a fresh value at the runtime, to generate a timestamp (Tr'). Then, it sends its public key (IDr), the generated timestamp (Tr') and the related signature ({IDr.

Figure 3. The rsu role specification for sub-case 1

```
role rsu (R, Vi: agent,
          IDr, Credvi: public_key,
          SND, RCV: channel(dy))
played_by R def=
local
State: nat,
Tr, Tvi: text
const authR1, authR2: protocol_id
init State := 0
transition
1. State = 0 /\ RCV(start) =|>
State' := 1 /\ Tr' := new() % R's timestamp
            /\ SND(IDr.Tr'.{IDr.Tr'}_inv(IDr))
            /\ witness(R, Vi, authR1, IDr.Tr')
2. State = 1 /\ RCV(Credvi.Tvi'.{Credvi.Tvi'}_inv(Credvi)) =|>
State' := 2 /\ SND(IDr.Credvi.{IDr.Credvi}_inv(IDr))
            /\ witness(R, Vi, authR2, IDr.Credvi)
end role
```

Figure 4. The vehiclei role specification for sub-case 1

```
role vehiclei (Vi, R: agent,
               IDr, Credvi: public_key,
               Memoryvi: (public_key.text.{public_key.text}_inv(public_key)) set,
               SND, RCV: channel(dy))
played_by Vi def=
local
State: nat,
Tr, Tvi: text
const authR1, authR2: protocol_id
init State := 0
transition
1. State = 0 /\ RCV(IDr.Tr'.{IDr.Tr'}_inv(IDr))
            /\ not(in(IDr.Tr'.{IDr.Tr'}_inv(IDr), Memoryvi)) =|>
State' := 1 /\ request(Vi, R, authR1, IDr.Tr')
            /\ Memoryvi' := cons(IDr.Tr'.{IDr.Tr'}_inv(IDr), Memoryvi)
            /\ Tvi' := new() % vi's timestamp
            /\ SND(Credvi.Tvi'.{Credvi.Tvi'}_inv(Credvi))
2. State = 1 /\ RCV(IDr.Credvi.{IDr.Credvi}_inv(IDr)) =|>
State' := 2 /\ wrequest(Vi, R, authR2, IDr.Credvi)
end role
```

Figure 5. The session role specification for sub-case 1

```
role session (R, Vi: agent,
              IDr, Credvi: public_key,
              Memoryvi: (public_key.text.{public_key.text}_inv(public_key)) set)
def=
local SR, RR, SVi, RVi: channel(dy)
composition
rsu (R, Vi, IDr, Credvi, SR, RR)
  /\ vehiclei (Vi, R, IDr, Credvi, Memoryvi, SVi, RVi)
end role
```

Figure 6. The environment role specification for sub-case 1

```
role environment()
def=
local
Memoryvi: (public_key.text.{public_key.text}_inv(public_key)) set
const authR1, authR2: protocol_id,
r, vi, i: agent,
idr, credvi, idi: public_key
init Memoryvi := {}
intruder_knowledge = {r, vi, idr, credvi, idi, inv(idi)}
composition
    session(r, vi, idr, credvi, Memoryvi)
/\ session(r, vi, idr, credvi, Memoryvi)
/\ session(i, vi, idi, credvi, Memoryvi) % intruder playing role of R
end role
```

Figure 7. The goal section specification for sub-case 1

```
goal
authentication_on authR1
weak_authentication_on authR2
end goal
environment()
```

Tr'}_inv(IDr)). In the second transition, after the reception of the public key (Credvi), the timestamp (Tvi') and the signature ({Credvi.Tvi'}_inv(Credvi)), R sends IDr and Credvi along with the corresponding signature ({IDr.Credvi}_inv(IDr)). In these transitions, we also find witness events that are described next. In fact, in this sub-case, two properties must be checked:

- Vi authenticates R with IDr concatenated with Tr' (IDr.Tr').
- Vi authenticates IDr concatenated with Credvi (IDr.Credvi) as built by R.

In HLPSL, the authentication goals are achieved through witness and their corresponding request events in the transitions of basic roles and the statement authentication_on in the goal section when freshness of exchanged messages is required. If no replay protection is needed, wrequest and weak_authentication_on are used instead of request and authentication_on.

As depicted in Figure 3, we use the witness events in the rsu role to confirm that R is a witness for IDr concatenated with Tr' (witness(R, Vi, authR1, IDr.Tr')), and for IDr concatenated with Credvi (witness(R, Vi, authR2, IDr.Credvi)). Here, authR1 and authR2 are labels of type protocol_id and they are used to distinguish different authentication goals.

Figure 4 shows the vehiclei role specification. In the list of role parameters, we notice that, differently from the list of parameters of the rsu role, we added the variable Memoryvi which is an array used to verify the freshness of the received messages (IDr.Tr'.{IDr.Tr'}_inv(IDr)). In fact, in our scheme, timestamps are used to check freshness; however, since HLPSL (and in particular AVISPA's back-ends) do not support time (Pura, Patriciu & Bica, 2009), we introduced Memoryvi to enable Vi to verify if it has already seen a received message or not. More details are provided next. When Vi receives the message (IDr.Tr'.{IDr.Tr'}_inv(IDr)), it first searches the received message in the array Memoryvi. If the message is found in Memoryvi, it means that Vi has already processed the same message, and hence the last received one is rejected. If the message is not found in Memoryvi (not(in(IDr. Tr'.{IDr.Tr'}_inv(IDr), Memoryvi))), Vi considers it as new and processes it by requesting a check of (IDr.Tr') through the statement (request(Vi, R, authR1, IDr. Tr')). Then, Vi saves the message in Memoryvi to be used in the next verifications (Memoryvi':= cons(IDr.Tr'.{IDr.Tr'}_inv(IDr), Memoryvi)). Now, Vi generates a timestamp (Tvi') and sends its message (Credvi.Tvi'.{Credvi.Tvi'}_inv(Credvi)). Upon receiving the message (IDr.Credvi.{IDr.Credvi}_inv(IDr)), Vi requests a check of (IDr.Credvi) as built by R through the statement (wrequest(Vi, R, authR2, IDr.Credvi)).

In Figure 6, which shows the specification of the environment role, we declare two valid identical session()'s in parallel to detect if replay attack exists. In addition, we introduce an active intruder that plays the role of agent R to detect if Man-in-the-Middle (MitM) attack exists.

In the goal section, represented by Figure 7, the statements (authentication_on authR1) and (weak_authentication_on authR2) enable the check of the aforementioned required authentication goals.

In order to check the absence of errors, we downloaded SPAN + AVISPA provided in the site of AVISPA. SPAN (Glouche, Genet & Houssay, 2006) refers to Security Protocol ANimator and it symbolically executes HLPSL specifications in order to have a better understanding of the specification and to verify if it is executable. We

Figure 8. Protocol simulation for sub-case 1

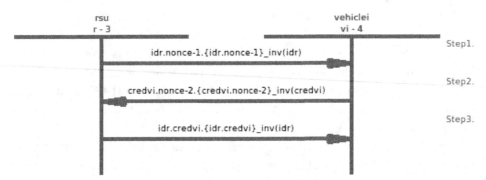

Figure 9. Validation output of OFMC for sub-case 1

```
% OFMC
% Version of 2006/02/13
SUMMARY
  SAFE
DETAILS
  BOUNDED_NUMBER_OF_SESSIONS
PROTOCOL
  /home/span/span/testsuite/results/vehicle_authenticating_RSU.if
GOAL
  as_specified
BACKEND
  OFMC
COMMENTS
STATISTICS
  parseTime: 0.00s
  searchTime: 1.38s
  visitedNodes: 522 nodes
  depth: 10 plies
```

use the protocol simulation of SPAN to build Message Sequence Charts (MSC) of our HLPSL specification. Figure 8 shows the provided MSC. Let us note that during the protocol simulation, no intruder's role has been introduced.

As for the security goals verification, the AVISPA execution, using the OFMC tool, proves the absence of errors and it indicates safe results. Figure 9 depicts the validation output of OFMC.

Sub-Case 2: An RSU Authenticates a Vehicle

The difference between this sub-case and the first sub-case is that we now focus on verifying that R authenticates Vi with: Credvi concatenated with Tvi' (Credvi.Tvi'). For this reason, we introduce modifications to the previous HLPSL specification. The specifications of the role rsu, the role vehiclei, the role session, the role environment and the goal section that correspond to this sub-case are provided in Figure 10, Figure 11, Figure 12, Figure 13 and Figure 14.

As shown in Figure 10, which depicts the specification of the rsu role, now agent R is the one that holds an array (Memoryr) to check the freshness of messages generated by Vi. In fact, upon receiving the message (Credvi.Tvi'.{Credvi.Tvi'}_ inv(Credvi)), R checks if this message exists in Memoryr. If the message is found, then it is discarded. However, if the message is not found (not(in(Credvi.Tvi'. {Credvi.Tvi'}_inv(Credvi), Memoryr))), then R requests a check of (Credvi.Tvi') through the statement (request(R, Vi, authVi, Credvi.Tvi')) where authVi is of type

Figure 10. The rsu role specification for sub-case 2

```
role rsu (R, Vi: agent,
          IDr, Credvi: public_key,
          Memoryr: (public_key.text.{public_key.text}_inv(public_key)) set,
          SND, RCV: channel(dy))
played_by R def=
local
State: nat,
Tr, Tvi: text
const authvi: protocol_id
init State := 0
transition
1. State = 0 /\ RCV(start) =|>
State' := 1 /\ Tr' := new() % R's timestamp
              /\ SND(IDr.Tr'.{IDr.Tr'}_inv(IDr))
2. State = 1 /\ RCV(Credvi.Tvi'.{Credvi.Tvi'}_inv(Credvi))
              /\ not(in(Credvi.Tvi'.{Credvi.Tvi'}_inv(Credvi), Memoryr)) =|>
State' := 2 /\ request(R, Vi, authvi, Credvi.Tvi')
              /\ Memoryr' := cons(Credvi.Tvi'.{Credvi.Tvi'}_inv(Credvi), Memoryr)
              /\ SND(IDr.Credvi.{IDr.Credvi}_inv(IDr))
end role
```

Figure 11. The vehiclei role specification for sub-case 2

```
role vehiclei (Vi, R: agent,
               IDr, Credvi: public_key,
               SND, RCV: channel(dy))
played_by Vi def=
local
State: nat,
Tr, Tvi: text
const authvi: protocol_id
init State := 0
transition
1. State = 0 /\ RCV(IDr.Tr'.{IDr.Tr'}_inv(IDr)) =|>
State' := 1 /\ Tvi' := new() % Vi's timestamp
              /\ SND(Credvi.Tvi'.{Credvi.Tvi'}_inv(Credvi))
              /\ witness(Vi, R, authvi, Credvi.Tvi')
2. State = 1 /\ RCV(IDr.Credvi.{IDr.Credvi}_inv(IDr)) =|>
State' := 2
end role
```

Figure 12. The session role specification for sub-case 2

```
role session (R, Vi: agent,
              IDr, Credvi: public_key,
              Memoryr: (public_key.text.{public_key.text}_inv(public_key)) set)
def=
local SR, RR, SVi, RVi: channel(dy)
composition
rsu (R, Vi, IDr, Credvi, Memoryr, SR, RR)
 /\ vehiclei (Vi, R, IDr, Credvi, SVi, RVi)
end role
```

Figure 13. The environment role specification for sub-case 2

```
role environment()
def=
local
Memoryr: (public_key.text.{public_key.text}_inv(public_key)) set
const authvi: protocol_id,
r, vi, i: agent,
idr, credvi, idi: public_key
init Memoryr := {}
intruder_knowledge = {r, vi, idr, credvi, idi, inv(idi)}
composition
    session(r, vi, idr, credvi, Memoryr)
/\ session(r, vi, idr, credvi, Memoryr)
/\ session(r, i, idr, idi, Memoryr) % intruder playing role of vi
end role
```

Figure 14. The goal section specification for sub-case 2

```
goal
authentication_on authvi
end goal
environment()
```

protocol_id. After that, R saves the message in Memoryr for future use (Memoryr':= cons (Credvi.Tvi'.{Credvi.Tvi'}_inv(Credvi), Memoryr)).

In Figure 11, which depicts the specification of the vehiclei role, Vi sends its message (Credvi.Tvi'.{Credvi.Tvi'}_inv(Credvi)) and it generates a witness event (witness(Vi, R, authVi, Credvi.Tvi')) to assert that it is a witness for (Credvi.Tvi').

As shown in Figure 13, in the specification of the environment role, we invoke two valid identical session()'s in parallel to detect if replay attack exists. We also introduce an active intruder that plays the role of agent Vi to detect if MitM attack exists.

In the goal section, provided in Figure 14, the statement (authentication_on authVi) permits the check of the abovementioned required authentication goal.

As shown in Figure 15, the AVISPA execution, using the OFMC tool, confirms safety.

Remarque: the MSC of the HLPSL specification of sub-case 2 is the same as the MSC of the HLPSL specification of sub-case 1.

Figure 15. Validation output of OFMC for sub-case 2

```
% OFMC
% Version of 2006/02/13
SUMMARY
  SAFE
DETAILS
  BOUNDED_NUMBER_OF_SESSIONS
PROTOCOL
  /home/span/span/testsuite/results/RSU_authenticating_vehicle.if
GOAL
  as_specified
BACKEND
  OFMC
COMMENTS
STATISTICS
  parseTime: 0.00s
  searchTime: 1.70s
  visitedNodes: 780 nodes
  depth: 10 plies
```

Case 2: The Authentication of a Sending Vehicle by a Receiving Vehicle During the Signature Generation and Verification Phase

This case is modeled to verify that a receiving vehicle authenticates a sending vehicle during the signature generation and verification phase. In this case, two basic roles are specified: the role vehiclei and the role vehiclej. The specifications of the role vehiclei, the role vehiclej, the role session, the role environment and the goal section are respectively shown in Figure 16, Figure 17, Figure 18, Figure 19 and Figure 20.

Figure 16. The vehiclei role specification for case 2

```
role vehiclei (vi, vj: agent,
               IDr, credvi: public_key,
               SND, RCV: channel(dy))
played_by vi def=
local
State: nat,
T: text,
M: message
const auth1, auth2: protocol_id
init State := 0
transition
1. State = 0 /\ RCV(start) =|>
   State' := 1 /\ T' := new() % vi's timestamp
               /\ M' := new() % vi's message content
               /\ SND(IDr.credvi.{IDr.credvi}_inv(IDr).M'.T'.
                  {credvi.M'.T'}_inv(credvi))
               /\ witness(vi, vj, auth1, IDr.credvi)
               /\ witness(vi, vj, auth2, credvi.M'.T')
end role
```

Figure 17. The vehiclej role specification for case 2

```
role vehiclej (vj, vi: agent,
               IDr, Credvi: public_key,
               Memoryvj: (public_key.message.text.{public_key.message.text}_inv(public_key)) set,
               RCV: channel(dy))
played_by vj def=
local
State: nat,
T: text,
M: message
const auth1, auth2: protocol_id
init State := 0
transition
1. State = 0 /\ RCV(IDr.Credvi.{IDr.Credvi}_inv(IDr).
               M'.T'.{Credvi.M'.T'}_inv(Credvi))
            /\ not(in(Credvi.M'.T'.{Credvi.M'.T'}_inv(Credvi), Memoryvj)) =|>
State' := 1 /\ wrequest(vj, vi, auth1, IDr.Credvi)
            /\ request(vj, vi, auth2, Credvi.M'.T')
            /\ Memoryvj' := cons(Credvi.M'.T'.{Credvi.M'.T'}_inv(Credvi), Memoryvj)
end role
```

Figure 18. The session role specification for case 2

```
role session (vi, vj: agent,
              IDr, Credvi: public_key,
              Memoryvj: (public_key.message.text.{public_key.message.text}_inv(public_key)) set)
def=
local SVi, RVi, RVj: channel(dy)
composition
vehiclei (vi, vj, IDr, Credvi, SVi, RVi) /\ vehiclej (vj, vi, IDr, Credvi, Memoryvj, RVj)
end role
```

Figure 19.The environment role specification for case 2

```
role environment()
def=
local
Memoryvj: (public_key.message.text.{public_key.message.text}_inv(public_key)) set
const auth1, auth2: protocol_id,
vi, vj, i: agent,
idr, credvi, idi: public_key
init Memoryvj := {}
intruder_knowledge = {vi, vj, idr, credvi, idi, inv(idi)}
composition
    session(vi, vj, idr, credvi, Memoryvj)
/\ session(vi, vj, idr, credvi, Memoryvj)
/\ session(i, vj, idr, idi, Memoryvj) % intruder playing role of vi
/\ session(i, vj, idi, idi, Memoryvj) % intruder playing role of both R and vi
end role
```

Figure 20. The goal section specification for case 2

```
goal
weak_authentication_on auth1
authentication_on auth2
end goal
environment()
```

As depicted in Figure 16, the specification of the vehiclei role begins with a list of role parameters: the name of the agent playing the vehiclei role (Vi), the name of the agent playing the vehiclej role (Vj), the public key of agent R (IDr), the public key of Vi (Credvi) and two variables of type public channel (SND and RCV) to send and receive messages. Next, we have the list of variables local to the role such as the timestamp of Vi (T) and the message content of Vi (M). Now, we focus on the transitions part. Vi uses the function new() to generate a timestamp (T') and a message content (M'). Then, it sends the public key (IDr), the public key (Credvi), the signature ({IDr.Credvi}_inv(IDr)), the generated message (M'), the generated timestamp (T') and the signature ({Credvi.M'.T'}_inv(Credvi)).

Note that in our proposal, the RSU (the agent R in our HLPSL specification) is the one that generates (IDr.Credvi.{IDr.Credvi}_inv(IDr)). However, we assumed that Vi already has this message from case1: the mutual authentication between an RSU and a vehicle.

Witness events are used to confirm that Vi is a witness for IDr concatenated with Credvi (witness(Vi, Vj, auth1, IDr.Credvi)) as well as Credvi concatenated with M' and T' (witness(Vi, Vj, auth2, Credvi.M'.T')) where auth1 and auth2 are labels of type protocol_id.

In the specification of the vehiclej role, shown in Figure 17, the variable Memoryvj is used to enable Vj to check the freshness of a received message (Credvi.M'.T'.{Credvi.M'.T'}_inv(Credvi)). In fact, when Vj receives (IDr. Credvi.{IDr.Credvi}_inv(IDr).M'.T'.{Credvi.M'.T'}_inv(Credvi)), it checks if (Credvi.M'.T'.{Credvi.M'.T'}_inv(Credvi)) is in Memoryvj. If the message is found, then it is discarded. However, if it is not found (not(in(Credvi.M'.T'. {Credvi.M'.T'}_inv(Credvi), Memoryvj))), Vj requests a check of (IDr.Credvi) as well as (Credvi.M'.T') through the statements (wrequest(Vj, Vi, auth1, IDr. Credvi)) and (request(Vj, Vi, auth2, Credvi.M'.T')) then it saves (Credvi.M'.T'. {Credvi.M'.T'}_inv(Credvi)) in Memoryvj for the following verifications (Memoryvj':= cons(Credvi.M'.T'.{Credvi.M'.T'}_inv(Credvi), Memoryvj)).

Figure 19 represents the environment role in which we declare two valid identical session()'s in parallel to detect if replay attack exists. We also introduce an active intruder that plays whether the role of Vi only or the role of both R and Vi to detect the existence of any MitM attack.

In the goal section, shown in Figure 20, the statements (weak_authentication_on auth1) and (authentication_on auth2) enable the check of the abovementioned authentication goal.

The built MSC of our HLPSL specification using protocol simulation of SPAN is shown in Figure 21. Let us note that during the protocol simulation, no intruder's role has been introduced.

As represented by Figure 22, the AVISPA execution using the OFMC tool exhibits safe results and it does not detect any vulnerability.

Figure 21. Protocol simulation for case 2

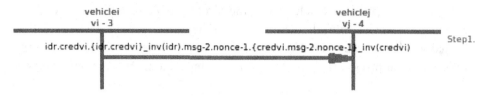

Figure 22. Validation output of OFMC for case 2

```
% OFMC
% Version of 2006/02/13
SUMMARY
  SAFE
DETAILS
  BOUNDED_NUMBER_OF_SESSIONS
PROTOCOL
  /home/span/span/testsuite/results/inter_vehicles_authentication.if
GOAL
  as_specified
BACKEND
  OFMC
COMMENTS
STATISTICS
  parseTime:  0.00s
  searchTime: 0.10s
  visitedNodes: 28 nodes
  depth: 5 plies
```

CONCLUSION

VANETs mainly seek to render road travelling safer by enabling vehicles to exchange safety related messages. Since these messages are of a delicate nature, they should be secured before being relied on. In this context, a major security requirement is the message authentication with conditional privacy preservation of the real identity of sending vehicles. To deal with this demand, we proposed in this chapter a scheme that enables vehicles to engage in communication with each other while preserving their privacy by using temporary tickets. However, when a misbehavior occurs, the TA is able to recover the real identity of involved vehicles. Then, RSUs handle the task of isolating them from the network. In fact, our scheme is constructed around five phases: (1) the network initialization phase during which the TA initializes the network, (2) the authentication phase which takes place between a vehicle and its current RSU each time the vehicle enters into a new domain and/or the present ticket of the vehicle expires, (3) the signature generation and verification phase during which vehicles sign their outgoing safety related messages and authenticate received ones, (4) the traceabilty phase which serves to recover, by the TA, the real identity of a misbehaving vehicle and (5) the revocation phase to discard, by RSUs, misbehaving vehicles from the network. An in-depth security analysis as well as a formal validation, using the AVISPA tool, were conducted to prove the security efficiency of our proposal. As a future work, we intend to implement our proposal.

REFERENCES

Abdelnur, H., Avanesov, T., & Rusinowitch, M. (2009). Abusing SIP authentication. *Journal of Information Assurance and Security, 4*(4), 311–318.

Armando, A., Basin, D., Boichut, Y., Chevalier, Y., Compagna, L., Cuéllar, J., ... Mödersheim, S. (2005, July). The AVISPA tool for the automated validation of internet security protocols and applications. In *International conference on computer aided verification* (pp. 281-285). Springer. 10.1007/11513988_27

Bellare, M., Namprempre, C., & Neven, G. (2004). Security proofs for identity-based identification and signature schemes. *Advances in Cryptology-EUROCRYPT*, 268-286.

Büttner, C., Bartels, F., & Huss, S. A. (2015, October). Real-world evaluation of an anonymous authenticated key agreement protocol for vehicular ad-hoc networks. In *Wireless and Mobile Computing, Networking and Communications (WiMob), 2015 IEEE 11th International Conference on* (pp. 651-658). IEEE.

Chen, J., Yuan, Q., Xue, G., & Du, R. (2015, April). Game-theory-based batch identification of invalid signatures in wireless mobile networks. In *Computer Communications (INFOCOM), 2015 IEEE Conference on* (pp. 262-270). IEEE.

De Fuentes, J. M., González-Tablas, A. I., & Ribagorda, A. (2011). Overview of security issues in vehicular ad-hoc networks. In *Handbook of research on mobility and computing: Evolving technologies and ubiquitous impacts* (pp. 894–911). IGI Global. doi:10.4018/978-1-60960-042-6.ch056

Dolev, D., & Yao, A. (1983). On the security of public key protocols. *IEEE Transactions on Information Theory, 29*(2), 198–208. doi:10.1109/TIT.1983.1056650

Fan, C. I., Sun, W. Z., Huang, S. W., Juang, W. S., & Huang, J. J. (2014, September). Strongly privacy-preserving communication protocol for VANETs. In *Information Security (ASIA JCIS), 2014 Ninth Asia Joint Conference on* (pp. 119-126). IEEE. 10.1109/AsiaJCIS.2014.24

Glouche, Y., Genet, T., & Houssay, E. (2006). SPAN–a Security Protocol ANimator for AVISPA–User Manual. *IRISA/Université de Rennes, 1*, 20.

Gotsman, A., Massacci, F., & Pistore, M. (2005). Towards an independent semantics and verification technology for the HLPSL specification language. *Electronic Notes in Theoretical Computer Science, 135*(1), 59–77. doi:10.1016/j.entcs.2005.06.004

He, D., Zeadally, S., Xu, B., & Huang, X. (2015). An efficient identity-based conditional privacy-preserving authentication scheme for vehicular ad hoc networks. *IEEE Transactions on Information Forensics and Security, 10*(12), 2681–2691. doi:10.1109/TIFS.2015.2473820

Islam, S. H., & Khan, M. K. (2016). Provably secure and pairing-free identity-based handover authentication protocol for wireless mobile networks. *International Journal of Communication Systems, 29*(17), 2442–2456. doi:10.1002/dac.2847

Liu, Y., Wang, L., & Chen, H. H. (2015). Message authentication using proxy vehicles in vehicular ad hoc networks. *IEEE Transactions on Vehicular Technology, 64*(8), 3697–3710. doi:10.1109/TVT.2014.2358633

Mejri, M. N., Achir, N., & Hamdi, M. (2016, January). A new group Diffie-Hellman key generation proposal for secure VANET communications. In Consumer Communications & Networking Conference (CCNC), 2016 13th IEEE Annual (pp. 992-995). IEEE.

Mrabet, K., El Bouanani, F., & Ben-Azza, H. (2015, October). A secure multi-hops routing for VANETs. In *Wireless Networks and Mobile Communications (WINCOM), 2015 International Conference on* (pp. 1-5). IEEE. 10.1109/WINCOM.2015.7381299

Pura, M., Patriciu, V., & Bica, I. (2009). Modeling and formal verification of implicit on-demand secure ad hoc routing protocols in HLPSL and AVISPA. *International Journal of Computers and Communications, 2*(3), 25–32.

SHA3-224. (n.d.). Retrieved from http://nvlpubs.nist.gov/nistpubs/FIPS/NIST. FIPS.202.pdf

Shao, J., Lin, X., Lu, R., & Zuo, C. (2016). A threshold anonymous authentication protocol for VANETs. *IEEE Transactions on Vehicular Technology, 65*(3), 1711–1720. doi:10.1109/TVT.2015.2405853

Tripathi, V. K., & Venkaeswari, S. (2015, April). Secure communication with privacy preservation in VANET-using multilingual translation. In *Communication Technologies (GCCT), 2015 Global Conference on* (pp. 125-127). IEEE.

Yasmin, R., Ritter, E., & Wang, G. (2014). Provable security of a pairing-free one-pass authenticated key establishment protocol for wireless sensor networks. *International Journal of Information Security*, *13*(5), 453–465. doi:10.100710207-013-0224-7

Younes, M. B., & Boukerche, A. (2015, March). SCOOL: A secure traffic congestion control protocol for VANETs. In *Wireless Communications and Networking Conference (WCNC)* (pp. 1960-1965). IEEE. 10.1109/WCNC.2015.7127768

Chapter 9

Toward a Security Scheme for an Intelligent Transport System

Amira Kchaou
SUPCOM, Tunisia

Ryma Abassi
SUPCOM, Tunisia

Sihem Guemara El Fatmi
SUPCOM, Tunisia

ABSTRACT

Vehicular ad-hoc networks (VANETs) allow communication among vehicles using some fixed equipment on roads called roads side units. Vehicular communications are used for sharing different kinds of information between vehicles and RSUs in order to improve road safety and provide travelers comfort using exchanged messages. However, falsified or modified messages can be transmitted that affect the performance of the whole network and cause bad situations in roads. To mitigate this problem, trust management can be used in VANET and can be distributive for ensuring safe and secure communication between vehicles. Trust is a security concept that has attracted the interest of many researchers and used to build confident relations among vehicles. Hence, the authors propose a secured clustering mechanism for messages exchange in VANET in order to organize vehicles into clusters based on vehicles velocity, then CH computes the credibility of message using the reputation of vehicles and the miner controls the vehicle's behavior for verifying the correctness of the message.

DOI: 10.4018/978-1-5225-7353-1.ch009

INTRODUCTION

A Vehicular Ad-hoc NETwork (VANET) is composed by several vehicles, interacting with other vehicles and the fixed equipment known as Roads Side Units (RSUs) (Singh et al. 2017). Two communications types exist in VANET: (1) Vehicle-to-Vehicle communication (V2V) where every vehicle can communicate with each other directly and (2) Vehicle-to-Infrastructure (V2I) where a vehicle can communicate with the static infrastructure. These types of communication are used for enhancing road safety, sharing information about vehicles and traffic conditions and for providing the ability to navigate services, to access internet, to get multimedia services (Azizian et al. 2016).

Vehicles have a high mobility in the roads which leads to a dynamic topology of network and due to the large number of vehicles and others some VANET characteristics, clustering can be applied to VANET. The aim of clustering mechanism in VANET is maintaining the connectivity between vehicles, making topology of VANET less dynamic and enhancing the stability of the network (Hadded et al. 2015). Hence, the clustering mechanism organizes the network into groups of vehicles based on similarities such as vehicles velocity and elects cluster heads (CHs) using the common vehicle between the neighbors of each vehicle. Unfortunately, malicious vehicles can easily propagate false information, modify or drop messages causing bad situations in roads such as accident, traffic congestion, collision, etc. In this chapter, we propose a trust management scheme to estimate the credibility of messages exchanged among vehicles by CHs for ensuring reliability and increasing confidence between entities. The credibility of message allows vehicles, which are around the event, to form an opinion about the quality and accuracy of the message based on the reputation of vehicles. Each vehicle has a reputation value evaluated through past actions and estimating its trustworthiness. However, computing the credibility of message only by the CH may not be enough to verify if an exchanged message is correct or no, a distributed scheme e.g. blockChain can be used for such task. This latter is managed by the fixed equipment in VANET, which are RSUs (miners) and is based on three steps: message transmission, block creation and block validation. During the first step, miner checks the message based on the behavior of the vehicles around the event, and receives the credibility of message by CH. Then, miner takes a decision about the message validation using the fuzzy logic (Ghafoor et al. 2013). This latter is a decision-making process based on two inputs, which are the credibility of message by CH and the flag value of the behavior of vehicle by miner, and a group of fuzzy rules. In addition, fuzzy logic is used to improve the decision-making process in order to determine the value of the Trust Message (TM) and reduce delays in computation (Altoaimy et al. 2014). The second step is used to build a block containing several messages validated by miner. The third step handles the validation of block by miner in order to form a chain of blocks.

The chapter has 6 sections: following this introduction, section 2 describes the clustering mechanism for VANET and baptized CMV. Section 3 presents the Trust management scheme for VANET based on CMV and baptized TCMV. Section 4 describes the distributed trust management for VANET based on TCMV and baptized DTCMV. Section 5 provides a critical overview of the related works for clustering, trust management, and BlockChain in VANET. And, section 6 provides conclusions.

A CLUSTERING MECHANISM FOR VANET: CMV

Recently, we proposed a Clustering Mechanism for VANET baptized CMV in order to maintain the stability of the network (Kchaou et al, 2018). CMV is built upon two steps:

- Clusters setting up based on vehicles velocity.
- Clusters maintenance.

Clusters Setting Up

Clusters setting up describes the steps of the formation of cluster. In VANET, each vehicle sends periodically a *BEACON _MSG* to the closest RSUs. This message is formalized as follows:

BEACON _MSG(IDv, position, direction, velocity)

where IDv is the identifier of vehicle, position corresponds to the position of vehicle using its GPS, direction corresponds to the direction of vehicle described with the degree of departure from north along the clockwise direction and velocity corresponds to the velocity of vehicle.

Each RSU receives this message and stores it in its *RSU_TABLE* depicted in Table 1.

Table 1.

IDV	Position	Direction	Velocity	Restricted neighborhood

Where IDv corresponds to the identifier of vehicle, position corresponds to the position of vehicle, direction refers to the direction of vehicle in the road and velocity corresponds to the velocity of vehicle and restricted neighborhood refers to the vehicle's neighbors such as all vehicles having the same value of velocity or more and less of α km/s. Initially, the restricted neighborhood field is empty.

RSU sends an *ACK_BEACON_MSG* containing vehicle's RSU. This message is formalized as follows:

ACK_BEACON_MSG (RSU)

Each RSU consults its *RSU_TABLE* especially the *velocity* of each vehicle and adds the vehicle's neighbors in the *restricted neighborhood*. After a certain time (timer=β second), the RSU sends to each vehicle the *NEIGHBORS_MSG* as follows:

NEIGHBORS_MSG(IDv, Restricted neighborhood)

where *restricted neighborhood* corresponds to vehicle's neighbors.

Then RSU searches the common vehicle in the *restricted neighborhood* and puts all *IDv* having the common vehicle in the same clusters. RSU organizes the vehicles into clusters having the similar velocity features and selects in each cluster the common vehicle between *restricted neighborhoods* as CH. This information is reported in the *RSU_CLUSTER_TABLE* shown in Table 2.

Where the *index* of cluster refers to each cluster, the *ID_CH* corresponds to the identifier of cluster's CH and *members* correspond to the members of cluster.

Once the cluster established, the RSU sends to each vehicle a *CH_MSG* to notify about CH. This message is formalized as follows:

CH_MSG(IDv, ID_CH)

Clusters Maintenance

The cluster maintenance step deals with two different scenarios:

Table 2.

Index	ID_CH	Members

1. **Cluster Joining**: When a novel vehicle (nv) joins the network, one of among RSUs detects it and chooses the cluster of nv based on its velocity. A *CH_MSG* is then sent to nv whereas a *NewV_MSG* is sent to the CH and to the cluster's members. This message is to notify the CH and the members of cluster about the new vehicle and is formalized as follows:

NewV_MSG (IDv, ID_CH, members)

where *IDv* refers the identifier of nv, *ID_CH* corresponds to identifier of CH of nv and members refers to the nv's *members* of cluster.

The CH receiving a *BEACON_MSG* from nv adds this latter to the *CH_MEMBER_TABLE* shown in Table 3.

2. **Cluster Leaving:** If the CH does not receive three successive *BEACON_MSG* from the same vehicle then this latter is considered as leaving. Therefore, the CH removes it from *CH_MEMBER_TABLE* and sends to the members and RSU an *ALERT_MSG* formalized as follows:

ALERT_MSG (ID_CH, IDv, Flag, [REP])

where *ID_CH* refers the moved vehicle, *IDv* corresponds to the identifier of the leaving moved vehicle, the *flag* value equal to 2 shown in Table 1 and *REP* corresponds to the reputation value of vehicle (this field is optional because it depends on the flag value).

If the members of cluster do not receive three successive *BEACON_MSG* from the CH. The members of cluster send an *ALERT_MSG* to RSU with *flag* value equal to 3. To retrieve data, RSU sends to the old CH a *RETRIEVE_MSG* as follows:

RETRIEVE_MSG (ID_CH)

where *ID_CH* corresponds to the old CH.

Table 3.

IDv	Position	Direction	Velocity

The old CH answers by an *ACK_RETRIEVE_MSG* as follows:

ACK_RETRIEVE_MSG (RSU, *REPUTATION_TABLE*, blacklist)

where *RSU* refers to the receiver of this message, The *REPUTATION_TABLE* contains the *IDv* of vehicle and its reputation value *REP*, and the *blacklist* contains the dishonest vehicles of the old CH.

Then, RSU gives the responsibility of old CH to one of the members, which has several *restricted neighborhood* in *RSU_TABLE*.

TRUST FOR CMV: TCMV

In this section, a Trust management scheme for VANET based on CMV and baptized TCMV in order to build a secured messages exchange in VANET. TCMV mechanism computes the credibility of the message based on the reputation of vehicles and then updates the reputation of vehicle, which sent the urgent message.

In VANET, Vehicles store exchanged *BEACON _MSG* in *VEHICLE_TABLE* depicted in Table 5.

When a vehicle *vx* detects an accident, a traffic jam or an obstacle in the road, it sends to CH an *URGENT_MSG*. CH receives this message and stores its in the *CH_VEHICLE_TABLE*. This message is formalized as follows:

URGENT_MSG (IDv, ID_CH, message, localization)

Table 4.

IDv	REP

Table 5.

IDv	Position	Direction	Velocity

Table 6.

IDv	ID_CH	message	localization

where *IDv* corresponds to the vehicle sending the message, *ID_CH* refers to the ID of CH; *message* corresponds to the event detected, *localization* refers to the position of event.

The *CH_VEHICLE_TABLE* has the same fields as *URGENT_MSG* and is presented in Table 6.

After a certain time (timer= β second), if CH does not receive any *URGENT_MSG* from other vehicles then it elects the vehicles which are near to the localization of event using the *position* field in *CH_MEMBER_TABLE* and sends to them an *EVENT_LOCATION_MSG* as follows:

EVENT_LOCATION_MSG (IDv, localization)

After the verification of existing an event, CH receives an *URGENT_MSG* from vehicles that are considered as observers of event and are included in the observers_list of CH. Then, CH computes credibility of the message when the number of observers *(NbrO)* is upper than a cryptography threshold, which equal to a quarter of number of members *(NbrM)* in cluster otherwise CH chooses other members close to the localization of the considered event.

Computing the Credibility of the Message

A CH consults the *REPUTATION_TABLE* and especially the reputation value of each observer in order to estimate the credibility of the message such as depicted by Figure 1.

- When the reputation value of observer *vi* is negative or equal to zero, this observer is ignored.
- If the reputation value of observer *vi* is positive and the observer *vi* agrees with the reported event, then the counter SUM_{yes} is incremented by 1 and the *IDv* of observer *vi* is included on the observers_list$_{yes}$. Else if the observer *vi* disagrees with the reported event then the counter SUM_{No} is incremented by 1 and the IDv of observer *vi* is included on the observers_list$_{No}$.

Figure 1. Formulas of credibility of message

$$CM_{vx} = \sum_{i}^{observers\_list_{yes}} (REP_{Vi} * (+1)) \div SUM_{YES}$$

$$CM_{vx} = \sum_{i}^{observers\_list_{NO}} (REP_{Vi} * (-1)) \div SUM_{No}$$

If SUM_{yes} is greater than SUM_{No} then the credibility of the message of the vehicle vx ($CMvx$) equals to the sum of reputation value of each an observer vi (REP_{Vi}) on the observers_list$_{yes}$ multiplied by +1. Else, $CMvx$ is computed using the sum of REP_{Vi} on the observers_list$_{No}$ multiplied by -1.

In fact, the observer vi agrees with the reported event that is why we choose to multiply with +1 whereas we multiply with - 1 when the observer vi disagrees with the reported event.

DISTRIBUTED TRUST MANAGEMENT FOR VANET BASED ON TCMV: DTCMV

A Distributed Trust Management scheme for VANET based on TCMV and baptized DTCMV. This latter is built upon the following three steps such as depicted by Figure 2:

Figure 2. DTCMV description

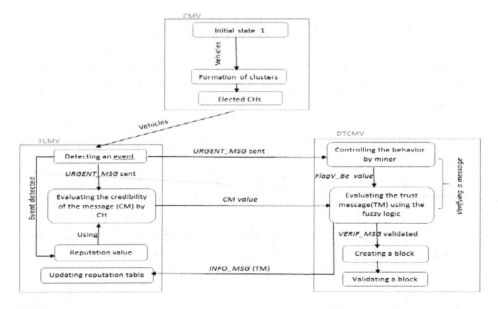

- Transmission of *VERIF_MSG* message.
- Block creation.
- Block validation.

Transmission of VERIF_MSG Message

After detecting an event (accident, traffic jam or obstacle) by vehicle *vx* and the CH appeals TCMV mechanism for computing the credibility of the message, it sends a *VERIF_MSG* to the closest RSU (called miner) in order to verify if this message is correct or no. This message is formalized as follows:

VERIF_MSG (IDvx, ID_CH, RSU, localization, message)

where IDvx corresponds to the vehicle sending the message, ID_CH refers to the CH; RSU refers to the closest miner relative to CH, localization is the position of event, and message corresponds to the event detected.

When miner receives a *VERIF_MSG* by CH, it consults the *RSU_TABLE* in order to control the behavior of the vehicle *vx* during a period z (needed by the CH in order to compute the credibility of the message). The behavior of the vehicle *vx* is given by three parameters: the direction of vehicle *vx*, the velocity of vehicle vx and finally the acceleration. These parameters will be used by a miner to determinate the flag value of the behavior of vehicle *vx* (*FlagV_Bevx*).

- If the vehicle *vx* moves in the same direction, and increases suddenly its velocity and the acceleration, then the *FlagV_Bevx* equals to +1;
- Else if the vehicle *vx* decreases its velocity and the acceleration during a period (z), and changes suddenly its direction, then the *FlagV_Bevx* equals to -1.

After computing the credibility of the message of vehicle *vx*, the CH sends to miner a *CM_MSG* containing the value of *CMvx*. This message is formalized as follows:

CM_MSG (CMvx)

When a miner receives this message and after controlling the behavior of vehicle *vx* for a predefined period (z), this latter takes a decision about the *VERIF_MSG* validation using the fuzzy logic. It has two inputs and four fuzzy sets. The two input parameters are *CMvx* and *FlagV_Bevx*.

- The *CMvx* consists of two fuzzy sets which are [-3,0] and]0,+3];
- The *FlagV_Bevx* can be +1 (positive) and -1 (negative).

The output fuzzy sets consist of two fuzzy sets: Correct Event (CE), Incorrect Event (IE). The rule sets are represented as follows:

- If the *CMvx* belongs to [-3,0], and the *FlagV_Bevx* equals to -1, then the TM (Trust Message) is CE;
- If the *CMvx* belongs to [-3,0], and the *FlagV_Bevx* equals to +1, then the *TM* is IE;
- If the *CMvx* belongs to]0,+3], and the *FlagV_Bevx* equals to -1, then the *TM* is CE;
- If the *CMvx* belongs to]0,+3], and the *FlagV_Bevx* equals to +1, then the *TM* is IE.

Let us note that *TM* has two fuzzy sets: CE, IE. If the *TM* is IE then the *VERIF_MSG* is not valid and miner sends to CH an *INFO_MSG* containing *TM* in order to ignore the message received by *vx* and to appeal the TCMV mechanism for updating the reputation value of vehicle *vx*, this message is formalized as follows: *INFO_MSG* (TM)where TM corresponds to CE or IE.

Else if the TM is CE then the *VERIF_MSG* is valid, miner sends to CH an *INFO_MSG*, broadcasts the message received by *vx* to all members of cluster and other CHs, and it adds the *VERIF_MSG* validated in the pending pool. This latter consists of several *VERIF_MSG* messages validated by miners and are not included in a block yet.

Each miner has a local data structure containing *VERIF_MSG* messages validated (i.e. are not included in a block yet and are selected randomly from the pending pool).

Block Creation

Periodically, each miner selects *VERIF_MSG* messages from local data structure and generates a new block. This block consists of several *VERIF_MSG* messages *Mi* validated as well as a link to the previous block that join these blocks (Lei et al. 2016). Block consists of the block header and the block body as shown in Figure 3.

The block header includes:

- The block version indicates the position of this block in the BlockChain.
- The Parent Block Hash (*Hprev*) is a hash value linking the block to the previous block.

Figure 3. Block structure

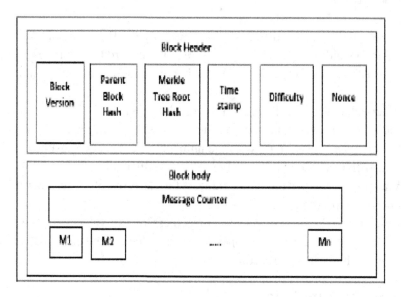

- Merkle tree root (*Hroot*) is a hash value of all the transactions included in the block.
- Timestamp records the time at which block is generated.
- Difficulty (*D*) is a metric to find a successfully hash. There are two ways of describing the difficulty. The first represents it as the number of zeros with starting the hash result of the block header, whereas the second measures an estimated difficulty target. The target is a 256-bit number of hash calculations to extract a block. Then, to accept block, the hash value must be below this target.
- The nonce (*N*) is a counter i.e. used in Proof Of Work (POW), usually starts with 0 and increases for every hash calculation.

The block body is built upon a *VERIF_MSG* counter and all verified *VERIF_MSG* messages *Mi*.

After its creation, the block must be signed with the private key of the creating miner and broadcast to all other miners of the overlay for verification. Then, it validated for chaining to the BlockChain such as detailed in the next step.

Block Validation

Each miner can generate a different block but only the first one solving its POW will be able to validate it. POW is a digital receipt i.e. hard to calculate but easy for others to verify (Zheng, et al. 2016). POW is built upon the following four steps:

1. Miner calculates a hash value of the block header.
2. The block header is hashed continuously using different nonce value until the calculated value starts with the numbers of zeros and must be equal to or smaller than a certain given value called the difficulty.
3. When miner reaches the target value, it forwards the block to other miners in order to verify the calculated value.
4. If all other miners confirm the correctness of the value then the block is validated and others would append this new block to the end of BlockChains using the hash of the preceding block.

Updating the Reputation

Each CH has a *REPUTATION_TABLE* containing its members with their reputations. The reputation value of vehicle is incremented or decremented according to *TM*. If *TM* equals to *CE* then the reputation value of vehicle *vx* is incremented by +0.2. Else if *TM* equals to *IE* then the reputation value of vehicle *vx* is decremented by -0.2.

If the reputation value of vehicle *vx* reaches the minimum value -3 then CH considers it as dishonest vehicle and puts it in the blacklist.

Therefore, CH broadcasts an *ALERT_MSG* with the flag value equal to 1 to notify members of cluster, their RSU and others CHs that exist a dishonest vehicle.

RELATED WORKS

Clustering Mechanism in VANET

Zhang et al. (2011) proposed a multi-hop clustering solution with a new mobility metric depending on relative mobility between vehicles in multi-hop distance. However, such proposal is not feasible for such dynamic networks. Likewise, Ucar et al. (2013) introduced a Vehicular Multi-hop algorithm for Stable Clustering in vehicular ad hoc networks called VMaSC. This algorithm deals with changes of mobility of vehicles, which is computed by finding the average of the relative velocity of all the similar direction neighbors. Arkian et al. (2015) proposed a new 2-layer clustering scheme using an adaptive multiple metric in VANET. In the first layer, the

RSU acts as static cluster head. In the second layer, vehicles form dynamic clusters and the dynamic cluster heads is chosen based on a new multiple metric (mobility and local Quality of Service metrics) called suitability value and the static cluster head (i.e. RSU) become its members.

Trust Management in VANET

Raya et al. (2008) introduced a framework for data-centric trust establishment. This system evaluates data trustworthiness reported by other entities rather than trust of the entities themselves. Given that each vehicle computes the report about an event, hence multiple reports relative to the single event from all vehicles are combined to estimate the probability of the event. However, this approach focuses only on the data and it does not take into account the trustworthiness of the sender or the forwarder of event messages. Huang et al. (2014) proposed a novel voting scheme. In this approach, each vehicle has different voting weight based on the distance between sender and event, and the closer vehicle to the event obtains larger weight, to absorb the Information Cascading and Oversampling (ICO). However, some vehicles, which are far to the event, give a false weight vote. In addition, this approach focuses on the voting weight based on the distance between sender and event rather than the reputation of vehicles. Lo et al. (2009) proposed an event-based reputation system in VANET to provide reliable traffic information and filter the false messages spread by malicious attackers in the network. This mechanism is introduced to calculate confidence, using the event reputation value, and trust threshold. The reputation value is incremented by 1 in the received message when a vehicle detects an event. The number of vehicles, which generate messages of the same event, represents the event confidence value. If the event confidence value and reputation value are equaled with the defined threshold, then the event will be considered a true event. However, the high mobility of vehicles in VANET will allow a short time to detect an event. Wei et al. (2012) proposed a RSU and beacon-based trust management model, called RaBTM where the fixed equipment knows as RSU determines the trustworthiness of event messages from cross-checking the verisimilitude of event messages and beacon messages. This approach aims to prevent malicious insiders from sending or forwarding falsified messages to other nodes into VANETs. However, RSU is a fixed equipment, cannot be responsible to manage for the coordination between vehicles due to the high change topology in VANET.

BlockChain in VANET

Rowan et al. (2017) proposed a BlockChain technology for securing inter-vehicles communication using side-channels. The proposed mechanism is verified using a new session cryptographic key, leveraging both physical side-channels and a BlockChain public key infrastructure. However, the communication is required for autonomous vehicles and these latter imply security issues. Dorri et al. (2017) proposed a BlockChain based architecture to ensure the privacy of the users by using changeable Public Keys (PK) and to enhance the security of the vehicular ecosystem. The architecture allows a novel automotive service and updates the wireless remote. However, this approach lacks practical issues for example membership management and scalability. Yong yuan, et al. (2016) proposed a BlockChain based intelligent transportation systems (ITS) to provide a secured, trusted and decentralized autonomous ecosystem. In addition, authors have designed an ITS-oriented, seven-layer conceptual model for BlockChain. However, intelligent transportation implies lack of trust where data is to be shared, thereby intermediaries have to be introduced leading an great complexity. Benjamin et al. (2016) have combined Vehicle Ad-hoc Networks and Ethereum's BlockChain. The proposed technology provides security, communication between vehicles without disclosing personal information, updates on traffic jams and weather forecasts and can use others VANET services. However, Benjamin et al. are not calculating the correctness message exchanged to check it.

In this chapter, the main focus is verifying the message considering the control of the vehicle's behavior by a miner and the credibility of message by CH in order to improve security of communication between entities in VANET.

FUTURE RESEARCH DIRECTIONS

Vehicular communications are expected to share different kinds of information between vehicles. However, the presence of dishonest vehicles in the route may lead to the drop or modification of the content of the exchanged messages. Thus, it is a challenge to find and maintain an efficient route for transmitting reliable information. It is aimed to propose a new routing protocol for VANETs based on trust. This protocol uses the trustworthiness of the path and the number of hops in order to find the optimal route.

CONCLUSION

In this chapter, we presented a secured and distributed clustering mechanism for messages exchange in VANET. The clustering mechanism is built upon two phases: the clusters setting up based on vehicles velocity and the maintenance of cluster (the displacement of a vehicle or the arrival of a new vehicle). The purpose is to ensure security of communication between vehicles based on the computing the credibility of message by CH using the reputations of observers and the controlling of the behavior of the vehicle by miner.

REFERENCES

Altoaimy, L., & Mahgoub, I. (2014, December). Fuzzy logic based localization for vehicular ad hoc networks. In *Computational Intelligence in Vehicles and Transportation Systems (CIVTS), 2014 IEEE Symposium on* (pp. 121-128). IEEE.

Arkian, H. R., Atani, R. E., Pourkhalili, A., & Kamali, S. (2015). A Stable Clustering Scheme Based on Adaptive Multiple Metric in Vehicular Ad-hoc Networks. *Journal of Information Science and Engineering, 31*(2), 361–386.

Azizian, M., Cherkaoui, S., & Hafid, A. S. (2016, April). A distributed d-hop cluster formation for VANET. In *Wireless Communications and Networking Conference (WCNC)* (pp. 1-6). IEEE. 10.1109/WCNC.2016.7564925

Dorri, A., Steger, M., Kanhere, S. S., & Jurdak, R. (2017). Blockchain: A distributed solution to automotive security and privacy. *IEEE Communications Magazine, 55*(12), 119–125. doi:10.1109/MCOM.2017.1700879

Ghafoor, K. Z., Bakar, K. A., van Eenennaam, M., Khokhar, R. H., & Gonzalez, A. J. (2013). A fuzzy logic approach to beaconing for vehicular ad hoc networks. *Telecommunication Systems, 52*(1), 139–149. doi:10.100711235-011-9466-8

Hadded, M., Zagrouba, R., Laouiti, A., Muhlethaler, P., & Saidane, L. A. (2015, May). A multi-objective genetic algorithm-based adaptive weighted clustering protocol in vanet. In *Evolutionary Computation (CEC), 2015 IEEE Congress on* (pp. 994-1002). IEEE.

Huang, Z., Ruj, S., Cavenaghi, M. A., Stojmenovic, M., & Nayak, A. (2014). A social network approach to trust management in VANETs. *Peer-to-Peer Networking and Applications, 7*(3), 229–242. doi:10.100712083-012-0136-8

Kchaou, A., Abassi, R., & Guemara El Fatmi, S. (2018). Towards a Secured Clustering Mechanism for Messages Exchange in VANET. *Proceedings of the 32-nd IEEE International Conference on Advanced Information Networking and Applications (AINA-2018).* 10.1109/WAINA.2018.00068

Lei, A., Ogah, C., Asuquo, P., Cruickshank, H., & Sun, Z. (2016). A secure key management scheme for heterogeneous secure vehicular communication systems. *ZTE Communications, 21*, 1.

Leiding, B., Memarmoshrefi, P., & Hogrefe, D. (2016, September). Self-managed and blockchain-based vehicular ad-hoc networks. In *Proceedings of the 2016 ACM International Joint Conference on Pervasive and Ubiquitous Computing: Adjunct* (pp. 137-140). ACM.

Lo, N. W., & Tsai, H. C. (2009). A reputation system for traffic safety event on vehicular ad hoc networks. *EURASIP Journal on Wireless Communications and Networking, 2009*(1), 9. doi:10.1155/2009/125348

Raya, M., Papadimitratos, P., Gligor, V. D., & Hubaux, J. P. (2008, April). On data-centric trust establishment in ephemeral ad hoc networks. In *INFOCOM 2008. The 27th Conference on Computer Communications. IEEE* (pp. 1238-1246). IEEE.

Rowan, S., Clear, M., Gerla, M., Huggard, M., & Goldrick, C. M. (2017). *Securing vehicle to vehicle communications using blockchain through visible light and acoustic side-channels.* arXiv preprint arXiv:1704.02553

Singh, M., & Kim, S. (2017). *Blockchain Based Intelligent Vehicle Data sharing Framework.* arXiv preprint arXiv:1708.09721

Ucar, S., Ergen, S. C., & Ozkasap, O. (2013, April). VMaSC: Vehicular multi-hop algorithm for stable clustering in vehicular ad hoc networks. In *Wireless Communications and Networking Conference (WCNC)* (pp. 2381-2386). IEEE. 10.1109/WCNC.2013.6554933

Wei, Y. C., & Chen, Y. M. (2012). Reliability and Efficiency Improvement for Trust Management Model in VANETs. In *Human Centric Technology and Service in Smart Space* (pp. 105–112). Dordrecht: Springer. doi:10.1007/978-94-007-5086-9_14

Yuan, Y., & Wang, F. Y. (2016, November). Towards blockchain-based intelligent transportation systems. In *Intelligent Transportation Systems (ITSC), 2016 IEEE 19th International Conference on* (pp. 2663-2668). IEEE. 10.1109/ITSC.2016.7795984

Zhang, Z., Boukerche, A., & Pazzi, R. (2011, October). A novel multi-hop clustering scheme for vehicular ad-hoc networks. In *Proceedings of the 9th ACM international symposium on Mobility management and wireless access* (pp. 19-26). ACM. 10.1145/2069131.2069135

Zheng, Z., Xie, S., Dai, H. N., & Wang, H. (2016). Blockchain challenges and opportunities: A survey. *Work Pap.*, 2016.

Chapter 10
Security Policies a Formal Environment for a Test Cases Generation

Ryma Abassi
SUPCOM, Tunisia

Sihem Guemara El Fatmi
SUPCOM, Tunisia

ABSTRACT

Specifying a security policy (SP) is a challenging task in the development of secure communication systems since it is the bedrock of any security strategy. Paradoxically, this specification is error prone and can lead to an inadequate SP regarding the security needs. Therefore, it seems necessary to define an environment allowing one to "trust" the implemented SP. A testing task aims verifying whether an implementation is conforming to its specification. Test is generally achieved by generating and executing test cases. Some automated testing tools can be used from which model checkers. In fact, given a system modeling and a test objective, the model checker can generate a counterexample from which test cases can be deduced. The main proposition of this chapter is then a formal environment for SP test cases generation based on a system modeling, a SP specification (test purpose), and the use of a model checker. Once generated, these test cases must be improved in order to quantify their effectiveness to detect SP flaws. This is made through the generation of mutants.

DOI: 10.4018/978-1-5225-7353-1.ch010

1. INTRODUCTION

The need for security is driven by the increasingly proportion of losses caused to the organizations due to various security incidents. One reason of this can be a lack of a global security environment that differentiate between the actions to authorize and those to deny trough a set of rules, generally grouped in a document referred to as security policy (SP). SP development is unfortunately, a sensitive task because it may contain errors, or may be generated by wrong decisions or wrong evaluations of the security organization needs. In order to avoid such problems a validation process is necessary before any deployment. SP validation consists in checking if the policy matches all the security needs i.e. are we building the right SP? In recent works, we proposed a three-step process allowing the validation of a SP (Abbassi & El Fatmi, 2008b, 2009). In the first step, we proved that the SP is consistent. The second step dealt with proving the completeness of the SP according to the initial requirements while in the third step, we proved the preservation of the security properties. However, validation is not enough to ensure that the SP is correctly enforced. In fact, once the SP is formally and correctly specified, it is essential to prove that it is correctly implemented in the system, too. This can be done by testing the enforced SP.

Moreover, we have found that the theory developed for this aim in the software engineering domain can be adapted for SP because several similarities exist between the expressions of the needs in the two domains as mentioned in several studies. In the software engineering domain, testing entails the execution of the software system in the real environment, under operational conditions (Belli & Guldali, 2004). It is used in order to verify whether an implementation is conforming to its specification (supposed correct) i.e. checking that the behavior of a real implementation is correct with respect to a specification (Calame, 2005). Such testing is carried out by test cases, i.e., ordered pairs of test inputs and expected test outputs (Felli & Guildali, 2004). By analogy, testing a given network configuration for compliance with a stated SP is a kind of conformance testing.

Furthermore, since testing task needs the use of automated tools, model checkers can be used. In fact, given a system model and a test criterion, the model checker can generate a counterexample from which test cases can be deduced. A model checker visits all reachable states of the model and verifies whether the expected system properties, specified as temporal logic formula, are satisfied over each possible path. If a property is not satisfied, the model checker attempts to generate a counterexample in the form of a trace as a sequence of states.

In this paper, we propose a framework to model a SP, to formally specify it and to test its implementation regarding some security exigencies and thus, using the model checking technique. This framework is based on the concept of Executable

Security Policies (ESP), that we introduced in Abassi and El Fatmi (2008a, 2008b, 2009) in order to model the behavior of a given SP before its actual implementation. More precisely, we take as input: (1) a formal model of a network together with its embedded ESP. This model is expressed in S-Promela, a Promela based language handling security aspects. (2) Some Test Purposes (TP) describing desired behaviors. TP are expressed by the Linear Temporal Logic LTL (Kroger, 1987). As output, we generate Test Cases (TC) in order to verify that the desired SP is correctly enforced in the considered network.

Moreover, we proposed a mutation analysis process based on some mutation operators and used in order to introduce flaws in the SP implementation. In fact, the use of policy mutants as substitutes for real flaws enables a first investigation of tested SP (Elrakaiby, Mouelhi & LeTraon, 2012). These operators are chosen to assess the ability of a TC to detect potential problems in the SP implementation. More precisely, for each one of the main rule components i.e. type, modality, subject, object, action, constraint and event we define a number of mutation operators injecting minimal errors. Thus, the inability of a TC to detect mutants would reveal its incapacity to detect SP enforcement errors.

The rest of this paper is organized as follows. In Section 2, we resume our propositions concerning the modeling of SP and more exactly of an ESP. In Section 3, our SP testing method is depicted based on a Promela based language: S-Promela, a TP modeling and a TC generation. Section 4 presents the mutation analysis associated to our testing method. A case study illustrating these theoretical concepts is given in Section 5 as a real application to what has been stated formally. Finally, Section 7 concludes this paper.

2. EXECUTABLE SECURITY POLICY MODELING

The RFC 2196 (Fraser, 1997) defines a SP as a "formal statement of the rules by which people who are given access to an organization technology and information assets must abide". More generally, the main objective of a SP is to maintain the principles of the organization's general security strategy. These principles cover several aspects such as detailed in Belli and Guldai (2004). Besides, SP and network specifications are generally based on a formal modeling. SP modeling constitutes a very important task because it helps the definition of the security rules and allows their management i.e. validation, test, etc.

2.1. Security Policies Basis

A SP is composed by a set of rules. According to the previous SP definition and considering the whole system in which a SP can be deployed, we have found in recent works (Abassi & El Fatmi, 2008a, 2008b, 2009), that a modeling task requires the definition of the following concepts: (1) subject s that represents an active entity in the system like human users, employees, processes, applications or programs (2) object o that represents a passive entity in the system like ports, data or hosts (3) action a that represents an action that can be performed by a subject on an object like connection or read and/or write requests (4) constraints c that we used to precise an action applicability scope and (5) events e that are triggered in order to induce a rule execution (6) type t that can be a request or an obligation and (7) a modality m that can be positive or negative.

$$R: t \times m \times s \times a \times o \times c \times e \tag{1}$$

These seven components can be used in order to model three rules types:

1. **Request Rule**: States that a given subject requests performing a given action on a given object. This request can be granted or denied. Formally, it is expressed as:

$$req(s \times a \times o \times [c] \times [e]) \rightarrow resp \tag{2}$$

where resp is the expected rule response. This response may evolve over time i.e. according to the satisfaction of certain constraints; it can be yes or no. For example, someone trying to withdraw money from his bank account can be authorized to do so or not depending on the availability of money in this account.

2. **Obligation Rule**: Following the occurrence of an event, a given action has to be performed. Formally, it is expressed as:

$$ob(s \times a \times o \times [c] \times e) \tag{3}$$

3. **Prohibition Rule**: SP prohibits the occurrence of a certain action in the protected system. The prohibition syntax is similar to the request rule syntax in that sense that it is a request made by a subject and to which the SP must respond. However, prohibition response is always 'no'. Formally, it is expressed by:

$$phb(s \times a \times o \times [c] \times [e]) \rightarrow no \tag{4}$$

Figure 1. ESP modeling

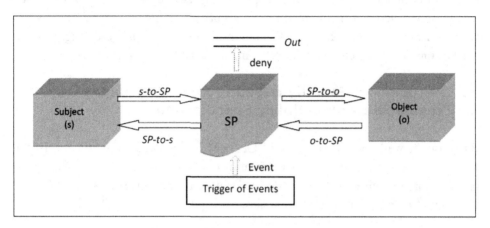

In Abassi and El Fatmi (2008a), we proposed the concept of Executable Security Policy (ESP) as a mean of SP validation. We defined an ESP as a SP model that can generate the expected behavior of a secured system communicating with its environment according to the security exigencies specified by the SP. When using ESP, the behavior of the SP can be observed and tested before it is actually enforced on the desired system.

Figure 1 represents an ESP as a mean of communication between two network components where the communication is made following the several rules composing the SP. In this Figure, four actors are depicted: the subject, the object, the SP and the trigger of events. All potential interaction between a subject and an object must be made through the SP i.e. a subject cannot interact directly with an object. In this Figure, the communication channel is split into four half duplex channels depending on the actor where the request come from and the actor where the request is addressed. A subject s submits his request via the channel *s-to-SP*. The SP verifies the legitimacy of the request from the set of SP rules. In the case where the request is granted, it is transmitted to the corresponding object o via the *SP-to-o* channel. The response of this request is then sent back by the object via the *o-to-SP* channel. Once received by the SP, this response reaches the subject s via the *SP-to-s* channel. In the case where the requested access is denied, the SP reject it into the out channel and delivers to the subject an error message without implying the *SP-to-o* and *o-to-SP* channels. Moreover, each channel can be accessed either for insertion or extraction. Hence, a mode is associated to each one of these operations: the write mode for insertion and the read mode for extraction.

The model represented by the Figure 1 considers also a trigger of events allowing the generation of all potential events for which the SP must react. These events are useful for obligation rules as explained previously. Hence, we assume the existence of a table, created and maintained by the security responsible, associating events with the rules they may trigger. Let's note that the model depicted by Figure 1 is a generic one. It can be customized following a particular rule type.

2.2. S-Promela: A Security-Based Promela Language for Executable Security Policy Specification

Based on the well-known, Promela (PROcess MEta Language) (Holzmann, 1991), we proposed a new executable SP specification language called S-Promela (Security-based Promela). This latter has well defined syntax and a precise semantics designed to fit with SP specification particularities.

2.2.1. S-Promela Syntax

Promela allows the description of a system as a composition of process instances which are executed in parallel and interact asynchronously through message passing (Holzmann, 1991). However as mentioned before, Promela as it is, is not adequate to handle the security specificities and an extension is needed. This extension is based on the original Promela syntax and adds some concepts basically for the specification of the rule types. In Figures 3, 4, 5, 6, 7, 8, 9 and 10 the S-Promela syntax is depicted in which the reader can recognize some Promela components: where (1) Declarations defining all needed variables such as channels, subjects, objects, etc. (2) Pre-defined terms defining known values such as Boolean terms, etc (3) Control flow constructors defining conditional expressions, repetition expressions, etc. and (4) Basic statements, expressing the elementary SP behavior that we will call SP primitives as well as other required statements such conditions, expressions, etc.

Let's note that in the following figures, '[]' introduces optional terms, '*' indicates zero or more repetitions of a term, '|' separates several choices and '" "' surrounds literals.

A rule describes actions that subjects can execute on objects when some constraints are fulfilled. This is depicted by Figure 3 where:

Figure 2. S-Promela specification structure

SP	S-PromelaSPec	::=	Procs	
	Procs	::=	Procd	| Procs
	Procd	::=	rule	

Figure 3. Rule syntax

Rules	*rule*	::=	*While' '('* Condition *')' 'do'* Sequence [*andor* Sequence]*	
	Condition	::=	*Expr*	*|Evt-occur*
	Expr	::=	*Expr*	*|Expr Binaop Expr*
			|Expr Andor Expr	*|Sequence*
	Evt-occur	::=	*'occurs' '(' event ')'*	
	Sequence	::=	*'{' Primitive '}'*	*| '{' pfm-action '}' | '{' Procd '}'*

- **Condition**: Represents a condition to the triggering of a rule.
- **Expr**: Represents a given expression.
- **Evt-Occur**: Represents the occurrence of an event.
- **Sequence**: Represents an execution sequence that may be a set of primitives, a function or a procedure execution.

Furthermore, each procedure is composed by four parts: declaration (Figure 4), predefined terms (Figure 5), control expressions (Figure 6) and basics declarations (Figure 7).

A declaration can have one of the following forms:

- **Channel**: Declares a communication channel. It is identified by the communicating entities which are the both ends of the channel, e.g. channel s-to-SP identifies a channel that carries a flow from the subject S and to the SP.
- **Action**: Declares an action (requested or that must be done) that a subject (try or has to) perform on an object.
- **Message**: Declares an action response from object.
- **Subject**: The subject interacting through the SP.
- **Object**: The object targeted by an action.
- **Event**: Declares a triggered event.
- **Procedure**: Declares a procedure having zero or one parameter, the triggered event. A procedure is instantiated through its name.
- **Notification**: Represents a notification sent by the SP to a subject.
- **Struct**: Declares a structure composed by two elements: the triggered event and its associated procedure dictating what actions should be performed when the event occurs.
- **Table**: Declares a table of struct.

Figure 4. Declarative part of S-Promela syntax

Declaration	channel	::=	name
		subject	::=	name
		object	::=	name
		action	::=	name
		message	::=	name
		event	::=	name
		constraint	::=	name
		notification	::=	name
		Procedure	::=	'procedure' name '(' [event] ')'
		Struct	::=	'struct' name '{' (event, Procedure) * '}'
		Table	::=	Struct name '[' integer ']'

A pre-defined term depicted by Figure 6 can be one of the following forms:

- **Boolean**: Represents the true and false values.
- **Comment**: Presents the syntax of a comment.
- **Skip**: Shorthand for a dummy, nill statement.
- **Pfm-Action**: An entity executes an action given in parameters. This function returns the result of the execution as a special message.
- **Name**: A set of characters and/or numbers.
- **Entity**: The entity performing the primitive. It can be a subject, an object or the SP.
- **Var**: Corresponds to an entity, an event or a message.
- **Parameters**: Constitutes the arguments of the primitive. Four parameters are used: channel, action, message, and event.
- **Condition**: Represents the guard of a selection/ repetition construct.
- **Expr**: Represents a given expression. The expression nil is the last element of a table.

A Control flow statement can have one of the following forms as depicted by Figure 6:

- **Conditional**: Declares a selection construct.
- **Repetition**: Declares a repetition construct.
- **Separator**: Declares a step separator.
- **Sequence**: Declares brackets to enclose an arbitrary block of code.

Figure 5. Predefined terms syntax

Pre-def terms	Boolean	::=	true		false
	| Comment	::=	/'*' comment '*' /		
	| skip	::=	'skip'		
	| nil	::=	'nil'		
	| Pfm-action	::=	'pfm-action' '(' Entity ',' Parameters ')'		
	| name	::=	char [char | number] *		
	| Entity	::=	subject	| object	| SP
	| Parameters	::=	channel ',' [action | message] ',' object		
			| action	| event	| constraint
	| Affectation	::=	Var '=' Expr		
	| Var	::=	Entity	| event	| message

- **Andor**: Declares the logical operators and, or.
- **Binarop**: Declares binary operators e.g equality, lesser than, greater than, different, etc.
- **'='**: An assignment statement which replaces the value of Var with the value of expr.

A basic statement can have one of the following forms as depicted by Figure 8:

- **Primitive**: Represents SP-based primitives used to model the interaction between subject, SP and object. Two primitives are depicted: write and read.
  - **Write**: An entity puts a message into a channel.
  - **read**: An entity extracts a message from a channel.
- **Evt-Occur**: Represents the occurrence of a given event specified by the associated parameter

Figure 6. Control expression syntax

Ctrl-flow	Conditional	::=	'If' '(' Condition ')' 'then' Sequence [andor Sequence]* ['else' Sequence]		
	| Separator	::=	Expr ';' Expr		
	| Andor	::=	'&&'	| '||'	
	| Binarop ::=	'=='		| '<'	| '>'
		| '≠'	| '≥'	| '≤'	

Figure 7. Basics statements syntax

Basic stmts	|*Primitive*	::=	*Write*	|*Read*
	|*Write*	::=	*entity '-' 'write' '(' parameters ')'.*	
	|*Read*	::=	*entity '-' 'read' '(' parameters ')'.*	

Let's note that obligation rules may be triggered by a single event or by a conjunction of events. This is depicted by Figure 8 where:

- Synchronization supports two operators:
  - '∧': Specifies the occurrence of two events independently of their occurrence order.
  - '∨': Specifies the occurrence of only one of the synchronized events.
- Precedence indicates that *event1* must be triggered before *event2*.
- Repetition: indicates that an event has to be triggered n times where n is an integer.

SP composition is a useful concept because it allows the reuse of rules already specified in order to create new SP and thus without writing them each time. SP composition is handled by S-Promela using operators defined in Figure 9:

- **Addition**: Returns the union of two rules. In such case, an action cannot be granted unless one of the two rules grant it. Similarly, an action is denied if at least one of the two rules denies it.
- **Product**: Returns the rules intersection implying that an action is granted (resp. denied) if one of the two rules authorizes (resp. denies) it.
- **Substraction**: Returns the components of the first rule not belonging to the second one.

For example:

Figure 8. Events composition operators Syntax

Evt operators	*Synchronization*	::=	∧	| ∨
	|*Precedence*	::=	*event1 → event2*	
	|*Repetition*	::=	*n * event*	

Figure 9. Composition Operators Syntax

Composition	Addition	::=	rule '+' rule
	|Product	::=	rule '*' rule
	| Substraction	::=	rule '-' rule

- *Subject user*1; declares a subject named *user1*.
- *req*{*user*1, *read, file*1} stands for a request rule where *user1* requests to read *file1*.
- *when*(*receive* − *mail*) *pfm*{*user, scan, mail*} stands for an obligation rule where a user is obliged to scan all received mails.

In the rest of this paper and according to what is stated by Promela, '!' represents an input and '?' represents an output.

2.2.2 S-Promela Semantics

By analogy to Promela, the S-Promela process semantic is an Extended Finite State Machine (EFSM) defined through a vocabulary $\sum$, a set of sates S, an initial state s_0 and a set of transitions T. In the following, an adequate EFSM for each rule type introduced previously is presented.

```
Positive request rules:
An EFSM associated to the positive request rule is formally
expressed as:
R^r = (∑^r, S^r, s_0^r, T^r)
in which:
S^r = s_0^r, s_1^r, s_2^r, s_3^r,
T_r = t_1, t_2, t_3 where t_1 = s_0^r, true, SP - read (S - to - SP, a, o, c), s_1^r;
                          t_2 = s_1^r, c, SP - write (SP - to - o, a, o),  s_2^r;
                          t_3 = s_1^r, ¬c, SP - write (out, a, o), s_3^r;
and accept = s_2^r, s_3^r.
Prohibition rules:
An EFSM associated to a prohibition rule is formally expressed
as:
R^ph = (∑^ph, S^ph, s_0^ph, T^ph)
in which:
S^ph = s_0^ph, s_1^ph, s_2^ph,
```

$T^{ph} = t_1, t_2$ where $t_1 = s_0^{ph}$, true, $SP - read$ $(S - to - SP, a, o, c)$, s_1^{ph};
$$t_2 = s_1^{ph}, c, SP - write (out, a, o), s_2^{ph};$$
and $accept = s_2^{ph}$.

We have to note that the prohibition rule is modeled similarly to the negative request rule. In fact, as explained before, the negative request rule can be modeled by a request for which we associate a negative response. Hence, it can be tested by the use of the EFSM R^{ph}.

Obligation rules:
In our model, we took as an assumption that an obligation is triggered by a temporal event. Hence, an EFSM associated to an obligation rule is formally expressed as:
$R^o = (\sum^o, S^o, s_0^o, T^o)$
in which:
$S^o = s_0^o, s_1^o, s_2^o,$
$T^o = t_1, t_2$ where $t_1 = s_0^o$, true, $occurs(e)$, s_1^o;
$$t_2 = s_1^o, true \; SP - write (SP - to - o, a, o), s_2^o;$$
and $accept = s_2^o$.

Based on this modeling, we introduce in the following our SP testing method.

3. A SECURITY POLICIES TESTING METHOD PROPOSITION

Most TC synthesis tools such as TGV (Jard & Jeron, 2005) follow the scheme of Figure 11: given a reference model, and some TP, they produce a set of TC (Ledru et al., 2001). The reference model is a specification of the intended behavior of the system under test. Synthesis tool's role is to select TC from the specification behavior. For this, a second input is needed: the TP depicting the functionalities to be tested. The tool's output is then a set of TC describing the behavior of the system under test and verdicts associated to those behaviors.

Our proposition is based on the same scheme while using a model checker: the reference model is a S-Promela model of the network with its SP, TP are the desired security exigencies and are specified using LTL, the used synthesis tool is SPIN and the generated counter example is the TC. Such approach benefits from the counterexample generation capability of model checkers for constructing TC. Thus, model checkers build a finite state transition system and exhaustively explore the reachable state space searching for violations of the properties under investigation. If a property violation is detected, the model checker produces a counterexample

Figure 10. General structure of the proposed testing method

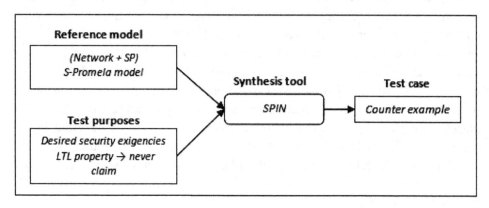

illustrating how this violation can take place. In short, a counterexample is a sequence of inputs that will take the finite state model from its initial state to a state where the violation occurs.

In this work, the reference model is the SP specification for which we proposed an adequate modeling language: S-Promela. The synthesis tool is SPIN, the model checker associated to Promela, which is one of the most advanced model checker when handling large state spaces (de Vries & Tretmans, 1998). SPIN is also, an on-the-fly model checker used to support system validation and verification by automatically assessing the validity of a property expressed in LTL (Holzmann, 1991). The test purposes are the desired security properties. They are described using LTL which is the classical SPIN property input. The SPIN output is then, a counterexample from which TC can be deduced.

A network can be modeled by (D, P) where D is a set of data messages and P is a set of process types. A Process is defined as an EFSM (Extended Finite State Machine) formalized as $(\Sigma, S, s_0, T) \in P$ where Σ is the input alphabet, S is a finite set of states, $s_0 \in S$ is the initial state and T is the transition set (Mallouli et al., 2007). A transition is defined as $(s, c, a, s') \in T$ where $s \in S$ is the source state; c is a constraint, a is an action and $s' \in S$ is the target state (Mallouli et al., 2007).

For the testing needs, two trap states are associated to an EFSM. A trap state is a state for which *trap:S→true, false* defined as $trap(s) = \forall(s, a, s') \in T(s = s')$ holds (Calame, 2005).

The trap state returning true is called *accept state* while the trap sate returning a false value is called *refuse state*. The notion of accept state is used to select targeted behaviors while the notion of refuse state is used to cut down the exploration of the specification state space when undesired actions are taken. Hence, a rule can be modeled by an EFSM equipped with two sets of trap states noted $accept^R$ and $refuse^R$.

The third needed notion is TP. A TP is "a prose description of a well-defined objective of testing, focusing on a single conformance requirement or a set of related conformance requirement" (ISO/IEC 9646-1/2/3, 1992). Average networks have a very large state space. Generating test cases just relying on this state space can be a very time-consuming activity producing a large number of test cases. Limiting the generated test cases to certain aspects of the whole system can speed up the generation process and leads to a much smaller result space. These aspects are defined as test purposes. In practice, TP are informal descriptions of behaviors to be tested. In our approach, we model TP by Büchi Automata since we intend generating TC by the use of the SPIN model checker. Formally, a TP is a Büchi Automaton formalized as:

$$TP = (S^{TP,} I^{TP}, T^{TP}, F^{TP}) \tag{9}$$

where: S^{TP}: set of states; $I^{TP} \in S$: set of initial states; $T^{TP}:S \rightarrow 2^S$ is a transition relation and $F^{TP} \in S$: set of accepting sates (Holzmann, 1991).

3.1. Test Purpose Generation

As mentioned above, TP are designed to represent functionalities of the system behavior. Hence, we associate a TP to each type of rule and we define them by LTL (Kroger, 1987) according to what is required by the model checker SPIN. TP can be expressed with LTL using Boolean operators and temporal modalities F and G. A TP is expressed by a logical formula built upon literals. Each literal can be either a constraint literal or an event literal (Kroger, 1987).

1. *Constraint literals* (C) express information about the rule's components i.e. subject, object and action. *Student*(x) for example, indicates that the subject x is a student where $has - password(X, Y)$ indicates that X has the password Y.
2. *Event literals* (E) express information about the occurrence of a transition in the system behavior.

In this work, we consider two events types: internal event representing the execution of an action and external event representing temporal events used as rules triggers.

Figure 11 depicts the proposed LTL modeling of TP using the assumptions presented above where $G \, \alpha$ stands for "always" i.e. always holds; and $F \, \alpha$ stands for "eventually" i.e. will hold in a given time in the future. A TP can then, have one of the following forms: $G \, req$: an authorization; $G \, oblig$: an obligation ad $G \, proh$: a prohibition.

A request rule is triggered by the fulfillment of a constraint C and leads to the occurrence, finally, of an internal event. It can be triggered also, by a conjunction

Figure 11. Test purpose's syntax

P	:=	$G\,req \mid G\,oblig \mid G\,proh$
Req	:=	$C \Rightarrow F\,Ei \mid C \wedge Ee \Rightarrow F\,Ei$
$oblig$	:=	$Ee \Rightarrow F\,Ei \mid C \wedge Ee \Rightarrow F\,Ei$
$proh$	:=	$C \Rightarrow G\neg Ei \mid C \wedge Ee \Rightarrow G\neg Ei$
E	:=	$Ei \mid Ee$
Ei	:=	$literal$
Ee	:=	$lieral \mid Ee \wedge Ee \mid Ee \vee Ee$
C	:=	$lieral \mid C \wedge C \mid C \vee C$

of a constraint C and an event E_e. We want to test whether each time that a subject s requests to perform the action a on the object o, he can do it. For example, a rule stating that *req(user, change, password, $-$, $-$)$\rightarrow$yes* meaning that *"each user can change its password"* can be expressed by the following TP as: *User(X)$\wedge$has $-$ password(X, Y)$\Longrightarrow$F change(X, Y)* and tests whether any user having a password can change it.

An obligation rule An obligation is triggered by the occurrence of an external event and leads to the occurrence finally, of a given internal event. It can be triggered by a conjunction of an event E_e and a constraint C too. We want to test whether each time an event e occurs, the action a is executed on the object o by subject s. For example, a rule stating that *ob (administrator, change, password, $-$, beginning $-$ month)* meaning that *"an administrator must change its password every beginning of month"* can be expressed by the following TP as: *User(X)$\wedge$has $-$ password(X, Y)$\wedge$Beginning $-$ month $\Longrightarrow$F change(X, Y)* and tests whether user is obliged to change its password every beginning of month.

A prohibition rule is triggered by the fulfillment of a constraint C and leads to the nonoccurrence of a given internal event. It can be triggered by a conjunction of a constraint C and an event E_e too. We want to test whether each time the action a is requested, it is not being executed. For example, a rule stating that

proh(user, change, password, not his, $-$)$\rightarrow$no meaning that *"user shall not change a password which is not his"* can be expressed by the following TP as: *user(X)$\wedge\neg$password(X, Y)$\Longrightarrow$G$\neg$change(X, Y)* and tests whether a user cannot change a password which is not his.

Figure 12. Proposed framework

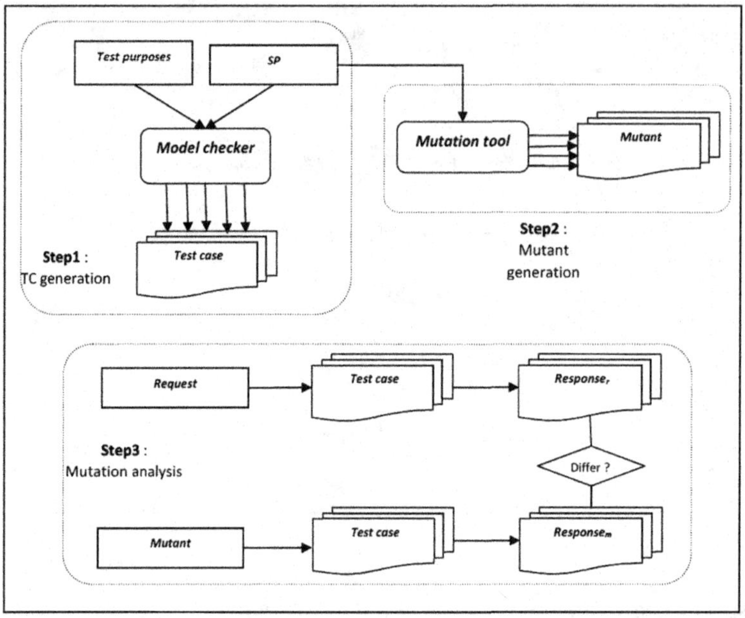

3.2. Test Cases Generation

TC generation is the third step in our SP testing process after network modeling and TP specification. A TC is defined as an elementary test targeted to testing a particular functionality (ISO/IEC 9646-1/2/3, 1992). This step is achieved by a classical model checking technique through the use of SPIN: having the system model and the negation of TP, SPIN produces a counterexample showing a trace where the negation of the TP does not hold and consequently, where the desired TP holds. This counterexample constitutes the desired TC. Moreover, two verdicts are associated to a TC: a Fail verdict denotes a divergence with the expected behavior and the ESP is rejected. A Pass verdict is returned if the observation is correct and the TP is reached.

In order to evaluate the efficiency of these TC, we propose to perform a mutation analysis.

4. MUTATION ANALYSIS

Mutation analysis applied to SP testing (Gomez-Abajo et al., 2018; Papadakis et al., 2017) can be described as follows: first, we inject errors relevant of most types of

Table 1. Proposed mutation operators

Mutation Operator ID	Definition	Explication
CRM	Change the Rule Modality	The rule modality is inverted.
ANR	Add a New Rule	A new rule is specified. The goal is to simulate the case where the implementation behaves in an unexpected way.
RER	Remove an Existing Rule	An existing rule is removed.
RCF	Remove the Constraint Field	Obligation rules will be applied without any restriction (to all situations).
REF	Remove the Event Field	Obligation rules will never occur while request rules will be applied without any restriction
CRF	Change Rule Field with a different one	One rule field (subject, object, action, constraint or event) is replaced by another according to the rule construction

faults that can occur in the program in order to create mutants' versions. Second, we execute TC again each mutant. Finally, we compute a mutation score which is the number of killed mutants divided by the number of mutants.

Figure 13 depicts the proposed framework. In Step1, TC are generated such as presented previously. In Step 2, mutants are generated using the tested SP and a mutation tool implementing some mutation operators. In Step3, these mutants are applied to the TC and the obtained response $response_m$ is compared to response of these TC when solicited by initial user requests $response_r$. If these responses are the same, then the mutant is killed otherwise it is alive.

Besides, based on the SP rules parameters, we propose seven operators representing the most frequently encountered errors. These operators are defined at a generic level independently from any security formalism. Let's note that we didn't define an operator allowing to invert rule type i.e. request becomes obligation and reciprocally because such kind of mutation generates equivalent mutants i.e. the mutant and the initial rule behave similarly. In fact, it is important to not consider equivalent mutants when computing the mutation score elsewhere this latter will be under-evaluated. That's why we choose to not consider this kind of operator.

5. CASE STUDY

In order to provide the reader with a real situation of testing a SP, we illustrate in this section, the previous concepts as a real application. Let's have a network architecture

Table 2.

Rule1: Users in LAN2 are allowed to access the Web server in LAN3.
Rule2: Users in LAN3 are prohibited to access the FTP server in LAN2.
Rule3: Users in LAN1 must scan any entering mail.

Table 3.

```
subject user-lan2, user -lan3, user-lan1;
object web-server, ftp-server, mails;
action access, scan;
event enter-mail;
if req{ user-lan2,access,web-server}
:: pfm\{ user-lan2,access, web-server}
fi
dny { user-lan3, access,ftp-server}
when (enter-mail)
:: pfm{ user-lan1, scan, mail}
```

composed by three segments LAN1, LAN2 and LAN3; a set a subjects *user-lan1*, *user-lan2*, *user-lan3*; three objects *ftp server*, *web server* and *mails*; two actions i.e. *access* and *scan* and a temporal event *enter-mail*.

5.1. S-Promela Rules

The desired SP for the above network architecture is namely:

The presented rules fall into one of the categories addressed in Section 3. They can be modeled using S-Promela as shown in Table 3.

EFSM can be derived for them, as showed by Figure 14, 15 and 16.

5.2. LTL Test Purpose

Let's recall that the second step of our testing process, depicted by Figure 13, is generating TP. Since TP is designed to represent a given desired functionality, we associate to each rule a TP. According to the same Figure 13, these TP are used as an input for the Spin model checker and are then, expressed using Linear Temporal Logic and more precisely our proposed syntax depicted in Figure12. Hence, corresponding TP can be expressed as following:

Let's recall that in the SPIN model checker, each LTL formula needs to be converted into a Büchi Automaton enclosed in a never claim. So, a necessary step must be performed which is generating the negation of these TP. In the following, a

Figure 13. Generated EFSM for Rule1

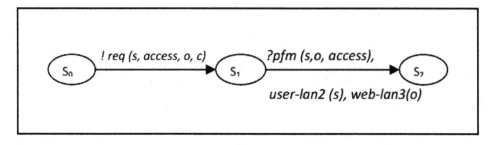

Figure 14. Generated EFSM for Rule2

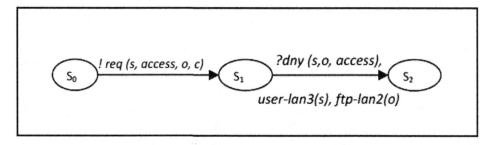

Figure 15. Generated EFSM for Rule3

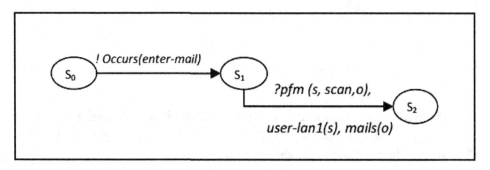

Table 4.

Rule1: *user − lan2(X)∧web − server − lan3(Y)⟹Faccess(X, Y)*
Rule2: *user − lan3(X)∧ftp − server − lan2(Y)⟹G¬access(X, Y)*
Rule3: *enter − mail(Y)∧user − lan1(X)⟹Fscan(X, Y)*

Figure 16.

```
Never /* authorization C⇒F Ei*/
 {
        T0_init:
                If
                :: (((!((user-lan2(X)))) || (((!((web-server(Y)))) || ((access (X, Y)))))))⟼ goto accept_all
                :: (1) → goto T0_S5
                Fi;
        T0_S5:
                If
                :: ((e)) → goto accept_all
                :: (1) → goto T0_S5
                Fi;
        Accept-all:
                Skip
}
```

Figure 17.

```
never {    /* interdiction C ⇒ G ¬ Ei*/
           accept_init:
           T0_init:
                   if
                           ::(! ((access (X, Y)))) -> goto accept_S3
                           :: (((! (((user-lan3(X)))) || (! ((ftp-server(Y)))))) -> goto accept_all
                   fi;
           accept_S3:
           T0_S3:
                   if
                           :: (!((e2))) -> goto accept_S3
                   fi;
           accept_all:
           skip
}
```

never claim corresponding to the first TP generated by SPIN is depicted. In this never claim, and for sake of simplicity, we use *#define* to declare the required elements. TP corresponding to Rule1 is modeled in Figure 16.

Similarly, we can generate TP for the two remaining rules. TP corresponding to Rule2 is modeled as in Figure 17.

Finally, TP corresponding to Rule3 is modeled in Figure 18.

Figure 18.

```
never {    /* obligation E, ∧C ⇒F Eᵢ*/
          T0_init:
               if
               :: ((((! ((mail(Y)))) || (((! ((enter-mail(Y)))) || (((! ((user-lan1(X)))) || ((sacn(X,Y))))))))) -> goto
                   accept_all
               :: (1) -> goto T0_S6
               fi;
          T0_S6:
               if
               :: ((e2)) -> goto accept_all
               :: (1) -> goto T0_S6
               fi;
          accept_all:
               skip
}
```

5.3. Test Cases

The last step is the TC generation. This is done by a classical model checking where SPIN generates a counter-example for each TP. A test verdict (Pass or Fail) is then associated to each TC to indicate whether its final state has been reached during its execution regard to an implementation (Jard & Jerson, 2005).

So far, we have not yet experienced this framework. However, expected TC can be depicted by Figure 179, 18 and 19. In Figure17, starting from an initial state, a request is submitted by a subject belonging to Lan2 in order to access the web server in Lan3. If this request is authorized and consequently, the action is performed then the test case concludes to a Pass verdict. Else, it fails.

Figure 20 depicts the generated TC for Rule 2. Starting from an initial state, a request submitted from a subject belonging to LAN3 for accessing the FTP server is

Figure 19. Generated Test Cases for Rule 1

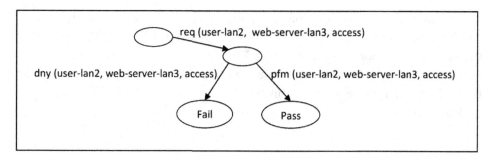

Figure 20. Generated Test Cases for Rule 2

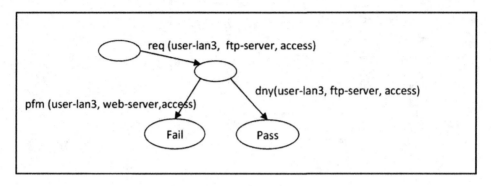

Figure 21. Generated Test Case for Rule 3

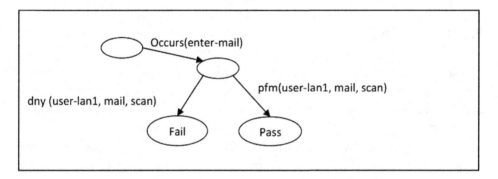

denied. This allows to the TC to conclude to a *Pass* verdict. However, if this request is accepted, then the TC concludes to the *Fail* verdict.

Figure 21 depicts the generated TC for Rule 3. This TC concludes to *Pass* verdict if when an email arrives, it is scanned by a user of LAN1. It concludes to *Fail* when a user belonging to LAN1 does not scan an incoming email.

5.4. Mutation Analysis

Using the same SP defined in the beginning of this section, 15 mutants were generated such as detailed in Table 2. In the following the new mutant SP is presented following the used operator. For instance, using the RER operator, the third rule was removed whereas using the CRF operator, a filled of each rule was changed i.e. the subject of rule1 and 2 and the event triggering rule3.

RER mutants:

- **Rule 1:** *req(user, web − server − lan3, access, user in LAN2) → yes*
- **Rule 2:** *req(user, ftp − server − lan2, access, user in LAN3) → no*

ANR mutants:

- **Rule 1:** *req(user, web − server − lan3, access, user in LAN2) → yes*
- **Rule 2:** *req(user, ftp − server − lan2, access, user in LAN3) → no*
- **Rule 3**: *ob(user, mail, scan, entering − mail, user in LAN1)*
- **Rule 4:** *req(user, mail, scan, user in LAN2) → no*

CRM mutants:

- **Rule 1:** *req(user, web − server − lan3, access, user in LAN2) → no*
- **Rule 2:** *req(user, ftp − server − lan2, access, user in LAN3) → yes*
- **Rule 3:** *ob(user, mail, scan entering − mail, user in LAN1)*

RCF mutants:

- **Rule 1:** *req(user, web − server − lan3, access) → yes*
- **Rule 2:** *req(user, ftp − server − lan2, access) → no*
- **Rule 3:** *ob(user, mail, scan, entering − mail)*

REF mutants:

- **Rule 1:** *req(user, web − server − lan3, access, user in LAN2) → yes*
- **Rule 2:** *req(user, ftp − server − lan2, access, user in LAN3) → no*
- **Rule 3:** *ob(user, mail, scan, user in LAN1)*

CRF mutants:

- **Rule 1:** *req(user, web − server − lan3, access, user in LAN3) → yes*
  - ○ Rule1-1: *req(user, web − server − lan3, format, user in LAN2) → yes*
- **Rule 2**: *req(user, ftp − server − lan2, access, user in LAN2) → no*
  - ○ Rule2-1: *req(user, ftp − server, access, user in LAN3) → no*
- **Rule 3:** *ob(user, mail, scan, sending − mail, user in LAN1)*
  - ○ Rule3-1: *ob(user, mail, read, entering − mail, user in LAN1)*

The next step is then to replace the existing rules by mutant rules. Test cases that are generated to validate the implementation are run against the mutated versions of the policy. A mutant is detected when a test case fails.

Table 5. Used mutants

Mutant Operator	Mutants Number
CRM	2
ANR	1
RER	1
RCF	2
REF	1
CRF	6
ALL	**13**

In the following, the mutation analysis results are summarized in Table 3. Using the RER operator, a rule was removed implying that the SP became incomplete and that when an email arrives no scan will be made. This mutant will not be killed since our testing process is not intended to detect missing rule. Using the ANR operator, a new rule is added to the SP. In such case, none of the generated TC is applicable. Using the CRM operator, the modality of rule 1 is inverted. In such case, the generated TC (Figure 20) fails implying that the mutant is killed. Using the RCF operator, the constraint was removed from the three rules. In such case, the TC will be applied, and the mutants killed. Using the CRF operator, mutants are killed except when the action field is changed. In fact, in such case, the TC is not used.

Obtained results are encouraging although the number of generated mutants is crucial. However, let's note that even undetected mutants are concerned with the SP completeness not its implementation. This property was considered in our previous work (Abassi & El Fatmi, 2009) and the contribution of this paper is a continuity of this latter and that in order to build a security process based on SP such as defined in Figure 22.

Table 6. Mutation analysis results

Mutant Operator	Mutants Number	Killed Mutants	score
CRM	2	2	100%
ANR	1	0	0%
RER	1	1	0%
RCF	2	2	100%
REF	1	0	0%
CRF	6	4	66%
ALL	**13**	**9**	**69%**

Figure 22. A network securing process based on SP

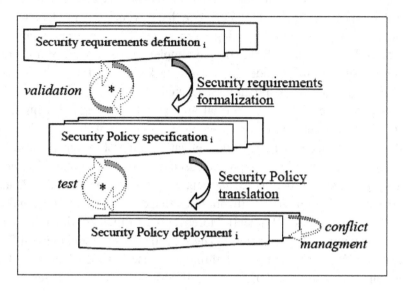

For each SP, security requirements definition is used in order to find all the requirements necessary to handle expected interactions between subjects and objects. Once defined, security requirements must be formalized through the use of an adequate formal specification language. This phase output is a formal SP specification. However, due to the human intervention, this SP specification may contain errors, omissions, contradictions, etc. Hence, a validation activity is necessary in order to state whether the SP specification is the good one according to the desired requirements. A validated specification is then translated before its real deployment on the corresponding network. At this stage, one must be able to check whether the specified SP is able to fulfill all the needed and desired security requirements. This is generally done through a test activity. Hence, we propose to generate elementary tests for a given SP according to desired functionalities.

Let's note that '*' in Figure 22 denotes that (1) validation (respectively test) must be repeated as many times as necessary until the specification is declared valid (respectively the test pass) and (2) the transition from one phase to another is made only when the validation (respectively test) is successful.

6. CONCLUSION

Developing a SP is a sensitive task because the policy itself can lead to security weaknesses if it is not conforming to the security properties. The validation task is not enough to ensure that the SP is correctly enforced. In fact, once the SP is formally and correctly specified, it is essential to prove that it is correctly implemented in the network, too. This can be done by testing the enforced SP. Appropriate techniques are necessary to check whether a SP is correctly implemented. Testing SP is a practical way to ensure such property. Indeed, SP testing task aims verifying whether a given network configuration is compliant with a stated SP.

In this paper, we presented a formal approach for testing SP using a model checker. This approach is based on an adequate modeling of the SP and especially of the three rules type e.g. authorization, obligation and prohibition. More precisely, we proposed three steps testing approach based on a SP modeling, a TP expression and finally, a TC generation. In the first step, we proposed to model the SP and that by the mean of a formal SP specification language based on Promela and called S-Promela (Security-based Promela). Moreover, we formally defined the syntax as well as the semantics of this language. The second step was then, the Test Purpose specification. We performed this task through the use of LTL where each TP type was formally expressed through events and constraints. The third step is the test cases generation achieved by a classical model checking technique. An important issue in testing SP is its efficiency proof. One strategy to evaluate this efficiency is to perform mutation analysis which has proved its effectiveness in many fields such as software engineering. Hence, we depicted in this paper, a mutation analysis based on the proposition of some mutation operators. These operators were used in order to inject faults in the SP in order to create mutants' versions.

REFERENCES

Abassi, R., & El Fatmi, S. G. (2008a). A Model for Specification and Validation of Security Policies in Communication Networks: the firewall case. Proceedings of ARES 2008, 467-473.

Abassi, R., & El Fatmi, S. G. (2008b). An Automated Validation Method for Security Policies: the firewall case. *Proceedings of The Fourth International Conference on Information Assurance and Security, (IAS 2008)*, 291-294.

Abassi, R., & El Fatmi, S. G. (2009). Towards a Test Cases Generation Method for Security Policies. *Proceedings of the International Conference on Telecommunication ICT 2009*, 41-46. 10.1109/ICTEL.2009.5158616

Abassi, R. & El Fatmi, S.G. (2009). Executable Security Policies: Specification and Validation of Security Policies. *International Journal of Wireless & Mobile Networks, 1*(1).

Belli, F., & Güldali, B. (2004). Software Testing via Model Checking. In *Proceedings of ISCIS*. Springer Verlag. 10.1007/978-3-540-30182-0_91

Calamé, J. R. (2005). Specification-based test generation with TGV. Technical Report, Amsterdam.

Darmaillacq, V., Richier, J. L., & Groz, R. (2008). Test Generation and execution for security rules in temporal logic. *Proceedings of ICSTW'08*, 252-259. 10.1109/ICSTW.2008.41

de Vries, R. G., & Tretmans, J. (1998). On-the-fly conformance testing using spin. *Fourth Workshop on Automata Theoretic Verification with the Spin Model Checker*, 115-128.

Elrakaiby, Y., Mouelhi, T., & LeTraon, Y. (2012). Testing Obligation Policy Enforcement using Mutation Analysis. *Proceedings of the IEEE Fifth International Conference on Software Testing, Verification and Validation*. 10.1109/ICST.2012.157

Fraser, B. (1997). RFC 2196, Site Security Handbook.

Gómez-Abajo, P., Guerra, E., de Lara, J., & Merayo, M. G. (2018). A tool for domain-independent model mutation. *Science of Computer Programming*, *163*, 85–92. doi:10.1016/j.scico.2018.01.008

Heimdahl, M. P. E., Rayadurgam, S., Visser, W., Devaraj, G., & Gao, J. (2003). Auto-generating Test Sequences Using Model Checkers: A Case Study. *FATES*, *2003*, 42–59.

Holzmann, G. J. (1991). *Design and Validation of Communication Protocols*. Prentice Hall.

ISO/IEC 9646-1/2/3 (1992) Open Systems Interconnection Conformance Testing Methodology and Framework - ISO/IEC 9646-1/2/3, 1992.

Jard, C., & Jeron, T. (2005). TGV: Theory, principles and algorithms. *International Journal of Software Tools for Technology Transfer*, *7*(4), 297–315. doi:10.100710009-004-0153-x

Jia, Y., & Harman, M. (2011). An analysis and survey of the development of mutation testing. *IEEE Transactions on Software Engineering*, *35*(5), 649–678. doi:10.1109/TSE.2010.62

Kequin, L., Mounier, L., & Groz, R. (2007). Test Generation from Security Policies Specified in Or-BAC. *Proceedings of COMPSAC 2007*.

Khamaiseh, S., Chapman, P., & Xu, D. (2018, July). Model-Based Testing of Obligatory ABAC Systems. In *2018 IEEE International Conference on Software Quality, Reliability and Security (QRS)* (pp. 405-413). IEEE. 10.1109/QRS.2018.00054

Kroger, F. (1987). *Temporal logic of programs*. Springer-Verlag, Inc. doi:10.1007/978-3-642-71549-5

Ledru, Y., Bousquet, L., Bontron, P., Maury, O., Oriat, C., & Potet, M. L. (2001). Test purposes: adapting the notion of specification to testing. In *Proceedings of the 16th IEEE International Conference on Automated Software Engineering*. San Diego, CA: IEEE. 10.1109/ASE.2001.989798

Mallouli, W., Orset, J. M., Cavalli, A., Cuppens, F., & Cuppens, N. (2007). A Formal Approach for Testing Security Rules. *SACMAT, 7,* 127–132. doi:10.1145/1266840.1266860

Papadakis, M., Kintis, M., Zhang, J., Jia, Y., Le Traon, Y., & Harman, M. (2017). Mutation testing advances: An analysis and survey. *Advances in Computers*.

Compilation of References

9 types of software defined network attacks and how to protect from them. (n.d.). *Router Freak.* Retrieved from: https://www.routerfreak.com/9-types-software-defined-network-attacks-protect/

Abassi, R. & El Fatmi, S.G. (2009). Executable Security Policies: Specification and Validation of Security Policies. *International Journal of Wireless & Mobile Networks, 1*(1).

Abassi, R., & El Fatmi, S. G. (2008a). A Model for Specification and Validation of Security Policies in Communication Networks: the firewall case. Proceedings of ARES 2008, 467-473.

Abassi, R., & El Fatmi, S. G. (2008b). An Automated Validation Method for Security Policies: the firewall case. *Proceedings of The Fourth International Conference on Information Assurance and Security, (IAS 2008)*, 291-294.

Abassi, R., & El Fatmi, S. G. (2009). Towards a Test Cases Generation Method for Security Policies. *Proceedings of the International Conference on Telecommunication ICT 2009*, 41-46. 10.1109/ICTEL.2009.5158616

Abdelnur, H., Avanesov, T., & Rusinowitch, M. (2009). Abusing SIP authentication. *Journal of Information Assurance and Security, 4*(4), 311–318.

Abercrombie, P., & Karaorman, M. (2002). jContractor: Bytecode instrumentation techniques for implementing design by contract in java. Electronic Notes in Theoretical Computer Science, 70.

Ajaeiya, G. A., Adalian, N., Elhajj, I. H., Kayssi, A., & Chehab, A. (2017). Flow-based intrusion detection system for SDN. In *IEEE Symposium on Computers and Communications (ISCC)*. IEEE.

Alechina, N., Alechina, R., Habner, J., Jago, M., & Logan, B. (2006). Belief revision for AgentSpeak agents. Proceedings of Autonomous Agents and Multi Agents Systems 2006, 1288 – 1290. doi:10.1145/1160633.1160868

Ali, S. T., Sivaraman, V., Radford, A., & Jha, S. (2015). A survey of securing networks using software defined networking. *IEEE Transactions on Reliability, 64*(3), 1086–1097. doi:10.1109/TR.2015.2421391

Alom, M. Z., Bontupalli, V., & Taha, T. M. (2015). Intrusion detection using deep belief networks. In *Aerospace and Electronics Conference (NAECON), 2015 National* (pp. 339-344). IEEE. 10.1109/NAECON.2015.7443094

Alpern, B., & Schneider, F. B. (1987). Recognizing safety and liveness. *Distributed Computing, 2*(3), 117–126. doi:10.1007/BF01782772

Al-Shaer, E., & Al-Haj, S. (2010). FlowChecker: configuration analysis and verification of federated openflow infrastructures. *3rd ACM Workshop on Assurable and Usable Security Configuration, SafeConfig 2010*, 37-44.

Altoaimy, L., & Mahgoub, I. (2014, December). Fuzzy logic based localization for vehicular ad hoc networks. In *Computational Intelligence in Vehicles and Transportation Systems (CIVTS), 2014 IEEE Symposium on* (pp. 121-128). IEEE.

Alur, R., Fix, L., & Henziger, T. A. (1994). A determinizable class of timed automata. In *Proceedings of 6th Conference on Computer Aided Verification (CAV'94)*. Springer. 10.1007/3-540-58179-0_39

Alvarez, G., & Petrovic, S. (2003). A new taxonomy of web attacks suitable for efficient encoding. *Computers & Security, 22*(5), 435–449. doi:10.1016/S0167-4048(03)00512-1

American Institute of Aeronautics and Astronautics. (2018). *Artificial Intelligence for Cybersecurity*. Retrieved 16 October 2018, from http://www.aiaa.org/protocolAI/

Ansel, J., Marchenko, P., Erlingsson, Ú., Taylor, E., Chen, B., Schuff, D. L., & Yee, B. (2011). Language-independent sandboxing of just-in-time compilation and self-modifying code. *Proceedings of the 32nd ACM SIGPLAN conference on Programming language design and implementation - PLDI '11*. 10.1145/1993498.1993540

Arkian, H. R., Atani, R. E., Pourkhalili, A., & Kamali, S. (2015). A Stable Clustering Scheme Based on Adaptive Multiple Metric in Vehicular Ad-hoc Networks. *Journal of Information Science and Engineering, 31*(2), 361–386.

Armando, A., Basin, D., Boichut, Y., Chevalier, Y., Compagna, L., Cuéllar, J., ... Mödersheim, S. (2005, July). The AVISPA tool for the automated validation of internet security protocols and applications. In *International conference on computer aided verification* (pp. 281-285). Springer. 10.1007/11513988_27

Arnold, A. (1987). Transition systems and concurrent processes. In *Mathematical Problems in Computation Theory* (pp. 9–21). Warsaw: Banach Center.

Artho, C., Havelund, K., & Biere, A. (2003). High-level data races. *Journal on Software Testing, Verification and Reliability, 13*(4).

Artho, C., Schuppan, V., Biere, A., Eugster, P., Baur, M., & Zweimuller, B. (2004). JNuke: Efficient Dynamic Analysis for Java. *Proceedings of 16th International Conference on Computer Aided Verification (CAV 2004)*, 462-465.

Artho, C., & Biere, A. (2005). Combined Static and Dynamic Analysis. *Proceedings of AIOOL '05*.

Artho, C., Biere, A., & Havelund, K. (2004). Using block-local atomicity to detect stale value concurrency errors. In *Proceedings of ATVA'04*. Springer. 10.1007/978-3-540-30476-0_16

Compilation of References

Avizienis, A., Larpie, J. C., & Randell, B. (2000). Fundamental Concepts of Dependability. *Information Survivability Workshop.*

Azizian, M., Cherkaoui, S., & Hafid, A. S. (2016, April). A distributed d-hop cluster formation for VANET. In *Wireless Communications and Networking Conference (WCNC)* (pp. 1-6). IEEE. 10.1109/WCNC.2016.7564925

Ball, T., Bjørner, N., Gember, A., Itzhaky, S., Karbyshev, A., Sagiv, M., . . . Valadarsky, A. (2014). VeriCon: towards verifying controller programs in software-defined networks. *SIGPLAN Conference on Programming Language Design and Implementation,* 282-293.

Bandara, A. K., Lupu, E. C., & Russo, A. (2003). *Using event calculus to formalise policy specification and analysis. In Proceedings of Policies for Distributed Systems and Networks* (pp. 26–39). Policy.

Banks, G., Fattori, A., Kemmerer, C., Kruegel, C., & Vigna, G. (2011). MISHIMA: Multilateration of Internet hosts hidden using malicious fast-flux agents. *Proceedings of Conference on Detection of Intrusions and Malware and Vulnerability Assessment (DIMVA).* 10.1007/978-3-642-22424-9_11

Baresi, K., & Guinea, S. (2005). *Dynamo: Dynamic Monitoring of WS-BPEL Processes.* ICSOC 05, *3rd International Conference On Service Oriented Computing,* Amsterdam, The Netherlands.

Baresi, K., Guinea, S., & Plembani, P. (2005). *Using WS-Policy in Service Monitoring.* TES 05, *6th VLDB Workshop on Technologies for E-Services,* Trodheim, Norway.

Barnett, M., & Schulte, W. (2001). Spying on Components: A Runtime Verification Technique. *Proceedings of OOPSLA 2001, Workshop on Specification and Verification of Component Based Systems.*

Barringer, H., Goldberg, A., Havelund, K., & Sen, K. (2004). Rule-Based Runtime Verification. *5th International Conference on Verification, Model Checking and Abstract Interpretation (VMCAI 04),* 44-57.

Bartetzko, D., Fischer, C., Moller, M., & Wehrheim, H. (2001). Jass -Java with assertions. *Electronic Notes in Theoretical Computer Science, 55*(2).

Bellare, M., Namprempre, C., & Neven, G. (2004). Security proofs for identity-based identification and signature schemes. *Advances in Cryptology-EUROCRYPT,* 268-286.

Belli, F., & Güldali, B. (2004). Software Testing via Model Checking. In *Proceedings of ISCIS.* Springer Verlag. 10.1007/978-3-540-30182-0_91

Bengio, Y., Simard, P., & Frasconi, P. (1994). Learning long-term dependencies with gradient descent is difficult. *IEEE Transactions on Neural Networks, 5*(2), 157–166. doi:10.1109/72.279181 PMID:18267787

Bennet, S. Y. (1997). *A Sanctuary for Mobile Agents.* Technical Report CS97-537. University of California in San Diego. Available at http://www- cse.ucsd.edu/users/bsy/index.html

Bhamare, D., Salman, T., Samaka, M., Erbad, A., & Jain, R. (2016, December). Feasibility of Supervised Machine Learning for Cloud Security. In *Information Science and Security (ICISS), 2016 International Conference on* (pp. 1-5). IEEE.

Bordini, R. H., Hübner, J. F., & Wooldridge, M. (2007). *Programming Multi-Agent Systems in AgentSpeak using Jason.* doi:10.1002/9780470061848

Bork, D., Pavlidis, M., & Utz, W. (2017). *Modeling Method Conceptualization within OMiLAB: The SecureTropos Case. In RCIS 2017* (pp. 470–475). Brighton: PDF.

Borselius, N. (2002). Mobile agent security. *Electron Commun Eng J, 14*(5), 211–218. doi:10.1049/ecej:20020504

Bouyer, P., Chevalier, F., & D'Souza, D. (2005). Fault Diagnosis using Timed Automata. *Proceedings of 8th Intern. Conf. on Foundations of Software Science and Computations Structures (FoSSaCS'05)*, 219-233. 10.1007/978-3-540-31982-5_14

Braga, R., Mota, E., & Passito, A. (2010). Lightweight DDoS flooding attack detection using NOX/OpenFlow. In *IEEE 35th Conference on Local Computer Networks (LCN)* (pp. 408-415). IEEE.

Bresciani, P., Perini, A., Giorgini, P., Giunchiglia, F., & Mylopoulos, J. (2004). Tropos: An agent-oriented software development methodology. *Autonomous Agents and Multi-Agent Systems, 8*(3), 203–236. doi:10.1023/B:AGNT.0000018806.20944.ef

Brisset, P. (2000). *A Case Study in Java Software Verification.* Appeared in Workshop on Security, Middleware, and Languages, Stockholm, Sweden.

Brooks, R. R. (2004). Mobile code paradigms and security issues. *IEEE Internet Computing, 8*(3), 54–59. doi:10.1109/MIC.2004.1297274

Brörkens, M., & Möller, M. (2002). Dynamic event generation for runtime checking using the JDI. *Electronic Notes in Theoretical Computer Science, 70*(4).

Büttner, C., Bartels, F., & Huss, S. A. (2015, October). Real-world evaluation of an anonymous authenticated key agreement protocol for vehicular ad-hoc networks. In *Wireless and Mobile Computing, Networking and Communications (WiMob), 2015 IEEE 11th International Conference on* (pp. 651-658). IEEE.

Calamé, J. R. (2005). Specification-based test generation with TGV. Technical Report, Amsterdam.

Canini, M., Venzano, D., Peresíni, P., Kostic, D., & Rexford, J. (2012), A NICE Way to Test OpenFlow Applications. *Proceedings of the 9th {USENIX} Symposium on Networked Systems Design and Implementation*, 127-140.

Capra, L., Emmerich, W., & Mascolo, C. (2001). Reflective middleware solutions for context-aware applications. In *Proc. of Reflection. The 3rd Int. Conf. on Meta-level Architectures and Separation of Crosscutting Concerns*. Kyoto, Japan: Springer-Verlag. 10.1007/3-540-45429-2_10

Capra, L., Emmerich, W., & Mascolo, C. (2003). CARISMA: Context Aware Reflective Middleware System for Mobile Applications. *IEEE Transactions on Software Engineering, 29*(10), 929–945. doi:10.1109/TSE.2003.1237173

Chang, E., Pnueli, A., & Manna, Z. (1994). Compositional Verification of Real-Time Systems. *Proc. 9th IEEE Symposium On Logic In Computer Science*, 458-465. 10.1109/LICS.1994.316045

Chen, F., & Rosu. (2003). *Towards Monitoring-Oriented Programming: A Paradigm Combining Specification and Implementation.* Academic Press.

Chen, J., Yuan, Q., Xue, G., & Du, R. (2015, April). Game-theory-based batch identification of invalid signatures in wireless mobile networks. In *Computer Communications (INFOCOM), 2015 IEEE Conference on* (pp. 262-270). IEEE.

Chen, X.-F., & Yu, S.-Z. (2016). CIPA: A collaborative intrusion prevention architecture for programmable network and SDN. *Computers & Security, 58*, 1–19. doi:10.1016/j.cose.2015.11.008

Chonka, A., Xiang, Y., Zhou, W., & Bonti, A. (2011). Cloud security defence to protect cloud computing against HTTP-DoS and XML-DoS attacks. *Journal of Network and Computer Applications, 34*(4), 1097–1107. doi:10.1016/j.jnca.2010.06.004

Cisco. (n.d.). Cisco open network environment for government. *Cisco.* Retrieved from: https://www.cisco.com/c/en/us/solutions/industries/government/us-government-solutions-services/software-defined-networking.html

Clavel, M., Durn, F. J., Eker, S., Lincoln Martí-Oliet, N., Meseguer, J., & Quesada, K. F. (1999). The Maude System. *Proc. of the 10th Inter. Conf. on Rewriting Techniques.*

Clements, P., Papaioannou, T., & Edwards, J. (1997). Aglets: Enabling the Virtual Enterprise. Proceedings of Managing Enterprises Stakeholders, Engineering, Logistics and Achievement (ME-SELA'97).

CNBC. (2018). *Weaponized drones. Machines that attack on their own. 'That day is going to come'.* Retrieved from https://www.cnbc.com/2018/07/20/ai-cyberattacks-artificial-intelligence-threatens-cybersecurity.html

Cohen, D., Feather, M., Narayanswamy, K., & Fickas, S. (1997). Automatic Monitoring of Software Requirements. *Proc. of the 19th Int. Conf. on Software Engineering.* 10.1145/253228.253493

Cohen, G., Chase, J., & Kaminsky, D. (1998). Automatic Program Transformation with JOIE. *Proc. of USENIX Annual Technical Symposium.*

Collberg, C., & Thomborson, C. (2000). *Watermarking, Tamper-Proofing, and Obfuscation Tools for Software Protection.* University of Auckland Technical Report 170.

Comuzzi, M., & Spanoudakis, G. (2010). Dynamic set-up of monitoring infrastructures for service based systems. *Proceedings of the ACM Symposium on Applied Computing*, 2414–2421. 10.1145/1774088.1774591 d'Amorim, M., & Havelund, K. (2005). Event-based runtime verification of Java Programs. In *Proc. of the 3rd Int. Workshop on Dynamic Analysis, WODA '05*. St. Louis, MO: ACM Press.

da Silva, A. S., Wickboldt, J. A., Granville, L. Z., & Schaeffer-Filho, A. (2016). *ATLANTIC: A framework for anomaly traffic detection, classification, and mitigation in SDN*. In *IEEE/IFIP Network Operations and Management Symposium (NOMS)*, (pp. 27-35). IEEE.

Damianou, N., Dulay, N., Lupu, E. C., & Sloman, M. S. (2001). *The Ponder Policy Specification Language*. Presented at Policy, in *Workshop on Policies for Distributed Systems and Networks*, Bristol, UK. 10.1007/3-540-44569-2_2

Darmaillacq, V., Richier, J. L., & Groz, R. (2008). Test Generation and execution for security rules in temporal logic. *Proceedings of ICSTW'08*, 252-259. 10.1109/ICSTW.2008.41

David, P. C., Ledoux, T., & Bouraqadi-Saadani, N. M. N. (2001). Two-step weaving with reflection using AspectJ. *OOPSLA 2001 Workshop on Advanced Separation of Concerns in Object- Oriented Systems*.

De Fuentes, J. M., González-Tablas, A. I., & Ribagorda, A. (2011). Overview of security issues in vehicular ad-hoc networks. In *Handbook of research on mobility and computing: Evolving technologies and ubiquitous impacts* (pp. 894–911). IGI Global. doi:10.4018/978-1-60960-042-6.ch056

de Vries, R. G., & Tretmans, J. (1998). On-the-fly conformance testing using spin. *Fourth Workshop on Automata Theoretic Verification with the Spin Model Checker*, 115-128.

Dean, D., Franklin, M., & Stubblefield, A. (2002). An algebraic approach to IP traceback. *ACM Transactions on Information and System Security*, *5*(2), 119–137. doi:10.1145/505586.505588

Deng, L. (2014). A tutorial survey of architectures, algorithms, and applications for deep learning. *APSIPA Transactions on Signal and Information Processing, 3*.

Dingwall-Smith, A., & Finkelstein, A. (2002). From Requirements to Monitors by Way of Aspects. *Proc. of 1st Int. Conf. on Aspect-Oriented Software Development*.

Dolev, D., & Yao, A. (1983). On the security of public key protocols. *IEEE Transactions on Information Theory*, *29*(2), 198–208. doi:10.1109/TIT.1983.1056650

Donalek, C. (2011). *Supervised and Unsupervised Learning*. Retrieved from http://www.astro.caltech.edu/~george/aybi199/Donalek_Classif.pdf

Dorri, A., Steger, M., Kanhere, S. S., & Jurdak, R. (2017). Blockchain: A distributed solution to automotive security and privacy. *IEEE Communications Magazine*, *55*(12), 119–125. doi:10.1109/MCOM.2017.1700879

Elrakaiby, Y., Mouelhi, T., & LeTraon, Y. (2012). Testing Obligation Policy Enforcement using Mutation Analysis. *Proceedings of the IEEE Fifth International Conference on Software Testing, Verification and Validation*. 10.1109/ICST.2012.157

Emmerich, W. (2000). Software Engineering and Middleware. A Roadmap. In *The Future of Software Engineering - 22nd Int. Conference on Software Engineering (ICSE)* (pp 117-129). ACM Press.

Esparza, O., Fernández, M., Soriano, M., Muñoz, L., & Forné, J. (2003). Mobile Agent Watermarking and Fingerprinting: Tracing Malicious Hosts. *Database and Expert Systems Applications (DEXA'03)*.

Esparza, O., Soriano, M., Muñoz, J. L., & Forné, J. (2003b). Host revocation authority: A way of protecting mobile agents from malicious hosts. Lecture Notes in Computer Science, 2722.

Esparza, O., Fernández, M., & Soriano, M. (2003a). Protecting mobile agents by using traceability techniques. *IEEE International Conference on Information Technology: Research and Education. ITRE 2003*. 10.1109/ITRE.2003.1270618

Fan, C. I., Sun, W. Z., Huang, S. W., Juang, W. S., & Huang, J. J. (2014, September). Strongly privacy-preserving communication protocol for VANETs. In *Information Security (ASIA JCIS), 2014 Ninth Asia Joint Conference on* (pp. 119-126). IEEE. 10.1109/AsiaJCIS.2014.24

Farmer, W., Guttman, J., & Swarup, V. (1996). Security for Mobile Agents: Authentication and State Appraisal. *Proceedings of the 4th European Symposium on Research in Computer Security*, 118-130. 10.1007/3-540-61770-1_31

Feather, M.S., Fickas, S., van Lamsweerde, A., & Ponsard, C. (1998). Reconciling System Requirements and Runtime Behavior. *Proc. of 9th Int. Work. on Software Specification & Design*.

Feather, M., & Fickas, S. (1995). Requirements Monitoring in Dynamic Environments. *Proc. of Int. Conf. on Requirements Engineering*.

Fiala, J. (2015). *A Survey of Machine Learning Applications to Cloud Computing*. Retrieved from http://www.cse.wustl.edu/~jain/cse570-15/ftp/cld_ml/index.html

Fiore, U., Palmieri, F., Castiglione, A., & De Santis, A. (2013). Network anomaly detection with the restricted Boltzmann machine. *Neurocomputing, 122*, 13–23. doi:10.1016/j.neucom.2012.11.050

Foster, N., Harrison, R., Freedman, M. J., Monsanto, C., Rexford, J., Story, A., & Walker, D. (2011) Frenetic: a network programming language. ICFP 2011, Tokyo, Japan. doi:10.1145/2034773.2034812

Fraser, B. (1997). RFC 2196, Site Security Handbook.

Gamer, T. (2012). Collaborative anomaly-based detection of large-scale internet attacks. *Computer Networks, 56*(1), 169–185. doi:10.1016/j.comnet.2011.08.015

Gao, N., Gao, L., Gao, Q., & Wang, H. (2014, November). An intrusion detection model based on deep belief networks. In *Advanced Cloud and Big Data (CBD), 2014 Second International Conference on* (pp. 247-252). IEEE.

Gartner. (2018). *Cybersecurity Q&A: The New World of Cyber*. Retrieved from https://www.gartner.com/smarterwithgartner/cybersecurity-qa-the-new-world-of-cyber/

Ghafoor, K. Z., Bakar, K. A., van Eenennaam, M., Khokhar, R. H., & Gonzalez, A. J. (2013). A fuzzy logic approach to beaconing for vehicular ad hoc networks. *Telecommunication Systems*, *52*(1), 139–149. doi:10.100711235-011-9466-8

Giannakopoulou, D., & Havelund, K. (2001). Automata-Based Verification of Temporal Properties on Running Programs. In *Proc. of Inter. Conf. on Automated Software Engineering (ASE'01)* (pp. 412-416). ENTCS. 10.1109/ASE.2001.989841

Glouche, Y., Genet, T., & Houssay, E. (2006). SPAN–a Security Protocol ANimator for AVISPA–User Manual. *IRISA/Université de Rennes, 1*, 20.

Goldberg, A., & Havelund, K. (2003). Instrumentation of Java Bytecode for Runtime Analysis. In Proc. Formal Techniques for Java-like Programs. In *Technical Reports from ETH Zurich* (Vol. 408). ETH Zurich.

Gómez-Abajo, P., Guerra, E., de Lara, J., & Merayo, M. G. (2018). A tool for domain-independent model mutation. *Science of Computer Programming*, *163*, 85–92. doi:10.1016/j.scico.2018.01.008

Goswami, K. K. (2017). *Intelligent threat-aware response system in software-defined networks* (Unpublished master's thesis). San José State University, San Jose, CA.

Gotsman, A., Massacci, F., & Pistore, M. (2005). Towards an independent semantics and verification technology for the HLPSL specification language. *Electronic Notes in Theoretical Computer Science*, *135*(1), 59–77. doi:10.1016/j.entcs.2005.06.004

Gouda, M.G. & Liu, A.X. (2006). Structured firewall design. *Computer Networks*. doi:10.1016/j.comnet.2006.06.015

Grastien, A., Cordier, M., & Largout, C. (2005). Incremental Diagnosis of Discrete-Event Systems. *15th Int. Work. On Principles of Diagnosis (DX05)*.

Gray, R. (2004). Mobile Agents: Overcoming the Early Hype and a Bad Name. *Proceedings of IEEE International Conference on Mobile Data Management (MDM)*, 302.

Gray, R. (1996). Agent Tcl: A Flexible and Secure Mobile-Agent System. *Proceedings of the Fourth Annual Tcl/Tk workshop (TCL 96)*, 9-23.

Grimes, R. (2004). *Authenticode*. Microsoft Corporation TechNet, Microsoft Authenticode Reference Guide.

Guerraoui, R., & Schiper, A. (1997). Software-based replication for fault tolerance. *Computer*, *30*(4), 68–74. doi:10.1109/2.585156

Gumus, F. (2016). *Congestion control in software defined networks with machine learning algorithms* (Unpublished master's thesis). Istanbul University, Istanbul, Turkey.

Gunter, C. A., Peter, H., & Scott, N. (1997). Infrastructure for Proof-Referencing Code. *Proceedings, Workshop on Foundations of Secure Mobile Code.*

Gurevich, Y. (1993). Evolving Algebras: An attempt to discover semantics. In G. Rozenberg & A. Saloma (Eds.), *Current Trends in Theoretical Computer Science* (pp. 266–292). World Scientific. doi:10.1142/9789812794499_0021

Gurevich, Y., Schulte, W., Campbell, C., & Grieskamp, W. (2001). *The Abstract State Machine Language.* Microsoft Corporation.

Hachez, G. (2003). *A Comparative Study of Software Protection Tools Suited for E-Commerce with Contributions to Software Watermarking and Smart Cards* (PhD thesis). Universite Catholique de Louvain. Retrieved from http://www.dice.ucl.ac.be/ hachez/thesis gael hachez.pdf

Hadded, M., Zagrouba, R., Laouiti, A., Muhlethaler, P., & Saidane, L. A. (2015, May). A multi-objective genetic algorithm-based adaptive weighted clustering protocol in vanet. In *Evolutionary Computation (CEC), 2015 IEEE Congress on* (pp. 994-1002). IEEE.

Hatcher, W. G., & Yu, W. (2018). A Survey of Deep Learning: Platforms, Applications and Emerging Research Trends. *IEEE Access: Practical Innovations, Open Solutions, 6*, 24411–24432. doi:10.1109/ACCESS.2018.2830661

Hatcli, J., & Dwyer, M. (2001). Using the Bandera tool set to model-check properties of concurrent Java software. *LNCS, 2154*, 39–58.

Havelund, K., & Rosu, G. (2001). Monitoring Programs using Rewriting. In *Proc. Int. Conference on Automated Software Engineering (ASE'01)* (pp. 135-143). Institute of Electrical and Electronics Engineers. 10.1109/ASE.2001.989799

Havelund, K., & Rosu, G. (2002). Synthesizing Monitors for Safety Properties. Tools and Algorithm for Construction and Analysis of Systems (TACAS), 342-356. doi:10.1007/3-540-46002-0_24

Havelund, K. (2008). Runtime verification of C programs. In *TestCom/FATES*. Springer-Verlag. doi:10.1007/978-3-540-68524-1_3

Havelund, K., & Rosu, G. (2001). Monitoring Java Programs with Java PathExplorer. *Proc. of the 1st International Workshop on Runtime Verification (RV'01), 1*, 97-114.

Havelund, K., & Rosu, G. (2004). An Overview of the Runtime Verification Tool Java PathExplorer. *Methods Syst. Des., 24*(2), 189–215. doi:10.1023/B:FORM.0000017721.39909.4b

He, D., Zeadally, S., Xu, B., & Huang, X. (2015). An efficient identity-based conditional privacy-preserving authentication scheme for vehicular ad hoc networks. *IEEE Transactions on Information Forensics and Security, 10*(12), 2681–2691. doi:10.1109/TIFS.2015.2473820

Heimdahl, M. P. E., Rayadurgam, S., Visser, W., Devaraj, G., & Gao, J. (2003). Auto-generating Test Sequences Using Model Checkers: A Case Study. *FATES, 2003*, 42–59.

Helsinger, A., Thome, M., & Wright, T. (2004). Cougaar: A Scalable, Distributed Multi-Agent Architecture. *IEEE, 2*, 1910–1917. doi:10.1109/ICSMC.2004.1399959

Hinton, G. E., & Salakhutdinov, R. R. (2006). Reducing the dimensionality of data with neural networks. *Science, 313*(5786), 504-507.

Hirschfeld, R., & Kawamura, K. (2004). Dynamic service adaption. *Proceedings of the Fourth IEEE International Workshop on Distributed Auto-adaptive and Reconfigurable Systems (with ICDCS'04).*

Hoare, C. (2004). *Communicating Sequential Processes*. Retrieved from http://www.usingcsp.com/cspbook.pdf

Hodo, E., Bellekens, X., Hamilton, A., Tachtatzis, C., & Atkinson, R. (2017). *Shallow and deep networks intrusion detection system: A taxonomy and survey.* arXiv preprint arXiv:1701.02145.

Hohl, F. (1998). Time Limited Blackbox Security: Protecting Mobile Agents From Malicious Hosts. In G. Vigna (Ed.), Mobile Agents and Security (pp. 92-113). Springer-Verlag.

Holzmann, G. J. (1991). *Design and Validation of Communication Protocols*. Prentice Hall.

Hu, H., Han, W., Ahn, G-J & Zhao, Z. (2014) FLOWGUARD: building robust firewalls for software-defined networks. *Proceedings of the workshop on Hot topics in software defined networking*, 97-102.

Huang, Z., Ruj, S., Cavenaghi, M. A., Stojmenovic, M., & Nayak, A. (2014). A social network approach to trust management in VANETs. *Peer-to-Peer Networking and Applications, 7*(3), 229–242. doi:10.100712083-012-0136-8

Imamverdiyev, Y., & Abdullayeva, F. (2018). Deep Learning Method for Denial of Service Attack Detection Based on Restricted Boltzmann Machine. *Big Data, 6*(2), 159–169. doi:10.1089/big.2018.0023 PMID:29924649

Ingram Micro Advisor. (2008). 7 advantages of software defined networking. *Ingram Micro Advisor.* Retrieved from: http://www.ingrammicroadvisor.com/data-center/7-advantages-of-software-defined-networking

Islam, S. H., & Khan, M. K. (2016). Provably secure and pairing-free identity-based handover authentication protocol for wireless mobile networks. *International Journal of Communication Systems, 29*(17), 2442–2456. doi:10.1002/dac.2847

ISO/IEC 9646-1/2/3 (1992) Open Systems Interconnection Conformance Testing Methodology and Framework - ISO/IEC 9646-1/2/3, 1992.

Ivanovic, M., & Ninkovic, S. (2017). Personalized HealthCare and Agent Technologies. *Proceedings 11th KES Conference on Agents and Multi-Agent Systems- Technology and Applications.*

Janicke, H., Siewe, K., Jones, F., Cau, A., & Zedan, H. (2005). Analysis and Run-time Verification of Dynamic Security Policies. AAMAS 05 workshop on Defence Applications of Multi-Agent Systems, Utrecht, The Netherlands.

Jankowski, D., & Amanowicz, M. (2016). On efficiency of selected machine learning algorithms for intrusion detection in software defined networks. *International Journal of Electronics and Telecommunications, 62*(3), 247–252. doi:10.1515/eletel-2016-0033

Jansen, W. (1998a). *Mobile Agents and Security*. National Institute of Standards and Technology. Retrieved April 8, 2005, from http://www.csrc.nist.gov/staff/jansen/pp-agentsecurityfin.pdf

Jansen, W., & Karygiannis, T. (1998). Mobile Agent Security. NIST Special Publication, National Institute of Standards and Technology, 800-19.

Jansen, W. (1998b). *Countermeasures for Mobile Agent Security, Computer Communications, Special issue on advanced security techniques for network protection* (Vol. 23). Elsevier Science.

Jansen, W. A. (2000). Countermeasure for mobile agent security. *Computer Communications, 23*(17), 1667–1676. doi:10.1016/S0140-3664(00)00253-X

Jard, C., & Jeron, T. (2005). TGV: Theory, principles and algorithms. *International Journal of Software Tools for Technology Transfer, 7*(4), 297–315. doi:10.100710009-004-0153-x

Jia, Y., & Harman, M. (2011). An analysis and survey of the development of mutation testing. *IEEE Transactions on Software Engineering, 35*(5), 649–678. doi:10.1109/TSE.2010.62

Johansen, D. (2004). Mobile Agents: Right Concept, Wrong approach. In *Proceedings of the 2004 IEEE International Conference on Mobile Data Management* (pp. 300-301). IEEE Computer Society.

Kaler, C., & Nadalin, A. (Eds.). (2005). *Web Services Security Policy Language (WSSecurityPolicy)*. Retrieved from http://www-128.ibm.com/developerworks/library/speci_cation/ws-secpol/

Kazemian, P., Chan, M., Zeng, H., Varghese, G., McKeown, N., & Whyte, S. (2013). Real Time Network Policy Checking Using Header Space Analysis. *Proceedings of the 10th USENIX Symposium on Networked Systems Design and Implementation*, 99—111.

Kchaou, A., Abassi, R., & Guemara El Fatmi, S. (2018). Towards a Secured Clustering Mechanism for Messages Exchange in VANET. *Proceedings of the 32-nd IEEE International Conference on Advanced Information Networking and Applications (AINA-2018)*. 10.1109/WAINA.2018.00068

Kequin, L., Mounier, L., & Groz, R. (2007). Test Generation from Security Policies Specified in Or-BAC. *Proceedings of COMPSAC 2007*.

Khamaiseh, S., Chapman, P., & Xu, D. (2018, July). Model-Based Testing of Obligatory ABAC Systems. In *2018 IEEE International Conference on Software Quality, Reliability and Security (QRS)* (pp. 405-413). IEEE. 10.1109/QRS.2018.00054

Kiczales, G., & Lampig, J. (1997). Aspect-oriented Programming. LNCS, 1241, 220-242. doi:10.1007/BFb0053381

Kiczales, G., Hilsdale, E., Hugunin, J., Kersten, M., Palm, J., & Griswold, W. G. (2001). An Overview of AspectJ. In *Proceedings of the 15th European Conference on Object-Oriented Programming* (pp. 327-353). Springer-Verlag.

Kim, J., Kim, J., Thu, H. L. T., & Kim, H. (2016, February). Long short term memory recurrent neural network classifier for intrusion detection. In *Platform Technology and Service (PlatCon), 2016 International Conference on* (pp. 1-5). IEEE.

Kim, M., Kannan, S., Lee, I., Sokolsky, O., & Viswanathan, M. (2001). Java-mac: A Runtime Assurance Tool for for Java Programs. Electronic Notes in Theoretical Computer Science, 55.

Kim, J., Kim, J., & Kim, H. (2015). An Approach to Build an Efficient Intrusion Detection Classifier. *Journal of Platform Technology, 3*(4), 43–52.

Ko, C., Ruschitzka, M., & Levitt, K. (1997). Execution Monitoring of Security-Critical Programs in Distributed Systems: A Specification-Based Approach. *Proc. of the IEEE Symp. on Security and Privacy*, 175-187.

Kotz, D., & Gray, R. (1999). Mobile Agents and the Future of the Internet. *Operating Systems Review, 33*(3), 7–13. doi:10.1145/311124.311130

Koulouris, T., Spanoudakis, G., & Tsigkritis, T. (2007). Towards a framework for dynamic verification of peer-to-peer systems. *Second International Conference on Internet and Web Applications and Services, ICIW'07.* 10.1109/ICIW.2007.63

Krivic, P., Skocir, P., Kusek, M., & Jezic, G. (2017). Microservices as Agents in IoT Systems. *Proceedings 11th KES Conference on Agents and Multi-Agent Systems- Technology and Applications.*

Kroger, F. (1987). *Temporal logic of programs.* Springer-Verlag, Inc. doi:10.1007/978-3-642-71549-5

Lange, D. (1998). Mobile Objects and Mobile Agents: The Future of Distributed Computing? In *Proceedings of the 12th European Conference Object-Oriented Programming (ECOOP)* (vol. 1445, p. 1). Springer-Verlag.

Lange, D., & Oshima, M. (1999). Seven Good Reasons for Mobile Agents. *Communications of the ACM, 42*(3), 88–89. doi:10.1145/295685.298136

Lazarevic, A., Kumar, V., & Srivastava, J. (2005). Intrusion Detection: A Survey. In *Managing cyber-threats: issues approaches & challenges.* Springer. doi:10.1007/0-387-24230-9_2

Leavens, G., Baker, A., & Ruby, C. (2003). *Preliminary Design of JML: A Behavioural Interface Specification Language for Java.* Technical Report 9806u. Iowa State University, Department of Computer Science. Retrieved from http://www.jmlspecs.org/

Ledru, Y., Bousquet, L., Bontron, P., Maury, O., Oriat, C., & Potet, M. L. (2001). Test purposes: adapting the notion of specification to testing. In *Proceedings of the 16th IEEE International Conference on Automated Software Engineering.* San Diego, CA: IEEE. 10.1109/ASE.2001.989798

Lee, D., & Yannakakis, M. (1996). Principles and Methods of Testing Finite State Machines – A Survey. *Proceedings of the IEEE, 84*(8), 1090–1123. doi:10.1109/5.533956

Lee, I., Kannan, S., Kim, M., Sokolsky, O., & Viswanathan, M. (1999). Runtime Assurance Based on Formal Specifications. *Proc. of the Int. Conf. on Parallel and Distributed Processing Techniques and Applications.*

Lei, A., Ogah, C., Asuquo, P., Cruickshank, H., & Sun, Z. (2016). A secure key management scheme for heterogeneous secure vehicular communication systems. *ZTE Communications, 21,* 1.

Leiding, B., Memarmoshrefi, P., & Hogrefe, D. (2016, September). Self-managed and blockchain-based vehicular ad-hoc networks. In *Proceedings of the 2016 ACM International Joint Conference on Pervasive and Ubiquitous Computing: Adjunct* (pp. 137-140). ACM.

Li, X., Zhang, A., Sun, J., & Yin, J. (2004). The Research of Mobile Agent Security. In *Second International Workshop on Grid and Cooperative Computing (GCC)* (vol. 3033, pp. 187-190). Shanghai, China: Academic Press.

Ligatti, J., Bauer, L., & Walker, D. (2005). Edit Automata: Enforcement Mechanisms for Runtime Security Policies. *International Journal of Information Security, 4*(1-2), 2–16. doi:10.100710207-004-0046-8

Lindholm, T., & Yellin, F. (1996). *The Java Virtual Machine specification.* Retrieved from http://www.javasoft.com/docs/books/vmspec/html/VMSpecTOC.doc.html

Liu, A. X. (2008). Formal Verification of Firewall Policies. *IEEE International Conference on Communications,* 1494-1498.

Liu, Y., Wang, L., & Chen, H. H. (2015). Message authentication using proxy vehicles in vehicular ad hoc networks. *IEEE Transactions on Vehicular Technology, 64*(8), 3697–3710. doi:10.1109/TVT.2014.2358633

Lo, N. W., & Tsai, H. C. (2009). A reputation system for traffic safety event on vehicular ad hoc networks. *EURASIP Journal on Wireless Communications and Networking, 2009*(1), 9. doi:10.1155/2009/125348

Lowe, G. (1995). An Attack on the Needham-Schroeder public-key authentication protocol. *Information Processing Letters, 56*(3), 131–133. doi:10.1016/0020-0190(95)00144-2

Mahub, K., & Spanoudakis, G. (2004). A Framework for Requirements Monitoring of Service Based Systems. *Proc. of the 2nd Int. Conf on Service Oriented Computing.*

Mallouli, W., Orset, J. M., Cavalli, A., Cuppens, F., & Cuppens, N. (2007). A Formal Approach for Testing Security Rules. *SACMAT, 7,* 127–132. doi:10.1145/1266840.1266860

Maña, A., & Muñoz, A. (2007b). Trusted Code Execution in Javacard. *International Conference on Trust, Privacy and Security in Digital Business. TrustBus 2007: Trust, Privacy and Security in Digital Business*, 269-279.

Maña, A., Muñoz, A., & Serrano, D. (2007). Towards Secure Agent Computing for Ubiquitous Computing and Ambient Intelligence. *Fourth International Conference, Ubiquitous Intelligence and Computing, Hong Kong (China) 2007.*

Maña, A., & Muñoz, A. (2006) Protected Computing vs. *Trusted Computing. In International Conference on Communication Systems Software and Middleware (COMSWARE'06).* New Delhi: IEEE.

Maña, A., Muñoz, A., & Serrano, D. (2009). Protected Computing Approach: Towards the Mutual Protection of Agent Computing. *7th International Conference on Practical Applications of Agents and MultiAgent Systems PAAMS 2009.* 10.1007/978-3-642-00487-2_57

Marrow, P., & Ghanea-Hercock, R. (2000). Mobile Software Agents – Insect-Inspired Computing. *BT Technology Journal*, *18*(4), 129–139. doi:10.1023/A:1026771012206

Marwan, M., Kartit, A., & Ouahmane, H. (2018). Security Enhancement in Healthcare Cloud using Machine Learning. *Procedia Computer Science*, *127*, 388–397. doi:10.1016/j.procs.2018.01.136

Mascolo, C., Capra, L., Zachariadis, S., & Emmerich, W. (2002). XMIDDLE: A Data-Sharing Middleware for Mobile Computing. *Journal on Wireless Personal Communications*, *21*(1), 77–103. doi:10.1023/A:1015584805733

Matulevicius, R., Mouratidis, H., Mayer, N., Dubois, E., & Heymans, P. (2012). Syntactic and Semantic Extensions to Secure Tropos to Support Security Risk Management. *J. UCS*, *18*(6), 816–844.

McKeown, N., Anderson, T., Balakrishnan, H., Parulkar, G., Peterson, L., Rexford, J., ... Turner, J. (2008). Openflow: Enabling innovation in campus networks. *Computer Communication Review*, *38*(2), 69–74. doi:10.1145/1355734.1355746

Mejri, M. N., Achir, N., & Hamdi, M. (2016, January). A new group Diffie-Hellman key generation proposal for secure VANET communications. In Consumer Communications & Networking Conference (CCNC), 2016 13th IEEE Annual (pp. 992-995). IEEE.

Meyer, B. (2000). *Object-Oriented Software Construction* (2nd ed.). Upper Saddle River, NJ: Prentice Hall.

Milojicic, D., LaForge, W., & Chauhan, D. (1998). Mobile Objects and Agents. *Proceedings of the Second USENIX Conference on Object Oriented Technologies and Systems (COOTS).*

Möller, M., Bartetzko, D., Fisher, C., & Wehrheim, H. (2001). Jass-java with assertions. In *Electronic Notes in Theoretical Computer Science* (Vol. 55). Elsevier Science Publisher.

Moszkowski, B. (1996). The programming language Tempura. *Journal of Symbolic Computation*, *22*(5/6), 730–733.

Mouratidis, H. (2011). Secure software systems engineering: The Secure Tropos approach. *Journal of Software, 6*(3), 331–339. doi:10.4304/jsw.6.3.331-339

Mouratidis, H., & Giorgini, P. (2009). Enhancing secure tropos to effectively deal with security requirements in the development of multiagent systems. In *Safety and Security in Multiagent Systems* (pp. 8–26). Springer Berlin Heidelberg. doi:10.1007/978-3-642-04879-1_2

Mouratidis, H., Kolp, M., Faulkner, S., & Giorgini, P. (2005). A Secure Architectural Description Language for Agent Systems. *AAMAS, 5*, 25–29.

Mrabet, K., El Bouanani, F., & Ben-Azza, H. (2015, October). A secure multi-hops routing for VANETs. In *Wireless Networks and Mobile Communications (WINCOM), 2015 International Conference on* (pp. 1-5). IEEE. 10.1109/WINCOM.2015.7381299

Muñoz, A., & Maña, A. (2009b). A Hardware Based Infrastructure for Agent Protection. 3rd Symposium of Ubiquitous Computing and Ambient Intelligence 2008. *Advances in Soft Computing, 51*, 39-47.

Muñoz, A., Anton, P., & Maña, A. (2011). Static mutual approach for protecting mobile agent. In Advances in Intelligent and Soft Computing (Vol. 91, pp. 51–58). Academic Press. doi:10.1007/978-3-642-19934-9_7

Munoz, A., Harjani, R., & Mana, A. (2011). Dynamic Security Monitoring and Accounting for Virtualized Environments. In *Int Workshop on Convergence Security in Pervasive Environments/ Int Workshop on Security on Security and Trust for Applications in Virtualized Environments*. Ubicación.

Muñoz, A., Maña, A., & Antón, P. (2010b). A solution based on cryptographic hardware to protect agents. In *Proceedings - 13th International Conference on Network-Based Information Systems, NBiS 2010* (pp. 400–407). Academic Press. 10.1109/NBiS.2010.115

Munoz, A., Mana, A., & Gonzalez, J. (2013). Dynamic Security Properties Monitoring Architecture for Cloud Computing. Security Engineering for Cloud Computing: Approaches and Tools, 1-18.

Muñoz, A., Maña, A., & Serrano, D. (2009). SecMiLiA: An approach in the agent protection. In *Proceedings - International Conference on Availability, Reliability and Security, ARES 2009* (pp. 341–348). Academic Press. 10.1109/ARES.2009.50

Muñoz, A., Maña, A., & Serrano, D. (2009c). Trusted Computing: The Cornerstone in the Secure Migration Library for Agents. *7th International Conference on Practical Applications of Agents and Multi-Agent Systems.*

Muñoz, A., Maña, A., & Serrano, D. (2009d). The Role of Trusted Computing in Secure Agent Migration. *3rd International Conference on Research Challenges in Information Science (RCIS 2009).*

Muñoz, A., Maña, A., Harjani, R., & Montenegro, M. (2009a). Agent Protection based on the use of cryptographic hardware. *IEEE 33rd International Computer Software and Applications Conference Ubicación.*

Muñoz, A., Gonzalez, J., & Maña, A. (2013). A Performance-Oriented Monitoring System for Security Properties in Cloud Computing Applications. *The Computer Journal, 55*(8), 979–994. doi:10.1093/comjnl/bxs042

Muñoz, A., & Maña, A. (2011b). TPM-based protection for mobile agents. *Security and Communication Networks, 4*(1), 45–60. doi:10.1002ec.158

Muñoz, A., Maña, A., & Antón, P. (2010). In the track of the agent protection: A solution based on cryptographic hardware. *Lecture Notes in Computer Science, 6258*, 284–297. doi:10.1007/978-3-642-14706-7_22

Naldurg, P., Sen, K., & Thati, P. (2004). A Temporal Logic Based Framework to Intrusion Detection. *Proc. of the Int. Conf. on Formal Techniques for Networked and Distributed Systems (FORTE)*.

Nanda, S., Zafari, F., DeCusatis, C., Wedaa, E., & Yang, B. (2016). Predicting network attack patterns in SDN using machine learning approach. In *IEEE Conference on Network Function Virtualization and Software Defined Networks (NFV-SDN)*. IEEE. 10.1109/NFV-SDN.2016.7919493

Necula & Lee. (1996). *Proof-Carrying Code*. Technical Report CMU-CS-96-165. Carnegie Mellon University.

Necula, G. C., & Lee, P. (1998). Safe, untrusted agents using proof-carrying code. In G. Vigna (Ed.), *Mobile agents and security, LNCS 1419* (pp. 61–91). Berlin: Springer. doi:10.1007/3-540-68671-1_5

Nguyen, K. K., Hoang, D. T., Niyato, D., Wang, P., Nguyen, D., & Dutkiewicz, E. (2018, April). Cyberattack detection in mobile cloud computing: A deep learning approach. In *Wireless Communications and Networking Conference (WCNC)* (pp. 1-6). IEEE. 10.1109/WCNC.2018.8376973

Ordille, J. (1996). When agents Roam, Who can You Trust? *Proceedings of the First Conference on Emerging Technologies and Applications in Communications*. 10.1109/ETACOM.1996.502505

Palangi, H., Ward, R. K., & Deng, L. (2016). Distributed Compressive Sensing: A Deep Learning Approach. *IEEE Transactions on Signal Processing, 64*(17), 4504–4518. doi:10.1109/TSP.2016.2557301

Papadakis, M., Kintis, M., Zhang, J., Jia, Y., Le Traon, Y., & Harman, M. (2017). Mutation testing advances: An analysis and survey. *Advances in Computers*.

Pavlidis, M., & Islam, S. (2011, June). SecTro: A CASE Tool for Modelling Security in Requirements Engineering using Secure Tropos. In *CAiSE Forum* (pp. 89-96). Academic Press.

Pavlovskaya, M., Gaisin, R., & Dautov, R. (2017). Finding Correlations Between Driver Stress and Traffic Accidents: An Experimental Study. *Proceedings 11th KES Conference on Agents and Multi-Agent Systems- Technology and Applications*.

Pearson, S. (2007). *How Can You Trust the Computer in Front of You? Technical Report Trusted E-Services Laboratory, HP Laboratories Bristol.* HPL-2002-222. Trusted Computing Group. TCG Specification Architecture Overview, Revision 1.4 (2007). Retrieved from https://www.trustedcomputinggroup.org/groups/TCG 1 4 Architecture Overview.pdf

Pencolé, Y., & Cordier, M. (2005). A Formal Framework for the Decentralised Diagnosis of Large Scale Discrete Event Systems & its Application to Telecommunication Networks. *Artificial Intelligence, 164*(1-2), 121–180. doi:10.1016/j.artint.2005.01.002

Pham, V., & Karamouch, A. (1998). Mobile Software Agents: An Overview. *IEEE Communications Magazine, 36*(7), 26–37. doi:10.1109/35.689628

Phan, T. V., Bao, N. K., & Park, M. (2016a). A novel hybrid flow-based handler with DDoS attacks in software-defined networking. In *Ubiquitous Intelligence & Computing, Advanced and Trusted Computing, Scalable Computing and Communications, Cloud and Big Data Computing, Internet of People, and Smart World Congress (UIC/ATC/ScalCom/CBDCom/IoP/SmartWorld), 2016 Intl IEEE Conferences* (pp. 350-357). IEEE.

Phan, T. V., Toan, T. V., Tuyen, D. V., Huong, T. T., & Thanh, N. H. (2016b). OpenFlowSIA: An optimized protection scheme for software-defined networks from flooding attacks. In *IEEE Sixth International Conference on Communications and Electronics (ICCE)* (pp. 13-18). IEEE. 10.1109/CCE.2016.7562606

Pino, L., Spanoudakis, G., Krotsiani, M., & Mahbub, K. (2017). Pattern Based Design and Verification of Secure Service Compositions. *IEEE Transactions on Services Computing*, 1–1. doi:10.1109/TSC.2017.2690430

Pnueli, A. (1977). The Temporal Logic of Programs. *Proc. of the 18th IEEE Symposium on Foundations of Computer Science*, 46-77.

Pura, M., Patriciu, V., & Bica, I. (2009). Modeling and formal verification of implicit on-demand secure ad hoc routing protocols in HLPSL and AVISPA. *International Journal of Computers and Communications, 2*(3), 25–32.

Raya, M., Papadimitratos, P., Gligor, V. D., & Hubaux, J. P. (2008, April). On data-centric trust establishment in ephemeral ad hoc networks. In *INFOCOM 2008. The 27th Conference on Computer Communications. IEEE* (pp. 1238-1246). IEEE.

Riordan, J., & Scheneider, B. (1998). Environmental Key Generation Towards Clueless Agents. G. Vigna (Ed.), Mobile Agents and Security. Springer-Verlag.

Robinson, W. (2002). Monitoring Software Requirements using Instrumented Code. *Proc. of the Hawaii Int. Conference on Systems Sciences.*

Roth, V. (1998) Secure recording of itineraries through cooperating agents. *Proceedings of 4th workshop on mobile object systems: secure internet mobile computations*, 147–154.

Rothermel, K., Hohl, F., & Radouniklis, N. (1997). Mobile Agent Systems: What is Missing? *Proceedings of the International Working Conference on Distributed Applications and Interoperable Systems (DAIS)*, 111-124.

Rowan, S., Clear, M., Gerla, M., Huggard, M., & Goldrick, C. M. (2017). *Securing vehicle to vehicle communications using blockchain through visible light and acoustic side-channels*. arXiv preprint arXiv:1704.02553

Rul, S., Vandierendonck, H., & De Bosschere, K. (2009). Towards automatic program partitioning. *Conference On Computing Frontiers*, *9*. doi:10.1145/1531743.1531759

Russo, A., Miller, A., Nuseibeh, B., & Kramer, J. (2002). An Abductive Approach for Analysing Event-Based Requirements Specifications. Presented at *18th Int. Conf. on Logic Programming (ICLP)*, Copenhagen, Denmark. 10.1007/3-540-45619-8_3

Said, H. M., Alyoubi, B. A., El Emary, I., & Alyoubi, A. A. (2016). Application of Intelligent Data Mining Approach in Securing the Cloud Computing. *International Journal of Advanced Computer Science and Applications*, *7*(9), 151–159.

Sander, T., & Tschudin, C. (1998). Protecting Mobile Agents Against Malicious Hosts. In G. Vigna (Ed.), Lecture Notes in Computer Science: Vol. 1419. *Mobile Agents and Security. Springer-Verlag*. doi:10.1007/3-540-68671-1_4

Sandhu, R., & Samarati, P. (1996). Authentication, access control, and audit. *ACM Computing Surveys*, *28*(1), 241–243. doi:10.1145/234313.234412

Saruhan Ozdag, F. (2017). *Detection of network attacks with machine learning method* (Unpublished master's thesis). Istanbul University, Istanbul, Turkey.

Sathya, R., & Abraham, A. (2013). Comparison of Supervised and Unsupervised Learning Algorithms for Pattern Classification. *International Journal of Advanced Research in Artificial Intelligence*, *2*(2), 34–38. doi:10.14569/IJARAI.2013.020206

Schlimmer, J. (Ed.). (2006). *Web Services Policy Framework (WS-Policy Framework)*. Retrieved from http://www.ibm.com/developerworks/library/speci_cation/ws-polfram/

Schmidhuber, J. (2015). Deep learning in neural networks: An overview. *Neural Networks*, *61*, 85–117. doi:10.1016/j.neunet.2014.09.003 PMID:25462637

Schneider, F. B. (1998). *Enforceable Security Policies*. Cornell University Technical Report TR98- 1664.

Schoder, D., & Eymann, T. (2000). The Real Challenges of Mobile Agents. *Communications of the ACM*, *43*(6), 111–112. doi:10.1145/336460.336488

Schwuttke, U. M., & Quan, A. G. (1993). Enhancing Performance of Cooperating Agents in Real-Time Diagnostic Systems. In *Proceedings of the Thirteenth International Joint Conference on Artificial Intelligence (IJCAI-93)* (pp. 332-337). Menlo Park, CA: Academic Press.

Sekar, R., Venkatakrishnan, V. N., Basu, S., Bhatkar, S., & Du Varney, D. (2003). Model-Carrying Code: A Practical Approach for Safe Execution of Untrusted Applications. *ACM Symposium on Operating Systems Principles*.

SHA3-224. (n.d.). Retrieved from http://nvlpubs.nist.gov/nistpubs/FIPS/NIST.FIPS.202.pdf

Shanahan, M. (1999). The Event Calculus Explained. *Artificial Intelligence Today*, 409-430. doi:10.1007/3-540-48317-9_17

Shao, J., Lin, X., Lu, R., & Zuo, C. (2016). A threshold anonymous authentication protocol for VANETs. *IEEE Transactions on Vehicular Technology*, *65*(3), 1711–1720. doi:10.1109/TVT.2015.2405853

Shepherdson, D. (2003). The JACK Usage Report. *Proceedings of the Autonomous Agents and Multi Agents Systems 2003 (AAMAS 03)*.

Singh, M., & Kim, S. (2017). *Blockchain Based Intelligent Vehicle Data sharing Framework.* arXiv preprint arXiv:1708.09721

Spanoudakis, G., & Mahub, K. (2006). Non Intrusive Monitoring of Service Based Systems. *Int. Journal of Cooperative Inform. Systems*, *15*(3), 325–358.

Stern, J. P., Hachez, G., Koeune, F., & Quisquater, J. J. (1999). Robust Object Watermarking: Application to Code. In *Proceedings of Info Hiding '99*. Springer-Verlag. Retrieved from http://www.dice.ucl.ac.be/crypto/publications/1999/codemark.pdf

Tang, T. A., Mhamdi, L., McLernon, D., Zaidi, S. A. R., & Ghogho, M. (2016). Deep learning approach for network intrusion detection in software defined networking. In *International Conference on Wireless Networks and Mobile Communications (WINCOM)*. IEEE. 10.1109/WINCOM.2016.7777224

Tardo, J., & Valente, K. (1996) Mobile Agent Security Telescript. In *Proceedings of IEEE COMPCON '96* (pp. 58-63). IEEE Computer Society Press.

Tarr, P. L., Ossher, H., Harrison, W. H., & Sutton, S. M. Jr. (1999). N degrees of separation: Multidimensional separation concerns. *International Conference on Software Engineering*, 107-119.

Toutouh, J., Muñoz, A., & Nesmachnow, S. (2018). Evolution Oriented Monitoring oriented to Security Properties for Cloud Applications. In *Proceeding of ARES 2018 Proceedings of the 13th International Conference on Availability, Reliability and Security*. ACM.

Tripakis, S. (2002). Fault Diagnosis for timed automata. *Proc. 7th Int. Symp. Formal Techniques in Real-Time and Fault Tolerant Systems*, 205-224. 10.1007/3-540-45739-9_14

Tripathi, V. K., & Venkaeswari, S. (2015, April). Secure communication with privacy preservation in VANET-using multilingual translation. In *Communication Technologies (GCCT), 2015 Global Conference on* (pp. 125-127). IEEE.

Ucar, S., Ergen, S. C., & Ozkasap, O. (2013, April). VMaSC: Vehicular multi-hop algorithm for stable clustering in vehicular ad hoc networks. In *Wireless Communications and Networking Conference (WCNC)* (pp. 2381-2386). IEEE. 10.1109/WCNC.2013.6554933

van Lamsweerde, A. (2006). Elaborating Security Requirements by Construction of Intentional Anti-Models. In *Proceedings of ICSE'04, 26th International Conference on Software Engineering*. ACM-IEEE.

Van, N. T., Bao, H., & Thinh, T. N. (2016). An Anomaly-based Intrusion Detection Architecture Integrated on OpenFlow Switch. In *Proceedings of the 6th International Conference on Communication and Network Security (ICCNS)* (pp. 99-103). ACM. 10.1145/3017971.3017982

Vigilson Prem, M., & Swamynathan, S. (2012). Securing mobile agent and its platform from passive attack of malicious mobile agents. In *IEEE-International Conference on Advances in Engineering, Science and Management* (pp. 605–609). ICAESM. Retrieved from http://www.scopus.com/inward/record.url?eid=2-s2.0-84863963880&partnerID=40&md5=c70f6cd57f57 3d678601718e70e13008

Vigna, G. (1997). Protecting mobile agents through tracing. *Proceedings of the 3rd ECOOP workshop on mobile object systems*.

Vigna, G. (2004). Mobile Agents: Ten Reasons for Failure. In *Proceedings of the 2004 IEEE International Conference on Mobile Data Management* (pp. 298-299). IEEE Computer Society.

Vincent, P., Larochelle, H., Lajoie, I., Bengio, Y., & Manzagol, P. A. (2010). Stacked denoising autoencoders: Learning useful representations in a deep network with a local denoising criterion. *Journal of Machine Learning Research*, *11*(Dec), 3371–3408.

Wagelaar, D. (2004). Towards a context-driven development framework for ambient intelligence. *Proceedings of the Fourth IEEE International Workshop on Distributed Auto-adaptive and Reconfigurable Systems (with ICDCS'04)*.

Wang, H., & Wang, C. (1997). Intelligent Agents in the Nuclear Industry. *IEEE Computer*, *30*(11), 28–34. doi:10.1109/2.634838

Wang, L., & Jones, R. (2017). Big data analytics for network intrusion detection: A survey. *International Journal of Networks and Communications*, *7*(1), 24–31.

Wang, T., & Chen, H. (2017). SGuard: A lightweight SDN safe-guard architecture for DoS attacks. *China Communications*, *14*(6), 113–125. doi:10.1109/CC.2017.7961368

Wei, Y. C., & Chen, Y. M. (2012). Reliability and Efficiency Improvement for Trust Management Model in VANETs. In *Human Centric Technology and Service in Smart Space* (pp. 105–112). Dordrecht: Springer. doi:10.1007/978-94-007-5086-9_14

White, J. (2004). *Mobile Agents White Paper, General Magic*. Retrieved March 17, 2004, from http://www.genmagic.com/agents/Whitepaper/whitepaper.html

Wooldridge, M. (1997). Agent-based Software Engineering. *IEE Proceedings. Software Engineering*, *144*(1), 26–37. doi:10.1049/ip-sen:19971026

Xu, C., Shen, J., Du, X., & Zhang, F. (2018). An Intrusion Detection System Using a Deep Neural Network with Gated Recurrent Units. *IEEE Access: Practical Innovations, Open Solutions*.

Xu, J., Li, H., & Zhou, S. (2015). An overview of deep generative models. *IETE Technical Review*, *32*(2), 131–139. doi:10.1080/02564602.2014.987328

Yang, Z., Cheng, B. H., Stirewalt, R. E., Sowell, J., Sadjadi, S. M., & McKinley, P. K. (2002) An aspect oriented approach to dynamic adaptation. *Proceedings of the ACM SIGSOFT Workshop On Self-healing Software (WOSS'02)*. 10.1145/582128.582144

Yasmin, R., Ritter, E., & Wang, G. (2014). Provable security of a pairing-free one-pass authenticated key establishment protocol for wireless sensor networks. *International Journal of Information Security*, *13*(5), 453–465. doi:10.100710207-013-0224-7

Yellin, F. (1996). *Low-level security in Java*. Retrieved from http://www.javasoft.com/sfaq/veri_er.html

Yin, C., Zhu, Y., Fei, J., & He, X. (2017). A deep learning approach for intrusion detection using recurrent neural networks. *IEEE Access: Practical Innovations, Open Solutions*, *5*, 21954–21961. doi:10.1109/ACCESS.2017.2762418

Younes, M. B., & Boukerche, A. (2015, March). SCOOL: A secure traffic congestion control protocol for VANETs. In *Wireless Communications and Networking Conference (WCNC)* (pp. 1960-1965). IEEE. 10.1109/WCNC.2015.7127768

Young, G. O. (1964). *Synthetic structure of industrial plastics*. In J. Peters (Ed.), *Plastics* (2nd ed.; Vol. 3, pp. 15–64). New York: McGraw-Hill.

Yousefi-Azar, M., Varadharajan, V., Hamey, L., & Tupakula, U. (2017, May). Autoencoder-based feature learning for cyber security applications. In *Neural Networks (IJCNN), 2017 International Joint Conference on* (pp. 3854-3861). IEEE.

Yuan, Y., & Wang, F. Y. (2016, November). Towards blockchain-based intelligent transportation systems. In *Intelligent Transportation Systems (ITSC), 2016 IEEE 19th International Conference on* (pp. 2663-2668). IEEE. 10.1109/ITSC.2016.7795984

Zhang, B., Yu, Y., & Li, J. (2018, May). Network Intrusion Detection Based on Stacked Sparse Autoencoder and Binary Tree Ensemble Method. In *2018 IEEE International Conference on Communications Workshops (ICC Workshops)* (pp. 1-6). IEEE. 10.1109/ICCW.2018.8403759

Zhang, Q., Yang, L. T., Chen, Z., & Li, P. (2018). A survey on deep learning for big data. *Information Fusion*, *42*, 146–157. doi:10.1016/j.inffus.2017.10.006

Zhang, Z., Boukerche, A., & Pazzi, R. (2011, October). A novel multi-hop clustering scheme for vehicular ad-hoc networks. In *Proceedings of the 9th ACM international symposium on Mobility management and wireless access* (pp. 19-26). ACM. 10.1145/2069131.2069135

Zheng, Z., Xie, S., Dai, H. N., & Wang, H. (2016). Blockchain challenges and opportunities: A survey. *Work Pap.*, 2016.

About the Contributors

Ryma Abassi received her engineering degree in Networks & Telecommunications in 2004, and her MSc and PhD degrees from the Higher Communication School, Sup'Com in 2006 and 2010, respectively. Currently, she is an Assistant Professor and the Associate Director at ISET'Com and member of the "Digital Security" unit at SUP'Com. Dr Ryma Abassi was a Fulbright scholar at Tufts University, MA, USA where she worked on formal methods for security protocols validation. Moreover, she obtained the SSHN grant two times in 2014 and 2017 and is a visiting professor at University of Limoges. Her current researches are focusing on MANET/VANET security, trust management, security protocols validation, IoT security, etc. She has more than 30 publications in impacted journals and classified conferences and is co-supervising four PhD students.

* * *

Ons Chikhaoui received her engineering degree in Telecommunications from the National School of Electronics and Telecommunications of Sfax (ENET'Com) in July 2015. Since October 2015, she is a PhD student at the Higher School of Communications of Tunis (Sup'Com) and a member of the Digital Security Research Laboratory.

Safak Durukan-Odabasi has received her Ph.D. degree on Computer Engineering from Istanbul University in 2013. Her research areas are next generation networks, cloud computing, IoT and cybersecurity. She is currently working as an Assistant Professor at Istanbul University – Cerrahpaşa.

Francisco Jaime started his professional development in 2006, when he finished his studies as a computer engineer at University of Málaga. That year he became part of the Computer Architecture department at University of Málaga, mainly focused over processors and memories architectures, compilers and image processing among others. Here he developed his activity for seven years as a researcher. During this period he combined his PhD activities together with some other interesting works regarding digital arithmetic, superscalar processors, multimedia extensions, design and development of digital circuits, FPGAs and cryptography. Finally, he received his PhD degree in 2011. In 2013 he became part of the Proteus research team at University of Málaga, within the Computer Science department, whose main workload lies in computer security and protection of information. There, he worked as a project manager for three years, where his assignments and responsibilities focused to coordination of tasks and resources of the PARIS project, besides actively participating in the technical execution of the project. This project was granted under the FP7 program with an interdisciplinary approach concerning security and privacy for video surveillance and biometric systems. At the same time, he collaborated in the making of European projects proposals for the Horizon 2020 program. Resulting of these years at University, he got a Master's degree in Software Engineering and Artificial Intelligence, several international publications and he also participated in several international conferences. He learnt several languages for the production of digital circuits, low level software development and high level modeling methodologies. In 2015 he is an equity partner of Safe Society Labs, a spin off company dedicated to make the most of the research results produced by the Proteus team, as well as the knowledge and technology transfer. His main role in the company related to the coordination of software development projects and the making of computer forensic reports for legal cases. In 2016 he joins CITIC to work in the technical aspects of a cybersecurity related project. He carried out this activity for about one and a half years. After that, in 2017, he joined again University of Málaga as a professor for a period of five months. Finally, he was an active part of a research team in the Computer Science department, developing new algorithms and methodologies regarding automatic recommendation.

Aman Jantan is an Associate Professor and Senior Lecturer at the School of Computer Science, Universiti Sains Malaysia, Malaysia. He specialises in Digital Forensics, Malware, IDS, Computer & network security. He has won several grants and awards in difference hemispheres within his field and beyond. Moreover, he has over 70 publications in highly indexed journals with hundreds of citations.

Amira Kchaou received her engineering degree in computer in 2016. Currently, she is a PhD student at the Higher Communication School (Sup'Com) and member of the "Digital Security" lab at Sup'Com. Her current researches are focusing on VANET security, trust management, etc.

Muhammad Kiru is a research scholar at the School of Computer Science, Universiti Sains Malaysia. He is currently pursuing PhD in Computer Science (Cybersecurity). He specializes in networks, cybersecurity and threat profiling. His other areas of specialization include malware analysis, hacking and penetration.

Antonio Muñoz is currently professor at University of Málaga. He cooperates as security expert for Ericsson. He has more than 15 years or experience as Cybersecurity Expert. He holds his PhD an MSc degree in Computer Science and a Postgraduate Master degree in Software Engineer and Artificial Intelligence, both of them from the University of Malaga. He has been researcher in the GISUM group at the University of Malaga since 2003. His principal research interests are in the area of Agent technology, Digital Content Protection, Cryptographic Hardware based Systems, Security Patterns and Security Engineering. Antonio was involved in the EU Sixth Framework Programme project within the projects Ubisec, Serenity, and in the EU Seventh Framework Programme projects. Excellent understanding of current enterprise software technologies and development practices and tools, including virtual environments, source control, remote development, issue tracking, build and test automation, and networking management. A true "roll up the sleeves and get it done" working approach; demonstrated success as a problem solver, operating as a result-oriented, self-starter.

V. Pavithra is currently pursuing master's degree in Computer Science and Information Security at Thiagarajar College of Engineering, Madurai. She completed Bachelor's degree in the stream of information Technology at Velammal College of Engineering and Technology. Her areas of interest are Security and Ethical Hacking. She presently doing research project in the area of Medical Image Security.

R. Guru Roja completed master's degree in Computer Science and Information Security at Thiagarajar College of Engineering, Madurai. Her areas of interest are Security and Ethical Hacking.

Nurefsan Sertbas holds a bachelor degree in Electronics and Telecommunication Engineering Department from Istanbul Technical University. In 2016, she graduated from the Computer Engineering department in the same university as her second major. Afterward, she received MSc. degree in Computer Engineering from Bogazici University in 2018. Currently, she is a PhD student in the same university. Her research interests include network security, software defined networks, information centric networking and artificial intelligence approaches.

M. Thangavel is an Assistant Professor presently working in the Department of Information Technology at Thiagarajar college of Engineering, Madurai. He presently holds 4.5 years of Teaching and Research experience in Thiagarajar college of Engineering, Madurai and 2 years of Teaching and Research experience in Madras Institute of Technology, Anna University - Chennai. He graduated as a B.E. Computer Science and Engineering from M.A.M College of Engineering, Trichy (Anna University - Chennai) and as an M.E. Computer Science and Engineering from J.J. College of Engineering and Technology, Trichy (Anna University - Chennai) and Pursuing his PhD from Madras Institute of Technology, Chennai under Anna University - Chennai. He is a Gold Medalist in UG and Anna University - First Rank Holder with Gold Medal in PG. His specialization is Cloud Computing, and Information Security. His Areas of Interest include DNA Cryptography, Ethical Hacking, Compiler Design, Computer Networks, Data Structures and High Performance Computing. He has published 5 articles in International Journals, 8 book chapters in International Publishers, 14 in the proceedings of International Conferences and 3 in the proceedings of national conferences /seminars. He has attended 38 Workshops / FDPs/Conferences in various Higher Learning Institutes like IIT, Anna University. He has organized 21 Workshops / FDPs /Contests/Industry based courses over the past 5 years of experience. He has been a delegate for Cyber Week 2017 organized by Tel Aviv University, Israel. He has been recognized by IIT Bombay; SAP CSR as SAP Award of Excellence with cash reward of Rs.5000/- for the best Participation in IITBombayX: FDPICT001x Use of ICT in Education for Online and Blended Learning. He shows interest in student counseling, in motivating for better placements and in helping them design value-based life-style.

Jamal Toutouh is a postdoc researcher in the University of Málaga. He recently granted with Marie Curie Fellowship in MIT (USA). He received his PhD in Computer Science with honors (cum laude) at University of Málaga. He completed two postgraduate M.S. degrees: Master in Information and Computer Sciences at University of Luxembourg and Master in Software Engineering and Artificial Intelligence at University of Málaga. Previously, he received a 5-year combined degree of B.Eng. and M.Eng. in Computer Science in the latter university. His PhD research hypothesis merited a Doctoral Consortium 2013 award given by the Spanish Association for Artificial Intelligence (AEPIA) and the PhD thesis was awarded with the best PhD thesis of the year (2016). Dr. Toutouh has published articles in several prestigious indexed journals, book chapters, and referred international conferences. Dr. Toutouh has participated in several national and international research projects. In turn, he has closely collaborated and collaborates with institutions in Luxembourg, Finland, Qatar, and Uruguay. Most of his research is focused on the use of natural inspired algorithms to address problems related to Smart Cities and cybersecurity.

Derya Yiltas-Kaplan received the BSc, MSc, and PhD degrees in computer engineering from Istanbul University, Istanbul, Turkey, in 2001, 2003 and 2007, respectively. She was a post-doctorate researcher at the North Carolina State University and she received postdoctorate research scholarship from The Scientific and Technological Research Council of Turkey during the period of April 2008-April 2009. She is currently working as a faculty member in the Department of Computer Engineering at Istanbul University – Cerrahpaşa.

Zuleyha Yiner received BSc degree Computer Engineering (English) from Anadolu University in Eskisehir, MSc in Computer Engineering from İstanbul University in Istanbul. Now, she is a PhD student in Istanbul University – Cerrahpaşa. Her research interests are artificial intelligence, machine learning, natural language processing.

Index

A

AVISPA 190, 206-207, 210-211, 213, 216, 218

B

BlockChain 222-223, 231, 233-234

C

cloud computing 63-68, 80-81, 180
cloud security 64, 67-69
clustering 129, 132, 140, 221-223, 232, 234
controller 86, 88-89, 107, 112-113, 118-120, 122, 125-128, 130-138, 141-142, 145, 147-150
credibility 221-222, 226-229, 234-235
cryptography 48, 177, 190-192, 227
Cyber Security 68, 159

D

Data Center 84
data plane 86, 107, 112, 114-115, 120, 125, 131-132, 135, 145
data set 67-68, 129-131, 133-134, 138, 140, 142, 145
deep learning 63, 70-73, 80-81, 138, 140
Defense-in-Depth 37
detection 11, 21, 23, 27, 37, 41, 49-50, 63, 67-68, 70, 72, 74-76, 78-81, 86, 124-125, 128-130, 132-137, 140-142, 159, 168-170, 176-177, 179

E

Exploit Kit 7, 37

F

feature selection 130, 140
formal 146-148, 159, 163, 165-166, 169, 171-175, 188, 190, 206, 218, 237, 239, 261-262

H

hacker 8, 15, 37

I

integrity 16, 45, 48-49, 51, 53, 163-164, 171, 177, 188-189
intrusion 21, 27, 41, 63, 68, 74, 76, 78-80, 86, 124-125, 128-129, 131, 137, 140, 142, 145, 169-170, 177
intrusion detection 21, 27, 41, 63, 68, 74, 76, 78-80, 86, 124-125, 128-129, 137, 140, 142, 169-170, 177

L

learning 3, 63, 67-73, 75, 77-81, 116, 124-125, 128-132, 135, 137-138, 140-142, 145, 178

M

machine learning 3, 63, 67-71, 78, 81, 116, 124-125, 128-132, 138, 140-142, 145, 178

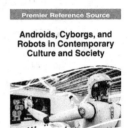

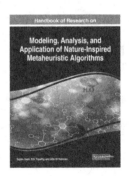

Ensure Quality Research is Introduced to the Academic Community

Become an IGI Global Reviewer for Authored Book Projects

Premier Reference Source

Emerging GIS Applications for Emergency and Disaster Management

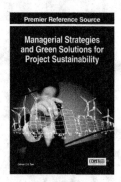

Premier Reference Source

Managerial Strategies and Green Solutions for Project Sustainability

Premier Reference Source

Comparative Approaches to Using R and Python for Statistical Data Analysis

Premier Reference Source

Solutions for High-Touch Communications in a High-Tech World

The overall success of an authored book project is dependent on quality and timely reviews.

In this competitive age of scholarly publishing, constructive and timely feedback significantly expedites the turnaround time of manuscripts from submission to acceptance, allowing the publication and discovery of forward-thinking research at a much more expeditious rate. Several IGI Global authored book projects are currently seeking highly qualified experts in the field to fill vacancies on their respective editorial review boards:

Applications may be sent to:
development@igi-global.com

Applicants must have a doctorate (or an equivalent degree) as well as publishing and reviewing experience. Reviewers are asked to write reviews in a timely, collegial, and constructive manner. All reviewers will begin their role on an ad-hoc basis for a period of one year, and upon successful completion of this term can be considered for full editorial review board status, with the potential for a subsequent promotion to Associate Editor.

If you have a colleague that may be interested in this opportunity, we encourage you to share this information with them.

Information Resources Management Association

Advancing the Concepts & Practices of Information Resources Management in Modern Organizations

Become an IRMA Member

Members of the **Information Resources Management Association (IRMA)** understand the importance of community within their field of study. The Information Resources Management Association is an ideal venue through which professionals, students, and academicians can convene and share the latest industry innovations and scholarly research that is changing the field of information science and technology. Become a member today and enjoy the benefits of membership as well as the opportunity to collaborate and network with fellow experts in the field.

IRMA Membership Benefits:

- **One FREE Journal Subscription**

- **30% Off Additional Journal Subscriptions**

- **20% Off Book Purchases**

- Updates on the latest events and research on Information Resources Management through the IRMA-L listserv.

- Updates on new open access and downloadable content added to Research IRM.

- A copy of the Information Technology Management Newsletter twice a year.

- A certificate of membership.

IRMA Membership $195

Scan code or visit **irma-international.org** and begin by selecting your free journal subscription.

Membership is good for one full year.

Printed in the United States
By Bookmasters